Varieties
of Jewish
Experience

ETZION FOUNDATION / YESHIVAT HAR ETZION
2013 ANNUAL DINNER

HONORING
RABBI DR. AHARON LICHTENSTEIN
IN CELEBRATION OF HIS UPCOMING 80th BIRTHDAY

HESHE AND HARRIET SEIF
GUESTS OF HONOR

RABBI YEHUDA '95 AND DR. MICHELLE SARNA
ALUMNUS OF THE YEAR

Sunday, March 10, 2013
Grand Hyatt Hotel

Varieties of Jewish Experience

BY
Rabbi Aharon Lichtenstein

KTAV Publishing House, Inc.
Jersey City, New Jersey

Library of Congress Cataloging-in-Publication Data

Lichtenstein, Aharon.
  Varieties of Jewish experience / Aharon Lichtenstein.

    p. cm.
  Includes index.
  ISBN 978-1-60280-186-8
  1. Judaism--21st century. 2. Orthodox Judaism--Relations--Nontraditional Jews. 3.
Orthodox Judaism. 4. Secularism. I. Title.
  BM562.L53 2011
  296.09'05--dc23

                        2011032149

Manufactured in the United States of America

Published by
KTAV Publishing House, Inc.
888 Newark Avenue, Suite 119
Jersey City, NJ 07306
orders@ktav.com
(201) 963-9524

Contents

Chapter 1

Of Marriage:
Relationship and Relations

I have written this piece, and I present it here, likewise, with a measure of ambivalence and trepidation. On the one hand, its subject is important, as a conceptual and ideological topic, *per se*. Moreover, beyond the theoretical, it impinges upon intimate chambers in the life of almost any and every halakhically committed Jew or Jewess. Finally, to the knowledgeable, the basic issues and primary texts are probably familiar, so that any attempt at grappling with the concerns and elucidating them may be welcome.

On the other hand, others may find parts of the discussion disturbing, if not objectionable. To some, it may appear to stand in violation of the mishnah's admonition, as elucidated by the gemara,[1] against public discussion of the arcane aspects of proscribed sexual liaisons. While the issues herewith treated have received fuller expositions in numerous Torah-oriented books and articles, every accretion may be challenged as an erosion of the proper level of *zeniut*. Of greater concern is the prospect that others, particularly the relatively less initiate, may find the essay unsettling. Perhaps, hitherto fully comfortable with the roseate tinge of some contemporary presentations of Jewish attitudes to sexuality, they may find their personal equipoise adversely affected by exposure to less positive sources. The result may be either some erosion in the quality and enthusiasm of married life; or, conversely, some slippage in respect for pillars of the halakhic world, such as the Rambam and the Ramban. And this might, in turn, undermine commitment to Halakhah in its totality.

On a broader, and possibly deeper, front, the differences noted between attitudes expressed by Hazal and later formulations raises issues concerning periodization and continuity within the halakhic system; and, for readers not wholly satisfied with suggestions I have tentatively advanced, by way of resolution, the impact may be, again, possibly unsettling.

Despite the ambivalence, I have, obviously, decided to proceed. I have done so not only in the interest of spiritual and intellectual candor but, additionally, on the sanguine assumption that, on balance, the effect will be constructive, inasmuch as most of the readers are already aware of the primary problems and will be spiritually enriched by its systematic analysis, their faith and commitment energized and fortified by the Torah discourse of *massa u-mattan be'divrei Torah*, rather than enervated or diluted. Nevertheless, where spiritual influence is at stake, a measure of trepidation persists. It is my hope and prayer that the Giver of Torah spare and save us from any fault or blemish in its dissemination.

Were I to respond, in full, to the overarching question presented to me — "What models are there in the classical rabbinic literature for relationships between men and women?" — I would preface my discussion with the observation that, as regards marriage (presumably, our primary focus), the models in evidence in Hazal are both few and partial. As to the sociological reality, there are, of course, interesting and possibly suggestive anecdotes. The story of the woman who was obligated to swear in Rava's *bet din* but was prevented from doing so when Rava's wife interfered to inform him that she was an untrustworthy *hashudah*,[2] tells us something about his wife's presence at the proceedings and about their relationship. Or again, the story of Rav Ze'ira's wife — who proffered some food to Rav Hiyya bar Ashi which he, evidently due to halakhic reservations, refused to eat, upon which she responded: "I made it for your *rebbe*, and he ate, and you don't eat?!"[3] — reflects a different sort of assertiveness.

Assorted evidence could unquestionably be addressed, some of it pointing in different directions. However, as far as full-blown normative models are concerned, I believe the harvest is scant. There is, of course, a corpus of *halakhot* spelling out the respective rights and duties; and these have been subsequently elucidated. However, as regards many of the issues which confront and concern many contemporary couples, we find relatively little imperative direction. These include the dynamics of the relationship proper — areas and degrees of authority and responsibility, the prioritization of respective individual interests, the nature of decision-making etc. — as well as aspects which extend beyond it: the place of the marriage within the broader context of life and activity, the scope and character of relations to others, be they children, general family, friends, or associates.

There exist, admittedly, some directives regarding some of these concerns. For the most part, however, they have been relegated to the realm of *devar ha-reshut*, an area not axiologically neutral but neither fully normative, with regard to which personal preference, with a possible eye upon meaningful variables, is characteristic. In a word, they are subject to the discussion, predilection, and decision of individual couples. Of course, romantic souls are scandalized by the thought that such issues may be "negotiated" at all, while pragmatists may be convinced that the abjuration of planning is a possible recipe for collision. My point is simply that there is room for flexibility and mutual choice. Whether the character of a marriage is dictated by convention, contemporary mores, or conscious limning is another matter.

Thus, the familiar description of an *ishah kesherah* as one who performs *rezon ba'alah*[4] in no way precludes a husband's declaring that his *razon* is precisely a desire for understanding and consensus. Or again, the gemara's suggested division between general and domestic, or between celestial and mundane, matters, as the domains of the husband and the wife, respectively, does not obviate a desire to cross those lines, where the proper qualifications exist. Nor would this come under the rubric of a *holekh ba'azat ishto*, for whom the gemara[5] anticipates dire consequences. The appellation and the strictures refer to a man who does not engage in serious discussion and decision, but instead blindly follows spousal counsel, whether, like the Antonys of the world, out of romantic passion, or out of sheer henpecked acquiescence. Barring that, consensus may be deemed both fairer and wiser, as טובים השנים מן האחד, "Two are better than one" (Kohelet 4:9); and there may be situations in which the peremptory command, כל אשר תאמר אליך שרה שמע בקלה, "Listen to all that she says" (Bereshit 21:12), applies inasmuch, as the midrash notes, שהיה אברהם טפל לשרה בנביאות, Avraham was secondary to Sarah in the realm of prophecy.[6]

It is difficult, and possibly presumptuous, therefore, to speak of absolute marital models in Hazal. Obviously, every Jewish home should be grounded upon the centrality of Torah, *avodah*, and *gemilut hasadim*, and dedication to these cardinal values must be assured in the structuring of its lifestyle. This is doubly true with respect to the homes of aspiring *talmidei hakhamim*, but is by no means confined to them. Much of the detail concerning the nature of the marital relationship, coincidence and distinctiveness, or balance and proportion, is, however, very much a *devar ha-reshut*.

This would be the gist of my preface were I tackling my overarching question in scope and in depth, even if only with respect to marriage. Having, however, been accorded the prerogative of devoting myself to a discussion of one of the subtopics delineated, I shall exercise that option and focus upon a narrower, albeit perhaps thornier, issue: "How shall we view possible models of the marriage relationship (love and companionship vs. procreation)?" This formulation strikingly parallels the opening of the Rav's essay, "Marriage," in *Family Redeemed*. "There are," the Rav notes, "two basic theories about the institution of marriage. One theory developed a *transeunt* axiology, that is, a value system that finds the meaning of matrimony *outside* of the matrimonial union. The other theory developed an *immanent* matrimonial value system, discovering meaning *within*."[7] The essay then proceeds to develop the distinction, explaining that the theories focus upon the welfare of the group or of the individuals — i.e., upon procreation and fellowship — respectively; and, drawing upon *humash* and Hazal, goes on to mold and posit a Jewish perspective upon the institution and its ideological base.

As we might have expected, the ideal subsequently espoused is inclusive and comprehensive. Resembling the ellipse rather than the circle, it has two foci. Moreover — and, within the essay, this point is both central and critical — both goals, and their corollaries, are integrally related: "Seen from the halakhic viewpoint, matrimonial community is not realized without embracing three personae. At this level, marriage redeems the productive urge from its animal species orientation and turns it into a spiritual tragic longing of man for his origin or source."[8] Hence, this position rejects not only the narrowing of *telos* to one of the elements, but also the inclination to regard marriage as the pursuit of two independent and possibly divergent aims, to be somehow balanced, in theory and in practice. It rather bears the stamp of a covenantal relationship — entered into between the parties, and with reference to the broader covenant between God and man, generally, and between the *Ribbono shel Olam* and *Knesset Yisrael*, particularly — within and through which twin goals are interactively achieved.

It is a stimulating piece, written with characteristic philosophic sophistication, psychological insight, and spiritual vision. Framed in simple terms, however, its central thesis, relating to the nature of marriage as both instrumental and intrinsic, is traditional, rather than innovative. The Tur opens his *Even Ha-Ezer*, whose first section deals with Hilkhot Piryah Ve-Rivyah with a brief paean to the Author of marriage — in both aspects:

יתברך שמו של הקדוש ברוך הוא שהוא חפץ בטוב בריותיו שידע שאין טוב לאדם להיות לבדו ועל כן עשה לו עזר כנגדו ועוד כי כוונת הבריאה באדם כדי לפרות ולרבות וזה אי אפשר בלא העזר ועל כן צוהו לדבק בעזר שעשה לו לכך חייב כל אדם לישא אשה כדי לפרות ולרבות.

Blessed is God that He desires the best for His creatures. For He knew that it is "not good" for man to remain alone and thus made for him a "fitting helper." Moreover, since an objective of human creation is reproduction, which is impossible without the "helper," God commanded that man cleave to the "helper" which He had created. Therefore every man must marry in order to reproduce.[9]

Whether, from a technical halakhic standpoint, marriage is necessary for the formal fulfillment of the *mizvah* of *peru u'revu*, is possibly a matter of debate. The Rosh was emphatic in stressing that it was not. In explaining the text of *birkat eirusin* and its convoluted content, he states that it does not relate to any particular *mizvah* — surely, not that of procreation, as קידושין בלא ורביה פריה מצות לקיים אפשר — as one could potentially fulfill the commandment to reproduce without marrying.[10] This view is palpably accepted by Rishonim who held, on the basis of a passage in the Yerushalmi,[11] that the *mizvah* could, *be'di'avad*, be fulfilled through an incestuous union, not amenable to matrimony. The Rambam, however, seems to have held otherwise. This is perhaps indicated by the inclusion of the *mizvah* within Hilkhot Ishut, but is fairly explicit in the heading to this section:

א) לישא אשה בכתובה וקידושין...
ד) לפרות ולרבות ממנה.

(1) To marry a woman with a *ketubbah* and *kiddushin*…
(4) To reproduce from her.

What is beyond question, however, is the fact that the institution is not designed solely in order to provide a licit channel for the perpetuation of the human, or the national, race.

The importance attached within *Yahadut* to the *mizvah* of procreation can hardly be overemphasized. It is conceived in religious, rather than primarily social, categories; and this, not simply as an affirmative response to a normative commandment, as any other *mizvah*, but as the implementation of the divine design in the creation of the world: תהו לא ברא לשבת יצרה, "He did not form it for waste, but created it for habitation."[12] Hence, willful abstinence is not regarded as merely the failure to do good but is equated with the perpetration of evil: דמים שופך כאילו אומר עזאי בן וממעט הדמות "Ben Azzai said: As though he sheds blood and diminishes the divine image;"[13] so severe is the judgment passed upon the shirker.

However, procreation is manifestly not the sole *raison d'être* for marriage. The verse in Kohelet (9:9) counsels אהבת אשר אשה עם חיים ראה, "Enjoy life with a woman you love," clearly referring to the realization of life rather than to its creation. Hazal correspondingly note that שרוי אשה לו שאין אדם כל טובה בלא ברכה בלא שמחה בלא "Any man who has no wife lives without joy, without blessing, and without goodness"[14] — again, focusing upon personal bliss *per se*. Moreover, Rav Huna's reproach of bachelorhood beyond a certain age, while explicitly motivated by the concern about the *hirhurei averah* of sexual fantasy,[15] probably also reflects the championing of the marital relation as such.

The significance of the interpersonal element is further reinforced by the substance of a familiar prooftext, twice cited in the gemara and codified by the Rambam:

האוהב את אשתו כגופו והמכבדה יותר מגופו... עליו הכתוב אומר וידעת כי שלום אהלך ופקדת נוך ולא תחטא.

> Whoever loves his wife as himself and honors her more than himself — of him Scripture says, "And you will know that your tent shall be in peace and you will visit your habitation, and not sin" (Iyov 5:24).[16]

The use of the accusative mode — as opposed to that of the more general ואהבת לרעך כמוך, which, as the Ramban[17] noted, bespeaks concern for another's welfare, but does not command loving his persona — underscores the emotional aspect of the amatory component in marriage. And whatever the referent of the intended *kibbud* — honor, esteem, service, or provision — it is patently clear that the institution is not perceived as a mere instrument to enable procreative sustenance of the human race. It is, of course, logically arguable that the *raison d'être* of marriage is indeed purely instrumental, but that the message of the gemara is simply a directive prescribing the desirable mode of attitude and conduct for a person who, by dint of whatever circumstance and for any reason, finds himself within its context. Nevertheless, it is surely difficult to sustain such a contention in the face of the Torah's prelude to its establishment: לא טוב היות האדם לבדו אעשה לו עזר כנגדו, "It is not good that the man should be alone; I will make him a help to match him."[18] As the Rav noted in this connection, the term "good" is here not confined to subjective psychological gratification but encompasses ethical and existential well-being as well. Describing the verse as an "ontological postulate," he expounds: "A lonely human existence is not good; it lacks God's sanction and exposes an imperfect form of being."[19] Hence, "Marriage is not just a successful partnership, but an existential community."

The sense and the experience of that community is, of course, multi-faceted. I have heretofore, following my questioner, paired love and companionship, distinguishing both from the procreative process as a motive for marriage. They are, however, far from synonymous, and differ markedly, with respect to both ground and substance. While each can relieve the pangs of loneliness, the power and intensity of love, given or received, is in no way comparable to the relatively dispassionate and pragmatically oriented character of companionship. Both, however, within the context of a marriage, provide not only emotional warmth but human meaning, not without spiritual significance. Hence, *Yahadut* has not regarded celibacy, even when religiously motivated, as an ideal. When, as Hazal interpreted, Aharon and Miriam implied that they, too, should abandon marriage, as had Mosheh Rabbenu, they were, in effect, told that his situation was unique, and had no bearing upon theirs,[20] which should remain normal:

> הא למדת שכל הנביאים כשהנבואה מסתלקת מהם חוזרים לאהלם שהוא צרכי הגוף
> כלם כשאר העם לפיכך אין פורשין מנשותיהם ומשה רבינו לא חזר לאהלו הראשון
> לפיכך פירש מן האשה לעולם ומן הדומה לה ונקשרה דעתו לצור העולמים ולא נסתלק
> מעליו ההוד לעולם וקרן עור פניו ונתקדש כמלאכים.

> We have thus learned that when the prophecy of [other] prophets dissipates, they return to their tents — meaning their bodily needs — like the rest of the nation. [The prophets] are thus not to separate from their wives. Our teacher Mosheh, however, did not "return to his tent"; he thus separated from his wife, and similar needs, altogether. [Instead] his mind was bound to the "Rock of Eternity," as God's glory never dissipated from upon him. His face radiated with light, and he became holy like the angels.[21]

There may be, subsequently, rare exceptions:

> מי שחשקה נפשו בתורה תמיד ושונה בה כבן עזאי ודבק בה כל ימיו ולא נשא אשה
> אין בידו עון.

> Whosever's soul craves Torah constantly, is obsessed with its study like Ben-Azzai, and clings to [Torah] his whole life, thus neglecting to marry, *ein be-yado avon* (bears no sin).[22]

Ein be-yado avon is the most that, even in such a case, the Rambam could assert. The valued norm is marriage, and its centrality is not at issue.

What does appear to be very much at issue is not the institution of marriage *per se* but its physical component. By way of example, I recall vividly a discussion with Rav Elimelekh Bar-Shaul. I went to see him during my first stay in Israel, in the summer of 1962. In the course of my visit, a kollel student entered and asked him about an aggadic account concerning David and Avigail, cited in the gemara in Megillah:

אלא מלמד שגילתה את שוקה והלך לאורה ג׳ פרסאות אמר לה השמיעי לי אמרה לו
לא תהיה זאת לך לפוקה.

> Rather it teaches that [Avigail] revealed her thigh and David walked three full *parsas* by its light. He said to her: "Please tell me." She responded: "Do not let this be a cause of stumbling."[23]

Quite apart from the *Tosafot's*[24] question as to how the conduct was becoming Avigail, could it be possible, he objected, that God's anointed, *ne'im zemirot Yisrael*, would have been affected by the stimulus? In response, Rav Bar-Shaul launched into a twenty-minute disquisition, waxing almost lyrical as he explained that the impact was perfectly human and thoroughly honorable; that sexuality was an integral aspect of divinely ordered and ordained personality; and that, far from being associated with shame, it was, and was intended to be, a reflection of healthy vigor, fully consistent with the cardinal value of *zeniut*. Upon the interlocutor's departure, I observed to Rav Bar-Shaul that his position was an accurate expression of our modern sensibility, but, I questioned, was it consonant and consistent with the prevailing tone of prominent Rishonim. Parrying the inquiry, he contended that indeed it was; and on that assertive note, the discussion concluded, and there the matter rested.

But does it truly rest? We are confronted by a singular phenomenon, one which, historically, has been the subject of animated controversy within the world of religious thought: the symbol of unbridled lust, to some, and of quasi-mystical ecstasy, to others; almost unparalleled for sheer visceral intensity, and yet enveloped with romantic passion; its attendant denudation eradicating the line between the human and the bestial, on the one hand, while enabling maximal bonding, on the other; the most productive of human activity, in one respect, and, on most occasions, the most predictably fruitless endeavor, in another. The topic has generated much discourse and elicited polar responses as well as an intermediate spectrum; and indeed it does not rest easily.

Contemplating our own Torah world, one is persistently struck by an apparent dissonance between the impression conveyed by Hazal and Rishonim, respectively. In surveying the gemara, we are struck by both its omissions and its assertions, general as well as halakhic. There is little in the way of either squeamish embarrassment or outright reservation. There is no revulsion from concupiscent pleasure nor recoil from romantic passion:

> ההוא דהוה קאמר ואזיל כי רחימתין הוה עזיזא אפותיא דספסירא שכיבן השתא דלא
> עזיזא רחימתין פוריא בר שיתין גרמידי לא סגי לן.

One was wont to say: "When our love was intense, a bed the width of a blade was room enough for both of us to lie upon. Now that our love is less intense, a bed, the width of sixty cubits, does not suffice."[25]

At one point, the gemara in Berakhot explores the possibility that sexual activity constitutes one of a triad of elements which convey a sense of *me'ein olam ha-ba*;[26] and while the designation is subsequently rejected, the reason given bears no taint of principled objection, but rather consists of the prosaic observation that sexual activity may be physically enervating. Several *blatt* later, it recounts how Rav Kahana surreptitiously entered the bedroom of Rav, his master, in order to observe his conduct, as תורה היא וללמוד אני צריך, "It is Torah, and I must learn," and noted the excitable passion which had suffused the relations.[27] Elsewhere, the gemara patently reproaches a person who sleeps in the same room with a married couple, thus precluding them, indirectly, from experiencing sexual pleasure.

> כל הישן בקילעא שאיש ואשתו שרויין בה עליו הכתוב אומר נשי עמי תגרשון מבית
> תענוגיה.

One who sleeps in an enclosure where a man and his wife lie, it is of him that the verse states, "You drive the women of My people away from their pleasant homes" (Mikhah 2:9).[28]

Indeed, it goes so far as to state that the critique applies even if the wife is a *niddah*, inasmuch, presumably, as the intrusive disruption of even aphysical intimacy is objectionable.

In a more purely aggadic vein, we note a remarkable portrait of postmortal embrace of Avraham and Sarah:

> רב בנאה הוה קא מציין מערתא כי מטא למערתא דאברהם אשכחיה לאליעזר עבד אברהם דקאי קמי בבא א"ל מai קא עביד אברהם א"ל גאני בכנפה (פירש רשב"ם: "בין זרועותיה") דשרה וקא מעיינא ליה ברישיה.

> Rav Bana'ah was marking out [burial] caves. When he reached that of Avraham, he encountered Eliezer, Avraham's servant, standing at the gate. He said to him, "What is Avraham doing?" He responded, "He is lying in Sarah's arms and she is peering at his head."[29]

And the point is further underscored with reference to the *avot* and *immahot* in another context. ולמה נתעקרו האמהות, "Why were the foremothers barren," asks the *midrash*; and, *inter alia*, it goes on to cite two complementary explanations related to our theme:

> רב עזריה משום ר' יוחנן בר פפא כדי שיהיו מתרפקות על בעליהן, בנויין... ר' הונא ור' אבון בשם ר' מאיר אמר כדי שיהנו בעליהן מהן שכל זמן שהאשה מקבלת עוברין היא מתכערת ומתעזבת.

> R. Azaryah said in the name of R. Yohanan bar Papa that it was in order that women should endear themselves to their husbands with their beauty.... R. Huna and R. Avun in the name of R. Mayer say that it was in order that their husbands should derive pleasure from them, for when a woman conceives she becomes disfigured and lacks grace.[30]

Finally, in a more explicitly ideological mode, we are of course all familiar with Rabbi Mayer's rationale for the prohibition of *niddah*:

> מפני מה אמרה תורה נדה לשבעה מפני שרגיל בה וקץ בה אמרה תורה תהא טמאה שבעה ימים כדי שתהא חביבה על בעלה כשעת כניסתה לחופה.

Why did the Torah ordain that the impurity of menstruation should continue for seven days? Because being in constant contact with his wife [a husband might] develop a loathing towards her. The Torah, therefore, ordained: Let her be unclean for seven days in order that she shall be beloved by her husband as at the time of her first entry into the bridal chamber.[31]

The assertion that, far from being meant to diminish the scope of marital sexuality, the injunction is rather intended to intensify it, speaks for itself.

Turning to halakhic contexts, we encounter a similar message. Relations on the holiest day of the week are not only permitted but encouraged, as תשמיש המטה מעונג שבת הוא, "marital relations are part of the Sabbath delight."[32] A prospective bridegroom is exempt from reciting *keri'at shema* for several days prior to his wedding, inasmuch as one who is engaged in performing one *mizvah*, whose discharge interferes with another,[33] is released from the latter. In his case, anticipatory contemplation of his initial marital encounter is defined as a legitimate dispensation from the need to concentrate upon *shema*, even though a person who has just lost a fortune enjoys no such dispensation, being rather ordered to transcend his voluntary despondency, regarded as a *tirda di'reshut*, and to focus upon his *avodat Hashem*.[34] Or again, Halakhah mandates that a pregnant or nursing woman may or must embrace otherwise problematic birth control. The dictum has spawned an extensive literature on the topic, but at no point has a responsible *posek* suggested that the couple simply abstain.[35]

Prima facie, another familiar dictum might be perceived as sounding a less positive note.

אמר רב חנן בר רב הכל יודעין כלה למה נכנסה לחופה אלא כל המנבל פיו ומוציא דבר נבלה מפיו אפילו נחתם לו גזר דינו של שבעים שנה לטובה נהפך עליו לרעה.

Said R. Hanan, the son of Rav: All know for what purpose a bride is brought into the bridal canopy. But whoever disgraces his mouth and utters a word of folly — even if a [divine] decree of seventy years of happiness was sealed [and granted] unto him — it is turned for him into evil.[36]

However, given the broader context we have noted, it is reasonable to assume that the stricture does not apply to verbal acknowledgment of the sexual aspect of marriage *per se* — after all, the gemara is replete with expositions of its halakhic and its physical minutiae — but rather to its lascivious if not pornographic savoring, with licentious titillation. Refrain from prurience need not issue in prudery.

This harvest stands in marked contrast to positions adopted by some of the foremost Rishonim. In a major chapter in *Mishneh Torah*, devoted to the rejection of excessive asceticism and positing the mishnah's dictum, וכל מעשיך יהיו לשם שמים, "Let all your actions be for the sake of heaven,"[37] as an overriding spiritual ideal, the Rambam evidently found no place for either love or companionship as the *raison d'être* of marital sexuality:

> וכן כשיבעול לא יבעול אלא כדי להבריות גופו וכדי לקיים את הזרע לפיכך אינו בועל
> כל זמן שיתאוה אלא כל עת שידע שהוא צריך להוציא שכבת זרע כמו דרך הרפואה
> או לקיים את הזרע.

> So, too, when one has sexual relations, he should act in order to maintain his health and to reproduce. Therefore, he should not have relations any time he desires, rather only during the time when he must produce semen as a medical need or for the sake of reproduction.[38]

In the *Moreh*, he ascribes the designation of Hebrew as *leshon ha-kodesh* to the paucity of its sexual nomenclature: "For in this holy language no word at all has been laid down in order to designate either the male or the female organ of copulation, nor are there words designating the act itself that brings about generation… No word at all designating, according to its first meaning, any of these things has been laid down in the Hebrew language, they being signified by terms used in a figurative sense, and by allusions."[39] The Ramban[40] challenged this judgment, although without explicitly confronting its underlying premise. Elsewhere, however, he, in turn, gives vent to the same general attitude. Remarkably, he does so in direct contradistinction from Rabbi Mayer's rationale for the prohibition regarding relations with a *niddah*:

> אסר הכתוב הנדה מפני טעם שהזכרתי שלא התירה התורה המשכב רק לקיום הזרע

והנה הולד נוצר מדם האשה כולו או רובו כאשר הזכרתי כבר, ומדם הנדות לא יהיה
נוצר כלל.

The verse prohibits [cohabiting] with a *niddah* for the reason I already
noted. For the Torah allows cohabitation only for the sake of reproduction. The fetus, moreover, is formed from either fully or mostly from
the woman's [real] blood; it cannot be formed from the menstrual
blood.[41]

This, on the heels of an earlier sweeping apodictic statement, ודע כי המשגל
דבר מרוחק ונמאס בתורה זולתי לקיום המין, "Know that sexual relations, in the
Torah, are remote and disgusting, unless they are for the sustenance of the
species."[42] Subsequently, he cites, with evident approval, a milder formulation of Ibn Ezra:

אמר ר"א כי המשגל לשלשה חלקים נחלק, האחד לפריה ורביה, והשני להקל מלחות
הגוף, והשלישי לתאוה הנמשלת לתאות הבהמות.

Said R. Avraham [Ibn Ezra]: There is a threefold purpose to sexual
relations: the first for reproduction; the second to ease the bodily
necessities; and the third for passion, which is likened to that of the
animals.[43]

Conceivably, however, the citation only presents a value-neutral classification; and, in any event, the bestial instinctual drive noted alongside the
procreative and the medicinal, is still poles removed from the world of
love and companionship.

Admittedly, a more balanced and even positive attitude finds expression in two *loci classici*, the fullest expositions of the subject in the writings
of Rishonim — the concluding chapter of the Rabad's *Ba'alei Ha-Nefesh*
and the anonymous *Iggeret Ha-Kodesh*, often erroneously attributed to the
Ramban. In his "*Sha'ar Ha-Kedushah*," the Rabad anchors the discussion
of marital sexuality within the broader context of the need to discipline
unbridled passional psychic and biophysical impulse in the quest for purgative sanctity:

ועל כן צריך האדם להתחזק ולהתגבר על יצרו ולעמוד על נפשו ולהלחם בתאוותיו
כדי שיהא לו מעלה בנפשו על נפש הבהמה שאין לה מעצור מכל אשר תשיג לתאוותה.

One must therefore overwhelm and conquer his inclination, standing upon his soul to fight his urges, in order that his soul should rise above that animalistic soul which has nothing which prevents it from obtaining all its desires.[44]

Significantly, this prefatory comment does not distinguish radically between various impulses, and sexuality is treated within the pale of the general spectrum, ranging between ascetic suppression and indulgent accommodation. Moreover, he does not delegitimize all unproductive relations. Nevertheless, of the four motivations whose value the Rabad acknowledges, the first two refer to procreation, the last to relieving pressures which might lead to sinful action and fantasy, and the third to responsiveness to a wife's romantic needs and advances:

> והשלישית... שהיא משתוקקת אליו והוא מכיר בה שהיא משתדלת ומרצה אותו
> ומתקשטת לפניו כדי שיתן דעתו עליה.

The third…that she desires him and he recognizes her attempts to please him. She adorns herself that he should notice her.[45]

This is still a far cry from Rav Bar-Shaul's cadences.

In contrast, a genuinely enthusiastic tone pervades the discussion of the *Iggeret Ha-Kodesh*. After an introductory chapter explaining the purpose and direction of the manual, he confronts the axiological issue head-on:

> דע כי חבור זה הוא ענין קדוש ונקי כשיהיה הדבר כפי מה שראוי ובזמן הראוי ובכוונה
> הנכונה, ואל יחשוב אדם כי בחבור הראוי יש גנאי וכיעור ח"ו... אבל כל בעלי התורה
> מאמינים שהשם ברא את הכל כפי מה שגזרה חכמתו ולא ברא דבר שיהיה גנאי או
> כיעור. שאם יאמר שהחבור הוא דבר של גנאי הנה כלי המשגל הם כלי הגנות והרי
> השי"ת בראם במאמרו דכתיב הוא עשך ויכוננך... ואם כלי המשגל גנאי היאך ברא
> הש"י דבר שיש בו משום חסרון או גנות חלילה.

Know that intercourse is clean and holy when it is done appropriately at the appropriate time and with the correct intentions. One should not think that appropriate intercourse contains anything shameful or ugly.… All those who hold fast to Torah believe that God created everything according to His wisdom and did not create anything

shameful or disgusting. For if intercourse is shameful, then the sexual organs are shameful organs, yet it was God who created them with His word, as it says "He created you, and prepared you" (Devarim 32:6)....
If the sexual organs were truly shameful, how could God have created something deficient or shameful, God forbid?[46]

However, I believe there is little question but that this chord, music to modern ears, is, in the medieval context, decidedly in the minority — not quite *sotto voce* but surely *pianissimo*. The selfsame Ba'al Ha-Turim who opens his magnum opus with the paean we have noted, paraphrases, in his *perush* to Vayikra,[47] the Ramban, without comment but, probably, with approval. And we have not so much as glanced at the renunciatory *hasidei Ashkenaz*, with their delegitimization of virtually all passionate sensory pleasure.

The attitudinal issue may perhaps be gauged by an additional parameter. While marital love is, hopefully, not readily quantifiable, the recommended frequency of relations presumably reflects, *inter alia*, how they are perceived, axiologically. halakhically, the matter is discussed within the context of the *mizvah* of *onah*, the normative duty incumbent upon a husband to satisfy his wife's sexual needs.[48] In sum, various standards are posited, albeit with a measure of flexibility, taking into account a number of variables: the husband's ability, on the one hand — depending upon vocation, strength, competing interests etc. — and the wife's needs, on the other, with a particular eye to expectations raised at the time of the marriage. Our present focus, however, is precisely the point at which duty is exhausted and transcended, the province, beyond halakhic norm, in which inclination, ideology, and aspiration hold sway.

In this connection, the primary *locus classicus* is generally perceived as the gemara in Berakhot, concerning the requirement that a *ba'al keri*, one who has experienced a seminal emission, immerse in a proper *mikveh* before he be permitted to study Torah.[49] This demand is not grounded in the laws of ritual purity, strictly defined, as no similar standard is set for persons who have attained a graver degree of *tum'ah*.[50] Rather, two factors are cited. The first is the need to sustain, in every encounter with Torah, the degree of awe which characterized its revelation at Sinai:

דתניא והודעתם לבניך ולבני בניך וכתיב בתריה יום אשר עמדת לפני ה' א-לקיך בחורב מה להלן באימה וביראה וברתת ובזיע אף כאן באימה וביראה וברתת ובזיע מכאן אמרו הזבים והמצורעים ובאין על נדות מותרים לקרות בתורה ובנביאים ובכתובים לשנות במשנה וגמרא ובהלכות ובאגדות אבל בעלי קריין אסורים.

As it has been taught: "And you shall make them known to your children and your children's children," and it is written immediately afterwards, "The day on which you stood before the Lord your God in Horev" (Devarim 4:10). Just as there it was in dread and fear and trembling and quaking, so too in this case it must be in dread and fear and trembling and quaking. On the basis of this they established that those with gonorrhea, lepers, and those who had intercourse with *niddot* are permitted to read the Torah, the Prophets, and the Hagiographa, and to study the Mishnah, Gemara, halakhot and haggadot; but a *ba'al keri* is forbidden.[51]

This reason may be of some relevance to our broader issue, but a second presumably addresses our specific question, immediately:

שלא יהו תלמידי חכמים מצויים אצל נשותיהם כתרנגולים.

That scholars should not frequent their wives like roosters.[52]

The Rambam understood this to mean that the requirement was intended to have a deterrent effect, discouraging frequent marital relations; and the text thus serves as a primary source for a general evaluation and recommendation:

אין דעת חכמים נוחה למי שהוא מרבה בתשמיש המטה ויהיה מצוי אצל אשתו כתרנגול ופגום הוא עד מאד ומעשה בורים הוא אלא כל הממעט בתשמיש הרי זה משובח והוא שלא יבטל עונה אלא מדעת אשתו ולא תקנו בראשונה לבעלי קריין שלא יקראו בתורה עד שיטבלו אלא כדי למעט בתשמיש המטה.

The Sages were displeased with one who engages in sexual relations excessively, and frequents his wife like a rooster. This reflects a very blemished character; it is the way boors conduct themselves. Rather, praiseworthy is one who diminishes his cohabitation; nevertheless, he should not be delinquent in his conjugal duties without his wife's consent. [The Sages] prohibited a seminally impure person from reading the Torah only so that he should diminish his sexual engagement.[53]

The interpretation and the inference are open to question, however. At one plane, the gemara does not state that the deterrent factor constituted the basic ground of the requirement. It recounts that other *tanna'im* held that a lesser purgative ritual, the pouring of a fairly small body of pure water upon the *ba'al keri*, sufficed, and that their students disagreed as to whether this ruling should be freely publicized. Only those who opposed publicizing this ruling were animated by concern over excessive sexuality.

At another plane, the gemara narrates that the *halakhah* was later rescinded — this, in accordance with the view of a later *tanna*:

תניא ר' יהודה בן בתירא היה אומר אין דברי תורה מקבלין טומאה... שנאמר הלא
כה דברי כאש נאם ה' מה אש אינו מקבל טומאה אף דברי תורה אינן מקבלין טומאה.

It has been taught: R. Yehudah ben Betera used to say: Words of Torah are not susceptible to impurity…as it says, "Is not My word like as fire" (Yirmiyahu 23:29). Just as fire is not susceptible to impurity, so words of Torah are not susceptible to impurity.[54]

This repeal invites two questions. First, in light of the principle that later *hakhamim* can rescind earlier legislation only if they are superior to their predecessors in wisdom and scope,[55] whence did Rabbi Yehudah ben Betera and his peers derive the authority to override Ezra's innovation? Second, derivatively, what was the rationale and the context of the repeal? The assertion that Torah is beyond defilement perhaps neutralizes the need for an analogue to Sinai. But what of the impact upon sexual habits? Does this remain in place or was this concern, too, rejected? As to the first question, *Tosafot* suggest two historical factors attendant upon the original ruling: Rabbi Yehudah ben Betera either challenged the historicity of Ezra's involvement, וי"ל דלמא סבר דלא תקן עזרא דבר זה; "perhaps he believed that Ezra did not establish this law;"[56] or, more moderately, that he had, from the outset, instituted a contingent requirement, explicitly leaving open the option of later repeal. The Rambam, however, presents a third alternative:

ולא פשטה תקנה זו בכל ישראל ולא היה כח ברוב הציבור לעמוד בה לפיכך בטלה.

This ordinance (*takkanah*) was not universally accepted among the people. Most were unable to observe it consistently and it was there-fore annulled.[57]

On the basis of *sugyot* in Avodah Zarah, he elsewhere[58] formulates quali-fications allowing for repeal of *takkanot* which had not taken root in the first place, particularly, if they proved to be excessively burdensome; and he applies those exceptions here.

Given this explanation, there is no reason to assume that the earlier reasoning had been subsequently rejected. Indeed, there need be no pro-cess of formal repeal by a later *bet din*, but only the determination of a sociological fact. However, the Meiri suggests a fourth alternative.

יש מפרשים הטעם שלא נאמר אין בית דין יכול לבטל וכו' אלא במה שנתקן מחמת גדר
אבל מה שנתקן ממקראות והם רואים לפרשם בדרך אחרת רשאים.

Some explain that the prohibition of a current bet din to revoke the *takkanah* of an earlier bet din applies only when the ordinance was passed as a safeguard. However, if it is an interpretive ordinance, the later *bet din* may interpret it differently.[59]

Having asserted that the limit upon a later *bet din*'s ability to rescind only refers to *takkanot* which were grounded upon a perceived need to safeguard Torah values and avoid violation, but not to the challenge of Scriptural interpretation, he goes on to specify how this qualification enabled rejection of the analogue to Sinai and of the ruling grounded upon it. The omission of any reference to the aim of inhibiting marital relations, leaves open the possibility that this rationale, too, is, finally, refuted; or, at the very least, that it is conceded, against the Rambam, that it had never been a *raison d'être* in the first place, but rather, at most, a disputed tactical reason for restraint in publicizing the repeal.

Perhaps most pressing, however, is a third consideration. While the Rambam, previously cited, counseled minimal sexuality for all, the gemara, even on the assumption that the *takkanah* was designed as a deterrent, only refers to *talmidei hakhamim*. This focus can, without much question, be understood in the Rambam's terms. While, on his view, sensual restraint is universally preferable, it is particularly advisable for a spiritual elite, to be held to a higher standard. The Rambam adhered to such a pattern in many contexts — notably, in Hilkhot De'ot of *Mishneh Torah*, in which, after four chapters devoted to molding the personality of the layman, he opens the fifth with a clear line of demarcation:

כשם שהחכם ניכר בחכמתו ובדעותיו והוא מובדל בהם משאר העם כך צריך שיהיה ניכר במעשיו במאכלו ובמשקהו ובבעילתו ובעשיית צרכיו ובדבורו ובהילוכו ובמלבושו ובכלכול דבריו ובמשאו ובמתנו.

Just as the wise man distinguishes himself from others with his wisdom and his temperaments and, in these, he stands apart from the rest of the nation, so, too, he should distinguish himself through his actions, his food and drink, his sexual relations, his bodily requirements, his speech, his walk, his dress, his maintenance, and his business dealings.[60]

Correspondingly, several *halakhot* later, he embodies this thesis with respect to sexuality:

אף על פי שאשתו של אדם מותרת לו תמיד ראוי לו לתלמיד חכם שינהיג עצמו בקדושה ולא יהא מצוי אצל אשתו כתרנגול אלא מלילי שבת ללילי שבת אם יש בו כח.

Though a wife is consistently permitted to her husband, a scholar should act with holiness and not frequent his wife like a rooster. [He should be with her], if he has the physical stamina, only from one Sabbath night to the next.[61]

However, it is entirely conceivable that *talmidei hakhamim* are singled out by the gemara for an entirely different reason.

The graduated list of required *onah*, with vocation designated as a primary variable, opens: העונה האמורה בתורה הטיילין בכל יום, "The times for *onah* prescribed in the Torah are: for *tayyalin* everyday." The gemara then asks, מאי טיילין; "What is meant by *tayyalin*," and, in response, cites divergent conceptions:

אמר רבא בני פירקי אמר ליה אביי מאן דכתיב בהן שוא לכם משכימי קום מאחרי

שבת אוכלי לחם העצבים כן יתן לידידו שנא ואמר רב יצחק אלו נשותיהן של תלמידי
חכמים שמנדדות שינה מעיניהם בעולם הזה ובאות לחיי העולם הבא ואת אמרת בני
פירקי אלא אמר אביי כדרב דאמר רב כגון רב שמואל בר שילת דאכיל מדידיה ושתי
מדידיה וגני בטולא דאפדניה ולא חליף פריסתקא דמלכא אבביה כי אתא רבין אמר
כגון מפנקי דמערבא.

What is meant by *tayyalin*? Rava replied: day students (*benei pirkei*). Said Abaye to him: [These are the men] of whom it is written in Scripture (Tehillim 127:2), "It is vain for you that you rise early, and sit up late, those that eat of the bread of toil; so He gives to those who chase their sleep away." "These," R. Yizhak explained, are the wives of the scholars, who chase the sleep from their eyes in this world and achieve thereby the life of the world to come. Yet you say [that *tayyalin* are] "day students!" [The explanation], however, said Abaye, is in agreement [with a statement] of Rav who said that [a *tayyal* is one] for instance, like R. Shemuel b. Shilat who eats of his own, drinks of his own, and sleeps in the shadow of his mansion and a king's officer never passes his door. When Ravin came he stated: [A *tayyal* is one], for instance, like the pampered men of the West (Israel).[62]

Ravin's definition — essentially, relaxed, effete, and possibly sybaritic men — is not surprising. Those of Rava and Abbaye probably are. With respect to *benei pirkei*, Rashi explains: תלמידים שהרב מצוי להם בעירן ושונים פרקם ולנים בביתם, "Students whose rabbi dwells in their town. They therefore may learn while living in their own homes." These are, in effect, roughly the equivalent of contemporary kollel students. And yet, Rava did not cavil at the thought that they, of all people, would be charged with nightly relations. Moreover, Abbaye does not challenge this conception on philosophic or axiological grounds. He does not address issues of spiritual decadence or passional surfeit. He simply contends, as Rashi explains, that the pressures of Torah learning and the time they need to devote to prolonged sojourn in the *bet midrash* clearly preclude nightly conjugal activity; or, conversely, as suggested by Talmidei Rabbenu Yonah,[63] that the effort expended in the course of intensive study, may be debilitating and enervating, no less than the energy exerted by the ordinary laborer. Moreover, Abbaye's exemplar is a *melammed tinnokot*, the instructor of children; and, with regard to him, too, daily *onah* is not regarded as inconsonant with his lofty spiritual career.

The implication is clear; and the brief interchange may suggestively explain why, in the gemara's discussion concerning *ba'al keri, talmidei hakhamim* are singled out. The formulation may simply be regarded as a variant of Abbaye's position. Read in this vein, the passage expresses neither revulsion from the carnal nor ideological recoil from the manifest blend of the physical, the psychic, and the spiritual of which sexual experience is comprised. The issue rather turns upon the conflict of resources and the consequent need to budget time, attention, and energy — fundamentally, the same type of concern that would arise with regard to any activity which would divert attention and capacity from the world of *talmud Torah*. Hence, the singling out of the *talmid hakham*, as opposed to the ordinary layman. The maintenance of a proper balance between mundane concerns, however innocent, and spiritual aspirations is, of course, a major axiological challenge in its own right; and the excessive preoccupation with the temporal is the object of criticism:

מניחין חיי עולם ועוסקין בחיי שעה.

Putting aside heavenly matters in favor of the mundane.[64]

This is radically different, however, from the rejection of a given sphere of activity as problematic *per se*.

Perhaps even more noteworthy is a parallel, and yet remarkably different, formulation in the Yerushalmi:

א"ר יעקב בר אבון כל עצמן לא התקינו את הטבילה הזאת אלא שלא יהו ישראל כתרנגולין הללו משמש מיטתו ועולה ויורד ואוכל.

R. Ya'akov bar Avun said: the only reason they instituted this *tevilah* (ritual immersion) was so the Israelites would not be like roosters, having relations, rising, then descending to eat.[65]

In contrast with the disdain for sexuality the Rambam elicited from the Bavli,[66] we encounter here an appreciation of its worth as the basis for the *takkanah* of *tevilah*. At the heart of the matter, lies the critical distinction between animal and human sexuality. For the cock, coitus constitutes, at most, an intense physiological experience, of brief duration and of no subsequent perceptible import. It is, in a word, casual. For man and woman, endowed with the capacity for "looking before and after," charged with the mandate to infuse even erotic activity with meaning, the same experience is framed within the context of an existential relationship, and, particularly when informed by religious content, invests the persons and their encounter with passional and spiritual purpose. It is precisely in order to underscore the significance of sexual relations, in order to focus attention upon their character and consequences, that *tevilah* was ordained. The restraints imposed sans *tevilah*, are intended to assure that relations *not* be casual. They generate interactive awareness which serves to ennoble and enhance sexuality, elevating it, redemptively, from the bestial to the human. And, inasmuch as this aspiration is not confined to an elite cadre of the learned, Rav Yaakov bar Abun speaks, comprehensively, of all:

שלא יהיו ישראל כתרנגולין הללו משמש מיטתו ועולה ויורד ואוכל.

So the Israelites would not be like roosters, having relations, rising, then descending to eat.

The question of frequency confronted — and, in a sense, confounded — a leading Ashkenazi *posek*, the thirteenth-century author of the *Or Zarua*. On the one hand, he quotes the gemara's explanation regarding *ba'al keri*, which he interprets, like the Rambam, as referring to the deterrent aspect of the *takkanah*, as well as the recommendation that the *onah* of *talmidei hakhamim* be לערב שבת מערב שבת. On the other hand, he cites a narrative from a gemara in Ketubbot, which seems to point in the opposite direction:

מיהו ההיא עובדא דמייתי בסמוך אתיא לי קצת בגמגום דמסיק התם יהודה בריה דרבי חייא חתניה דר' ינאי הוה אזיל ויתיב בבי רב וכל בי שמשי הוה אתא לביתיה וכי הוה אתי הוה קא חזי קמיה עמודא דנורא יומא חדא משכתיה שמעתיה כיון דלא חזי ההוא סימנא אמר להו כפו מטתו שאלמלי יהודה קיים לא בטל עונתו הוי כשגגה שיצאה מלפני השליט ונח נפשיה משמע שמעליותא היא שהיה תדיר אצל אשתו.

However, that certain case that the Talmud relates (Ketubbot 62b) is a bit unclear to me. There it concludes that Yehudah the son of R. Hiyya and son-in-law of R. Yanai was sitting in the house of learning. "*Kol bei shimshei*," [Yehudah] went to his house only to be confronted by [the vision of] a pillar of fire. One day he became engrossed in his learning [and remained] and did not see the sign. They said to turn over his bed [like a mourner], for were Yehudah alive, he would not have missed his marital requirement. It was like "an error committed by a ruler" (Kohelet 10:5) and he died. We can conclude that it was praiseworthy that he was often with his wife.[67]

Unlike Rashi, who, elsewhere[68] interprets *kol bei shimshi* as "weekly," the *Or Zarua* understood the phrase, more literally, as "nightly;" hence, his difficulty.

We, for our part, are confronted by a quandary of our own; and it is dual. At one plane, we ask ourselves, within the context of our learning, תורה היא וללמוד אנו צריכים, it is Torah, and we must learn, a simple and straightforward question: In light of the predominant evidence we have noted from Hazal — and, particularly, from its halakhic component, how and why did the Rambam, the Ramban, and some other Rishonim, deviate so markedly from their prevalent attitude? With reference to *yezer* — generic in connotation but defined by Rashi as *shel tashmish* — Hazal identify it as one of a triad which, optimally, תהא שמאל דוחה וימין מקרבת, "let the left hand deflect and the right hand bring close."[69] One sometimes gets the impression that the proportion was subsequently inverted.

The allure of facile historicistic solutions — in our case, of ascription to Sufi or Scholastic influences, regarding worldliness, in general, or sexuality, in particular — is palpably self-evident. In dealing with giants, however, we strive to avoid succumbing to its alluring temptations.

To be sure, post-Hazal *gedolim*, Rishonim or Aharonim may be affected by the impact of contact with a general culture to which their predecessors had not been exposed and to whose content and direction they respond. Upon critical evaluation of what they have encountered, they may incorporate what they find consonant with tradition and reject what is not. In the process, they may legitimately enlarge the bounds of their *hashkafah* and introduce hitherto unperceived insights and interpretations. Noone questions Aristotle's impact upon the Rambam or Kierkegaard's upon the Rav. In our case, however, we are seemingly dealing with apparent contravention rather than nuanced accretion; hence, while we may assign some weight to the historical factor, this will hardly suffice, and we must entertain other factors as well, seeking resolution in other directions. Probably the most promising is the suggestion that the sources I have cited were, in the eyes of some Rishonim, qualitatively outweighed by others. Most significantly, we might note his wife's account of Rabbi Eliezer's marital conduct and attitude which, as a paradigm, figures prominently in the *Ba'alei Ha-Nefesh*.

וכשהוא מספר מגלה טפח ומכסה טפח ודומה עליו כמו שכפאו שד.

> When he "converses," he uncovers a *tefah* while concurrently hiding a *tefah*, and is as though he were compelled by a demon.[70]

According to some interpretations, cited by the Rabad, the concluding phrase signifies an admixture of recoil reflected in brevity:

פי' דומה כמי שהבעיתו שד ונבעת והניח את המעשה, כל כך היה מקצר את התשמיש.

> Meaning it is as if the demon kicked him and he acts, and then relinquishes the action. That is how much he shortened sexual relations.[71]

However, other interpretations abound — some going so far as to suggest that the procedure was intended to increase, rather than diminish, passion;[72] and, in any event, one is still perplexed by the positive attitude presumably reflected in the relevant *halakhot*. This evidence is sometimes deflected by the contention that the encouragement of, say, relations on Shabbat is grounded in the fulfillment of conjugal obligation rather than in axiological approval. This is strange doctrine, however. It seems odd that Halakhah would recommend engaging in activity conceived as דבר מרוחק ונמאס בתורה זולתי לקיום המין "distant and disgusting in the Torah, unless performed for the maintenance of the species" solely in order to satisfy perceived wifely infirmity — and that this should be performed, of all times, on Shabbat. Hence, while the conjecture I have advanced appears to me reasonable and likely, much of the difficulty remains.

To the extent that we do succeed in harmonizing the positions of
Hazal and of Rishonim, we ameliorate the pressure of one issue but exac-
erbate that of another. For we are brought, in turn, to a second quandary
— our own. While I have conducted no empirical survey, I believe there is
little question regarding the sensibility of the contemporary Torah world,
irrespective of camp and orientation. We stand, fundamentally, with Rav
Bar-Shaul. We assert the value of romantic love, its physical manifestation included, without flinching from the prospect of concomitant sensual
pleasure; and we do so without harboring guilt or reservations. We insist,
of course, upon its sanctification — this, within the context of suffusive
kedushah of carnal experience, generally. We do not, in any sense and
form, join Blake, Lawrence, and their ideological confreres in celebrat-
ing lusty passion in isolation, and, on both halakhic and ethical grounds
— which are, in a meaningful sense, themselves halakhic — reject non-
marital sexuality as transient, vulgar and possibly exploitative, devoid of
interpersonal commitment or social and legal sanction. Moreover, even
with reference to the context of marriage, we recoil from the supposed
transmutation of the erotic into a quasi-mystical experience, bordering on
the transcendental, encountered in some quarters. Conceptually and historically, such associations are idolatrous rather than Jewish. With regard
to the basic phenomenon of sexual experience, however, our instincts and
our attitude are clearly positive. We have no qualms. Relatively few are
familiar — or, perhaps even comfortable with the substance or rhetoric
of the Shelah's formulation:

עניין הזיווג כשהוא בקדושה ובטהרה הוא קדוש במאד מעורר למעלה; מתקדש מלמטה
מעט מקדשין אותו מלמעלה הרבה, ומקיים קדושים תהיו כי קדוש אני ה' א-לקיכם כל
כל זיווג הוא מעין זיווג אדם וחוה הנעשה בצלמו ודמותו יתברך.

With respect to copulation, when enacted with holiness and purity,
it is most holy, bestirring [matters] above; a person sanctifies himself in the nether [realm], and he is sanctified greatly from the upper
[realm], and he fulfills [the commandment], "You shall be holy, for I
am the Lord your God am holy" (Vayikra 19:2). For every copulation
resembles that of Adam and Eve, performed in His form and image.[73]

But as to the fundamental attitude, we are very much attuned.

This attitude is clearly manifest in a section from Rav Kook's *Orot Ha-Kodesh*, aptly titled, הנטיה המינית לעתיד (The Future of Sexual Inclination):

הנטיה המינית הולכת היא וזורמת אל העתיד, אל שכלול החיים, שיביא הזמן, את חיי העולם הבא בעולם הזה. ומתוך שהחיים העתידים הנם מלאים הוד ונעם מלא, על כן גדולה היא שאיפת החפץ ועז הרצון של נטית עולמים זאת, והקדושה המגמתית רק עליה היא משרה את אורה. והנפש הטהורה מנהגת את נטיה זו למגמתה.

> The sexual inclination goes and pours forth toward the future, toward the perfect existence; it will bring a time when the existence of the world to come will be present in this world. For the future existence is filled with splendor and pleasantness. Great, therefore, is this intense desire, this powerful longing of the eternal inclination; and the tendentious Holiness settles its light only upon [this desire]. And the pure soul steers this desire towards its destination.[74]

The passage presumably reflects a general tendency to affirmative "world-acceptance," but its thrust, with respect to this particular area is, for our purposes, nonetheless noteworthy.

Readers of these lines are probably more familiar, however, with the Rav's formulations — less florid but sharper, more comprehensive, and more explicit. The fullest treatment appears in the chapter on "The Redemption of Sexual Life," in the posthumously published volume, *Family Redeemed*. The essay confronts the prospect of shame, distinguishing radically between it and the shyness embodied in *zeni'ut*; interweaves sexuality and community; harnesses sensibility to nuanced interpretation of phrases in the opening chapters of Bereshit, regarding the human and the animal order, respectively; and concludes with a striking declaration: "Oneness of the flesh is a metaphor indicative of complete unity, of a community of souls which comes into existence under the pressure of the sexual urge."[75]

The theme had been developed, however, in writings published during the Rav's lifetime, typified by a sub-chapter on the topic within the context of the discourse on *ha'ala'at ha-guf*, towards the conclusion of *U'vikashtem Mi-sham*:

הן הפילוסופיה היוונית והן הנצרות לא תפסו את הבחינה המיטפיסית־מוסרית
בהזדווגות המינית. רק בהלכה יש לפעולה זו יסוד מוצק בחיים הדתיים – מצוות פרו
ורבו היא מצוה ראשונה שבתורה. חיי נשואין הם חיים טהורים ומבורכים. חייו של
הרווק, אף על פי שלא חטא מעולם, נוגדים את תפיסת ההלכה. כל מי שאינו נושא
אשה שרוי בלא שמחה, בלי ברכה ובלי תורה.

Neither Greek philosophy nor Christianity grasped the moral and
metaphysical aspects of the sexual union. Only the Halakhah gives
this act a solid basis in religious life; the commandment to "be fruitful
and multiply" (Bereshit 1:28) is the first one in the Torah. Marital life
is pure and blessed. The life of a bachelor, even if he has never sinned,
runs contrary to the view of the Halakhah. One who is not married
has no joy, no blessing, and no Torah (Yevamot 62b).[76]

Moreover, while the terminology and the rationale might vary — and the
readiness to deal with the topic explicitly, at all, considerably limited — I
have the distinct impression that the situation is not significantly different
within the haredi world. Rav Yosef Epstein's *Mizvot Ha-Bayit*[77] — his is an
authentic voice of the *yeshivot ha-mussar* — serves as a prime example. He
opens the section entitled *mili di'zni'uta* with a passage from the Shelah
which sings the praises of חיבור קטן הכמות ורב האיכות "quantitatively a small
treatise, yet qualitatively large" — to wit, the *Iggeret Ha-kodesh*; continues
with the passage I quoted previously from the *Iggeret* proper, and follows
this with a citation from Rav Yaakov Emden's collection of responsa, *Mor
U'Keziah*. Speaking of marital relations, the latter writes:

וחכמים האמתיים, העומדים בסוד ה', יודעים שהוא פועל חשוב טוב ומועיל גם לנפש,
אין ערוך אליו בכל מעשה בשר ודם, כשיופעל בכונה טהורה, ומחשבה זכה נקיה, קדוש
יאמר לו ודאי, ואין בו דופי פחיתות כל עיקר ולא גנאי, אדרבה הרבה יקר וגדולה יותר
מדאי נעשה לו לאדם השותף עם קונו ומתדמה לו במעשה בראשית, כמ״ש נעשה אדם.

True scholars, who stand in God's confidence, know that this act
(sexual union) is important and good and is advantageous to the soul
as well. There is no comparable value in all other acts of man when this
act is performed with pure intentions and innocent and wholesome
thoughts; certainly it is called holy. There is in it no flaw, nor deprecia-
tion, nor reproach. On the contrary, [this act] is so precious and great

that man becomes a partner with his Maker, and becomes akin to Him in the act of creation, as it says (Bereshit 1:26), "Let us make man."[78]

The conclusion clearly refers to the procreative aspect of sexuality, but, just as clearly, the passage as a whole expresses appreciation of the relations *per se*: ומועיל גם לגוף. Much the same spirit pervades Professor Yehudah Levi's *Ish, Ishah U'Mishpahah*,[79] warmly approbated by Rav Zalman Nehemiah Goldberg and Rav Yehoshua Neuwirth, and sprinkled with references to the Steipler's epistles. While the book is conceived as an antithesis to modernism (it is subtitled, *Modernah Mul Mesoret*), its thrust is, with respect to our issue, very much in line with contemporary winds of doctrine.

Assuming these facts to be correct — as regards my own spiritual environs, I can attest directly — we ask ourselves: How and why do we depart from positions articulated by some of our greatest, אנו מפיהם אשר חיים ומימיהם אנו שותים, "from whose mouths we live and from whose waters we drink" and, is this departure legitimate? Are we victims of the Zeitgeist, swept along by general sociohistorical currents? Do we tailor our attitude on this issue to conform to appetitive convenience and erotic desire? Have we, in this case, adopted a self-satisfying posture of facile world-acceptance clothed in culturally correct garb?

To the extent that I am capable of candid self-awareness, I trust these questions can and should be answered in the negative. Our commitment to sexuality, properly sanctified, redeemed and redeeming, does not derive from libidinous passion but is, rather, grounded in profound spiritual instincts — upon our recognition that וירא א־לקים את כל אשר עשה והנה טוב מאד, — "God saw all that He created, and behold it was very good" (Bereshit 1:31), on the one hand, and our quest for meaningful interpersonal commingling, on the other. It is, for us, not merely an instrument for parallel intense enjoyment, nor a vehicle for reciprocal consumption. It is, rather, a fundamental component in a comprehensive relationship — at once, both itself an aspect of that relationship and a means toward molding its totality. This is our honed perception of ודבק באשתו והיו לבשר אחד — "cleaving to his wife that they become one flesh" (Bereshit 2:24) — partly carnal, in one sense, and yet powerfully existential in another.

As to the basis of our attitude's legitimacy, within the context of authoritative tradition, several factors may be cited. At one plane, we are buttressed, be it only subliminally, by the conviction that we are siding with Hazal, and they with us. At another, we are assuaged by the sense that while, at worst, we may be disregarding the attitudinal counsel of some Rishonim, we are not countermanding their *pesak*; and that, with respect to issues of *hashkafah*, reliance upon minority views is more of a legitimate option than as regards specific halakhic matters.

Probably most significant, however, is our reliance upon our own mentors. Sensing that modern *gedolim, ha-shofet asher be'yamekha* — for our purposes, most notably, the Rav, but not he, alone — have examined the issue and the evidence and adopted a positive stance, we, ordinary students of Torah, follow in their footsteps, as we identify with their position. Whether they felt justified in accepting, out of the depths of their own conviction, a minority view; whether they held that our topic was essentially a matter of hashkafic proclivity, not necessarily amenable to the normal procedures of *pesak*; or whether some other unknown but imagined element — might, for instance, the hospitable climate of Kabbalistic sources, have had some impact — is a matter for conjecture. That the authority of our mentors can inform and sustain our sensibility is not.

I am left, nonetheless, with a lacuna. Even while adhering to the Rav's position, one may freely concede wishing that he had done for us what we have been challenged and constrained to do here: examine the various tiers of tradition and elucidate the basis for his own judgment and commitment. Admittedly, the need for such a confrontation recedes significantly, if one ascribes the *Iggeret Ha-Kodesh* to the Ramban. That would change the alignment of major *ba'alei mahshavah* amongst Rishonim appreciably, isolating the Rambam somewhat. That is a most unlikely assumption, however. Even if no other evidence existed — and it does[80] — the citations from his *perush* on Vayikra which I have adduced are strong enough ground, in and of themselves, for rejecting the ascription; and the Rav, for one, probably knew that.

As to the Rambam, the Rav did relate to his views, and sought to enlist

him in his own ranks. In a footnote appended to the passage I quoted from
U'vikashtem Mi-sham, he adds:

לאמיתו של דבר גם הרמב"ם, על אף נטיותיו האסקטיות, שבאו לידי ביטוי בייחוד
במורה, כשתיאר שמה התנגשות יצרי הגוף עם כמיהת הרוח לא-לוקים, תפס עמדה
חיובית לגבי החיבור המיני. הוא גינה את הבולמוס המיני וההתגרות המינית, ורבנו
תובע מאת האדם העלאת החיים המיניים וקידושם על ידי הטבעת מגמה הלכתית
עליהם.

Actually, even Maimonides, despite his ascetic tendencies — which
were expressed particularly in his *Guide of the Perplexed*, where he
described the clash between the bodily instincts and the spirit's longing
for God — had a positive attitude to sexual intercourse. He denounced
sexual overindulgence and sexual provocation. He demanded that
man uplift and sanctify his sexual life by stamping it with a halakhic
purpose.[81]

He then proceeds to list a three-pronged purpose for sexuality: physiological, procreative, as a social-religious end, and teleological, as a means to
the realization of historico-spiritual destiny. It must be conceded, however,
that the attempt is far from convincing, with the reference to excerpts
cited highly selective, bordering on the tendentious. So, in this respect,
the lacuna persists.

It may of course be rejoined that the gap I have noted with respect
to the Rambam does not relate to sexuality *per se*, but is to be perceived
within the broader context of asceticism and other-worldliness, with reference to which, both within the Torah world and that of general religious
thought — ours is, after all, a universal topic — different camps, with varying orientations and emphases, assuredly exist. Such an approach would
probably expand the authoritative base of *ba'alei mahshavah* upon which
one could presumably rely.

This is unquestionably true, but not wholly reassuring. Indeed, from
a certain perspective, the contention, far from ameliorating our concern,
possibly exacerbates it. For we are brought to confront, honestly and
squarely, and across a broader front, Wordsworth's lament, "The world is
too much with us, late and soon." Whether the account is true is, for the

modernist, in particular, "a question to be asked;" whether, in the process of being, pragmatically and ideologically, in the world, we do not, as the sonnet continues, "lay waste our powers."

That self-examination is, collectively and personally, a religious imperative. Nevertheless, with respect to our specific issue, we remain true to our abiding spiritual intuitions. We cannot, as the Shelah could not, acquiesce in the sense that so fundamental an aspect of physical and psychic reality is, by and large, merely a snare. We cannot, as the author of the *Iggeret Ha-Kodesh* could not, abandon the conviction that so central a component of human nature is not part of the *tov me'od* of primordial creation. Consequently, impelled by our spiritual instincts and animated by the faith instilled in us by our Torah mentors, we opt for consecration rather than abstinence. In this most sensitive area, we strive for a life which is energized rather than neutralized — not merely sterilized and sanitized but ennobled and ennobling. We are challenged to sanctify — by integrating sexuality within total sacral existence, characterized by the systole and diastole of divinely ordained denial and realization; and by infusing the relationship itself with human and spiritual content. This is by no means the easier course. May we have the wisdom and the commitment to render it the better.

Notes

1. See Hagigah 11b.
2. See Ketubbot 85a; cf. Rambam, Sanhedrin, 24:1.
3. See Shabbat 140a.
4. The description — with a possibly implicit prescription — does not appear in the gemara. It is found in Tanna De'vei Eliyahu, and thence, in the Rambam, Ishut 15:20, and in *Hagahot Maimoniyot, ad locum*. See also Keritut 28a: האב קודם לאם בכל מקום מפני שהוא ואמו חייבין בכבוד אביו — "In all cases the father precedes the mother; for the mother is herself required to honor the father." This refers, however, to service rather than subservience.
5. See Eruvin 18b.
6. Shemot Rabbah, 1:1.
7. Rav Joseph B. Soloveitchik, *Family Redeemed: Essays on Family Relationships* (New York, 2000), p. 31. The implicit equation between the antinomies of instrumental vs.

intrinsic and group vs. individual welfare is, I believe, open to question. A marriage may serve as a means to the attainment of personal desiderata which lie beyond its pale.

8. Ibid, p. 35.

9. *Tur Even Ha-Ezer*, 1. The proem is absent in the *Shulhan Arukh, Even Ha-Ezer*, which plunges directly into the normative mode. However, the Rema does add, as a codicil:

וכל מי שאין לו אשה שרוי בלא ברכה ובלא תורה כו' ולא נקרא אדם וכיון שנושא אשה עונותיו
מתפקפקים שנאמר מצא אשה מצא טוב ויפק רצון מה'.

One who has no wife is left without blessing, without Torah…he may not even be called a person. However, once he is married, his sins are "doubted" by God, as it is written (Mishlei 18:22): "One who has found a wife has found goodness, and has received the desirous doubt of God."

10. *Pesakim*, Ketubbot 1:12.

11. See Yevamot 2:6; Rashba and Ritba, Yevamot 22a. These may possibly refer only to incest *de'rabbanan*. See also *Minhat Hinnukh*, 1:8, in the Machon Yerushalayim edition; and Maharit Algazi, Hilkhot Bekhorot, 9:65, which deal with this issue with reference to the problem of *mizvah ha-ba'ah ba'averah*.

12. Yeshayahu 45:18; see Gittin 41b, Megillah 27a, and Bava Batra 13a.

13. Yevamot 63b.

14. Yevamot 62b.

15. See Kiddushin 29b. Indulgence in such fantasy has received serious consideration — most notably in the gemara's assertion that הרהורי עבירה קשו מעבירה, "Licentious thoughts are more troubling than the exercise of [sexual] license," see Yoma 29a. This is often understood, in accordance with Rashi's interpretation, *ad locum*, as referring to the difficulty of restraint. However, the Rambam explains that the thoughts constitute a more serious offense, inasmuch as they entail a defilement of the noblest part of human personality, as opposed to that of a carnal organ. See *Guide*, 3:8.

16. Sanhedrin 76b; see Rambam, Ishut 15:19.

17. See his comment on Vayikra 19:17.

18. Bereshit 2:18; see Ramban, *ad locum*. Rashi cites the *midrash* as interpreting the statement with reference to cosmic, rather than personal, good.

19. *F. R.*, p. 17.

20. See Bamidbar 12:1–8. The Rav quoted his father as stressing that the focus of the narrative is not the exposition of *lashon ha-ra* but, rather the challenge to Mosheh's uniqueness.

21. Rambam, Yesodei Ha-Torah, 7:6. With respect to Aharon and Miriam, in this connection, see Avot De'Rabbi Natan, 9:2.

22. Rambam, Ishut 15:3.

23. Megillah 14b. For a different, but no less striking, interpretation of the verse cited, see Yerushalmi, Sanhedrin 2:3.

24. S.v. *she'gilletah.*
25. Sanhedrin 7a.
26. See 57b. The impact of the passage is somewhat muted however, by the subsequent conclusion: relief from bowel pressure.
27. See Berakhot 62a.
28. Eruvin 63b.
29. Bava Batra 58a. The portrayal needs to be viewed within the context of the gemara's subsequent comment, א״ל זיל אימא ליה בנאה קאי אבבא א״ל ליעול מידע ידע יצר בהאי עלמא ליכא, "He said: Go and tell him that Bana'ah is standing at the entrance. Said Avraham to him: Let him enter; it is well known that there is no passion in this [after] world." Avraham's assent to admit Rav Bana'ah, even though this would entail his being seen in an intimate pose, is explained on the basis of the knowledge that sexual passion does not exist in "this (after) world." Hence, the import of the stance and the encounter is, in effect, desexualized. Nevertheless, the passage remains significant.
30. Bereshit Rabbah, 45:4.
31. Niddah 31b.
32. Rambam, Shabbat 30:14.
33. This condition is posited by *Tosafot* in many places. See e.g., Sukkah 25a, s.v. *u-ve'lekhtekha.* However, some Rishonim assume the dispensation applies even if one could manage to perform both, provided that he is seriously engaged in the performance of the first *mizvah.* See *Or Zarua,* Hilkhot Sukkah, 2:299, and *She'elot U'Teshuvot Maharah Or Zarua,* 161, 163, 183. The latter view was adopted by the Rema; see *Orah Haym* 38:8.
34. See Berakhot 11a and 17b, and Sukkah 25a-b. See *Hiddushei Ha-Rashba,* Berakhot 11a, s.v. *be'lekhtekha,* for a possible distinction between the exemption in the course of the actual performance of a *mizvah* and that granted due to perturbation in anticipation of a *mizvah.*
35. See Ketubbot 39a.
36. Ketubbot 8b.
37. Avot 2:12
38. De'ot 3:2. The sense of the Rambam's formulation in this *halakhah* — and, to an extent, throughout the chapter — seems somewhat unclear. He opens by stating, צריך האדם שיכוון לבו וכל מעשיו לידע את השם ברוך הוא בלבד — "A man must focus his mind and the totality of his actions towards the recognition of God alone," evidently leaving no room for any other motif, be it even intermediate or secondary, unless one reads ויכוון "to focus" as an overall direction. He goes on to assert, וכן כשיאכל וישתה ויבעול לא ישים בלבו לעשות דברים האלו כדי ליהנות בלבד, "so too when he eats, drinks, or has relations he should not act solely for pleasure," clearly implying that the desire for pleasure is legitimate, if only it is not the exclusive motive. However, in the spirit of the segment I have quoted in my text, he continues, אלא ישים על לבו שיאכל וישתה כדי להברות גופו ואיבריו

בלבד "Rather one should concentrate his acts of eating and drinking for bodily health alone." A similar ambiguity exists in an earlier formulation of the same general theme in *Shemonah Perakim*, ch. 5. As to the reference to medical benefit, see, conversely, the elaborate enumeration of the medically problematic aspects of sexual excess, in Deʾot 4:19.

    For a brief and balanced summary discussion of the broader issue of asceticism with respect to the Rambam, see my late brother-in-law R. Yitzchak (Isadore) Twersky's *Introduction to the Code of Rambam* (New Haven, 1980), pp. 459–468, including, in relation to our specific focus, the judgment: "Generally, his attitude towards sex is very stringent" (p. 466).

39. 3:8; in Shlomo Pines' translation, p. 435.
40. See his comment on Shemot 30:13.
41. Vayikra 18:19.
42. Vayikra 18:6.
43. Vayikra 18:20.
44. *Baʿalei Ha-Nefesh*, ed. Ephraim Buckwold (Bnei Brak, 1992), p. 171.
45. Ibid, p. 174.
46. Ibid. (the *Iggeret* is printed in Buckwold's edition of the *B. H.*), pp. 195–196; ch. 2.
47. See *Perush Ha-Tur Ha-Arokh al Ha-Torah*, Vayikra 18:6 and 18:19. The brief paraphrases lack the verve of the Ramban's comments, but the spirit and the substance are clear.

    Interestingly, Rabbenu Bahye ben Asher, in his comment upon Vayikra 18:6, paraphrases the Ramban, with a yet sharper formulation — ומכאן אתה למד שענין המשגל אסור מדין התורה זולתי לקיום המין בלבד; "From here we learn that sexual relations are biblically prohibited, unless performed for the purposes of promulgation of our species" and, after challenging this position, cites the Rabad as an alternative, referring to the four motivations he had recognized. However, he then adds: והחמישי והוא אסור דרך תענוג ותאוה כתאות הבהמות "And the fifth, which is that [sexual relations] for pleasure, comparable to bestial desire, are prohibited." Textually, it is not clear whether the comparison qualifies the *taʿanug ve-taʾavah*, as it is only the bestial kind which is prohibited; or whether all such pleasure is proscribed, as it is inherently bestial in character. The latter seems more likely, however.

48. See Ketubbot 61b-62b.
49. See Berakhot 20b and 22a, where the status of a *baʿal keri* is treated with regard to *tefillah*, *keriʾat shema*, and *birkat ha-mazon* as well. Elsewhere, the ordinance is attributed to Ezra; see Bava Kamma 82b. This historical fact is, however, omitted from the *sugya* in Berakhot — presumably, as being irrelevant to the purely halakhic discourse.
50. See Berakhot 26a.
51. Berakhot 22a. The focus upon the element of tremor at Sinai, and the consequent emphasis upon maintaining it when encountering it is also expressed elsewhere. See,

e.g., Avot De'Rabbi Natan, 1:1 and 6:2, Yoma 4b and Rambam, Hagigah 3:6. Obviously, however, this element needs to be counterbalanced by the sense of joy and privilege. This important topic lies beyond my present bounds, however.

52. *Loc. cit.*
53. Issurei Bi'ah 21:11.
54. Berakhot 22a. Rishonim disagreed as to whether the repeal was limited to Torah study or encompassed *tefillah* as well.
55. See Avodah Zarah 36a and Rambam, Mamrim, ch. 2.
56. Bava Kamma 82b, s.v. ata.
57. Keri'at Shema 4:8.
58. See Mamrim, 2:7–8, where it would appear that, in certain instances, no formal repeal is even necessary and the ordinance lapses, having been invalid from the outset.
59. *Bet Ha-Behirah*, Berakhot 22a, s.v. *tevilah*. On the other hand, it is of course possible that the goal of restraint remains a desideratum but is overridden by the higher priority of fuller *talmud Torah*.
60. De'ot 5:1. The elitist element is of course much more fully articulated in the *Moreh*.
61. De'ot 5:4.
62. Ketubbot 62a.
63. See the citation in *Shitah Mekubbezet, ad locum.*
64. See Bezah 15b, where the criticism is applied to those who leave a *shi'ur* in order to enjoy a *se'udat yom tov*; and, even more remarkably, Shabbat 10a, where Rava comments negatively upon a colleague's devoting too much time to *tefillah*, which is presumably focused upon petition for temporal needs.
65. Yerushalmi, Berakhot 3:4.
66. It is conceivable that the Bavli, too, should be interpreted in light of, and in accordance with, the Yerushalmi. I have not encountered this view in Rishonim, however.
67. *Or Zarua*, Hilkhot Niddah, 360.
68. See Rashi, Ketubbot 103a, s.v. *bei.*
69. Sotah 47a.
70. Nedarim 20b.
71. B. H., Sha'ar Ha-Kedushah, p. 176. The Rabad goes on to cite an alternative interpretation that the description refers to insistence upon a significant measure of dress during relations — this, notwithstanding the fact that Rav Huna had designated such insistence as grounds for divorce; see Ketubbot 48a, and *Shulhan Arukh, Even Ha-Ezer* 76:13 and commentaries thereon.
72. See the comment of the Ritva, cited in *Shitah Mekubbezet*, Nedarim 20b.
73. Rav Yeshayahu Horwitz, *Shenei Luhot Ha-Berit* (Jerusalem 5730), "Sha'ar Ha-Otiyot," 384, 72b.
74. Vol. 3, sha'ar 2, seder 3, sec. 38; p. 299, in the standard edition.
75. P. 104.

76. *Ish Ha-Halakhah, Galuy Ve'nistar* (Jerusalem, 1979), p. 213; translation from *And From There You Shall Seek* (Jersey City, 2008), p. 115. The passage includes prominent mention of *piryah ve'rivyah* but its broader positive thrust is clear.
77. See Rav Yosef Dov Epstein, *Mizvot Ha-Bayit: Helek Sheni* (New York, 1966), pp. 247–248.
78. *Orah Haym*, 240.
79. See Yehudah Levi, *Ish, Ishah U'Mishpahah* (Bet El, 2001), especially, pp. 51–62.
80. See Rav Chavel's introduction to the *Iggeret* in his edition of *Kitvei Ha-Ramban*.
81. *Ish Ha-Halakhah, Galuy Ve'Nistar*, pp. 213–4; *And From There You Shall Seek*, p. 199.

Chapter 2

Talmud and Ma'aseh in *Pirkei Avot*

The relation between *talmud* and *ma'aseh*, study and implementation, can hardly be deemed a specifically modern concern. Nor does it constitute a uniquely Jewish issue. Endemic to the understanding of the spiritual life and its priorities, it recurs in varied civilizations and multiple contexts. Within the Western world, it constitutes a major crux of Greek — and, particularly, Athenian — philosophic speculation. During the Middle Ages, it engendered much debate among the Scholastics; and the claims of the *vita activa* and the *vita contemplativa* were subsequently perceived as central to the chasm dividing Christendom after the Protestant Reformation. Finally, in the modern period, echoes of the contretemps continue to reverberate — be it, often, in secular tones — at the planes of both theory and practice.

In our own Torah world, concern with the subject has been no less persistent, the discourse no less animated, and the attempt to attain a seemingly elusive resolution a major challenge. In Tanakh we do not encounter full-blown and directly explicit exposition of the issue, but many have sought to draw conclusions from their perspective upon the narrative portraying the lives and preoccupations of central figures within *Humash* or *Nevi'im*, or to identify prooftexts in *Ketuvim* as sources supporting their position. Hazal, however, report evidently charged debate, both extensive and intensive, on the question of priority and stature of *talmud* and *ma'aseh*, respectively:

וכבר היה רבי טרפון וזקנים מסובין בעלית בית נתזה בלוד, נשאלה שאלה זו בפניהם
תלמוד גדול או מעשה גדול נענה רבי טרפון ואמר מעשה גדול נענה רבי עקיבא ואמר
תלמוד גדול נענו כולם ואמרו תלמוד גדול שהתלמוד מביא לידי מעשה.

And Rabbi Tarfon and some [elders] were once convened in the upper story of the house of Nithza in Lod, and this question was posed before them: Which is greater, *talmud* or *maʿaseh*? Rabbi Tarfon responded and said, "*Maʿaseh* is greater." Rabbi Akiva responded and said, "*Talmud* is greater." The group responded and said, "*Talmud* is greater inasmuch as *talmud* leads to *maʿaseh*."[1]

In light of the presumably sound Aristotelian dictum that the end should be regarded as axiologically superior to a means that serves as its instrument, the conclusion cited, its formulation notwithstanding, apparently predicates the primacy of implementation. This was indeed assumed by Rashi in Bava Kamma.[2] Elsewhere, however, he appears to take a more literal approach and assigns priority — or, at the very least, parity — to study, through which both aims are achieved.[3] The Rambam, however, aligns himself with the gemara more fully and espouses its judgment consistently, as is reflected in his comment, appended, pursuant to citation of the gemara: לפיכך התלמוד קודם למעשה בכל מקום — "Therefore, everywhere, *talmud* precedes *maʿaseh*."[4] Subsequently, debate continued unabated, with *baʿalei halakhah*, *baʿalei mahshavah*, and *baʿalei mussar* — halakhists, philosophers, and ethico-pietists — deeply engaged, down to the present. If a contemporary exemplar needs to be singled out, Rav Soloveitchik's first major essay, *Ish Ha-Halakhah*, may serve as an apt specimen;[5] but it hardly stands alone.

Despite the universal component, the issue does bear a characteristically Jewish cast, for while both aspects are deeply ingrained within general religious sensibility and experience, as has been noted, each is especially prominent within *Yahadut* and hence the discourse is particularly relevant to Jewish tradition. On the one hand, Torah study, conceived as both normative duty and spiritual value, is posited as a central pillar of existence — personal, national, and even cosmic:

על שלשה דברים העולם עומד, על התורה, על העבודה, ועל גמילות חסדים.

The world is grounded upon three matters: *Torah*, *avodah*, and *gemilut hasadim*.[6]

Moreover, this conception is not confined to a narrow coterie of *majores ecclesiae* but is defined in broad social and communal terms:

וכל בניך למודי ה' ורב שלום בניך.

And all your sons are instructed by Hashem, and great is the peace of your sons.[7]

To a degree unparalleled in comparable cultures, the ordinary Jew is traditionally encouraged and expected to serve the *Ribbono shel Olam* with intellectual faculties and cognitive tools no less than with physical organs and material goods, as he comes to grips with the niceties of often arcane legal minutiae.

On the other hand, the Jew's responsibility to the realm of *ma'aseh* is also more comprehensive than that of his Gentile counterpart. Whereas for the latter, *vita activa* largely denotes participation and initiative in the rough and tumble arena of public life, to the Jew it suggests primarily fulfillment of the divine will as expressed in the pervasive halakhic regimen which penetrates every facet of the mundane order, its venue coexistent with the scope of life itself. In light of the greater range and intensity of both factors, study and practice, the incremental Jewish component of our problem may indeed be significant.

This brief essay is obviously not intended to provide either an exhaustive analysis of the problem or a comprehensive survey of its history. Its focus will be far more modest. I shall attempt to delineate a bird's eye view of the issues, as reflected in relevant passages excerpted from one of the most familiar of Rabbinic texts, *Pirkei Avot*. Familiarity is not the basis of its selection, however. Rather, I have chosen this tractate for three unrelated reasons. The first concerns its character. Perhaps best regarded as the Talmudic equivalent of Scriptural Mishlei, this amalgam of fully normative *halakhot*, moral wisdom, hortatory challenge, and outright prudential counsel is, in one sense, the least demanding of *massekhtot*, and in another, precisely because of its relatively amorphous nature, the most demanding.

Second, Avot confronts cardinal issues, at once fundamental and comprehensive, regarding the character and content of human life and the optimal mode of molding ideal personality. In a casual comment upon a mishnah which, *prima facie*, is unrelated to these concerns, the Rambam nonetheless diverts its substance to this channel, noting that it stimulates תקון נפשו במעלות המדות ובמעלות השכליות, שזו היא כונת המסכתא, "For this, that is, perfection of the soul, morally and intellectually, is the aim of this trac-tate."[8] And indeed the bedrock question of the determination of priority regarding the spiritual quality of the good life is explicitly posed at several points. Rabbi Yehudah Ha-Nasi, often simply denominated "Rabbi" — presumably, the *massekhet's* editor and compiler — raises it as the opening wedge of the second chapter:

רבי אומר אי זו היא דרך ישרה שיבר לו האדם, כל שהיא תפארת לעושה ותפארת לו
מן האדם.

Rabbi [Yehudah Ha-Nasi] said: Which is the right path which a person should select? That which reflects the luster of its pursuer, and redounds to him luster from others.[9]

Several *mishnayot* later we learn that Rabbi Yohanan ben Zakkai had five premier disciples, whom he confronted with a dual challenge:

צאו וראו אי זו היא דרך טובה שידבק בה האדם;

Go out and perceive which is a good path to which a person should adhere.

And, obversely:

צאו וראו אי זו היא דרך רעה שיתרחק ממנה האדם.

Go out and perceive which is a bad path, from which a person should distance himself.[10]

The responses vary widely. Rabbi's own formulation, "that which glorifies its agent, and confers upon him glory from others," is ambiguous insofar as it posits an ultimate goal but presents neither details regarding in what this *tif'eret* consists, nor any guideline concerning how the desideratum may be attained. In the latter mishnah, the variety is of another sort. The factors cited range from designation of an overarching factor, "a good heart," be it *telos* or means, to selection of elements which can, tactically and instrumentally, lead to the promised land: companionship and/or community, or the capacity to anticipate the future. For our purposes, however, most important is the attention riveted upon the question and some of the premises implicit within it, since it is this focus that leads naturally to weighing the merits of *talmud* and *ma'aseh*, respectively, and limning the contours of their interaction.

The third reason for choosing this tractate is grounded in the *massekhet*'s elements. *Pirkei Avot* constitutes an anthology, within whose parameters are cited epigrams ascribed to a broad range of *tannaim*, some central and others relatively marginal. Obviously, the respective authors expressed themselves with regard to numerous issues, touching upon the entire corpus of *halakhah* and/or *mahshavah*. Is it conceivable that Hillel's or Rabbi Akiva's dicta could be counted on the fingers of one hand? That the ethical legacy of giants in the forefront of our tradition consists of scattered morsels ascribed to each, and the composite compressed within five brief chapters? Evidently, in the process of selection and editing, attention was focused upon statements categorized as מרגלא בפומיה דרבי פלוני, recurrently repeated by a given *tanna*, as singled out by him for special awareness and dissemination, and, hence, characteristically identified with him. Given all three factors, we approach this treasure trove with an anticipatory eye for encountering distinctive insights.

To begin with the status of *talmud Torah*, independently considered, in Avot, there is no paucity of assertions trumpeting its prominence. Its designation as one of the pillars sustaining universal existence has already been noted,[11] but it is only the opening salvo. That is followed in short order by the admonition that one not credit himself as he contemplates his own virtue, expressed through learning much Torah, as לכך נוצרת, "it is to that end that you have been created;"[12] by the exhortation to persist diligently — הוה שקוד ללמוד תורה — in Torah study; by declaration that the absence of "Torah words" at a social gathering or a meal renders them מושב לצים, a "rogues' session," or זבחי מתים, "mortuary sacrifices," respectively, whereas, by contrast, Torah-centered gatherings ensure the presence of immanent *Shekhinah* in their midst.[13] This, in turn, is succeeded by the frightening asseveration that if, because of negligence and/or apathy rather than as a natural result of oblivion, one forgets any segment of the Torah he has learned, he is, figuratively, deemed as having endangered his soul.[14] Subsequently, Rabbi Mayer urges minimizing commercial activity so as to enable concentrated Torah study;[15] while in the tractate's penultimate counsel Ben Bag Bag exhorts, evidently as classical *mefarshim* consensually assumed, with reference to the pursuit of Torah, הפך בה והפך בה דכולא בה, "Delve into it, and delve into it, for all is within it."[16] Much ink has been spilled in attempt to expound this much-debated charge, but whatever the details, the scope ascribed to *talmud Torah* and the status correspondingly accorded to it is beyond question.

The focus upon the value of Torah study is matched, however, by acknowledgment, both implicit and explicit, of the worth of *ma'aseh*. In Hazal's usage, the term denotes at least four distinct yet related referents. At its broadest, it signifies the full gamut of activity, including intellectual labor, as opposed to perception, observation, or total passivity. Somewhat more narrowly conceived, the term still encompasses the full range of physical action, to the exclusion of verbal or cerebral initiative. In a related and yet still more limited sense, it refers to a very specific act, often regarded as more significant than a comparable passive state. Thus a לאו שיש בו מעשה, a transgression of a negative prohibition, such as purchasing or leavening *hametz* on Pesah, is more seriously regarded — and is concurrently more subject to sanction — than failure to destroy *hametz* that had already been owned prior to Pesah,[17] or than the neglect to eat matzah on the first night. Finally, *ma'aseh* may simply be synonymous with an incident or its narrative.

All four senses appear in the text of Avot. However, for our purposes we shall focus primarily upon the first and shall discuss the last least. That first aspect alone, however, is abundantly reflected in numerous dicta strewn throughout the *massekhet*. And while it seems patently clear that not every mishnah is equally and directly relevant to every reader, at either the personal or the collective plane, the composite image is one which certainly bespeaks and even exudes range and vibrancy in confronting the human condition. Thus we note from the outset that, in the mishnah previously cited as defining the metaphysical legs of a universal tripod, both ritual and beneficence[18] stand firmly alongside Torah. As we read on, we sense consistently that engagement of the recipient of proffered guidance within the realm of the temporal and even the carnal order, whether out of choice or from necessity, is taken for granted as the point of departure for dialogue. He may be a judge or a plaintiff, a scholar or a tradesman, a host or a guest, a neighbor, good or ill, a teacher or a disciple, a friend or an adversary, indolent or energetic, humble or condescending, *homo economicus* and *homo religiosus*. With respect to all of these capacities and relations, the Jew is confronted, addressed, and advised, as concerns both scope and modality, as to how best to organize and lead a life of ethical rectitude, religious obligation, and practical accomplishment, which will enhance the prospect for entry into the order of felicity of the eternal abode. The citations vary considerably as to theme and range of their message. Some are pinpointed:

הוי מתפלל בשלומה של מלכות שאלמלי מוראה איש את רעהו חיים בלעו;

Pray for the welfare of government, as, were it not for fear of it, each would swallow his fellow alive;[19]

others are mostly general and sweeping, as they postulate the element whose constant contemplation can instill the spirit and modality which will maximize, if not assure, virtue:

הסתכל בשלשה דברים ואין אתה בא לידי עברה – דע מאין באת ולאן אתה הולך ולפני מי אתה עתיד ליתן דין וחשבון

Regard three matters and you avoid lapsing into sin: from whence you have come, whither you are headed, and before whom you are destined to present judgment and accounting.[20]

Some are descriptive, many prescriptive, while in others the description, given the values presumably energizing the reader, implicitly infers the mandated resolution. Throughout, however, the emphasis upon both *talmud* and *ma'aseh* is crucial.

The prominence of *talmud* and *ma'aseh*, each absolutely and independently considered and evaluated, is not, however, our sole — or even
our primary — topic. We need to examine more fully their interaction
and possible conflict. In this respect, it is important that the traditional
parameters of discourse be borne in mind, especially as they include
an asymmetrical component. *Yahadut* optimally espouses and assumes
the conjunction of *talmud* and *ma'aseh*, but the import of their severance is unevenly perceived. While enactment of the halakhic regimen,
unaccompanied by learning and not buttressed by understanding, is
regarded as inadequate but worthy, the obverse — *talmud Torah* bereft of
faith and commitment to implement — is viewed as sacrilege, bordering
upon blasphemy. In its milder form, this dissonance finds expression in
two statements ascribed to the most frequently cited of *amoraim*, Rava.
Commenting upon the *pasuk*,

ראשית חכמה יראת ה' שכל טוב לכל עושיהם.

Fear of Hashem is the origin of wisdom, [a source] of right thought
for those who implement it (Tehillim 111:10).

he comments, ללומדיהם לא נאמר אלא לעושיהם, "The verse does not say, 'For
those who study them,' but rather, 'For those who implement them.'"[21] Or,
in a somewhat sharper vein, we note his admonitory plea to his students,
במטותא מינייכו לא תירתון תרתי גיהנם, "I implore you, do not inherit a double
Hell"[22] — to wit, as Rashi expounds, don't lead a life of self-sacrifice in the
pursuit of Torah in this world, only to lapse postmortem into the inferno
of the nether, if you have flagged in observance here. Elsewhere, however,
we encounter far more extreme formulations, well beyond the pale of
lassitude and retribution. Hazal saw the message writ large in a divine
reproach to the wicked — variously identified in midrashim with Do'eg
and Elisha ben Avuyah — in verses of Tehillim:

ולרשע אמר א-לקים מה לך לספר חקי ותשא בריתי עלי פיך. ואתה שנאת מוסר ותשלך
דברי אחריך.

But to the wicked, God says, "What have you to do with pronouncing

My statutes, and that you bear My covenant upon your mouth? And you have reviled guidance, and have thrust My words behind you."[23]

And in a more general vein, the point is driven home graphically in a declaration cited as a challenge to the practice of Rabbi Shimon bar Yohai, who occasionally, and perhaps even habitually, abstained from reciting *Shema*, if it interfered with his learning:

> ולית ליה לרשב״י הלמד על מנת לעשות ולא הלמד שלא לעשות שהלמד שלא לעשות
> נוח לו שלא נברא.

> And does not Rabbi Shimon bar Yohai acknowledge that he who studies with intent to perform [is to be valued], but not he who studies without intent to perform, as, if one studies without intent to perform, it were preferable for him not to have been born.[24]

Genuine severance is clearly no option. No matter how well motivated, it undermines the most fundamental premises of normative halakhic existence; and in addition to defiling commitment, interferes with the process of its realization, thus eviscerating both personal and communal spiritual well-being.

Prima facie, this assertion seems to be contravened by an inference possibly suggested by Rabbi Yishmael's statement in the fourth *perek*:

> הלומד על מנת ללמד מספיקין בידו ללמוד וללמד והלומד על מנת לעשות מספיקין
> בידו ללמוד וללמד לשמור ולעשות

> He who studies [only] with intent to teach is afforded the opportunity to study as well as to teach; but he who studies with intent to perform is afforded the opportunity to study, to teach, to preserve, and to perform.[25]

The impression conveyed by the opening comment is that, while inferior in comparison with the personage described later, he who pursues knowledge with an eye to teaching, but not, evidently, to implementing, will be rewarded with support in realizing his aim, inasmuch as what he is doing, while partial, is nonetheless meritorious. But Rabbenu Yonah, *ad locum*, noted the implication and was consequently horrified:

פי׳ חס ושלום שאין זה מדבר בלומד על מנת ללמד ולא לעשות שזה אין מספיקין בידו
לא ללמוד ולא ללמד.

> To wit: The mishnah does not speak, Heaven forbid, of one who stud-
> ies with the intent to teach but with no intent to perform, for such is
> denied the opportunity even to study or to teach.

Hence he goes on to explain that at issue is the quality and level of commitment, but not its bare existence. This view may strike some as a bit
forced and apologetic. In this respect the interpretation of the *Mahzor
Vitry, ad locum,* may be more palatable. Its author suggests that we are
dealing either with a person who is fully committed to observe but may
be prevented from doing so or who plans to fulfill but is motivated to
teach by extraneous factors:

שאין דעתו לקיים לפי שאינו יכול או אפילו יכול אינו עושה אלא לעשות לו שם על
מנת שיקראהו ר׳ ללמוד וללמד ולא יותר.

> [The mishnah refers to] one who does not expect to perform [only]
> because he lacks the wherewithal; or, alternatively, of one who is able
> [and does expect] to perform but shall do so solely in order to establish
> his reputation as a master of learning and teaching, but for no other
> reason.

As to why he then is assured of support, he explains:

שהמעשה עיקר כמו שמצינו בפ״א לא המדרש הוא עיקר אלא המעשה.

> For *maʿaseh* is the main thing as we have encountered earlier (1:17),
> "The main thing is not exposition but implementation."[26]

This reference introduces another issue, that of objective formal observance versus inwardness, with a long history of its own, but not to our
present purpose. In any event, one is hardly inclined to discard so deeply
rooted and widely held an attitude on the basis of a single problematic
inference.

The nature of the desired interaction is in one sense almost self-evident. The twin elements relate to varied aspects of human personality and
diverse areas of personal and collective existence. Either is ignored at peril,

and it is only their joint scope that enables us, like Arnold's Sophocles, to see life steadily and to see it whole — or rather, to live it as such. And yet, several strands may be discerned. In Avot, as elsewhere, we ought not perceive *talmud* and *ma'aseh* as merely twinned in shared and spiritual coexistence. Rather, within the halakhic tradition, they are regarded as entwined and fructifying; and reciprocally so. Thus on the one hand the mishnah postulates, almost stridently, that לא עם הארץ חסיד, the unschooled cannot attain the higher levels of piety. On the other hand, with reference to the selfsame category of *hasid*, Rava asserts, in a somewhat complementary vein, that he who would attain it should *inter alia* enact the precepts of Avot.[27] Beyond that, the mishnah proper states that the priority, presumably both chronological and axiological, of reverence to wisdom and the quest for it is a condition for the long-term viability of that wisdom-not of the reverence solely, but of the wisdom:

> ר' חנינא בן דוסא אומר כל שיראת חטאו קודמת לחכמתו חכמתו מתקיימת, וכל
> שחכמתו קודמת ליראת חטאו אין חכמתו מתקיימת.

Rabbi Hanina ben Dosa stated, "If one prioritizes fear of sin to wisdom, his wisdom survives, but if his wisdom is prioritized to his fear of sin, it does not survive."[28]

And we note that the assertion is presented as a fact and not just as a concern. The statement resembles attitudes encountered in a variety of parallel traditions but it is, for us, particularly noteworthy, precisely because the low-key and practically oriented tone of most of Avot is poles removed from the mystical mode.

Moreover, in this vein we might proceed a step further. The reciprocal dependency of *talmud* and *ma'aseh* is clearly stated. As, on the one hand, their conjunction, even at the vocational plane, constitutes a befitting mode of personal life:

> יפה תלמוד תורה עם דרך ארץ שיגיעת שניהם משכחת עון;

Talmud Torah goes handsomely with civility, as their joint pursuit obliterates sin.[29]

so, on the other hand, the absence of one derails the other:

ר' אלעזר בן עזריה אומר אם אין תורה אין דרך ארץ, אם אין דרך ארץ אין תורה.

Rabbi Elazar ben Azaryah said: "If Torah is absent, there shall be no *derekh eretz*; if *derekh eretz* is absent, there shall be no Torah."[30]

The implicit message of the *mishnayot* in Avot is that *talmud* and *ma'aseh* are not just a *sine qua non* of each other. Each is, beyond that, a manifest realization of the other. *Talmud Torah* bears a dual aspect. It is both an independent value as a central aspect of *avodat Hashem*, fusing cognition and religiosity, and as a specific normative performance, a *mizvah* in its own right — indeed, if properly motivated and faith-grounded, among the weightiest and noblest. Conversely, a life of submissive religious commitment provides the infrastructure for insight and perception and serves as an invaluable instrument of Torah learning and education.

While harmonious interaction can be idealized, the prospect of potential conflict cannot be averted. The possibility of internal contradiction must of course be anticipated by any legal system, and prescription for resolution is clearly requisite. In this regard, Halakhah is no exception. For the purpose of our discourse, however, it is essential that the substantive nature of the conflict under consideration be properly understood.

Primarily, the halakhist copes with two categories of conflict. In the first, itself divided into multiple subsections, the specific normative demands of diverse codicils stand in direct opposition. The *mizvah* of eating matzah on Pesah might, for instance, mandate eating a particular specimen if no other is available, while, if the specimen in question was baked with untithed flour, the prohibition against eating *tevel* proscribes its consumption. Similarly, the *mizvah* of *zizit* prescribes adorning a four-cornered garment with woolen strings even if its fabric is linen, whereas the injunction against wearing *sha'atnez* precludes it. Such conflicts abound and make their mark as a significant halakhic topic, and, depending upon variables such as the source and grade of commandment and restriction, respectively, are differentially resolved.

Very little of this rigorous discussion, however, finds its locus in the

relatively flexible and less technical context of Avot. The conflict encountered in its *mishnayot* is focused upon the broader concerns of policy,
attitude, values, and context. Inherently accidental head-on clashes are
not so much at issue. Attention is riveted rather upon immanent questions
— ideological, axiological, and practical — regarding the fabric and composition, the content and the direction, of human life as perceived from a
Torah perspective. Hence conflict relates to the budgeting of energy, time,
resources, and commitment, to the realization, both tragic and challenging, that *ars longa, vita brevis*, or, in the language of Rabbi Tarfon in Avot,
that עצלים והפועלים מרובה והמלאכה קצר היום — "The day is short, the task is
extensive, and the laborers lazy."[31] Hence our implicit charge with respect
to ourselves is to ensure that the workers not be indolent.

At stake, however, is more than a laudable work ethic and pervasive
dedication. The human agent qua agent, even if we momentarily omit
fulfillment of David's charge to Shlomo, ועבדהו אביך א-לקי את דע, "And know
the God of your father and serve Him" (I Divrei Ha-Yamim 28:9), is mandated to be not only conscientious but wise, both passionately committed
and intelligently perceptive, insightful as well as efficient — all of this
presumably part of the labor which has been thrust upon his shoulders.
And over all this effort the need to prioritize and the shadow of possible
clash looms large.

If direct halakhic conflict is barely cited in Avot, diverse emphases
and, at times, contradictory hashkafic formulations are nevertheless in
evidence. The radical tinge of המעשה אלא עקר המדרש לא, as filtered through
Rabbenu Bahye's interpretation, serves to exemplify:

> כלומר אין תכלית הידיעה ועמלו של אדם שילמוד תורה הרבה, אין התכלית אלא
> שיביא הלימוד לידי מעשה, הוא שכתוב ולמדתם אותם ושמרתם לעשותם בא להורות
> כי תכלית הלימוד אינו אלא כדי שיעשה.

To wit: The *telos* of knowledge and one's related labor is not the study
of much Torah [*per se*]. The purpose is but translating the study into
implementation. Hence, it is written, "And you shall learn them and
preserve them," in order to instruct us that the end of study is but that
one should act, [halakhically].[32]

To Volozhiner purists, this exposition of narrowness is sheer anathema. But even the less sensitive can readily agree that the message is hardly identical with that of הפך בה והפך בה דכולא בה; and neither mishnah merely replicates the reciprocity of אם אין תורה אין דרך ארץ, אם אין דרך ארץ אין תורה. Or again, the gut response to דרך ארץ of Rabban Gamaliel's assertion that יפה תלמוד תורה עם דרך ארץ differs markedly from that of Rabbi Nehunyah's declaration that כל המקבל עליו עול תורה מעבירין ממנו עול מלכות ועול דרך ארץ, "Whoever accepts the yoke of Torah is released from the yoke of government and from that of *derekh eretz*."[33] The cognitive content of the two can unquestionably be reconciled. The feeling — tone is palpably different, however — a matter of no small moment.

Over all looms the magisterial sweep of the demand that וכל מעשיך יהיו לשם שמים, "And all your actions should be for the sake of Heaven."[34] This directive, justly singled out by the Rambam as the linchpin of religious living,[35] unquestionably encompasses *talmud* as well as *maaseh*, particularly insofar as intellection too is included in the realm of activity. And yet, as is amply attested in the details cited in the Rambam's presentation, whether in *Shemonah Perakim* or in Hilkhot Deot, the focus is upon *maaseh*, more narrowly defined:

> נמצא המהלך בדרך זו כל ימיו עובד את ה' תמיד אפילו בשעה שנושא ונותן ואפילו בשעה שבועל מפני שמחשבתו בכל כדי שימצא צרכיו עד שיהיה גופו שלם לעבוד את ה'...ועל ענין זה צוו חכמים ואמרו וכל מעשיך יהיו לשם שמים.

> He who pursues this path all his days thus finds himself serving Hashem constantly, even while engaged in trade or even in the midst of sexual relations, inasmuch as with respect to all he does he thinks how can he best meet his needs so that his body will be sound in order to serve Hashem.... And it is with respect to this that the Sages asserted, "And all your actions should be for the sake of Heaven."[36]

Hence, the overarching formulation serves to secure the position of the *vita activa*, while yet promoting the conjunction of our two topics.

And there is, of course, subtler diversity. Commenting upon a series of *mishnayot* in the fourth *perek*, Rav Yizhak Abravanel suggests that the core issue is the relation of our twin topics:

ואומר שהכונה הכוללת בפרק הזה היא לבאר במה יקנה האדם שלימותו בתורה כי אחר
שהתבאר בפרקים הקודמים ששלימות האדם ותכליתו הוא בקנין התורה וקיומה נשאר
לבאר אם העיקר בה הוא העיון והחכמה התוריית או המעשה וקיום המצות ולכן באו
דעות השלמים האלה כל אחד כפי שטתו וסברתו.

> And let me say that the overall thrust of this chapter is to determine
> how one best attains his perfection with regard to Torah. For after
> it has been explained, in prior chapters, that the perfection of man
> and his ultimate purpose consists in the acquisition of Torah and its
> realization, we still need to determine whether the most essential is
> the probing and knowledge of Torah or its realization and the perfor-
> mance of *mizvot*. Hence we encounter here the views of these noble
> persons, each in accordance with his theory and perception.[37]

This perception should neither surprise nor alarm us. While some *bnei
Torah*, fully acculturated to the welter of *mahloket* at all level of halakhic
discourse, prefer to imagine that in the area of *emunot ve-deʾot* — or even
of *mahshavah* generally — comity and unanimity are *de rigueur*, the distinction belies both theory and fact. Surely there is no reason to entertain
it with respect to our particular topic. Even the advocacy of seemingly
diverse values can be readily and variously understood. Given the prevalence of controversy as a staple of rabbinic discourse, it can be obviously
contended that the variety confronted in Avot ought best be perceived
as an exemplar of this characteristic, which at times constitutes a dispute
over a relatively local issue, and at other times may emanate from conflict
over fundamental *Weltanschauung*. In its more extreme formulation, this
interpretation would hold that conflicting *mishnayot* argue over the adoption of one value and the concomitant negation of another, and vice versa.
A milder version could be content with controversy over priority and
emphasis. In either case, however, the reader or the student is encouraged
to regard his endeavors in sifting the texts as a selective quest for a single
and overriding phalanx of constricted guidelines.

Such a reading is grounded, generally, upon certain premises, both
methodological and ideological, regarding the respective merits of dialecti-
cal, monistic, and harmonistic canons of exposition; and specifically upon
one's grasp of particular texts and issues confronted in Avot. Allowing

for some analogy between the realms of Halakhah and *mahshavah* as regards *mahloket*, the possibility of unanimity or clear-cut recognition of advocacy of one contested value to the relative neglect of a rival can still not be ruled out. Nevertheless, in this case, given my own perspectives and proclivities regarding both halakhic training and hashkafic orientation, I freely admit to an inclination to multifaceted resolution and to the challenge of complexity. Even in the absence of such bias, I cannot fathom how the ethical life in its entirety could be encapsulated within the sphere of normative *talmud Torah* alone. Surely we, as advocates of Hazal's tradition, have nothing to gain and much to lose by any attempt to abandon, mute, or diminish the claims of both contemplation and action upon our consciences and upon our lives. In learning the *massekhet*, we err grievously in positing emphasis upon the two as diametrically opposed rather than conjoined. Surely, whatever the thrust of a particular text, the overall message in Avot is one of bonded values, and we shall lead purer and richer lives if we heed its call.

The linkage manifest in citations strewn through our *massekhet* foreshadows, in certain respects, its more explicit formulation in an early exposition penned by the first truly systematic master within our philosophic tradition. I refer, of course, to the Rambam and to the first of his major introductory prefaces. As the preface to his commentary upon the mishnah draws to its conclusion, the Rambam feels impelled to raise the crucial issue, both ethical and teleological, of the purpose and nature of human existence. Tersely stated, in response, he states, "The end of our world and of that which is within it is 'a wise and good person.'"[38] After the contention that this conclusion is equally grounded in prophetic revelation and philosophic thought, the discussion moves, not surprisingly, toward judiciously balanced resolution of the relations of *talmud* and *maʿaseh*. First, in the spirit of Hazal, the Rambam emphasizes that, if it is to be genuine and meaningful, the quest for wisdom must be grounded in existential commitment and its concomitant lifestyle. Despite its enormous intrinsic value, learning that is bereft of religiously and ethically mandated discipline is fraught with arrogance and invites Yirmiyahu's critique:[39] איכה תאמרו חכמים אנחנו ותורת ה' אתנו וכו' "How can you say, 'We are wise and Hashem's Torah is with us?'" etc. However, in the reverse case, inasmuch as the relation is asymmetrical, while this option is imperfect because it may not be wholly bound to "the path of truth and certitude," the course has merit. Nevertheless, given the imperfection, as to the question of chronological priority, learning takes precedence: "Throughout the Torah, the למדתם comes before לעשותם, wisdom before practice, since through wisdom one attains practice, but practice does not induce wisdom. Hence Hazal's formulation, שהתלמוד מביא לידי מעשה, 'For *talmud* leads to *ma'aseh*.'"[40] On this balanced note — *ma'aseh* being acknowledged as the more essential, but *talmud* assigned sequential priority — the discussion ends, having made a number of salient points, but, like *Pirkei Avot*, having left a number of others open.

This brief synopsis of the Rambam's exposition strikes several familiar chords, the gist of the argument paralleling points that have been noted with respect to the treatment of Avot. At this point, however, the analogy is in large measure arrested. The themes are similar, but the contexts as well as the respective audiences are quite different. As to the latter, the *hakdamah* is presumably oriented to readers who, while not all professional scholars, are apparently highly literate and sophisticated. With regard to Avot, the identity of the predominant projected audience is evidently in dispute. The Rambam envisioned it as aimed primarily at *dayyanim*;[41] and unquestionably a number of *mishnayot* relate directly to the formal judicial process. In all likelihood, however, the more prevalent view is that of the *Mahzor Vitry*, whose twelfth-century author prefaces his commentary upon Avot with the conjecture that the custom of reciting a *perek* on Shabbat afternoon derives from the limitations of the *hoi polloi*, for whom more difficult texts might be too challenging and who therefore imbibe requisite spiritual guidance from the milder fare of Avot.

לפי שעמי הארץ נאספים לקרית התורה, ומשמיעים אותם מידות תרומות השנויות
במסכת זו פרק ליום.

For the ignorant are gathered in order to hear *keri'at ha-Torah*, and ideal virtues which are discussed in this tractate are expounded to them, one chapter at a time.[42]

At a more significant level, however, we take note of distinctions concerning tone and content. With respect to the latter, note must of course be taken of the fact that the *hokhmah* or *talmud* as well as the *ma'aseh* of Avot all refer primarily to the world of Torah and Halakhah, while the Rambam's discussion includes this dimension but is certainly not confined to it. And as to the aura, the systematic mode, characteristic of much of the Rambam's writing, is of course largely absent in Avot, as is the relatively more imperious tone of the Rambam's *hakdamah*. In Avot, the prevalent human touch — reflected in direct personal guidance, much of it advisory, addressed by a *tanna* to a receptive listener in a fairly relaxed atmosphere, and, equally, in the absence of rigorous philosophic discourse or sharply honed argument — is in meaningful evidence. These observations do not obtain with respect to all of Avot, but I believe they are valid concerning a large segment, and assuredly with regard to this particular topic.

In a sense, the character of the interaction between author and reader — or shall we say between speaker and listener — contains the secret of Avot's appeal and power. As in other respects, the collection's normative level is marked by diversity, the statements ranging from pragmatic advice:

הוו זהירים ברשות שאין מקרבין לו לאדם אלא לצרך עצמן, נראין כאוהבין בשעת הנאתן ואין עומדין לו לאדם בשעת דחקו

Be wary of governing authorities, as they only befriend a person in their own interests, and feign empathy when it is to their advantage, but do not stand by a person in his moments of stress.[43]

which could have earned the assent of Lord Chesterfield or Machiavelli; through ethico-religious homily:

יהי כבוד חברך חביב עליך כשלך, ואל תהי נח לכעוס, ושוב יום אחד לפני מיתתך

May your peer's honor be as dear to you as your own, do not anger easily, and repent, [even] on the eve of death;[44]

to outright halakhic imperative:

הוי זהיר בקרית שמע ובתפלה, וכשאתה מתפלל אל תעש תפלתך קבע אלא תחנונים לפני המקום ברוך הוא.

Be careful with respect to *keri'at Shema* and *tefillah*; and when you pray, do not render your prayer as a matter of rote, but, rather, as pleas addressed to Hashem, *Barukh Hu*.[45]

The dominant chord, however, is relatively muted, in both tone and volume. We encounter little Sturm-und-drang. Voices are barely raised, threats hardly issued, fists largely impounded. The demands made upon us are far from minimal, in regard to both *talmud* and *ma'aseh*, and the standards to which we are held accountable are frequently imposing; and yet, even in *mishnayot* that present a panoramic view of the course of human life, inviting us to infer the consequences, we sense that by and large they provide knowledge, focus attention, and emphasize priorities but stop short of rubbing our noses in funerary earth. We are indeed reminded that

ולאך אתה הולך למקום עפר רמה ותולעה;

And whither are you headed? To a locus of earth, decay, and worms.[46]

but there is no danse macabre or Yorick to flesh out a *memento mori*.

The ability of *Pirkei Avot* to inculcate fundamental religious values within its relaxed atmosphere is in many respects quite remarkable, particularly with regard to values as central to Torah life as *talmud* and *ma'aseh*. However, I intuit that this fusion is, in no small measure, enabled by the broader context. The quietism of Avot, is in part very real but in part rather illusory, for the committed Jew indeed learns and absorbs the *massekhet* in its listener-friendly mode, but concurrently he captures its cadences as an aspect of his total religious experience. His ear is attuned to the קול דממה דקה, "the sound of evanescent silence," heard in the course of apparition to Eliyahu,[47] because that resonates with the קולות וברקים, the voices and flashes heard and seen at Sinai. Likewise, that ear is sensitive to the *sotto voce* tones of Avot, inasmuch as it experiences them against the background of the stern and imperative declaration emanating from Mount Horev:

אמר רבי יהושע בן לוי בכל יום ויום בת קול יוצאת מהר חורב ומכרזת ואומרת אוי להם
לבריות מעלבונה של תורה שכל מי שאינו עוסק בתורה נקרא נזוף.

Rabbi Yehoshua ben Levi stated: Daily, a celestial voice emerges from Mount Horev and declares and pronounces, "Woe to persons over the affront to Torah, as anyone who does not engage in Torah is chastised."[48]

Those to whom the din of the *bet midrash* is foreign may content themselves with the comment of Lionel Trilling — an interpreter, admittedly, drawn from outside the halakhic orbit, but surely an astute observer — that Avot "is not a system of ethics at all but simply a collection of maxims and pensees, some quite fine, some quite dull, which praise the life of study and give advice on how to live it."[49] And as to the quietism, they could readily accept his assertion that "we find in the tractate no implication of spiritual struggle. We find the energy of assiduity but not the energy of resistance.... Man in *Aboth* guards against sin but he does not struggle against it, and of evil we hear nothing at all."[50] Denizens of those *batei midrash*, to whom the challenging voices of tradition are an intrinsic facet of their perennial soundtrack, would rather apprehend and appreciate this quietism through the prism of the penultimate mishnah of the first chapter in Avot:

כל ימי גדלתי בין החכמים ולא מצאתי לגוף טוב אלא שתיקה ולא המדרש הוא העקר אלא המעשה וכל מרבה דברים מביא חטא.

Throughout, I was raised among sages, and found nothing better than silence for a person. And it is not exposition but implementation which is most important. And he who speaks profusely invites sin.[51]

The quiet I have touched upon is more ethical than auditory, and by no means literal *shetikah*. But good for one's constitution and good for the soul, its tenor reverberates through Avot nonetheless; and therein lies, paradoxically, the source of much of its impact, its power, and its fascination.

Notes

1. Kiddushin 40b and Sifri, Eikev, sec. 5 (in the edition of the Netziv). The two texts differ significantly in the details of the discourse described — as to location, individual ascription, etc. — but the basic thrust of the two narratives is largely identical.

Of greater import is an impression possibly conveyed by an earlier statement in the Sifri: ולמדתם אותם ושמרתם לעשותם שהמעשה תלוי בתלמוד ואין תלמוד תלוי במעשה וכן מציינו שענש הכתוב על התלמוד יותר מן המעשה — "'And you shall study them and take heed to perform them'. The *pasuk* hereby declares that *ma'aseh* is dependent upon *talmud*, but *talmud* is not dependent upon *ma'aseh*. Likewise, we find that Scripture reports greater punishment over *talmud* than over *ma'aseh*." This formulation raises the possibility that the priority of *talmud* derives from its superior worth and need not be grounded in its impact upon *ma'aseh*.

2. 17a, s.v. *mevi*.

3. See Kiddushin 40b, s.v. *she-ha'talmud*, where Rashi explains the superiority of *talmud* as grounded on the fact that it enables the attainment of both goals.

4. Talmud Torah, 3:3; c.f. ibid., 1:3. Two other suggestions for reconciling the implication and the statement of the gemara might be briefly mentioned. One explains that the question raised in the gemara in Bava Kamma relates to the sequence to be pursued, on a specific occasion, if one is confronted with both, rather than to overall policy. See *Tosafot*, Bava Kamma 17a, s.v. *ve-ha'amar*. This solution seems problematic, since sequence does not necessarily rest upon importance or reflect it, but may be due to other considerations. We eat a fruit cup before the main course but don't regard it as central. The second suggestion, cited in *Tosafot*, Kiddushin 40b, s.v. *talmud* and *Shittah Mekubezet*, Bava Kamma 17a, in the names of Rabbenu Perez and Rabbenu Yeshayah, introduces another variable, that is, the stage in life with regard to which the question arises. This view found echoes in later centuries and is particularly relevant for the modern period, marked by lengthy schooling and training.

5. The Rav was pulled in conflicting directions on this issue. He was, on the one hand, a scion of Volozhin and Brisk, with their focus on *Torah lishmah*, as well as under the impact of a highly abstract neo-Kantian orientation. On the other hand, the family tradition included a strong social conscience and activist streak, to which the Rav was both personally attracted and philosophically committed. The resultant tension is palpable in *Ish Ha-Halakhah* and elsewhere.

6. Avot 1:2. It is noteworthy that Rav Haym Volozhiner severely circumscribed the scope of this dictum; see his qualifications in his commentary, *Ru'ah Haym*, ad loc. The last two terms cited are not easily translated, since each has a broader and a narrower compass. The former could refer to some specific aspects of the ritual of *mikdash*, to the regimen of *mikdash* in its totality, or to part or all of the full range of service of God. The latter could be confined to specific assistance extended to one's fellow, material or spiritual, or to all actions, performed directly or indirectly, on his behalf. Commentators have differed as to the scope intended in this mishnah.

7. Yeshayahu 54:13.

8. Avot, 5:2.

9. 2:1. In part, the thrust of the mishnah consists in the fact that the opportunity and onus of conscious choice are assumed altogether.

10. 2:9. The question posed by Rabbi Yohanan resembles Rabbi's but is clearly narrower in scope. It is noteworthy that both texts speak of man universally, and not of the Jew alone.

11. I am assuming that the term *Torah* refers here to its study, as an activity parallel to the other elements, and not to the supportive existence of the Torah proper. This was apparently the understanding of the Rambam and Rabbenu Bahye, but clearly not of Rabbenu Yonah.

12. 2:8. This formulation need not imply that future learning constitutes the sole *raison d'être* for personal creation, but it is a strong statement, on any reading. It should also be noted that Rabbenu Yonah adds that the caveat against self-satisfaction is not confined to *talmud* but applies equally to *ma'aseh.* וזאת המדה גם כן היא על המצות שאם עשית מצות הרבה אל תחזיק טובה לעצמך כי לכך נוצרת — "And this mode applies equally to *mizvot*, that if you have performed many *mizvot* do not credit yourself, for it is to this end that you were created."

13. 3:2–4, 6. These are not, strictly speaking, halakhic rulings, and they are not cited in the Rambam's *Mishneh Torah*. The axiological statement is, however, clear and forceful.

14. 3:8. This statement, too, was not codified by the Rambam, as defining a specific halakhic violation. However, the Ramban, in commenting upon the *pasuk* cited (Devarim 4:9), did categorize it as such and included such forgetting as one of the 613 *mizvot*. This, however, is only with respect to forgetting the events of *ma'amad har Sinai*, not regarding anything else that one has learned.

15. 4:10. Cf. the narrative implicitly criticizing some of Hazal who did not adopt this course — e.g., Ta'anit 21a, and Avot De'Rabbi Natan 1:1.

16. 5:22. See, e.g., Rambam (in the common printed editions; in Rav Y. Shilat's edition of פירוש הרמב"ם לאבות, this mishnah does not appear altogether), Rabbenu Bahye, and Meiri.

17. See Rambam, Hamez U-Matzah 1:3.

18. As was previously noted, both terms are difficult to translate in this context, since they have multiple meanings. I have here used roughly accurate but not particularly elegant translations.

19. 3:2. The resemblance to Hobbes is striking, but while the underlying base rests upon premises regarding unfettered human nature, I feel impelled to assume some difference. Hazal have no Rousseauistic illusions but also did not subscribe to extreme pessimism on this issue.

20. 3:1. See 2:1, where similar counsel is offered, but with regard to a different trio.

21. Berakhot 17a (on the alternate *girsa* cited there in the marginal note).

22. Yoma 72b. For a list of other primary sources in this spirit, see the references cited in Rav E. R. Zeeny's edition of *Magen Avot*, the commentary of the author of the Tashbez

on *Avot* 1:17, pp. 74–76. To this we might add a remarkable interpretation of Rabbenu Bahye in his *perush* upon Devarim 30:15.

23. See Tehillim 50:16–17. For the identification, see Sanhedrin 106b and Hagigah 15b, respectively.

24. Yerushalmi, Berakhot 1:2. In reply, the rejoinder given is that R.S.b.Y. regarded the *mizvah* of reciting *shema* as being of a piece with Torah study, and hence all *talmud Torah* could be a vehicle of its fulfillment. זה שינון וזה שינון. The Bavli, however, has a contrary factual tradition, according to which R.S.b.Y. abstained only from fulfilling Rabbinic *mizvot*. See Shabbat 11a, and Moʿed Katan 9a-b and *Tosafot* s.v. *kan* thereon.

25. 4:5. The opportunity cited as being afforded or denied refers, of course, not to a decision within the context of a formal proceeding but to providential intervention.

26. Section 427, commenting on Avot 4:5.

27. See 2:8 and Bava Kamma 30a, respectively.

28. 3:9. The latter statement obviously invites the question of how the quantity is to be measured. But this is not my immediate concern.

29. 2:2. It should be noted, however, that the reason cited focuses upon avoiding evil rather than upon creating good. The term *derekh eretz* has, in Hazal, a wide scope of meanings, ranging from social conduct — what Coventry Patmore denominated "the traditions of civility" — to productive labor, conceived in both economic and quasi-metaphysical terms. Here, it probably refers to integration within the work force, which provides both economic sustenance and virtuous engagement in fulfilling God's primordial mandate to humanity, to place its stamp upon the natural order.

30. 3:17. The difference between the last two formulations is significant, but they obviously share a pietistic bent.

31. 2:15. Cf. 3:16 and 4:22.

32. 1:17.

33. 3:5. Here too, the referent is providential intervention.

34. 2:12.

35. See *Shemonah Perakim* chs. 4–5 and Deʿot, 3:3, respectively. It may be noted that much of the ideological controversy currently sundering the Torah world turns on the interpretation of to what extent does this dictum define what to do or how and why.

36. Deʿot 3:3.

37. *Nahalat Avot* (New York, 1953), p. 212; on 4:1.

38. My own English rendering of Rav Yitzchak Shilat's Hebrew translation of the original Arabic. See his edition of (ירושלים, תשנ"ז) הקדמות הרמב"ם למשנה, p. 57.

39. 8:8. The following *pasuk* continues: הבשו חכמים חתו וילכדו הנה בדבר ה' מאסו וחכמת מה להם — "Lo, the wise are shamed, disheartened, and captured. Lo, they have contemned Hashem's word and what have they of wisdom?"

40. *Hakdamot* p. 58.

41. This assumption serves as much of the basis for the Rambam's explanation of the position of Avot in *Seder Nezikin*, just after Sanhedrin. See *Hakdamot*, pp. 47–49. Of particular relevance to our discussion, we might note the Rambam's perception of *Avot*: בזו המסכתא מוסרי כל חכם מן החכמים עליהם השלום.

42. Section 424.

43. 2:3. This counsel may, to some extent, have been stimulated and sharpened by the catalyst of current historical events, but it hardly seems confined to a specific political constellation.

44. 2:9. The triad differs widely with respect to content and focus, but the overall direction is common to all three counsels.

45. 2:12. With respect to the motive force and character of *tefillah* as plea, cf. Berakhot 28b-29b.

46. 3:1.

47. See I Melakhim, 19:11–12.

48. 6:2. The citation is drawn from a chapter known as *kinyan Torah*, as it catalogs a list of 48 elements helpful to the acquisition of Torah. While not originally part of *Avot*, in the course of time it was linked to it as an appendage and is frequently printed with it.

    It is not clear from the text who is being addressed: universal humanity, collective Jewry, or those who lapse in *talmud Torah*.

49. "Wordsworth and the Iron Time," in *Wordsworth: Centenary Studies* (Princeton, N.J., 1951), p. 136.

50. Ibid, p. 140.

51. 1:17.

Chapter 3

Communal Governance, Lay and Rabbinic: An Overview

In the Torah world, the prospect of total Halakhah arouses ambivalence. It is, on the one hand, unquestionably appealing; and this, in two respects. First, we take great pride in the comprehensive scope of the halakhic order. *Yahadut*, the Rav was wont to state insistently, is not confined to the customary parameters of the *homo religiosus*. It relates to life in its kaleidoscopic diversity, as it legislates for the marketplace and the bedroom no less than for the *bet ha-kenesset* or the *bet ha-midrash*. It is animated by a spirit of integration, informing a system within which the sacred and the secular, *hayyei olam* and *hayyei sha'ah*, are distinct but not disjunct, both constituting, on both the personal and the collective plane, aspects of an organic whole.

Moreover, it is those who are, in some way, oriented to elements of the modern spirit, who espouse this theme most vigorously. The Rav and Rav Kook — each, admittedly, relating to the modern world variously, and each approaching our issue from his own perspective — share a common faith in the permeating sweep of Halakhah. Focusing upon the redemptive creation of sanctity or its illuminating discovery, respectively, their affirmation of the vitality and value of the range of human experience contrasts markedly with the residual other-worldliness often encountered in *ba'alei mahshavah* less exposed and less attuned to the modern temper. And small wonder. The inclination to a measure of world-acceptance, often excessive, is, after all, one of the characteristic traits of modernity.

Second, the Torah world, regardless of its perception of the modern, is attracted to total Halakhah because of our overwhelming espousal of the normative. The concept of *mizvah*, our stance vis-à-vis the *Ribbono shel Olam* as commanded beings, as sons and servants both, lies at the epicenter of Jewish existence. Not only do we glorify servile fealty to divine orders but — following Hazal, and in the face of intuited common morality — we revel in the contention that action in response to the halakhic call is superior to the same act, voluntarily undertaken. *Gadol ha-mezuveh ve-oseh.*[1] And this, presumably, not — or, not only — because, as some Rishonim held, it assures a more conscientious implementation,[2] but because, over and above the practical result, the halakhic charge renders the act intrinsically and qualitatively superior, inasmuch as it engages the agent in a dialogic encounter with his Master.[3]

On the other hand, we respond to the prospect of total Halakhah with reservation, if not recoil. The thought that everything has been programmed, all eventualities anticipated, so that we can rest assured that if only we mine long enough and deep enough we will discover the definitive right solution, is staggering, in one sense, and stifling in another. It emasculates us intellectually and — in some respects, religiously — because it effectively denies genuine spiritual choice and thus severely limits responsibility. We are reduced to deciphering possibly encoded messages and to implementation of detailed orders.

Jewishly and humanly, we yearn for more. We have been nurtured on the centrality of free will in the Torah life; and we instinctively assume that the creative impulse finds expression not only in the elucidation and explication of concepts and texts but in the process of their application as well. A committed Jew obviously does not arrogate autonomy. He regards *behirah hofshit* as the capacity to accept or reject Halakhah, but not as the right to do so. He does, however, presume that, in addition to being charged with navigating his ship, he has some latitude in charting its course.

This inclination, too, moreover, is reinforced by the link to modernity. While much of modern culture is grounded in determinism, that which is not, ranging from existentialism to humanism, is imbued with an enhanced sense of human worth and impelled by the conviction that this worth is, in no small measure, bound up with man's creative capacity. On the religious plane, this capacity can be harnessed toward self-sanctification, enabled precisely because the whole of the spiritual life has not been preempted by the explicitly normative. *Kaddesh azmekha ba-muttar lekha.* "Sanctify yourself through that which is licit for you."[4] One need hardly identify with Dostoevsky or Berdyaev to appreciate the value of the spiritual increment added by a dimension of freedom; and the contention that radical servitude is fully compatible with a modicum of legitimate choice is, from a Torah perspective, thoroughly tenable. *Avadai hem*; and yet, *herut al ha-luhot.*

This ambivalence provides a context within which we can confront the primary question posed to us: Is there an ideal model that can be culled from halakhic sources of how the Jewish community should be governed? To maximalists, the answer is self-evidently positive. From their perspective, the Halakhah has addressed itself, comprehensively, to far lesser matters; and to so grave and central a concern, *a fortiori*. And if a search fails to unearth the desired formulation, the failure is to be ascribed to the shortcomings of its initiator rather than to the content of the material, which is, *a priori*, present.

My own perception is quite different. Whatever our proclivities, and our wishes notwithstanding, we should acknowledge that, in fact, the Halakhah has left many issues — possibly, even entire tracts — largely open. These omissions, furthermore, are not confined to mere trivia. Consider, for instance, the sphere of family relations. The *mizvot* of *kibbud* and *mora* with regard to parents, of course, place a clear and, in time, detailed charge upon children. This, in turn, is counterbalanced by the conclusion that, unlike a regent, a parent is empowered to absolve his children of this duty, either generally or specifically.[5] To the best of my knowledge, however, nowhere do we encounter a clear halakhic ruling concerning the advisability of such forfeiture as to whether, optimally, a father should play the Bismarckian "autocrat of the breakfast table," in Holmes's phrase, or, if he prefers, may or even should adopt the role of an elder chum, laughing along with his children even as he is lampooned by them. Or again, much has been set down concerning marital relations and their reciprocal rights and responsibilities. But where is the codicil that translates into practical, normative terms the exhortation to love one's wife as oneself and to respect her more than oneself?[6] Which will delineate, ideally, the degree and scope of intimacy, the extent to which a couple leads parallel lives or a fused existence, how much time, and quality time, is spent together, and by what process they arrive at critical decisions? Whatever its appeal, the quest for total Halakhah is chimerical. There is, of course, a sense in which, as Rabbeinu Bahye emphasized, the whole range of human activity is fraught with spiritual import, if only because every act can be weighed against possible alternatives; so that the Rambam could confidently assert that the exemption of *yirat shamayim* from providential governance encompasses all that a person does. This is a long way, however, from the assumption that "had we but world enough and time," a clear halakhic position could be staked out on every issue.

Hazal had a halakhic term for this presumably non-halakhic sphere: *devar ha-reshut*. It should be noted, however, that the category is multi-faceted. At times, it refers to phenomena that are wholly neutral, devoid of either religious or axiological content. Thus, with respect to oaths, the mishnah predicates that they can devolve upon matters of *reshut*, such as the eating of an apple or abstinence thereof, as contradistinguished from a *devar mizvah*, upon which they cannot take effect.[7] On the other hand, *reshut* may denote entities — such as *tefillat arvit* (in Talmudic times), *korban pesah* for women, or the *hagigah* accompanying the *pesah*[8] — which are, intrinsically, *mizvah* elements *per se*, but whose performance is not mandatory for the person. Intermediately, it includes initiatives that are legally optional but, far from being axiologically, ethically, or religiously immaterial, are weighted with possibly portentous spiritual content. Thus, we are familiar with *milhemet reshut*;[9] maiming oneself is subsumed, on one view, under *reshut*;[10] while Rabbi Akiva includes under this rubric manumission of an *eved kenaʾani*, initiating *sotah* proceedings, and the defilement of a *kohen* in order to bury a close relative.[11] These nuances are clearly significant; but for our purposes it will suffice to establish sheer halakhic recognition of the category.

Given this perspective, we can approach our question — in effect, we need to determine whether a community's adoption of a particular sociopolitical authority falls under *reshut,* and if so, of which strain — without preconceptions. In light of the paucity of basic sources relating to the communal sphere, we might do best to begin our examination on the national plane, addressing ourselves to two primary issues: Does the Halakhah prescribe any specific form of civil government? What is the nature of the relation between religious and lay authority?

The first question is generally regarded as subject to controversy among *tanna'im* in the Tosefta, cited therefrom in the gemara in Sanhedrin. Rabbi Yehudah lists a triad of *mizvot* that became incumbent upon entry into Eretz Yisrael, the appointment of a king being the first; while Rabbi Nehorai rejoins that the relevant *parshah* is not normative, and was only stated in order to present a response in anticipation of a hypothetical complaint by a people in search of a leader.[12]

As might be expected, no definitive decision is adopted by the gemara, and, from the Geonim on, the disagreement persisted.[13] Geonic views on the matter, through statement or omission, are a bit murky, but the Rishonim were more explicit. Foremost among the advocates of the establishment of royalty as a *mizvah* was the Rambam, who opens Hilkhot Melakhim U'Milhamoteihem by citing the statement concerning the three *mizvot* that devolved *bi'shat kenisatam la-aretz.*[14] Others, however — admittedly of far lesser stature as *baalei Halakhah* — disagreed. Some leading *parshanim* — possibly under the negative impress of the account of Shaul's selection in I Shemuel, and, hence, impelled to interpret *ve-amarta* conditionally rather than normatively — were inclined to tone down the element of *mizvah.* Thus, Ibn Ezra summarily notes, *Som tasim reshut.*[15] Rabbeinu Bahye (b. Asher), for his part, opens his comment on the *pasuk* by stating that *al derekh ha-peshat zo mizvat asei*[16] that there be a king in Israel; goes on to contend, however, that this *mizvah* relates to the will of Israel and does not reflect the divine will, which much prefers that there be no sovereign among us but God; and, by way of expanding on the point, concludes by cataloguing the doleful tribulations caused by a list of Biblical monarchs.

Leading the opposition, however, was a late *parshan,* Rav Yitzhak

Abravanel, who — drawing, in part, upon observation of the tergiversa-
tions of Renaissance monarchies — argues vehemently that selection of a
king is, at most, permitted; and he goes so far as to contend that this view
can also be ascribed to the Rambam. In considerable detail, he analyzes
the needs for a ruling body and the purposes for which such a body would
presumably be established; examines, on both religious and philosophical
grounds, the merits of various options; surveys the historical development
of monarchy in Israel; and concludes not only that there is no positive
commandment to appoint a king but even that the license to do so is,
like that of *yefat to'ar*, a grudging concession to baser instincts; *Lo zivetah
ha-Torah alav gam lo zivetah al azivato, lefi she-dibberah Torah ba-zeh
ke-neged ha-yezer ha-ra.*[17]

A significantly modified variant of this position is espoused by the
Ramban. Commenting upon the *pasuk, ve-amarta asimah alai melekh*, he
notes that, on Hazal's view, the phrase has normative content, "For it is a
mizvah that they [i.e., the people] should come before the *kohanim* and
the *leviyim* and to the judiciary and say to them, 'It is our desire to place
a king over us.'"[18] This points, in one sense, in a normative direction, as
the people are told to present their desire for royalty. On the other hand,
any *mizvah* of royal appointment proper is muted, for it only takes effect
after the *vox populi* has made its appeal.

In our own time, such a condition was predicated (although, to the
best of my knowledge, without reference to the Ramban) by Rav Mosheh
Soloveichik, who sought to adduce historical evidence. He noted that
during *bayit sheni*, Hazal evidently made no effort to reestablish the monarchy; all such initiatives came from very different sources. He conjectured that this omission could be ascribed to the lack of requisite popular
demand, in the absence of which no *mizvah* of *minnuy melekh* obtains.[19]
Moreover, he was inclined to assume as a further, objective, condition
that it is only in force when pressing needs, such as security and social
order, require. It is, of course, arguable that even where no personal monarch is chosen, any ruling body, as Rav Kook held,[20] assumes the position
and prerogative of *melekh*, so that the *mizvah* is, in a sense, fulfilled. But

that is precisely the point. The end is crucial; the specific means, possibly optional.

In sum, the question of whether a particular form of national government is halakhically mandatory or even preferable is shrouded in a measure of uncertainty. No similar question beclouds a parallel seat of power — the rabbinic. Both the obligation to establish a central *bet din* when conditions are ripe and the status of its authority are firmly grounded in the *parshah* in Devarim,[21] as elucidated by Hazal and later sources. The point was especially driven home by the Rambam at the opening of Hilkhot Mamrim: "The Great *Bet Din* in Jerusalem is the mainstay of *Torah she-beal peh*, and they are the pillars of [instructive] decision, and from them statute and law emanate to all of Israel; and it is with respect to them that the Torah has prescribed, 'According to the law which they will teach you' — this is a positive commandment. And everyone who believes in Mosheh Rabbenu and his Torah is enjoined to ground the matter of religion upon them and to rely upon them."[22]

What is ambiguous, however, is the degree and character of the interaction between the respective authorities. The issue is, of course, immanent, and, as European history amply attests, has been the source of considerable tension. Regrettably, however, it was scantily addressed by Hazal, and, until the rise of the State of Israel, was not subsequently discussed extensively. The *pasuk* prescribes that the monarch be guided by rabbinic leadership, writing his *sefer Torah, mi-lifnei ha-kohanim ha-leviyim*, "from before the *kohanim*, the *leviyim*."[23] However, the nature of the relation is unclear. Do *hakhmei ha-sanhedrin* instruct, inspire, or order — and with respect to which realms? Presumably, they exercise "judicial review," invalidating initiatives that countermand Halakhah. But do they otherwise engage in the process of civil government? The mishnah specifies that a royal declaration of *milhemet ha-reshut* requires the Sanhedrin's imprimatur.[24] This palpably bespeaks a measure of involvement — at least at the level of "advise and consent." By the same token, however, it is clearly implied that they are generally not enmeshed in affairs of state, these being properly rendered to Caesar.

Such a division still leaves open the possibility of a role both in enforcing Halakhah and in legislating, incrementally, to extend and adopt it, thus effectively subjecting the citizen and the community to the authoritative demands of divergent and possibly competing jurisdictions. As is well known, this seemingly problematic prospect was indeed, in a limited vein, envisioned by the Rambam in the *Moreh*,[25] and was much more fully articulated by one of the foremost of latter-day Rishonim, albeit in a non-halakhic context. Expounding in his *derashot* upon the twin *parshiyot* in Shoftim concerning the establishment of organs of governmental authority, the Ran constructs a model of parallel legislative and judicial systems, each with its own laws, sanctions, and canons of evidence.[26] Rav Herzog was understandably perturbed by the prospect of a civil judiciary in disregard of halakhic standards, and even strained to deny that the Ran had ever intended this.[27] More salient, however, is the fact that the proposed overlap leaves open the question of how much coincidence is envisioned and unresolved the thorny issue of how a possible clash is to be confronted.

So much for the national plane. We need to ask ourselves, however, whether and to what extent it can serve as an archetypal model for lower echelons of communal government. This question resolves, in turn, into two components: (1) the mode and choice of rabbinic and lay authority, respectively; and (2) the nature of their interaction. Before focusing on our primary concern, the local community, we might briefly examine the intermediate tribal level. The possibility of divergence from the national model may already be entertained with respect to each *shevet*. Admittedly, the Ramban, drawing upon both the language of the word, *li'shvatekha*, in the *mizvah* of appointing *shoftim* and upon proof-texts from Hazal, contends that each tribe had its own miniature Sanhedrin, serving in both a legislative and a judicial capacity, much like state legislatures and courts in modern America: "And it is possible to interpret that the text requires the appointment of a *bet din* for the entire *shevet*, and it will judge all of them.... And if it be necessary to amend or to impose a matter upon their *shevet* they amend and impose, and this will be for the *shevet* as is the import of the Great Sanhedrin for the whole of Israel."[28] However, it is highly questionable that a similar parallel exists on the civil side. The term *nasi* appears in *Tanakh* in many contexts with respect to the ruler of a *shevet*, but this may not be to our purpose. First, the halakhic implications of this fact are unclear. With respect to the special *korban hattat* brought by a *nasi*, as opposed to that of an ordinary sinner, the mishnah specifies that only the *melekh*, qua supreme ruler, is included.[29] Similarly, with respect to the *pasuk, ve-nasi ve-ammekha lo taor,* "Nor shall you curse a ruler of your people,"[30] prohibiting cursing of a *nasi*, over and above the injunction against cursing in general, the Rambam confines it to the monarch and the head of the Sanhedrin;[31] and while the *Minhat Hinnukh* contends that the statute should extend to a tribal *nasi*,[32] there is no basis for this position in the Rishonim.

Second, even should one regard this point as open, what I believe is indisputable is the fact that there is no *mizvah* to appoint such a *nasi* in the first place. Whatever may be the case with respect to a *melekh*, the position of *nasi* is, to the best of my knowledge, purely optional, the form of tribal government being left to the discretion of the governed.

If this be so with respect to tribal rule, subordinate within a federal structure but still an overarching entity, it is, I believe, *a fortiori* true of the local scene. Here, too, the *mizvah* of appointing a *bet din* — initially, the presumed local Torah authority — obtains.[33] And here, too, there is no clear halakhic norm designating a particular form of lay civil government mandatory or, possibly, even preferable. We can, of course, looking back at the initial national model, have recourse to it for spiritual guidance that, by analogy, will point the direction local government should optimally pursue. We are mindful of the midrashic call for a pattern of precedent that should direct us with regard to details not formally included in the halakhic corpus. Relating to the proximity of the *parshiyot* of *nazir* and *sotah*, the Midrash explains that they are linked by a common thread. It posits that, fundamentally, only wine should have been proscribed for a *nazir*, grapes being essentially neutral. Nevertheless, he is enjoined from partaking of anything "which comes from the grapevine" in order to distance himself from possible transgression; and therein lies a general directive of specific relevance to *sotah*. "Do not say, 'Inasmuch as I am [only] proscribed from having relations with a [married] woman, I shall grasp her and have no sin, or I shall fondle her and have no sin, I shall kiss her and have no sin,' so the Holy One, Blessed Be He, says: 'Just as a *nazir* vows not to drink wine, and yet it is forbidden for him to eat grapes, or anything which comes from the grapevine, so it is wholly forbidden to touch a woman who is not yours.'" [34] The thrust of the passage — and there is no dearth of parallel texts — is clear, and its message is of possible bearing upon our issue.[35]

In the same vein, it is arguable that communal governance should be patterned after the national, as regards both the structure of rabbinic and lay authority, respectively, and the character of their interaction. However, if that is the contention, an examination of the degree of similarity is very much in order; and I venture to suggest that if it be conducted, significant differences will be readily apparent. We are not dealing, either in the basic halakhic sources or in our own modern context, with classical Athens or Renaissance Venice. The community under discussion differs from a state in character no less than in scope. It has no truck with foreign policy or military security; and, if voluntary, does not even impose taxes. On the other hand, it is more deeply engaged than remote central government in the human realm, in shaping and administering the *modus operandi* of servicing the ordinary citizen and coping with his demands. Hence, as the challenges differ, so may the solutions.

Contemporaneously, this distinction is more vividly apparent in the Diaspora than in Eretz Yisrael. Historically, there have, of course, been periods during which Jewish communities enjoyed a large measure of local autonomy, and possibly even a modicum of national autonomy, which achieved a level of halakhic recognition. *Rashei galuyot she-be'Bavel*, the Rambam pronounces, *bi'mekom melekh hen omedim* "Babylonian heads of the Diaspora community stand in stead of a king."[36] However, in the modern era, there is no pretense even of any Diaspora *kehillah*'s serious involvement in running a town. That is readily and wholly ceded to the general municipal authorities, leaving the Jewish community and its leadership to cope with purely internal affairs. However, while this dichotomy is sharper in the *Golah*, a point possibly reflected, halakhically, in the sufficiency of the establishment of provincial courts, as opposed to the need for local *batei din* in Eretz Yisrael,[37] it is, in our context, fundamentally valid in Israel as well.

Briefly stated, a current Jewish community does not engage in government but in internal governance; not in the exercise of power to regulate affairs of state, national or local, but in the organization and direction of the ebb and flow in the life of institutions and individuals within its confines and under its aegis. Even in contemporary Israel, there is a clear line of demarcation between the local general council, entrusted with the maintenance and development of its urban or rural locus, and the *moʾezah datit*, the religious council, not genuinely voluntary and yet not fully empowered, which superintends activity in narrow bands of human life. Hence, even if we should conclude, contrary to my own perception, that there are clear halakhic guidelines controlling and delimiting the mode of local political government, that need hardly be the case with respect to the institutions confined to limited social governance.

Of governance, in particular, halakhic sources, in their legal and formal aspect, have relatively little to say. Halakhah can live, and has lived, on the rabbinic side, with local *batei din*, fixed or ad hoc, and with superior *batei vaʿad*; with independent congregational rabbis, national synods, and, intermediately, *rabbanei ir*; with acknowledged but undesignated *gedolim* no less than with formally empowered masters. On the lay side, it can function, and has functioned, with patrician *rashei avot* as with popular town meetings; with elected *parnasim* or *tuvei ha-ir* as with appointed plenipotentiaries; with oligarchic property-owners as with the compound of membership and board currently in widespread vogue.

The form and structure of the respective seats of authority is, essentially, a *devar ha-reshut* — which is not to say, we remind ourselves, that it is a matter of indifference. There are, unquestionably, important axiological considerations, both moral and religious; and at any given station, some modes of government are more consonant with the spirit and substance of Halakhah than others. The point is that we need to approach the issue contextually and teleologically, with an eye to optimal results rather than to presumed rules. To be sure, there are aspects of the political realm upon which some specific *halakhot* impinge, normatively. The primary question posed to us, the quest for a composite ideal polity, is not, however, among them.

We are free, then, to deal with our issue not without preconceptions but without preconditions. In doing so, we can approach it in the spirit of Plato, conceiving, *ex nihilo*, the model of an ideal polity, although, Burke's critique of abstract constitutions ringing in our ears, not unmindful of the historical course of Jewish communal governance as it has evolved organically. Were we writing, or creating, our own *Republic*, we would obviously do what Plato did: grapple with the fundamental issues of political philosophy and social theory in light of moral and religious premises. We would define and prioritize the ends of a *polis* and of its structured governance, and then seek to determine which means best realize their attainment. In determining *telos*, we would obviously draw upon Torah sources, and then move to a distinctively — although, perhaps, not uniquely — Jewish conclusion. With respect to modalities, however, our hands would not be tied — not because our commitment is deficient but because the statutory norms that might bind us are, broadly speaking, simply nonexistent.

I believe we may go a step further. The flexibility I envisage is not confined to the plane of technical implementation. It encompasses attitudinal elements relating to some of the core issues of political theory: the distribution of power and the mode of its apportionment; the balance of rights and duties, entitlement and obligation; the parameters of governmental interference in individual life; the tension between personal will and the *volonte generale*; the ultimate human source of authority; the antithesis between liberty and equality; the ground of civic responsibility. With respect to this gamut of cruces, Halakhah, in its welter of detail and the legal and axiological principles immanent within it, may define the parameters of discourse, but without prescribing a definitive conclusion. In formulating that, hashkafic inclinations, moral sensibility, and even pragmatic evaluations may play a legitimate role in the determination of priorities and preference.

The point may be exemplified by reference to a wholly different sphere: religious asceticism. A halakhic order that mandates that on the holiest day of the week a person should eat heartily, and as well add a meal to his daily regimen; that postulates that *Tashmish ha-mittah me-oneg Shabbat hu, lefikhakh onat talmidei hakhamim ha-beri'im meshamshim mi-leilei Shabbat le-leilei Shabbat,* "Sexual relations are an aspect of Shabbat delight; therefore the *onah* of healthy *talmidei hakhamim* is on Shabbat eves,"[38] obviously precludes espousal of extreme ascetic views. It does not, however, ensure *a priori* unanimity on the issue; and, in fact, that has not been historically achieved. Much the same may be postulated with regard to our cluster of concerns.

This is particularly true of communal governance and the degree of its democratization. Obviously, there are *halakhot*, especially with respect to the degree of personal liberty, which run counter to democratic theory and practice; and these reflect the theocratic aspect of our *hashkafah*, particularly when authority is exercised, coercively, by an organ of governance rather than within a voluntary communal context. Nevertheless, the cardinal premises are fully sustainable, and, if a community so wills, may be applied in practice. The twin pillars of democratic theory — a) the factual assumption that, in the long run, the people know best, and b) the ethical assertion that even if the results are poorer it is their right to decide — and the faith in the common man, as well as the priority assigned to his interests, that undergirds them, can be accepted or rejected by a Jewish polity; it can be adopted at one point and renounced at another. At issue is, indeed, *devar ha-reshut*.

Nor should we be appalled if we intuit that a given structure has been adopted because of its provenance in the broader culture. It is, indeed, entirely possible that a given format is morally and politically preferable because it is attuned to the *Zeitgeist* and therefore more palatable to the governed. Let us bear in mind that when the Torah envisioned the backdrop for the selection of a monarch, it projected an expressed desire for *melekh ke-khol ha-goyim asher sevivotai*. So long as the phrase simply depicts a familiar phenomenon and does not denote the imitative rationale for the initiative, no problem is posed. The injunction of *u-ve'hukkotehem lo telekhu* applies to sheer aping, with the concomitant loss of distinctive cultural identity; or, as in the case of Egyptian and Canaanite mores cited in the *pasuk*, with respect to undesirable or immoral practices. It has no bearing upon the favoring of institutions deemed to have social worth. The key is, on the one hand, motivation, and, on the other, spiritual consonance with halakhic and hashkafic priorities.[39] The distinctive Jewish character may be reflected in the composite gestalt of the policy and its relation to the complex of Torah values rather than in the source of its formal structure. I lack the sociological expertise to assess the effect of the rise of democracy, for instance, upon Jewish models of governance; and I lack the imperative impulse to dictate what it should be. What I can state from the vantage point of the *bet midrash* is that, within limits, the option exists; and let the decision about exercising it be made with intelligence, sensitivity, and commitment.

The latitude I have assumed with respect to the organs of lay governance exists, similarly, in the rabbinic realm. Here, it is perhaps more circumscribed, as it is subject to a broader range of *halakhot* concerning the personal qualifications of a *rav* or a *dayyan*, the composition of a *bet din*, or the delineation of the areas of rabbinic jurisdiction. In principle, however, the fundamental analogy holds. Quite apart from the choice of the basic format of spiritual leadership — a *rav*, a *marbiz Torah*, a *bet din*, a *moreh-zedek*, a *shtat-maggid*, or any combination thereof — there is much flexibility at the level of detail. Many Rishonim take it for granted that a community may waive formal specifications and engage a *rav* who does not technically qualify. Contrarily, a community or its spiritual leaders might choose to impose additional requirements. Thus, at one time European *rabbanim* refused to grant *semikhah* to bachelors, some going so far as to defer the recognition until the recipient had been married for eleven years.[40] Or again, the common *bet din* consists of three members, but the number is not sacrosanct. The Rambam states, "Although a *bet din* of three is a complete *bet din*, whenever there are more, it is laudatory."[41] The Ramban goes so far as to suggest that where litigants disagree upon the venue within which their case is to be adjudicated, whoever insists upon going to a larger *bet din* has the upper hand, as this is equivalent to pressing for a qualitatively superior court.[42] The point arises with respect to interpersonal quarrels but, if anything, would presumably apply *a fortiori* on the communal plane.

The clearest evidence for the element of *reshut* in this area lies, however, in the paucity of *halakhot* governing it. And, indeed, historically there has been considerable variety. We are very much accustomed to the currently prevalent model of a *rav*, however selected or appointed, engaged contractually to a community as its titular spiritual leader, with a range of duties including *pesak*, teaching, preaching, pastoral care, reproof and inspiration, performance of life-cycle rituals, administration and supervision of requisite religious services, and representation of his community vis-à-vis others, Jewish or general. This archetype has not always been the rule, however. The dawn of spiritual leadership in Eretz Yisrael, and the balance therein between *hakham* and *navi*, can only be dimly perceived; and the picture with respect to the period of Hazal is likewise somewhat murky. The identification of a given locale as the bailiwick of a *tanna* or *amora*, so that its residents are guided by his halakhic decisions *le'kula* or *le'humra*, is assumed by the gemara in several contexts,[43] so that the familiar concept of *mara de-atra* has some early basis. That is still a far cry, however, from the station of *rabbanut* as we know it. That does not appear to have evolved in Europe until the central or late Middle Ages. Estimates range from the twelfth to the latter fourteenth century, with the causes suggested varying accordingly — the maturing of independent *kehillot* and the attainment of a measure of autonomy or their decline as a result of plagues and persecutions.[44] Later, *rabbanim* were appointed for larger tracts, resulting, with the rise of the modern nation-state, in the institution of chief rabbis for entire countries. In Eretz Yisrael, this development issued in the establishment of a *Rabbanut Rashit*, as Rav Kook, impelled by a blend of messianic fervor and a passion for putting the religious house in order, sought to restore centralized spiritual and halakhic leadership.

Retrospectively, even so brief a survey of the professional rabbinate invites consideration of the relationship between a *bet din*, generally communal, and the local *rav*. While, as has been noted, the origins of *rabbanut* as we know it are shrouded in some uncertainty, the prevalent perception of a shift in the center of gravity from institutional *batei din* to personal *rabbanim* is, broadly speaking, accurate. Appointment of the former, even in a fairly small community, is halakhically mandatory — particularly in

Eretz Yisrael, but also, albeit possibly on a smaller scale, in the Diaspora.[45] No comparable charge is cited in the gemara with respect to the selection of a *rav*; and presumably, in Hazal's time, selecting one was not *de rigueur*. Contemporaneously, by contrast, almost every *shul* or community has a *rav*, while *batei din* are relatively scarce; and in much of the Jewish world, this situation has obtained for some time.

Nevertheless, the contrast should not be overdrawn; nor should the import of the shift, applauded by some and deplored by others (it has been suggested that the change sapped the vitality of the general organic *kehillah*), be exaggerated. While no reference is made to formal professional status, the gemara does identify certain towns as the bailiwick of a specific *tanna* or *amora*; and thus evidently subject to his halakhic and spiritual authority. On the other hand, even in the modern era, religious power is often shared by the *rav* and a *bet din*, with the former often heading the latter. And even where that is not the case as, to cite a prominent example, in London, a tensile balance between the two, ranging between cooperation and confrontation, may generally exist.

In this connection, the scope of the classical local *bet din*'s functions should be borne in mind. Rishonim differed as to the primary impetus for its appointment. Commenting upon the *mizvah* to establish *shoftim ve-shoterim...be-khol she'arekha*, the Ramban notes that, inasmuch as the Torah speaks elsewhere of settling interpersonal disputes in a court of law, "Evidently, it is a *mizvah* that Israel have [such] courts."[46] This formulation emphasizes the narrow adjudicative aspect of a *bet din*'s responsibility and activity. The Rambam, however, while including this aspect,[47] focuses his summary exposition of the *raison d'être* for the establishment of *batei din* upon their role — partly educational and partly coercive — in molding the character of Jewish society and shaping its mores.[48] On this view, the *bet din* is not so much involved in legal judgment as in spiritual governance. Hence, the institutional differentiation between a complex of *batei din* and the professional rabbinate has traditionally been nowhere nearly as sharp as current practice might suggest. We would be wise, therefore, to acknowledge a historical transition without exaggerating it.

The point may be exemplified by reference to two diverse and yet analogous citations from the Rambam's *Mishneh Torah*. Setting forth the aims of the establishment of civil monarchy and, for that matter, of the monarch himself, he concludes:

ובכל יהיו מעשיו לשם שמים ותהיה מגמתו ומחשבתו להרים דת האמת ולמלאות
העולם צדק ולשבור זרוע הרשעים ולהלחם מלחמות ה'.

> And all his actions should be for the sake of Heaven, and his purpose and thought to elevate the religion of truth, and to fill the world with justice, and to break the strong arm of the wicked, and to fight the battles of God.[49]

Elsewhere, the Rambam assigns similar functions — apart, of course, from the military — to a *bet din*. In describing the schedule of a fast-day mandated because of some public calamity, present or threatened, the gemara states that during the early part of the day "we survey civic affairs" (*mi-zahara le-palgei de-yoma me'ayninan be-milei de-mata*).[50]

The Rambam cites this *halakhah* but expands it significantly:

בית דין והזקנים יושבין בבית הכנסת ובודקים על מעשי אנשי העיר מאחר תפלת
שחרית עד חצות היום ומסירין המכשולות של עבירות ומזהירין ודורשין וחוקרין על
בעלי חמס ועבירות ומפרישין אותן ועל בעלי זרוע ומשפילין אותן וכיוצא בדברים אלו.

> The *bet din* and the elders sit in the *bet ha-knesset* and survey the activity of the townspeople, from after the *shaharit* prayer until mid-day; and they remove the obstacles of sins, and warn and investigate and question with respect to agents of plunder and sinfulness and divest them [from these], and with respect to the strong-armed and humiliate them, and similar sundry matters.[51]

Not just some impersonal overview of vaguely conceived town matters, but concrete steps initiated by a conclave of *bet din* and civic fathers to investigate, admonish, enforce, and above all, like the monarch, to humble the agents of evil and break their power, as part of the community's spiritual purgation.

It should, in any event, be clear that in dealing with the professional rabbinate, we are, in a very real sense, confronted by a *devar ha-reshut* — not only with respect to the selection of a mode or a person for the exercise of rabbinic authority, but as regards the very establishment of the post of *mara de-atra*. Lest I be misunderstood, let me make my point crystal-clear. Of course, a *kehillah* should have a *rav* in its midst and, presumably, at its head. Would it occur to a community to be bereft of a physician or an engineer? Hazal list an authorized *bet din*, alongside a doctor, a blood-letter, and a scribe, as elements in whose absence a *talmid hakham* ought not to reside in a town.[52] That does not, however, render the inclusion of these components mandatory. The mishnah's exhortation, *asei lekha rav*, "Establish for yourself a *rav*,"[53] constitutes, like much of Avot, counsel rather than decree, is addressed to the individual rather than to the public, and, on most views, refers to the adoption of a teacher-mentor rather than to commitment to a *posek* or the creation of a position. As regards a chief rabbinate, I have, in a previous contribution to the Orthodox Forum, expressed the view that even if one should assume that residents of Israel are bound to accept the rulings of the *Rabbanut ha-Rashit*,[54] a questionable proposition in its own right, it is clear that there is no collective obligation to establish it in the first place.

We are left to deal, finally, with the relation between the respective seats of authority, with their balance and their interaction. On the national plane, analysis of this issue ought begin with a survey of the cooperation or confrontation between kings and prophets during *bayit rishon*, or between Hazal and civil rulers, whether the Hasmonean dynasty or a Babylonian *resh galuta*, subsequently. However, for our purposes, focusing upon the local arena, we shall cut a narrower swath. Even a more limited survey, however, should presumably include two primary issues. The first concerns the process of selection of the persons of authority in the respective realms, and the extent, if any, to which each sector exerts influence in manning the other.

The halakhic data concerning these processes are unclear, inviting the impression that we are, once again, confronting a *devar ha-reshut*. With respect to the choice of lay leadership, the gemara in Berakhot postulates that *ein ma'amidin parnas al ha-tzibbur ella im ken nimlakhim ba-tzibbur*, "no *parnas* is appointed over the public without consulting the public."[55] It is questionable, however, that we can glean much relevant evidence from this dictum. *Prima facie*, the consultation has a democratic ring, resonating with consent of the governed.[56] By the same token, however, it appears that someone other than the consulted public is doing the appointing. Just who this might be, and whether his identity has halakhic foundation, is left ambiguous, however. The Me'iri states, somewhat cryptically, that the statement admonishes *yahid oh yehidim* against imposing their candidate upon a reluctant populace, but offers no hint of their identity.[57] It appears likely that the *zibbur's* spiritual mentors were, in some measure, involved, but this remains a matter of conjecture. Moreover, while the Rif cites the statement, the Rambam and the Rosh, followed by the *Tur* and the *Shulhan Arukh*, omit it. Further, the role of *parnas* itself is shrouded in uncertainty. Unlike *tuvei ha-ir*, it may very well fuse spiritual and political authority. The gemara defines the level of knowledge requisite for a *talmid hakham* in order to qualify for appointment as a *parnas*,[58] and it is quite high; and elsewhere Mosheh Rabbeinu and David Ha-Melekh are designated as singular *parnasim*.[59] Hence, the process of selection of lay leadership in Hazal's time — to the best of my knowledge, nowhere amply discussed — remains undefined, like the analogous process of the choice of the *kohen gadol*.[60] Subsequently, this lacuna was filled in, and various procedures, including reasonably democratic elections (albeit often by a limited electorate), were adopted. In the absence of Hazal's sanction, these remained essentially optional, however, the mode of choice and the degree of rabbinic intervention varying significantly, at the discretion of the community or in consonance with the prevalent custom.[61]

The mode of rabbinic selection, once the position was instituted, was, by contrast, relatively clear. As a prospective employee, a *rav* was generally chosen by the laity. This may be grating to some and regarded as demeaning by others, but it is a fact of life in most of the contemporary Jewish world, and has been for some time. To be sure, the Rambam defines classical *semikhah* as *minnuy ha-zekenim le-dayyanut*, "the appointment of elders to serve as *dayyanim*,"[62] indicating that appointment is in the hands of *masmikhim* rather than the community. This should not confuse us, however. Whether a person qualifies to serve as a *dayyan* at all is determined by his Torah masters, who, in effect, certify him. However, the decision about who occupies which post more likely rests with the community to be serviced. Some lament the dependency that, *ab initio* and perhaps subsequently, is inevitably immanent, but the advantages of correspondence and symbiosis between a spiritual mentor destined, alternately, to shepherd his flock and to impose normative demands upon a possibly unruly populace, are equally self-evident. Leading *rabbanim* frequently endeavor to use their influence to push their preferred candidate. But it is the community and its lay constituency that, justly, has the final word.

We are left, in conclusion, to examine the exercise of rabbinic and lay authority, respectively, in dealing with the division of jurisdiction and the degree of interaction. In this connection, I have been presented with twin questions — Why grant authority to laypeople? Why grant authority to rabbis over questions of communal governance and policy? — that proceed from conflicting assumptions and move along diametrically opposite lines. The point of departure of the first is the presupposition that in a Jewish community, laypeople should have no authority, and consequently, that if any authority is nonetheless granted to them, a rationale is necessary in order to justify the initiative. The latter, contrarily, patently presumes, at least with respect to the realm of "communal governance and policy," however defined, that rabbis, as such, ought be precluded from the exercise of authority, this presumably being the prerogative of the laity, and that it is this which requires explanation.

I must confess that I find myself palpably malcontent with both presuppositions. The first seems blatantly patronizing and paternalistic. It evidently assumes that, regardless of the issue, the *majores ecclesia* always know best with respect to both ends and means. Consequently, the power of decision should be concentrated in their hands, and in their hands alone.

I may be overstating the case, but this is the clear implication of the question; and one need not be Jefferson or Voltaire to find it untenable. Even if we assume that spiritual oligarchs indeed know best, it does not necessarily follow that the imposition of their will is always advisable. Even in the public sector, poorer but self-determined results may be preferable to a superior dictated bottom line. Nor is this merely a question of stroking egos. There is moral and religious value in according dignity and responsibility to citizens or *shul* members; and there may be communal benefit, pragmatic and spiritual, in the engagement and involvement of *ba'alei battim* in processes of decision. Provision must obviously be made to ensure that choices be halakhically and hashkafically acceptable. This is clearly the province of rabbinic leadership, particularly with respect to the difficult and sensitive area of initiatives that are not in outright violation of Halakhah and yet not fully consonant with its tone and spirit. This is a far cry, however, from precluding lay governance entirely.

I find the second presupposition equally unpalatable, although for very different reasons. It clearly implies, as a point of departure, a restricted role for the rabbi and a constricted conception of his person. While the existence of areas, presumably halakhic, of rabbinic jurisdiction is evidently recognized, the perception of the rabbi, insofar as matters of communal policy are concerned, as a legal specialist, seems inescapable. He will be heard and heeded, so long as he addresses his congregants from the platform of the *Shulhan Arukh* as their *posek*. Barring that, however, he carries no more weight than any of them. *Devar ha-reshut* is just that purely optional in every sense.

I find this position unconscionable. It does violence to Halakhah, and it does violence to its rabbinic representatives. The notion that whatever has not been explicitly proscribed is implicitly licit, and thus not subject to rabbinic judgment, is morally and religiously abhorrent. It obviates sensitivity to *lifnim mi-shurat ha-din*, in its multifaceted manifestations,[63] obliterates meta-halakhic considerations, and potentially eviscerates the ethical and axiological components of Torah spiritual life. It invites not only Pauline and Buberian charges of arid legalism but Hazal's scathing comment, *lo harevah Yerushalayim ella al she-danu bah din Torah*.[64] It diminishes the image and the reality of the rabbi's stature, and emasculates his position as the spiritual and pastoral leader of his community.

Rabbinic involvement in areas of communal governance and policy, and lay recognition that it is not only legitimate but desirable, is essential to the optimal viability and vibrancy of a *kehillah*. This should be self-evident when issues of ethical import, of social justice or economic exploitation, arise. But the point is germane even in areas seemingly devoid of such considerations. Are budgetary planning and the concomitant assignation of priorities off-limits for a *rav*? And is *shul* architecture beyond his ken?

That a rabbi's judgment should be definitive regarding communal issues of clear halakhic import, and that these issues can be distinguished from broader spiritual questions, should be obvious. While there may be some question as to whether the *pesak* of a local *rav* must be the final word governing the personal life of every member of his *kehillah* or whether, as is increasingly the case today, a congregant may opt to follow other, possibly greater, *poskim*, is perhaps debatable. With respect to public *she'elot*, however, his decision is definitive. If recourse is indeed to be had to superior *poskim*, that cannot be the result of lay surfing of the Internet, but a freely chosen initiative of the rabbi. If the laity insists upon defiantly relying on its own sources, a rabbi should resist and, if necessary, resign.

However, the assertiveness of the *rav* as *posek* — analogous to the Sanhedrin's judicial review, on the national plane — does not exhaust his role as a spiritual authority. That role is threefold. The first aspect, just noted, entails the exercise of a formal halakhic role in the rendering of halakhic judgments on the basis of halakhic resources. Akin, and yet clearly distinct, is the exercise of personal authority, possibly binding, and yet not necessarily through the medium of applying halakhic rulings to proposed initiatives.

This aspect is manifested within a context now relatively neglected (although some regard it as relevant to the current Israeli scene) but very significant in Jewish life in the premodern period: the institution of *takkanat ha-kahal*. The institution, and the authority inherent therein, is rooted in early sources, and recourse to it presumably prevailed in Hazal's time. However, to the best of my knowledge, solid historical evidence on the matter is flimsy; and it appears likely that the provenance of community-initiated ordinances was limited, the sphere of *takkanot* in Babylonia and its environs being largely regarded as the province of spiritual leadership. It was not until the early medieval period that the institution truly flourished.

The kernel, however, is in Hazal, albeit as considerably expanded by later authorities. The gemara in Bava Batra states that "a town's residents are empowered to set down conditions with respect to measures, prices, and wages, and to punish those who violate them."[65] A number of Rishonim extrapolated from this and generalized regarding a measure of local authority in the socioeconomic realm. Thus, the Rashba, in one of numerous relevant *teshuvot*, postulates: "Whatever has been agreed upon by the community with respect to economic matters, they are empowered [to innovate]; and it is thus agreed upon and valid as if it were *din* proper, as their agreements are transformed into *din*, provided that this is done with public consent."[66] As is well known, the instrument of *takkanat ha-kahal*, which, in the sphere of social and particularly economic activity, could circumvent halakhic norms or even deviate from them, proved, historically, a powerful mode of enabling the imposition of local jurisdiction with a measure of flexibility.

This authority inhered, essentially, in the hands of the laity, acting either directly or through elected representatives, such as *shiv'at tuvei ha-ir*.[67] There was possibly, however, a significant limitation upon this lay authority. The gemara subsequently relates that a butchers' guild imposed certain rules and corresponding penalties governing its sphere, but that Rava invalidated its decrees. The rationale advanced by Rav Papa is that such *takkanot* can only take effect in the absence of an *adam hashuv*, "an important personage," presumably in some leadership capacity; "However, where there is an *adam hashuv*, they have no right to posit conditions."[68] No indication is given concerning the identity of this *adam hashuv*. However, in the specific case cited, it was presumably Rava himself; and in any event, a number of Rishonim assumed that the term refers to a halakhic figure. Thus, the Rashba states, "But if there is a *talmid hakham* there, his consent must be obtained."[69] Somewhat earlier, Rabbeinu Mayer Halevi speaks more broadly of *bi-reshut hakhameihem u-gedoleihem*, "with the consent of their scholars and their leaders."[70] Hence, while on the one hand the *sugya* affirms lay authority in critical areas of civic life — let us bear in mind that in the absence of superintending spiritual leadership, the populace can proceed independently — this is, perhaps, severely qualified by the veto power granted their rabbinic mentor.

I say "perhaps" because the qualification, in turn, is, on some views, significantly limited. First, the Rashba ruled that rabbinic consent was disposable where the entire community agreed upon an initiative.[71] Second, some Rishonim did not identify *adam hashuv* with Torah scholarship alone. Thus, the Ri Migash is quoted as explaining, *adam hashuv: talmid hakham ha-memunneh parnas al ha-tzibbur*, "a *talmid hakham* who has been appointed as a *parnas* over the public;"[72] and the *Yad Ramah* states explicitly that if only one of these two conditions is satisfied, the wishes of the individual in question may be disregarded.[73] The Rambam, presumably following his master, speaks of a *hakham hashuv le'taken ma'aseh ha-medinah u-le'hatzliah darkhei yosheveha*, "an important scholar, [in a position] to direct the activity of the *polis* and bring success to the ways of its inhabitants."[74] Third, it is entirely conceivable that the veto only applies when a community exercises its prerogative to issue economic directives resulting in a bottom line at variance with the one at which Torah law would arrive. It might be irrelevant with respect to *takkanot* in a social or economic vacuum. Finally, and perhaps most significantly, the Rivash contends that consent was only required for rules instituted by a specific group, such as a guild; and he notes that it was only in this connection that the Rambam spoke of *adam hashuv*.[75] Otherwise, where general local authorities sought to enact statutes, no further consent is necessary.[76]

Contemporaneously, *takkanot ha-kahal* are nowhere nearly as prominent as they once were; and yet an account of rabbinic relation to them may be of relevance as we seek to sketch models of mixed rabbinic and lay authority. The model empowers the laity to take the initiative in establishing ground rules governing much of the world of *Hoshen Mishpat* as well as neutral areas, while at the same time — on some views, and in certain circumstances — investing the rabbi with the right, and therefore the responsibility, to endorse or reject their proposals. The implications for, say, formulating synagogical by-laws should be apparent.

It is, however, possible that in such an instance, approval of an *adam hashuv* may not be necessary. It will be recalled that the Rivash held that it was only requisite for *takkanot* of a limited group but not to those of the general community. This distinction can presumably be based on one of two factors. Quite simply, we may ground it upon the differing levels of authority of a local government and of a mere syndicate. The Rivash him- self, however, relates it to a comment of the Ramban that Rava invalidated the guild's directives because they might conceivably have been enacted in order to advance its members' special interests, at the expense of the broader population.[77] In the case of the by-laws, then, over and above the limitations upon the need for *adam hashuv* previously cited, we might suggest, given the first interpretation, that rabbinic approval would be essential, while if we assume the second, it may very well be superfluous.

Be that as it may, the role of *adam hashuv*, however delimited, consti- tutes a second aspect of rabbinic involvement in general communal affairs. It should be stressed again that while the rabbi might base his decision upon non-halakhic considerations, his role as such is firmly anchored in Halakhah. We can, however, note a third aspect: rabbinic engagement in areas of communal governance and policy that is not, narrowly speaking, halakhically mandated. We are brought full circle to my gut reaction to the query, "Why grant authority to rabbis over questions of communal governance and policy?" and its implicit denial of a rabbinic role in this sphere.

It may be noted that we are confronted, *mutatis mutandis*, by a com- munal version of the problem of *da'at Torah*, which, in recent years, has generated considerable interest and a measure of controversy. In one form, the discussion has centered upon the status of general opinions formulated by *poskim* on the basis of public policy considerations, rather than those of Halakhah, narrowly defined. In its most prevalent guise, however, at issue has been the force of specific pronouncements issued by *gedolim* regarding social and political questions, especially where these have hinged on an evaluation of the facts rather than upon an analysis of theoretical issues.

The debate is presumably familiar, and the respective arguments can be summed up briefly. It turns, in part, upon historical factors. Opponents contend that the concept is of recent vintage, *sans* any basis in classical theory or practice; and they offer historicistic and sociological explana- tions to account for its rise. Traditionally, they argue, the line of demarca- tion between *mili di-shmaya* and *mili de-ara* was acknowledged, as typified

by a comment of the Baal Ha-Tanya: *He-hayetah ka-zot mi-yemot olam,
ve-ayeh eifo mezatem minhag zeh be-ahad mi-kol sifrei hakhmei Yisrael ha-
Rishonim ve-ha-Aharonim lihiyot minhag ve-tikkun lishol be-etzah gashmi-
yut ke-dat mah la'asot be-inyanei ha-olam ha-gashmi, af li-gedolei hakhmei
Yisrael ha-rishonim ke-tanna'im ve-amora'im asher kol raz lo anas le-hu
u-nehorin le-hon shevilin di-rekia ki im li-nevi'im mamash.* "Has there been
anything of the sort from time immemorial, and where have you found
this custom in any of the books of the scholars of Israel, be they Rishonim
or Aharonim, that there should be a custom and an institution to ask for
material counsel concerning what to do regarding issues of the material
world even of the greatest of the primal scholars of Israel, such as *tannaim*
and *amoraim*, to whom no secret was arcane and celestial paths familiar,
with the exception of actual prophets?"[78] Proponents, by contrast, concede that the term is new but claim that the phenomenon is not. *Gedolim*
from time immemorial asserted leadership in all walks of communal life;
masters "who had decided questions of *Yoreh Deah*," as the Rav stated at
an early stage, "had decided serious and complex questions of political
conduct."[79] And we could readily point to exemplars such as Rav Saadya
Gaon or the Hatam Sofer for evidence.

Primarily, however, the debate has been substantive. Advocates hold,
first, that *gedolim* are imbued with a greater sensitivity to the sacral, and so
assess situations from the perspective of more spiritual priorities; second,
that, apart from their concern, they have better insight whether because,
on the quasi-mystical plane, they have been blessed with *sod Hashem
li-yirei'av*, or because, in more rational terms, the illumination of Torah
charges their entire being and thus their wisdom is more critical than mere
information. Third, the submissive quest for *da'at Torah* may be regarded
as constituting a fulfillment of the precept of *u-vo tidbak*, "And you shall
cleave unto Him," which Hazal related to Torah masters:

מצות עשה להדבק בחכמים ותלמידיהם כדי ללמוד ממעשיהם כענין שנאמר ובו תדבק
וכי אפשר לאדם להדבק בשכינה אלא כך אמרו חכמים בפירוש מצוה זו הדבק בחכמים
ותלמידיהם.

It is a positive commandment to cleave unto the wise and their students in order to learn from their behavior, as it is analogously stated, "And you shall cleave unto Him." Is it possible to cleave unto the *Shekhinah*? Rather, thus have our scholars interpreted this *mizvah*: "Cleave unto the wise and their students."[80]

Finally, it is contended that independently of the merits of a particular decision, as with parenting, great importance is to be attached to the maintenance of hierarchical authority *per se*. Hence, acceptance of *da'at Torah* is, quite possibly, halakhically mandatory, or, at the very least, pragmatically advisable.

Opponents advance a two-pronged rebuttal. In part, they challenge some of the relevant factual assertions; and they point, empirically, to what they regard as a questionable modern track record. Primarily, however, they rejoin that even if the factual claims be admitted, the conclusion is invalid, inasmuch as other factors are overriding. General insight is important, but it cannot be divorced from intimate knowledge, and no level of intuited perception can substitute for the grasp enabled by familiarity. In case of a leak, you call a plumber rather than an architect, and when your car breaks down you prefer a mechanic to a physicist. And, as to the maintenance of Torah authority, that will not be eroded if exaggerated claims for it are not pressed in the first place. No intelligent child loses respect for a father who sends him to an orthodontist for treatment. In any event, on critical issues, the price of possible error is too high a premium for the enhanced reverence, and that needs to be enhanced by other means.

Personally, I share much of the faith of the advocates in the illuminative character of Torah and their concern with spiritual priorities. I freely admit, however, that, under present circumstances, I have difficulty in its application. Much as I humbly admire the fusion of saintliness and *lomdut* manifested in some *gedolim*, it is now less adequate to the challenges of governmental decision than heretofore. Two factors are primarily responsible. First, the issues have, exponentially, become far more complex, requiring a greater measure of expertise or, at least, access to it. Second, the relation of many *gedolim* to their ambient sociopolitical context, to the world about which they are, presumably, to be charged to decide, has changed drastically. In the premodern period, a *gadol* generally stood at the apex of a pyramid. He grew out of a society and a culture that he understood and that understood him, whose language he spoke and whose respect he enjoyed, whose lifestyle and sensibility were familiar, and whose concerns were perceived and often experienced. Today, by contrast, many *gedolim* are distanced from the general community and this, not by accident, but by design. Many first-rate *talmidei hakhamim* lead, from cradle to grave, highly sheltered lives. They receive a cloistered education, not only insulated from the general society but isolated from it. Their education has much to commend it, and may confer significant spiritual and intellectual benefits, but in many cases, it does not provide adequate preparation for in-depth understanding of the ambient culture and of the issues confronting it. The unfortunate result may be failure to appreciate long-term social dynamics, and the attendant responses and reactions, on the domestic plane, or to comprehend the consequences of proposed initiatives on the geopolitical plane.

Given these circumstances, reservations about comprehensive adherence to *da'at Torah* are understandable. However, the situation is significantly different at the local level. On the one hand, the issues are far less complex, and the potential consequences far less grave. On the other hand, chemistry with the laity and the degree of empathy with its concerns ought not be problematic. Presumably, a *kehillah* selects a *rav* who is on its cultural and ideological wavelength; and, hopefully, residence in its midst should reinforce mutual and reciprocal understanding. Consequently, it is both a *rav*'s prerogative and his responsibility to exercise moral and religious authority in relating to issues of communal governance and policy. On many questions, the community may not be halakhically compelled to accept his judgments. It is, however, bound to give them a serious hearing. Hence, he is both entitled and bound to give his judgments a serious airing sensitively, judiciously, responsibly, and clearly.

To some, this lending of ears to spiritual counsel does not constitute the granting of authority at all, and is, consequently, irrelevant to our discussion. I think it is quite relevant, but I have no interest in logomachy.

So long as the substance is clear, I shall not argue over the nomenclature. What is clear is the fact that if a rabbi is worth his salt, counsel is a highly effective means of having an impact upon communal affairs; and one need not fully subscribe to Chief Rabbi Jacobovits' dictum concerning the trade-off between power and influence to affirm this truth.

This mode of rabbinic and lay interaction falls short of full imposition of authority, and yet is fraught with spiritual and communal significance. And thus we conclude as we began — with a dual perception. On the one hand, the awareness of the scope and meaning of the concept of *devar ha-reshut* as applied to our problem is reiterated. On the other hand, we sharpen the recognition that this fact does not absolve rabbis and the laity from collective responsibility but possibly intensifies it. It is often, indeed, precisely with respect to the optional but not neutral that thought and guidance are most crucial. We note that the portions of the Torah that deal with promissory oaths and vows, the archetypal venue of *devar ha-reshut*, are channeled to the general community through the *rashei ha-matot*, the tribal chieftains, whose wisdom and direction are especially valuable in this critical context. We are not currently familiar with the institution of tribal chieftains. However, the element of spiritual leadership that, on Hazal's view,[81] they represent, is a perennial aspect of our Torah world, and the mode of its integration within a Jewish community a perpetual challenge.

Notes

1. Kiddushin 31a.
2. See *ad loc., Tosafot*, s.v. *gadol*.
3. See *ad loc., Tosafot Rosh*, s.v. *gadol*; Ritva, s.v. *de-amar*; and cf. *Derashot Ha-Ran*, ed. A.L. Feldman (Jerusalem, 1977), pp. 88–90.
4. Yevamot 20a.
5. Kiddushin 32a.
6. Sanhedrin 76b.
7. Shevu'ot 27a.
8. Berakhot 27b, Pesahim 91b, and Pesahim 69b, respectively.
9. Sotah 44b.

10. Bava Kamma 91a-b.

11. Sotah 3a.

12. Sanhedrin 20b; and cf. Sifre, on Devarim 17:14.

13. For a brief summary of geonic views, see Yaakov Blidstein, *Ekronot Mediniyim Be-Mishnat Ha-Rambam* (Ramat Gan: Bar-Ilan University, 1983), pp. 21–22; and cf. Rav Y.F. Perlow's commentary on *Sefer Ha-Mizvot Le-Rav Saadya Gaon*, 3:229–236.

14. Hilkhot Melakhim U'Milhamoteihem 1:1; and see Blidstein, pp. 19–31.

15. Devarim 17:15.

16. Devarim 17:15. In a sense, the argument, echoing I Shemuel, 8:6–7 and 10:19, against the choice of any human political authority would also militate against the selection of a president. Obviously, however, it cuts more sharply with respect to a monarch.

17. *Perush Ha-Torah*, ed. A. Schottland (Jerusalem, 1999), pp. 271–279. The reference concerning the Torah's concession is to Kiddushin 21b.

18. Devarim 17:14.

19. This was cited by the Rav in the name of his father, in a lecture delivered in 1969.

20. *Mishpat Kohen* 144:15.

21. Devarim 17:8–11.

22. Hilkhot Mamrim 1:1.

23. See Devarim 17:18.

24. Sanhedrin 2a, 16a.

25. *Moreh Ha-Nevukhim* 3:40.

26. Derashah 11.

27. Rav Yitzhak A.H. Herzog, *Tehukah Le-Yisrael Al Pi Ha-Torah* (Jerusalem, 1989), 2:75–83.

28. Devarim 16:18.

29. Horayot 10a.

30. Shemot 22:27; and see Ramban, *ad loc.*

31. *Mishneh Torah*, Hilkhot Sanhedrin 26:1.

32. *Mizvah* 71:1.

33. Sanhedrin 16b and Rambam, Sanhedrin 1:3–4.

34. Shemot Rabbah 16:1.

35. The passage assumes that the concept of *seyag* is not only counsel addressed to *hakhamim* on a *de-rabbanan* plane, with which it is familiarly associated, but is operative *mi-de'oraita*. There are a number of analogues, but for an explicit statement, see *Avot De-Rabbi Natan* 2:1. However, while the Rambam (*Sefer Ha-Mizvot, lo ta'aseh* 353 and Hilkhot Issurei Bi'ah 21:1) assumes that the text there deals with a *de-oraita*, many Rishonim held that the injunction cited is only of rabbinic origin.

It may also be noted that the Midrash regards lesser forms of sexuality as proscribed only as a safety measure to ensure that no full sexual relations occur, rather than as an axiological extension, prohibited, albeit at a lower level, for the same reason as actual relations.

36. Hilkhot Sanhedrin 4:13. The unqualified formulation conveys the impression that his authority extends beyond Babylonia. This is, of course, very problematic; see *Kesef Mishneh ad loc.*

37. See Makkot 7a; Rambam, Sanhedrin 1:2 (but note the textual variants; *ella be-khol pelakh u-pelakh* clearly makes the most sense and has the support of manuscripts); and Ramban, Devarim 16:18.

38. Rambam, Shabbat 30:14, on the basis of Ketubbot 62b. In this context, the Rambam's premise only leads to the conclusion that marital relations should be part of the Shabbat experience, but posits nothing regarding their optimal frequency at other times. However, in the gemara the reference to Shabbat appears in connection with the delimitation of the minimal conjugal duty of a *talmid hakham* vis-à-vis his wife; and this was cited by the Rambam, Ishut 14:1. This point touches upon broader issues that lie beyond my present scope.

39. See Vayikra 18:3 and Rashi *ad loc.*; Sanhedrin 52a and Avodah Zarah 11a; Rambam, Avodat Kokhavim 11:1 and *Kesef Mishneh*; and *Shulhan Arukh Yoreh Deah* 178:1 and *Be'urei Ha-Gra*, 7. The nuances of motivation are difficult to define in both theory and practice, and the issue requires greater elucidation than I can give here.

40. Rav Simha Assaf, *Be-Ohalei Yaakov* (Jerusalem, 1943), p. 30.

41. Hilkhot Sanhedrin 2:13.

42. See his comment on Devarim 1:12.

43. E.g., Shabbat 130a, Hullin 53b, Eruvin 94a.

44. Yisrael Yuval, *Hakhamim Be-Doram* (Jerusalem, 1989), chap. 1.

45. Tosefta, Sanhedrin 3:5, cited in Makkot 7a. Rambam, Sanhedrin 1:2, according to one textual reading, holds that the *mizvah* does not obtain in the Diaspora. This is the reading with which the Ramban was familiar; and thus in an introductory remark in his commentary on Devarim 16:18, he challenges the Rambam's view as running counter to the Tosefta. However, another reading, probably more genuine, aligns the Rambam with the Ramban's view, based on the Tosefta and the gemara. See the textual variants in the Frankel edition.

46. Introduction to *parshat Shoftim*, Devarim 16:18.

47. *Sefer Ha-Mizvot, asei* 176.

48. I believe it is more than likely that the Ramban would have argued that this aspect was within a *bet din*'s province, but that he did not regard it as the focus of the normative demand for its establishment.

49. Hilkhot Melakhim 4:10.

50. Megillah 30b.

51. Ta'aniyot 1:17.

52. Sanhedrin 17b.

53. Avot 1:6 and 1:17.
54. See my "The Israeli Chief Rabbinate: A Current Halakhic Perspective," *Tradition* 26:4 (1992): 33–34. For a different view, see Rav Shaul Yisraeli, *Ammud Ha-Yemini*, chap. 6; and see the articles by Rav Eliyahu B. Doron, Ithamar Wahrhaftig, and Aviad Hakohen in *Ha-Rabbanut Ha-Rashit Le-Yisrael*, ed. I. Wahrhaftig and S. Katz (Jerusalem, 2002).
55. Berakhot 55a.
56. It is clear that the dictum is not based on a concern for possible error, because the precedent cited is the divine nomination of Bezalel to be in charge of the construction of the *mishkan*.
57. *Bet Ha-Behirah ad loc.*
58. Shabbat 114a.
59. Yoma 86b.
60. Yoma 12b, *Tosafot*, s.v. *kohen*.
61. In this connection, reference should be made to the procedure for the selection of a monarch. See Rambam, Melakhim 1:3, and the reference cited in the *Sefer Ha-Mafteah* of the Frankel edition.
62. Sanhedrin 4:3.
63. This is of particular concern with respect to the quasi-normative aspects of the concept, but the concern is not limited to them.
64. Bava Mezia 30b.
65. Bava Batra 8b. See also Tosefta, Bava Mezia 11:12 and Bava Kamma 116b. On some views, the authority to impose sanctions only applies to recalcitrants who initially consented to the decrees but now fail to abide by them. There is no basis, however, for a group's imposing its will upon an individual in the first place. Obviously, such a position has alarming quasi-anarchic implications. This issue lies beyond my present scope, however.
66. *She'elot U'Teshuvot Ha-Rashba Ha-Meyuhasot Le'ha'Ramban* 65.
67. For a succinct and lucid account of the institution, as well as its sources and parameters, see Rav A. Karlin, "Shiv'ah Tuvei Ha-Ir: Tafkidam U-Maamadam Ha-Mishpati," *Ha-Torah Ve-ha'Medinah* 1 (1949): 58–66. For a much fuller treatment see Rav Yosef Goldberg's comprehensive monograph, *Tuvei Ha-Ir* (Jerusalem, 5760), fully annotated and replete with wide-ranging bibliographic references.
68. Bava Batra 9b.
69. *She'elot U'Teshuvot Ha-Rashba Ha-Meyuhasot Le'ha'Ramban* 65.
70. *She'elot U'Teshuvot ha-Ramah* 302.
71. *She'elot U'Teshuvot Ha-Rashba Ha-Meyuhasot Le'ha'Ramban* 65.
72. Cited in *Shittah Mekubetzet ad loc.*, and in *She'elot U'Teshuvot ha-Rashba* 5:125.
73. *Ad loc.*
74. Mekhirah 14:11.

75. *She'elot U'Teshuvot Ha-Rivash* 399. See *Siftei Kohen* 231:4, who cites many opposing views.

76. In this connection, perhaps note should be taken of another possible variable. The Rivash, in the *teshuvah* previously cited (399), asserts that a community's right to legislate ordinances and to impose sanctions for their violation obtains even in the Diaspora, for he points out that the incident regarding the butchers' guild occurred in Babylonia. The need to make the assertion and to prove it seems to imply that a contrary position might be tenable. This could be based on the principle that certain punitive laws, *dinei kenasot*, are not adjudicated in the absence of *dayyanim semukhin*, specially ordained judges who are not ordinarily found outside of Eretz Yisrael. However, this contention seems dubious, inasmuch as there presumably are no such *dayyanim* among the townspeople in question in any event, so why should the location be significant? Alternatively, it may be based on the fact that, for certain halakhic purposes, the term *kahal* is reserved for residents of Eretz Yisrael, because it is only there that the character of an organic community is fully realized; see Horayot 3a.

    While the Rivash rejects this distinction, it may nevertheless be of relevance in more limited terms. In explaining his position, the Rivash argues that שהדבר שהסכימו עליו בני העיר הרי הוא כאלו קבלוהו כל אחד על עצמו ונתחייבו בו. "For as regards the matter which has been agreed upon by the townspeople, it is as if each person had obligated himself to it and they are bound by it." This formulation can be understood to focus upon personal commitment as a variant of a social contract rather than on the collective *vox populi* as the basis of the binding force of *takkanot ha-kahal*. This could translate, although it need not, into the view ascribed to Rabbenu Tam that actual individual commitment is necessary in order to subject a person to the sanctions included in a *takkanah*. The upshot of this line of reasoning might conceivably be that Rabbeinu Tam's view could be accepted with respect to the Diaspora but not as regards Eretz Yisrael, where the full weight of an organic *kahal* could be harnessed.

    For a full exposition of the scope of the need for an *adam hashuv*, see Rav Goldberg, *Tuvei Ha-Ir*, pp. 324–328, and especially Appendix 4, pp. 459–496.

77. Ramban, Bava Batra 9a, s.v. *ha*.

78. *Iggeret Ha-Kodesh*, sec. 22.

79. From the eulogy delivered in 1940, of Rav Hayim Ozer, in *Divrei Hagut Ve-Ha'arakhah* (Jerusalem, 1982), p. 192. He later changed his attitude on the topic.

80. Rambam, De'ot 6:2, on the basis of Ketubbot 113b. The Rambam's didactic emphasis in this connection is absent in the gemara, and may be viewed as problematic. Surely, were any level of cleaving to God possible, its value would be intrinsic as a purgative and beatific experience, irrespective of whatever lessons could be derived therefrom. The same should presumably be true of encounters with *talmidei hakhamim*, insofar as they are regarded as a substitute.

81. Nedarim 78a.

Chapter 4

Jewish Philanthropy — Whither?

Were I, my distinctive assignment notwithstanding, to undertake a properly comprehensive account, be it only for the purpose of context and background, of the character and scope of *zedakah*, I should probably include some minimal account of several basic issues. At the very least, these should include definition of the term, as it appears, textually and conceptually, in primary sources; some description of the place the phenomenon occupies within the overall complex, communal and personal, of moral and spiritual life, as halakhically conceived; and discussion of the degree and character of interplay between the several distinct senses of *zedakah* — among them, credit, virtue, fidelity, or supererogatory conduct. Given my limited focus, however, I shall largely confine myself, as sufficient for our purposes, to the primary prevalent denotation: philanthropy.

Posing the Question

If I read my marching orders — within the broader context of this conference's structure — correctly, I fear that I have been assigned a nearly impossible task. We are informed that the issues relating to "a halakhic analysis of Jewish charity law," to include a panoply of pressing questions such as the balance between luxury and philanthropy or between *aniyei irekha* and Israeli needs; or, in a different vein, the impact of globalization upon the theory and practice of *zedakah*, will be discussed under another aegis. I have been dealt the seemingly broader and yet possibly blander hand of discourse regarding a single, admittedly major, concern: "Should the Jewish, and particularly the Orthodox, community be inward-looking, focused on self-preservation, or outward looking, seeking to influence the broader world through philanthropy?" The implication that my topic should be treated sans recourse to the halakhic codex is clear; but, given my training and perspective, the prospect that this course will be implemented is palpably dark. The *mizvah* and value which were singled out by the *Ribbono shel Olam* Himself as a prime basis for Avraham Avinu's election:

כי ידעתיו למען אשר יצוה את בניו ואת ביתו אחריו ושמרו דרך ה' לעשות צדקה ומשפט

> For I know him, that he will command his children and his household after him, and they shall keep the way of the Lord, to do *zedakah* and judgment;[1]

which, in light of that verse, *inter alia*, was daringly accorded singular normative status by Rambam:

> Our obligations with regard to the *mizvah* of *zedakah* are greater than our obligations to any other *mizvot*.[2]

whose observance, in the face of presumably relevant principles of coercion, could apparently be compelled;[3] that, of all *mizvot*, is to be analyzed beyond the scope of Halakhah? I apprehend, in any event, the crux and parameters of our respective foci, and shall strive to minimize possible duplication. But should I falter in this respect, the reader will at least have been forewarned by an anticipatory caveat. Beyond that, *mea culpa*.

Philanthropy in Tanakh and Halakhah

Implicit in the formulation of the question posed for my consideration is the assumption that both suggested options have merit. Each is endowed with ethical and religious content, each entails a response to genuine needs, and each enriches the human arena in accordance with the will of its Creator. Conceived in formal halakhic terms, narrowly defined, the specific gravity of the respective choices may seem quite disparate. The former enjoys the status of a clear *mizvah* — indeed, of several; and of the most prominent, to boot. Its status is most sharply delineated by Rambam, previously cited; but the emphasis finds ample precedent in Hazal, as well. It is variously described as the harbinger of redemption — "*Zedakah* is great because it hastens the redemption,"[4] and as endowed with the power to avert divine wrath,

אמר רבי אלעזר גדול העושה צדקה בסתר יותר ממשה רבינו דאילו במשה רבינו כתיב
כי יגורתי מפני האף והחמה ואילו בעושה צדקה כתיב מתן בסתר יכפה אף.

R. Eleazar said: A man who gives charity in secret is greater than Mosheh our Teacher, for of Mosheh it is written, "For I was afraid because of the anger and the wrath" (Devarim 9:19), and of one who gives charity [secretly] it is written, "A gift in secret subdues anger" (Mishlei 21:14). (Bava Batra 9b)

Conversely, the failure to respond to its challenge is equated with the gravest of sins: "One who averts his eyes from an opportunity to give *zedakah* is as one who worships idols."[5]

The latter, by contrast, is devoid of such credentials; and this factor surely deserves consideration. Nevertheless, we could be gravely in error were we to leap to the conclusion that, in and of itself, this point can resolve our issue apodictically or provide categorical guidelines, dictating the details of philanthropic budgets. The point may be clarified by reference to the concept, familiar to Halakhists, as *shevet*, "inhabitation," the mandate for "enlarging the bounds of human empire," in Bacon's language, by amplifying man's presence (and, to some extent, mastery), within the natural world, through procreation. Obviously similar to the command of *peru u-revu*,[6] it nevertheless differs insofar as the latter was evidently interpreted by Hazal as a personal obligation, while the former denotes a general charge, confronting humanity collectively.[7] The term derives from a verse in Yeshayahu, "Not for chaos has He created it, for habitation has He molded it" (45:18), which, patently, does not address its audience in a normative mode. Nevertheless, in a number of contexts, the gemara,[8] on *Tosafot*'s view, singles it out as particularly significant; as being, for instance, only one of three *mizvot* for whose fulfillment it is permissible to sell a *sefer Torah* or emigrate from Eretz Yisrael.

Or, again, to note a very different analogy, the Gaon of Vilna explicates the conclusion of *Megillat Esther* by focusing upon the nature and status of *tov* and *shalom*, respectively:

דרש טוב. הוא מעשים טובים ומדות טובות והמדות טובות הן יותר מכולן כמ"ש שלא נכתבו המדות טובות בתורה כי הם כוללין כל התורה כמ"ש כל הכועס כאלו עובד עבודה זרה וכל המספר לשון הרע ככופר בעיקר וכן כולם הוא כלל הכלי לכל המדות והוא הלבוש של כל המדות... והמדות הם כלל של המצות ובירך אותם בשלום שיהיו יכולים לקבל את התורה.

"Seek the *tov*, good," this refers to good deeds and proper *middot*, for proper *middot* are more crucial than all the [actions], as I have written, that the proper *middot* are not written explicitly in the Torah, for they underlie the entire Torah, as the gemara states (Shabbat 105b), "One should regard one who gets angry as an idolater" and (Arakhin 15b), "One who gossips is considered like a heretic," and the same goes for all the *middot*. *Shalom*, peace, is the general means to all the *middot* and the garb of all the *middot*... While the *middot* are the means to all the *mizvot*, and He blessed them with *shalom* to facilitate the receipt of the Torah.[9]

The attempt to explain the Torah's relative silence with respect to cataloguing ethical mores is interesting in its own right. However, the assertion that the omission can be ascribed to the fact that these — goodness and the quest for peace being singled out, particularly — were omitted because they are so basic and comprehensive, is almost startling. Hence, it illustrates our point graphically; and the conclusion that the *mizvah* aspect of *zedakah* invariably militates its preference to other courses of public policy may be over-hasty, indeed.

From an alternate perspective, the potential weight of the "outward-looking" option needs, unfortunately, to be emphasized for a very different reason. The ethical charge of *Nevi'im* and the example of wellsprings of our very existence notwithstanding, many in the Torah world persist in remaining oblivious to *hesed*'s universal aspect. I have lamented this tendency in a previous Forum essay, but the point needs to be hammered home, repeatedly: "The tendency," I wrote then and I reiterate now, "prevalent in much of the contemporary Torah world, in Israel as in much of the Diaspora, of almost total obliviousness to non-Jewish suffering is shamefully deplorable."[10] The insouciance springs, in part, from failure, often grounded in a blend of ignorance and prejudice, to appreciate the scope and value of Gentile *avodat Hashem* and spirituality.

Unquestionably, the complex of demands and opportunities divinely conferred upon Jewry is unique: "*Ha-Kadosh Barukh Hu* wanted to increase the merits of Yisrael, therefore He gave them a large number of *mizvot*." Clearly, however, this fact hardly warrants or even justifies the widespread disdain frequently experienced and expressed in relation to normative Gentile religious existence, as halakhically formulated. How many of our confreres are aware that, quite apart from the minimal core seven Noahide *mizvot*, Ramban and Rema held that Gentiles are committed to fulfilling much of the civil law encoded in *Hoshen Mishpat*?[11] Or that Rambam stated that any Gentile performance of any *mizvah* would be rewarded — "Every *mizvah* that a Gentile performs is rewarded, but he is still not like one who is obligated and performs?"[12] And of course, the most basic strains of religious experience — *ahavah, yir'ah, devekut, tefillah, korbanot, teshuvah* — as well as the demands of veracity and sensitivity, are incumbent upon the non-Jew as upon ourselves. Similarly, the cardinal *mizvah* of *talmud Torah* bears a universal aspect. It is sharply reflected in Rambam's vision of the Messianic era as one during which the whole world will be exclusively engaged in pursuing knowledge of God: "And the entire world will be involved in nothing else besides the pursuit of knowledge of God."[13] More explicitly, it emerges from R. Mayer's assertion that Gentile Torah study is on a par with its Jewish counterpart:

היה רבי מאיר אומר מניין שאפילו עובד כוכבים ועוסק בתורה שהוא ככהן גדול שנאמר אשר יעשה אותם האדם וחי בהם כהנים לויים וישראלים לא נאמר אלא האדם הא למדת שאפילו עובד כוכבים ועוסק בתורה הרי הוא ככהן גדול.

R. Mayer used to say. Whence do we know that even a heathen who studies the Torah is as a High Priest? From the verse, "[You shall therefore keep My statutes and My judgments,] which, if man do, he shall live in them" (Vayikra 18:5). Priests, Levites, and Israelites are not mentioned, but men: hence you may learn that even a heathen who studies the Torah is as a High Priest![14]

Whatever the causal nexus, we ask ourselves, in disbelief: Are the *midrashim*, imbibed from childhood, recounting Avraham Avinu's *gemilut hasadim*[15] — including the well-worn homily that his hospitality was superior to Lot's, inasmuch as he thought that his noontime guests were dusty nomads, while his nephew knew they were angelic — of no practical moment? Was the test of Rivkah's sensitivity futile, as it involved no Jews? Are we to regard Mosheh Rabbenu's bold defense of a group of Midianite lasses merely a chivalrous gesture by an aspiring shepherd? And is the divine rebuke to Jonah solely a phase of our Yom Kippur ritual, to be heard on *yom zomah rabbah*, only to remain unheeded on the morrow?

There are, of course, rationalizing rejoinders. It may be contended, for instance, that whatever preceded *mattan Torah* doesn't count, as the normative thrust of Sinai reoriented priorities. But can men or women of professed faith and ethical sensibility be content with such self-serving ripostes? For committed Orthodox Jews — and, *a fortiori*, for serious *bnei Torah* — the utter dismissal of universally oriented *hesed* as an expression of *avodat Hashem* cannot be accounted a live option. Our polestar is, rather, Rambam's invocation of the divine order as an implicit norm, in the spirit of "*ve-halakhta bi-drakhav*," *imitatio Dei*, informing our actions and perceptions:

הרי נאמר טוב ה' לכל ורחמיו על כל מעשיו ונאמר דרכיה דרכי נועם וכל נתיבותיה שלום.

For it is stated, "God is good to all, and His mercy extends to all his works" (Tehillim 145:9) and it is stated, "Its ways are ways of pleasantness, and all its paths are peace" (Mishlei 3:17).[16]

Divine universal beneficence and the Biblical focus upon the Torah's symbiotic relation to peace and harmony are more than a model. They constitute a charge.

Acknowledgment of our multiple philanthropic obligation lies, then, at the heart of our issue — as a point of departure at one plane, and as a possible conclusion at another; and it serves in that role because it constitutes the core of our theoretical perception of the scope of our commitment to *gemilut hasadim*. The ground of that commitment may be viewed from two perspectives. It may be regarded as deriving, exclusively, from our specifically Jewish identity, as a linchpin of the legacy of the patriarchal fountainhead of *Knesset Yisrael*, in general, and of its ethic, in particular; of Avraham, whose progeny and disciples are devoted to the realization of "And they shall keep the way of the Lord, to do *zedakah* and judgment" (Bereshit 18:19). Alternatively, it may be construed as a reflection of a Jew's dual identity, comprised of both universal and particularistic components. In this connection, we may ponder the import of a relevant passage in the Mekhilta. Commenting upon the verse, "one who hits another man and kills him will surely die," the *tanna*, Issi ben Akiva, notes:

קודם מתן תורה היינו מוזהרים על שפיכות דמים לאחר מתן תורה תחת שהוחמרו הוקלו? באמת אמרו פטור מדיני בשר ודם ודינו מסור לשמים.

> Before the Torah was given we were warned regarding bloodshed [of any human]. Is it conceivable that after the Torah was given we shall now be more lenient? Indeed they taught that he [a Jew who murders a Gentile] is exempt [from punishment] in the human court but his case comes before the Heavenly court.[17]

This was identified by the *Bet Yosef*, in his commentary on *Mishneh Torah*, as the source of Rambam's view that murder of a Gentile is punishable by divinely ordained death;[18] but its ramifications extend far beyond the confines of this specific judgment. It is probably reflected, for instance, in the gemara's wonder at the possibility that consumption of the meat of an animal which has been slaughtered halakhically, but is still alive and active biologically, might be proscribed for Gentiles but licit for a Jew. "Is there, then, anything," Rav Aha ben Yaakov asks rhetorically, "which is permitted for a Jew but forbidden for an idolater?"[19] Presumably, the underlying premise is that *mattan Torah* and concomitant election of *Knesset Yisrael* were intended to superimpose a higher level of obligation, rooted in newly acquired identity, but not to supersede prior commitment, grounded in preexisting, universal identity.[20]

On this reading, the possible ramifications for our implementation of *hesed* should be self-evident. Rishonim disagreed as to whether, over and above the seven Noahide *mizvot*, a non-Jew, as perceived from a halakhic perspective, is enjoined to give *zedakah*. Possible evidence elicited from the gemara is sparse and inconclusive. However, the message is seemingly encoded in a rebuke addressed by Yehezkel to treasonous Jerusalem, and it is sharp and telling. The royal city, proclaims the prophet, has rebelled more grievously than the paradigm of sin, classic Sodom; and it is worthy of correlative punishment. And what constituted the epitome of Sodomite vice? Failure to support the indigent:

הנה זה היה עון סדם אחותך גאון שבעת לחם ושלות השקט היה לה ולבנותיה ויד עני ואביון לא החזיקה

Behold, this was the iniquity of your sister Sodom: pride, surfeit of bread, and abundance of idleness was in her and in her daughters; and she did not strengthen the hand of the poor and needy.[21]

Manifestly, contends the author of *Hiddushei Ha-Ran*,[22] its citizenry ought, normatively, to have sustained the poor, and their abstinence became the cause of their destruction.

Given our prior premise, the import of this critique, at once instructive and devastating, bears upon the Jewish world — whom Yehezkel is castigating — as well. The *ani ve-evyon*, the poor and the impoverished, deserted by Sodom's smug and affluent bourgeoisie, is, of course, Gentile. Applying, therefore, Issi ben Akiva's principle to philanthropy, the population we would have been commanded to support prior to Sinai, remains, in light of our vestigial universal component, an aspect of our moral responsibility.

The point is greatly reinforced if we contemplate the full range of our commitment to the pursuit of *zedakah* and *hesed*. That commitment is doubly rooted. Most obviously, it is oriented to assist the recipient needy; and that is palpably the primary thrust of both of the *parshiyot* which

deal with the obligation to give *zedakah* — that of וכי ימוך אחיך ומטה ידו
עמך, והחזקת בו גר ותושב וחי עמך, "And if your brother has become poor, and
his means fail with you; then you shall relieve him; though he may be a
stranger, or a sojourner; that he may live with you" (Vayikra 25:35), or that
of כי לא יחדל אביון מקרב הארץ על כן אנכי מצוך לאמר פתח תפתח את ידך לאחיך לעניך
ולאבינך בארצך, "For the poor shall never cease out of the land; therefore I
command you, saying, You shall open your hand wide to your brother, to
your poor, and to your needy, in your land" (Devarim 15:11), respectively.
Concomitantly, however, it is intended to educate the affluent donor —
primarily, by engaging him in *imitatio Dei*, emulation of, *mutatis mutandis*, the ethical qualities which, by dint of both prophetic revelation and
personal intuition, we ascribe to the *Ribbono shel Olam*. That character,
and the role He has chosen to assume in history is, however, as amply
manifested in the *siddur*, itself dual. The concluding chapters of Tehillim,
recited daily as the backbone of *pesukei de-zimra*, alternate between the
predominantly universal strains of "*Ashrei*" to the largely national focus
of "*Ki Tov Zammerah*" or "*Shiru La'Shem Shir Hadash*." The fusion of
the universal and the particular in *malkhuyot, zikhronot*, and *shofarot* in
musaf of Rosh Hashanah engendered the Hafets Haym's reputed remark,
that if the *goyim* knew how much we pray for them, they would rush to
print *mahzorim*. Most prominently and most familiarly, the same theme
is struck in the twinned assertions with which *shema Yisrael* opens. And
most daringly, we are witness to the conjunction of seemingly incongruous statements in a remarkable verse in Yeshayahu (54:5):

כי בעליך עשיך ה' צ-באות שמו וגאלך קדוש ישראל א-לקי כל הארץ יקרא.

> For your Maker is your husband; the Lord of hosts is his name; and
> your redeemer the Holy One of Israel; He is called the God of the
> earth.

Here is the most intimate and visceral relationship aligned, side-by-side,
with the attribution of abstract mastery and sovereignty.

That fusion does not, however, entail benign neglect of the broader
venue. To be sure, "Yisrael is my son, my firstborn" (Shemot 4:22), and the

reciprocity of "You have avouched the Lord this day," and "The Lord has avouched you this day" (Devarim 26:17–18) as reflected in the asseveration of "Who is like Your nation Israel, one nation upon the land," in *minhah* of Shabbat, is essential to our perception of God's relation to us and of our relation to Him. But there are other children as well. They, too, need to be fed; and, in contemplating His bounty, we express the faith that places have been set for them at the table:

אהב צדקה ומשפט, חסד ה' מלאה הארץ; הזן את העולם כולו בטובו בחן ובחסד
וברחמים הוא נותן לחם לכל בשר כי לעולם חסדו; פותח את ידך ומשביע לכל חי רצון.

He loves righteousness and judgment; the earth is full of the goodness of the Lord (Tehillim 33:5); Who sustains the whole world with good-ness, kindness and mercy, He gives food to all creatures, for His *hesed* endures forever (Grace after meals); You open your hand, and satisfy the desire of every living thing (Tehillim 145:16).[23]

If that is our paradigm, can we confine our principled concern to our confreres alone?

At the level of concern, our answer must be resoundingly negative. Insouciance to suffering, regardless of its locus, is unconscionable. If the halakhic order took into account the anguish of brute animals — accord-ing to most Rishonim, Biblically so[24] — surely, *a fortiori*, it instills empa-thy for Gentile pain. And indeed, this inference is clearly implicit in the gemara. Within the context of a discussion as to whether the *halakhot* regarding response to possible animal pain is mandated *mi-de'oraita*, the *sugya* cites a prooftext which notes that the *mizvah* of coming to the aid of a fellow's animal, be he even an enemy, only applies to a Jewish enemy, but not to an idolater. But, asks the gemara, if concern for the animal is a factor, why discriminate?

If you say that the prohibition of causing distress to is *mi-de'oraita*, then what is the difference between one who despises Yisrael and one who despises idolaters?[25]

As this very passage clearly indicates, mandatory sensitivity may be overridden by other elements — revulsion from idolatry figuring most prominently among them. Independently considered, however, it exists.

The Problem of Priorities

At the level of implementation, however, the translation of concern into contribution is neither automatic nor certain. For here the analogy between the divine and human spheres breaks down. The crux of ethical living, in general, and of philanthropy, in particular, is the problem of priority — at once, the tragedy and the challenge, the bane and the glory, of groping and coping, within the context of confrontation, with choice. "Many are the needs of your people, and their minds limited" (*Ne'ilah* prayer), intones the lament and plea of the *piyut*. And of course, it is not only wisdom that is limited. Likewise lifespan, likewise powers, likewise talents and resources. No such issue confronts the *Ribbono shel Olam*, however. His initiative can inundate the world, in a positive or negative vein. Absent this boundless bounty, however, man or woman is impelled to choose; and, as regards the world of Halakhah, in particular, choice is the quintessential key. Every hour devoted to any activity, preempts every other; every ounce of energy expended in the pursuit of one value, obviates, as of that moment, all possible alternatives; every fellowship dollar granted to one aspiring candidate, is denied every rival. Hence, whether in the budgeting of personal activity or in regulating disbursement to others, we are impelled — at times, against our better judgment or inclination, and with little penchant for possibly supercilious evaluation — to grade. Moreover, we frequently are constrained to grade not only individuals but their contexts — with whom they associate, which causes they espouse and possibly represent, what will be the likely result of our predilection.

Choice, as either process or result, can be exhilarating as well as cruel. As manifest in the realm of triage, it aids one sector at the expense of another, it saves one life but discards numerous others; and, in extreme cases, satisfactory resolution being deemed impossible, may entertain the prospect of apparent absurdity, in preferring the sacrifice of all to the arbitrary selection of one. Hence, as applied to philanthropy, in particular, determining the validity and value of a given initiative still leaves us in need of principled guidance and operative direction. I take it that we are gathered here in search of such direction, with an eye to mapping strategy, in light of current reality, as well as establishing some basis for axiological priority.

My own assignment has been largely confined to a single question regarding the relative merits, pragmatic and spiritual, of insular and catholic philanthropy, respectively. In coming to grips with the issue, let me stress at the outset that, on the one hand, it does not constitute an endemic Jewish problem; yet, on the other hand, its Jewish component is probably more significant than the comparable cognate factor relevant to other communal contexts. The core question relates to the blend of collective altruism or egoism; and, as such, whether as a fundamental orientation or as delicately nuanced, constitutes one of the chestnuts of general ethical theory and of its religious variants. Concurrently, it bears a distinctly Jewish mien; and this, for at least two primary reasons. First, the focus upon special election and the privileged uniqueness of Jewry both provides a conceptual base and induces a psychic mindset which is conducive to intensifying insular sensibility. Second, this proclivity is further buttressed by sociohistorical factors — the record of millennia of persecution and the concomitant struggle for survival, on the one hand, and the reality of Diaspora dispersion, bonding across borders and oceans, defining "us" and "the other" differently than for the denizens and citizens of a delineated geopolitical entity.

Our first task, therefore, shall entail reflecting upon this general issue, and its possible implications for contemporary Jewish, and particularly, Orthodox, philanthropy. Subsequently, we shall strive to relate to some of the nuts-and-bolts of the question of more specific priority, harnessing, to that end, paradigms of the relevant *halakhot*, as formulated in principal sources. No conspectus of the laws of *zedakah* and *hesed* is hereby offered, and there is no pretense of exhaustiveness. Hopefully, however, even a cursory survey can shed some light on the principled issues here under consideration.

The General Issue

Our first question itself bears a dual aspect. Its primary thrust relates, presumably, to the venue of Jewish philanthropy and to the identity of the beneficiary community. As formulated, however, it also touches upon a second factor — the *telos* of the respective options. The questioner asserts that the inward Jewish focus is geared to self-preservation, while the outward looking emphasis aims "to influence the broader world." It is evidently assumed that the two issues are intrinsically and intimately related. I, for one, am far from certain that this is indeed the case. It is entirely conceivable that some historical and/or sociological bond can be perceived. Universalist philanthropists may indeed be more likely to be impelled by an ideological manifesto than their insular counterparts. Nevertheless, who is being serviced and to what end are, logically, separate concerns. Self-preservation may very well be defined as encompassing both physical and spiritual components. Conversely, engagement with the broader world may include — and perhaps even primarily incline to — meeting the personal physical, economic, and cultural needs of the destitute, the underprivileged, and the disenfranchised, quite apart from impacting upon their ambient milieu. Moreover, we should assuredly beware of the tendencies associated with the impulse to influence. It may, unquestionably, be motivated by pure *yirat shamayim*, by the paradigm of Avraham Avinu's call — ויקרא שם בשם ה' א-ל עולם, "And called there on the name of the Lord, the everlasting God" (Bereshit 21:33). However, it may also be adulterated by selfish urges, tinged with a modicum of what Steven Schwarzschild used to denominate "the imperialism of the soul." At worst, it may even entail some patronizing and paternalistic exploitation of distress in order to push the envelope of one's supposedly enlightened agenda.

These reservations notwithstanding, the formulation does touch upon a cardinal truth — upon a truth, moreover, which rests on a firm halakhic base. Philanthropy is oriented to two distinct — albeit, possibly intertwined — aims. At one plane, it strives to ameliorate suffering and to enable, more equitably, prevalence of a reasonably satisfactory standard of living. Alternatively, it seeks to enhance the quality of life by advancing cultural, intellectual, moral, and spiritual values, at both the personal and the institutional planes.

Halakhic equivalents of these twin goals find expression in various sections of the Torah, as elucidated by Hazal and subsequently codified by classic *mefarshim* and *poskim*. Our first aspect, the *mizvah* of aiding the poor, appears in two *parshiyot* — that which opens, וכי ימוך אחיך, "And if your brother has become poor," in Vayikra (25:35), and the much fuller exposition, related to the prospect of, כי יהיה בך אביון מאחד אחיך באחד שעריך, "If there is among you a poor man of one of your brothers inside any of your gates," and strikingly focused upon Eretz Yisrael, in Devarim (15:7). Both, however, are complemented by prior discourse, narrative as well as normative, regarding contribution to the establishment of the *Mishkan* and its appurtenances. *Prima facie*, one might have thought that the latter bears no connection to *zedakah* at all, and is rather subsumed under another category. However, Hazal evidently assumed otherwise, as, in dealing with certain halakhic minutiae, the gemara in Arakhin[26] conjoins funding a *bet ha-knesset* with assisting the indigent. Moreover, Rambam, who paid scrupulous attention to classification, included both in his Hilkhot Mattenot Aniyyim.[27] Hence, formulation of an ethic of Jewish philanthropy needs to consider policy with respect to both axiological and socioeconomic ramifications.

The question of separatism confronts us here in two respects. It needs to be examined, historically, through the prism of a survey of our past; and it challenges us, contemporaneously, with an eye to our current status, with regard to which this discussion is being conducted. As to the former, it has unquestionably been identified *ab initio* — regarded by some as a source and reflection of strength and, by others, as a manifestation of turpitude — as a hallmark of our existence. Hazal's view of Avraham — "R. Yehudah says: Everyone in the world was on one side and he was on the other side"[28] — as well as their perception of jealously guarded singularity in Egyptian bondage; perhaps even Bilam's depiction (who knows, by which impulse driven)[29] of *Knesset Yisrael* as the עם לבדד ישכן ובגוים לא יתחשב,

"people who shall live alone, and shall not be reckoned among the nations" (Bamidbar 23:9); Haman's angry portrayal of clannish resistance to dicta of the imperial melting pot; the phalanx of *takkanot* and *gezerot* legislated in order to avert significant social intercourse — all attest to prominence of our separatist streak; and it has, of course, served, since Paul, as a crux of Jewish-Christian polemic.

To this trait, we freely admit, and, from our point of view, it requires no apologia. A kindred point needs to be addressed, however, and briefly expounded. The critique of our posture is not confined to separatism *per se*. We are subject to moral reproach as well, charged with being not only clannish but selfish; obsessively, and, if need be, unethically, concerned with promoting our own interests, even to the point of exercising duplicity and adopting double standards.

On this score, I find myself conceding some factual assertions, but rejecting the assessment of "guilty as charged," deriving from them. Admittedly, if judged by the canons of professed Christian ethics, we may be found wanting. We advocate neither transfer of one's only cloak nor turning the other cheek. This, however, not out of moral lassitude but out of principled conviction. We certainly preach the centrality of *gemilut hasadim* and strive to practice it, as both the linchpin of personal character and as the bond of social cohesion. We can admire munificent individuals or communities who share their bounty with the less fortunate, and then some. Nevertheless, ours is a balance of altruism and egotism, which is grounded in distinctly Jewish roots and tradition, and which owes no fealty to alien value systems. We neither espouse nor cultivate Franciscan penury, and harbor no guilt over the omission. Up to a critical point, we do indeed recognize the primacy of personal interest — and this, not only at the national plane, in the spirit of Reinhold Niebuhr's *Moral Man and Immoral Society*, but at the individual level as well. "As a *tanna* has stated," notes the gemara,

שנים שהיו מהלכין בדרך וביד אחד מהן קיתון של מים אם שותין שניהם מתים ואם
ישתה אחד מהן מגיע ליישוב דרש בן פטורא מוטב שישתו שניהם וימותו ואל יראה

אחד מהם במיתתו של חבירו עד שבא רבי עקיבא ולימד וחי אחיך עמך חייך קודמין
לחיי חבירך.

If two are travelling on a journey [far from civilization], and one has
a pitcher of water, if both drink, they will [both] die, but if one only
drinks, he can reach civilization — Ben Petura taught: It is better
that both should drink and die, rather than that one should behold
his companion's death. Until R. Akiva came and taught: "That your
brother may live with you" (Vayikra 25:36): your life takes precedence
over his life.[30]

Moreover, this credo is not confined to life-and-death situations, such as
that of the duo exposed to the ravages of dehydration, with only sufficient
water to enable survival of one. It is legitimized with respect to far milder
contexts, applying likewise to mere financial matters, such as the *mizvah*
of *hashavat avedah*:

אבדתו ואבדת אביו אבדתו קודמת אבדת אביו ואבדת רבו שלו קודם... מנא הני מילי
אמר רב יהודה אמר רב אמר קרא אפס כי לא יהיה בך אביון שלך קודם לשל כל אדם.

If his own lost article and his father's lost article [need attention], his
own takes precedence; his own and his teacher's, his own takes precedence.... Whence do we know this? — R. Yehudah said in Rav's
name: the verse states, "Save that there shall be no poor among you"
(Devarim 15:4), yours takes precedence over all others.[31]

The principle was most sharply articulated by Ramban. Commenting
upon the charge of "You shall love your brother as yourself," he expounds:

וטעם ואהבת לרעך כמוך הפלגה כי לא יקבל לב האדם שיאהוב את חבירו כאהבתו
את נפשו ועוד שכבר בא רבי עקיבא ולמד חייך קודמין לחיי חבירך אלא מצות התורה
שיאהב חבירו בכל ענין כאשר יאהב את נפשו בכל הטוב.

"You shall love your neighbor as yourself" is an expression by way of
hyperbole, for a human heart is not able to accept a command to love
one's neighbor as oneself. Moreover, R. Akiva has already come and
taught, "Your life takes precedence over the life of your fellow." Rather,
the *mizvah* in the Torah means that one is to love one's fellow in all
matters, as one loves all good for oneself.[32]

Ramban's description of R. Akiva's *"kelal gadol ba-Torah"* as "hyperbolic" *haflagah* is astonishing; and, precisely for that reason, it attests, dramatically, to the depths of his moral realism, which recognizes the right to pursue one's own interest more than one's fellow's. And this, notwithstanding the fact that concern for the welfare of others constitutes a *mizvah*, whereas pursuit of self-interest presumably does not.

The principle of *hayyekha kodemin* attains further significance — and particular relevance for our own discussion — by dint of its incorporation into the *Shulhan Arukh*. At the apex of the pyramid of worthy recipients of support, Rema places the prospective "donor" himself:

> One's own livelihood takes precedence over all others, and one does not have to give *zedakah* until he has his needs.[33]

Even allowing for the assumption that the exemption is not total, it retains considerable import.

The Practical Issue

The implications for our problem are self-evident. I have earlier stressed that outward-looking philanthropy, that which is sensitive to privation beyond our community and strives to share in its amelioration, should be acknowledged and encouraged as an aspect of our responsibility to *hesed*; that we should internalize the full force of Hazal's designation of *"mizvah le-hahayoto,"* as including the non-Jew;[34] that the normative ideal of *imitatio Dei* as grounded in *"ve-halakhta bi-drakhav"* charges us to strive to emulate divine munificence. I remain firmly committed to these positions. However, in practice, these demands inevitably clash with meeting the multifaceted needs of our own community. These ordinarily enjoy priority on several grounds.

First, they are our own — a blend, in a sense, of self-interest, insofar as donor and recipient are fused in an organic entity, and of altruistic concern, insofar as, at the personal plane, the two are differentiated. Second, as we invoke the principle of *"efshar la'asotah al yedei aherim,"*[35] the prospect that a given need can and, hopefully, will be met by others, dilutes my own obligation and releases energy and resources for other ends, frequently affecting the balance between inward and outward looking responses. Many universal causes have, almost by definition, broader appeal and a wide spectrum of potential supporters. Specifically Jewish institutions, by contrast — and especially those related to sacral *devarim she-bi'kedushah* — can only draw upon a far more limited base. Finally, to a significant extent, support of our brethren as a fulfillment of the *mizvah* of פתח תפתח את ידך לאחיך לעניך ולאבינך בארצך, "You shall open your hand wide to your brother, to your poor, and to your needy, in your land" (Devarim 15:11), serves to advance the cause of the *zedakah* of *Mishkan* as well, by sustaining and empowering the community of its adherents. Hence, the dictates of priority may militate maintenance of an inward focus after all.

Nevertheless, the difference between the course I am espousing and the one I have rejected should be readily apparent. At one plane, it is attitudinal — possibly, of little interest to treasurers and bursars, but of great import to persons of spirit and educators. Whether an individual fails to extend support because he lacks the means or because he lacks commitment, he leaves the indigent in equally dire straits. The respective options are of momentous significance, however, as regards the philosophic and ethical stance of the "non-donor." To share in the agony of general need, wishing that one could ameliorate it, and confident in the assumption that, were financial response feasible, it would constitute a fulfillment of the *mizvah* of *zedakah*, is, even if one defers and demurs, one thing. To assume that the suffering is immaterial and its relief purely neutral, insofar as the parameters of *zedakah* are concerned, is something else entirely.

Moreover, there is some pragmatic fallout as well. If an inward-looking focus is dictated by the necessity of priority, it should presumably be subject to its limits as well. The factors governing priorities of *zedakah* — and, presumably, *gemilut hasadim* — are varied and, in detail, numerous. Broadly speaking, however, they fall under five rubrics:

1. The personal identity and level, however determined,[36] of the prospective recipient *per se*, with the spiritual hallmarks of a *talmid hakham*, presumably Torah scholarship and virtue, at the pinnacle.

2. The degree of relation — be it familial linkage, interaction issuing in indebtedness, e.g., a student-teacher relationship, common residence, etc. — between the donor and recipient.
3. The nature of the need, as regards kind and degree, whether evaluated in accordance with objective or subjective standards, with an eye to determining utility and worth.
4. Apart from the "points scored," within the scale of *zedakah*, on the basis of the foregoing, the possible interposition and impact of other norms — such as *kibbud av ve-em*, within a situation of *hesed*.
5. The weight possibly assigned to relatively adventitious general guidelines, such as, e.g., the sequential order of "*ein ma'avirin al ha-mizvot*"[37] (the halakhic equivalent of "first come, first served."

All are relevant to the world of *hesed* and all enter into decisions necessary to that world, my preceding reflections included. In this regard, however, an important qualification must be borne in mind. The gemara in Eruvin 63a states that a person who channels all of his *Mattenot kehunah* to a single *kohen* "brings hunger unto the world;" and this statement served Rishonim as a source for proscribing the donation of all of one's *zedakah* to a single pauper — presumably, even if he was among his prioritized relatives. This view has been authoritatively set down in the *Shulhan Arukh*: "One should not give all his charity to a single poor person."[38] Evidently, a clear and essential distinction is hereby postulated. The list of criteria recognized by Halakhah, properly and sensitively applied, collectively determine what should be done in a particular situation. However, general policy, whether personal or communal, needs to be conducted with a broader perspective; and if, for instance, repeated application of the formal criteria will issue in exclusive concentration upon one sector and the desiccation of others, the mix requires revision. How that is to be effected, whether by recourse to a reserve objective pattern, or by resort to subjective intuition, obviously needs to be judged thoughtfully, as do many other questions of priority. My point is simply that, with regard to our question, an inward-looking focus ought not to necessarily preclude the inclusion of general needs of a broader clientele in the implementation of a philanthropic strategy. I am firmly convinced that, for the foreseeable future, an inward-looking focus — to which, under ordinary circumstances, I am committed — should continue to characterize our philanthropic policy. Concurrently, I contend that our community needs to be more forthcoming in recognizing the needs of others and responding to them more generously than we are currently doing. This is doubly true with respect to periods of relative affluence, but ought not to be confined to them.

The prospect of possible practical ramifications is reinforced if we take account a limitation of the principle of *hayyekha kodemin*. In the gemara — and subsequently, in *Shulhan Arukh* — no mention is made of the respective stakes. In the archetypal case of desert thirst, there is, ordinarily, no difference. However, with respect to *hashavat avedah*, there certainly can be a very substantial gap. I may have lost a Timex watch and my fellow, the Hope diamond. And yet, this factor goes largely ignored.[39] The mishnah does state that the finder may strike a deal with his fellow, whereby he volunteers to forgo recovering his own object on the condition that he be reimbursed for its loss; and the *Mehabber* states that, under the circumstances, the finder should be accommodating. But he is not legally required to initiate the concordat.

> ואף על פי כן יש לו לאדם ליכנס לפנים משורת הדין ולא לדקדק ולומר שלי קודם אם
> לא בהפסד מוכח ואם תמיד מדקדק פורק ממנו עול גמילות חסדים וסוף שיצטרך
> לבריות.

Nonetheless, one should act *lifnim mi-shurat ha-din*, in a supererogatory manner, and should not be stringent and say, "My own takes precedence," if there is no manifest loss; for if one is always stringent, one divests oneself of the practice of *hesed* and will, in the end, require the assistance of others.[40]

This moral counsel, too, however, is proffered *lifnim mi-shurat ha-din*.

The *Ba'al Ha-Tanya*, conversely, regarded such behavior as unconscionable — even at the level of *din*. Addressing himself to reports of a Jewish community which had evidently suffered an economic downturn, as a result of which its elite had cut back on charity, even as their own lifestyle remained largely intact, he rebukes their conduct and takes pains to conjecture and condemn their possible rationale:

ועם כל זה לא זה הם עושים לנפשם לפי הנשמע אשר קפצו ידם הפתוחה מעודם עד היום הזה ליתן ביד מלאה ועין יפה לכל הצטרכות ההכרחיים לדי מחסורי האביונים נקיים אשר עיניהם נשואות אלינו ואם אנו לא נרחם עליהם ח"ו מי ירחם עליהם וחי אחיך עמך כתיב ולא אמרו חייך קודמין אלא כשביד אחד קיתון של מים וכו' שהוא דבר השוה לשניהם בשוה לשתות להשיב נפשם בצמא. אבל אם העני צריך לחם לפי הטף ועצים וכסות בקרה וכי האי גוונא כל דברים אלו קודמין לכל מלבושי כבוד וזבח משפחה בשר ודגים וכל מטעמים וכב"ב ולא שייך בזה חייך קודמין מאחר שאינן חיי נפש ממש כמו של העני שוה בשוה ממש כדאיתא בנדרים דף פ'. והנה זהו עפ"י שורת הדין גמור.

Nonetheless, they are not acting rightly unto their soul according to the reports that they close their hand which, all their life long, to this very day, was open to give with a full hand and benevolence toward all essential necessities to satisfy the needs of the destitute whose eyes are lifted unto us. If, Heaven forefend, we will not have mercy on them, who will show them compassion? For it is written, "That your brother may live with you" (Vayikra 25:36). The rule, "Your life takes precedence," only applies to the case of "One has a single pitcher of water" (Bava Mezia 62a), that is, when the same thing is equally essential to both, to drink in order to restore their soul from thirst. But when the poor needs bread for the mouths of babes, and wood and clothes against the cold, and the like, then all these take precedence over any fine clothes and family-feasts, meat and fish, and all the delicacies of man and any members of his household. The rule, "Your life takes precedence," does not apply in such a case, because all these are not really essential to life, as are the needs of the poor. They [the wealthy and the destitute] are truly equal, as mentioned in Nedarim 80b. Now all this is according to the strict measure of the law....[41]

Adoption of this qualification would obviously greatly enlarge the gap between the opposed positions previously outlined.

In principle, therefore, I fully agree that Jewish, including Orthodox, philanthropy should feel a measure of responsibility for universal causes, and should act on that feeling. However, when confronted by the arguments in favor of an outward-looking focus encapsulated in the question posed to me, I find that my assent is quite limited. Surely, we ought to share in "funding environmental causes, alternative energy sources or medical research." And this, for two complementary reasons — one selfish, and one altruistic. The former relates to the fact that we are beneficiaries of these initiatives, and should recognize that, in all fairness, we ought to pull our oar in enabling them.

Moreover, even if we should have no compunctions about parasitism, it is not inconceivable that the broader world will not allow us the luxury. A major American transplant center is reported to have warned that if Orthodox Jews will fail to donate organs, they will be denied their receipt; and similar caveats might be issued elsewhere. Hence, quite possibly, not only our reputation but also our welfare could be on the firing line.

The altruistic motif inheres in the awareness, previously noted, that we are ethically charged to assist in sustaining and improving the quality of life for the inhabitants of this planet as an expression of *hesed*, and to aid in "enlarging the bounds of human empire," as our contribution to *yishuvo shel olam*, one of the two central aims which Rambam designated as exclusively worthy of persistent pursuit: "it is not appropriate for a person to engage in anything except the pursuit of wisdom and *yishuvo shel olam*."[42] I am mindful of the fact that some contend that, having been designated as "a priestly kingdom and sacred nation," we, like *kohanim*, deserve to receive while exempt from giving. However, there are surely more appropriate areas — spiritual, ethical, and religious — to manifest our clerical status.

The second contention relates to the prospect of using outward looking philanthropy "to instill Jewish values into social programs." At this point, I find myself in somewhat of a quandary. I confess that I was already a little confused by the first suggestion. I had rather naïvely assumed that an outward looking focus was not solely bound with research and development, but was in some way related to helping suffering individuals cope with privation; that it was even akin to Emma Lazarus' invitation to "teeming millions" to partake of the New World's cornucopia and share in the realization of the American dream; that it entailed funding Lambaréné or Biafra and extending a helping hand to U.N.I.C.E.F. Having readjusted my sights on that score, as I am now confronted by researchers in white coats, laboring in state-of-the-art facilities as they grapple with extending the frontiers of scientific and technological achievement, I still find myself befuddled by the second suggestion.

What is the scope and magnitude of the social programs under consideration? Presumably, if the focus is indeed outward looking, seeking to influence the broader world, very extensive. In that case, however, is the prospect of instilling Jewish values, desirable as it may be, truly realistic? I am inclined to assume that such an enterprise requires very substantial sums. Exceeding the capacity of the ordinary Maecenas, and on the assumption that the Gateses and the Buffetts of this world are not included in our discussion, a meaningful change of focus could very well result in sapping the viability and strength of existing Jewish enterprises, while barely making a dent in the values and direction of the broader world. I don't believe that this game is worth the candle.

If, on the contrary, the programs involved are far more constricted — referring, for instance, to the secular Jewish world and its institutions — the prospective impact could conceivably be far more substantial. Even so, however, my intuitive response remains skeptical. Any major shift would, in all likelihood, issue, axiologically, in costs exceeding benefits. However, as I am barely a neophyte in this area, I prefer to receive guidance from veteran laborers in the vineyards before making any but a tentative assessment.

Conclusion

Let me briefly submit a further response to the question posed to me. In relating to it, I believe a dual perspective is not only legitimate but highly advisable. As formulated, the question has a clear contemporary ring, as reflected in both its general thrust and the very contemplation of a major revision in the direction and substance of Jewish philanthropy. Clearly, no such prospect would have been seriously entertained by our forefathers in the pre-modern era. The live option herein presented would probably not even have occurred to insular Jewish communities in Poland or Morocco. On the one hand, they both lacked the means to expand their philanthropic activity significantly, and, given their relatively limited interaction with the broader world, were also generally bereft of the impulse to do so. On the other hand, inasmuch as the general welfare state within which post-Emancipation Jewry could find its niche had yet to assume part of the burden of supporting Jewish individuals and institutions, the obligation of family and indigenous *kehillah* to minister to our own was more keenly felt. Rambam attested that while he knew that not all communities had a *tamhui* to provide daily needs to the indigent, "we have never heard of a Jewish community that did not have a *kuppah shel zedakah* of its own."[43] None of us would have to travel any great distance to find a community which, *mirabile dictu*, manages without a *kuppah* to distribute weekly stipends.

To us, the question occurs. And we convene here, in the hope that out of our conference will emerge, if not conclusive resolutions, at least, a measure of direction — without pontification, without presumption, without pretense; but with animated commitment, with sharpened responsibility; with an acute perception of what we owe the *Ribbono shel Olam* and what we owe our people; and with a prayer that we may be worthy of the *siyyata di-shmaya*, which we so desperately need.

Against this background, particularly given the realization that we are so deeply immersed in issues of priority, it is essential, I repeat, that we maintain a dual perspective. Clearly, the objectives encoded within *sifrei psak*, buttressed by much historical precedent, are, for us, a polestar. They assign relative value and provide guidance in the implementation of *zedakah*. Nevertheless, we should beware of excessively mechanical application. By their very nature, the details are not all etched in stone, and the total picture very frequently includes many variables. The question of weighing the respective claims of *Mishkan* and of *aniyyim*, for instance, epitomized by Maharik's decision[44] to permit the diversion of funds earmarked by their contributor for the poor to the reconstruction of a fire-gutted shul, can obviously be treated at the abstract plane of the formulation of general policy. But can anyone seriously contend that an identical answer will obtain in all situations? Indeed, even as concerns Maharik's specific *teshuvah*, in reading and analyzing the responsum, we note that major consideration, so spiritually and psychologically understandable, but without significant roots or standing in Hazal — was given to the fact that the envisioned shul was to replace the recently destroyed *bet ha-knesset* in the heart of Jerusalem. Can we fail to take account of the impact of any decision upon the population and regard its likely response as irrelevant? And what of the donor? Ought we to suppose that the balance between his spiritual enrichment through engagement in *hesed* and pragmatic ameliorating of the tragedy of destitution will always remain in identical equilibrium? How do we factor heroic relief for the prioritized or most acutely agonized few against the routine needs of a multitude? Finally, can the depth of spiritual or material need of a given town be ignored? Is the level of danger of assimilation or starvation of no moment?

The answer to these rhetorical questions is clear. In this area, in particular, the variables are numerous and too substantive to admit disregard. And they are, collectively, sufficiently flexible both to warrant consideration and to enable it. Halakhic guidelines will certainly be invoked in determining philanthropic policy and practice. However, their application needs to be sensitive and contextual, with an eye to a constellation of relevant factors which we ignore at our peril — spiritual and material, personal and communal. Historically, first-class *poskim* have marshaled ingenuity and responsibility in confronting frequently delicate and controversial issues of *zedakah*; and theirs can hopefully serve as an instructive model.

Such an approach is rendered even more essential if we bear in mind the possible impact of an additional factor — not specifically related to *zedakah* but, nevertheless, of critical moment in almost every meaningful area of our religious life. I refer to the prospect of *kiddush ha-Shem* — or, sadly, the reverse — in the broad sense of the term: impact upon regard for Torah and *avodat Hashem*. Precisely because of its position at the interface of the private and public sectors, how distributive justice is meted out by the committed and their leadership can influence the standing of tradition and its adherents. We perhaps ought not to exaggerate this factor. Decision should, possibly, be preferably grounded in substantive elements rather than in promotional terms; and, contrary to much popular sentiment, the impact upon *shem Shamayim* proper can result from the measure of consonance of an action with the immanent divine presence, rather than with its public relations effect. Nevertheless, we remember that Hazal, following many *pesukim*, attached great significance to the status of divine names and their public standing. This is reflected in relation to oaths, often intimately linked to use of *shem Shamayim*.[45] Thus, on the one hand, Rambam describes a proper link as a hallowing process:

שהשבועה בשמו הגדול והקדוש מדרכי העבודה היא והידור וקידוש גדול הוא להשבע בשמו.

> For taking an oath in His great and holy name is one of the paths of His service. It is a great measure of glorification and sanctification to take an oath in God's name.

Conversely, abuse of that link constitutes a mode of blasphemous defamation, regarded as the nadir of sin:

עון זה מן החמורות הוא כמו שבארנו בהלכות תשובה אף על פי שאין בו לא כרת ולא מיתת בית דין יש בו חילול השם המקודש שהוא גדול מכל העונות.

> This sin is considered one of the severe transgressions, as explained in Hilkhot Teshuvah. Although it does not involve *karet* or execution by the court, it involves the desecration of God's holy name which is more severe than all other sins.[46]

Hence, judicious and sensitive decision is critical; and so, likewise, with respect to our specific issue.

* * *

As this paper draws to a close, it suddenly dawns upon me that it has not quite succeeded in its mission. With respect to the preferable direction of contemporary Jewish philanthropy, I trust I have adequately clarified that

I believe it should be animated, *inter alia*, by a principled recognition of universal responsibility for *zedakah* and *gemilut hasadim*, to be reflected, in some measure, by efforts to respond to that obligation; but that, in practice, it should focus primarily upon meeting Jewish needs. However, insofar as I have emphasized the importance of contextual judgment in the light of significant variables, I have fallen short of unequivocal delineation of the precise optimal balance some readers may have sought. I was asked a simple question, susceptible of definitive response, and I'm afraid I only proffer a qualified response. However, at least the basic direction of my position and the preference expressed and reflected in it, should be clear. And as to the flexibility, I cite, by way of precedent, two supportive analogous sources: a gemara in Berakhot regarding the dissemination of Torah; and, closer to our immediate topic, Ramban's recourse to a text concerning a balance between *talmud Torah* and *gemilut hasadim*. "*Tanya*," opens the first citation, of a passage from the Tosefta:

הלל הזקן אומר בשעת המכניסין פזר בשעת המפזרים כנס ואם ראית דור שהתורה
חביבה עליו פזר שנאמר יש מפזר ונוסף עוד ואם ראית דור שאין התורה חביבה עליו
כנס שנאמר עת לעשות לה׳ הפרו תורתך

> Hillel the Elder said: When the scholars gather in the Torah [i.e., they do not teach it to the broader public], you shall disseminate it; and when they disseminate it, you shall gather it in. If you see a generation which is eager for the knowledge of the Torah, spread it about, as it says, "There is that scatters and yet increases" (Mishlei 11:24). But if you see a generation which takes no interest in the Torah, keep it in to yourself, as it says, "It is time to do for the Lord, [for] they make void Thy law" (Tehillim 119:126).[47]

Qualification with respect to so primary and prominent a duty places the need for proper assessment and knowledgeable perception in bold relief.

And, finally, we note Ramban, in his treatise, *Torat Ha-Adam*, dealing with the possible interruption of Torah study in order to pay homage to a funeral cortege, cites a relevant prooftext — drawn from the Yerushalmi in Kil'ayim:

תני אין מדקדקין במת ולא בכלאים בבית המדרש ר' יוסי היה יתיב מתני והוה תמן
מיתא מאן דנפיק ליה לא אמר כלום מאן דיתיב ליה לא אמר ליה כלום.

It was taught: One is to concern oneself about neither a corpse nor
prohibited admixtures in the study hall. R. Yosi was sitting and teaching, and there was a corpse [passing by]. He said nothing to those
[students] who went out [to accompany the funeral], and he said nothing to those who remained seated [in the study hall].[48]

In certain circumstances, that recoil from rigidity, determined but in no
sense carefree, constitutes the incarnation of responsible decision.

Notes

1. Bereshit 18:19. For a crucial discussion of the link to election, see Ramban, *ad locum*.
2. Hilkhot Mattenot Aniyyim, 10:1.
3. See Bava Batra 8b, and Ketubbot 48a and 50a. Many Rishonim assumed, on the basis of a gemara in Hullin 110b, that positive commandments whose reward is explicitly stated in the Torah, are not subject to coercion; and many also included *zedakah* in this category. Some therefore concluded that it could not indeed be compelled while others sought to explain why it was nonetheless actionable. See *Tosafot*, Bava Batra 8b, s.v. *akhpeh*; Ritva, Rosh Hashanah 6a, s.v. *ve-asita*; Rambam, Hilkhot Mattenot Aniyyim 7:10, and Hilkhot Nahalot 11:10–11 and *Kesef Mishneh* thereon; and *Kezot Ha-Hoshen* 290:3.
4. Bava Batra 10a.
5. Bava Batra 10a. The equation with idolatry is not, of course, to be understood too literally. Similar statements appear in Hazal in diverse contexts, in some of which, indeed, the analogy relates to a clearly grievous sin, and may have halakhic ramifications. Thus, for instance, with respect to a *mehallel Shabbat* who, for certain purposes, is treated as if he were a non-Jew; see Hullin 5a and Rambam, Shabbat 30:15. However, in other cases, despite the equation, no such sanctions are ever envisioned. See. e.g., Shabbat 105b, with respect to a person who is subject to fits of violent anger, with the resultant loss of self-control; or, a similar critique of one marred by the blight of inflated pride; see Sotah 4b and Rambam, De'ot 2:2; or again, of one who demeans (*ha-mevazzeh*) the holidays, even, as Rashi explains (Sanhedrin 99a), be that only as regards *hol ha-mo'ed*; see Pesahim 118a and Sanhedrin 99a. Obviously, however, the equations are nonetheless pregnant with ethical and religious import.
6. See Yevamot 65b, and *Tosafot*, s.v. *ve-lo*. The possibility that the *pasuk* can be

interpreted as a blessing rather than as a command has been entertained; see Maharsha, Sanhedrin 59b, s.v. *gemara va-harei*. This has not been accepted normatively, however.

7. On my view, this distinction is reflected in the position, endorsed by some Rishonim, that even persons exempt from the *mizvah* of *peru u-revu* are included in the commandment to engage in procreation, within the parameters dictated by *shevet*. In a similar vein, the midrash's citation of *shevet*, rather than *peru u-revu*, as the grounds for compelling the master of a servant, prevented from raising a family by his status, to manumit him (see Gittin 41a), is best understood in the light of this suggestion. The owner could not be charged to act in order to enable the servant to fulfill the latter's personal obligation but could be coerced on the basis of his own responsibility to the general mandate.

    On a totally different note, the sixteenth-century author of *Shenei Luhot Ha-Berit*, took this *pasuk* to discourage asceticism while legitimizing worldly experience. See Sukkah, *Ammud Ha-Shalom*, II:76 (5623 ed.).

8. See Megillah 27a, Avodah Zarah 13a, Yevamot 62a-b, and Gittin 41a-b. See also Avodah Zarah 13a, *Tosafot*, s.v. *lilmod*, which cites and rejects a diametrically opposed view that the *mizvot* cited are of lesser gravity, and the intent of the gemara is to innovate that even they are sufficient to warrant the sale or the departure.

9. *Perush Ha-Gra*, Esther 10:3. See Shabbat 105b; cf. Rambam, De'ot, 2:3, where he postulates that the *via media* he generally advocated did not apply to anger, from which one should distance himself maximally; and Teshuvah 7:3, where it is included among traits which require penitence.

10. *Jewish Perspectives on the Experience of Suffering* (Northvale, N.J.: 1999) p. 59, reprinted in *Leaves of Faith*, Volume II, p. 47.

11. See Ramban's commentary on Bereshit 34:13, and *She'elot U'Teshuvot Ha-Rema*, Resp. 10, respectively.

12. *Teshuvot Ha-Rambam*, ed. Y. Blau, 148. Cf. also *Perush Ha-Mishnayot*, Terumot 3:9.

13. Hilkhot Melakhim 12:5.

14. Sanhedrin 59a. For ancillary reasons, the gemara goes on to restrict the range of the Torah material included in the license. This has no bearing, however, upon the principled view of Torah study as such.

15. During the course of this essay, I have not distinguished between *zedakah* and *gemilut hasadim*. The gemara does clearly differentiate them, as the former is largely confined to financial assistance given to the poor while the latter encompasses many forms of aid and support, even if extended to the affluent. See Sukkah 49b. However, as I sensed that this distinction was not particularly relevant to my presentation, I assumed the liberty of interchanging the terms indiscriminately.

16. Hilkhot Melakhim 10:12; cited with reference to *zedakah* for Gentiles. Cf. De'ot 1:5–6, and *Hanukkah* 4:14. In this connection, a recent monograph encompassing both the

general principles and the detailed minutiae of *zedakah* — and, to a lesser extent, of *gemilut hasadim* — is noteworthy. Rav Menachem Kasdan's *Yesodei Ha-Zedakah* (Jerusalem, 5769), presents a comprehensive survey, both erudite and astute, which touches upon almost every significant aspect of the topic, and constitutes a valuable contribution to its halakhic and hashkafic understanding and analysis. Moreover, narrative sections depicting exemplars of optimal fulfillment of *zedakah*, clearly presupposes that support of Gentiles is included in the broader parameters of the *mizvah* and of the ideal; see, e.g., p. 587. And yet, as even a cursory glance at the index clearly reveals, in the body of the discourse, this specific issue is largely ignored. It is to be hoped that the lacuna will be covered in subsequent editions.

17. *Mishpatim, massekhta di-nezikin*, sec. 4; in the Horowitz-Rabin ed., p. 263.

18. See Roze'ah U'Shemirat Nefesh, 2:11, and *Kesef Mishneh, ad locum*.

19. See Hullin 33a.

20. See *mori ve-rabbi*, R. Yitzchak Hutner, *Pahad Yizhak, Pesah* (Brooklyn, N.Y.: 1988) p. 145, who assumes this position generally, but regards Shabbat and *yamim tovim* as exceptions.

21. Yehezkel 16:49. Note the acerbity with which previous *pesukim* chastise Jerusalem for being worse than Sodom. Cf. Yeshayahu, 1:9–10.

22. See his comment on Sanhedrin 56b, s.v. *va-yezav*. The editor of the Mossad Harav Kook edition (Jerusalem, 2003) notes, however, that Rambam may have felt otherwise, as he evidently classifies *zedakah* as meritorious but voluntary for a Gentile. See Hilkhot Melakhim 10:10, and the discussion listed in the *Sefer Ha-Mafte'ah* of the Frankel edition.

23. The omission of any ethnic reference in the familiar midrashic statement that the *Ribbono shel Olam* only rises to judgment (as opposed, figuratively, to a sedentary posture) in response to outcries of the poor, is perhaps also noteworthy. See Bereshit Rabbah, 75:1, and Shemot Rabbah, 17:4.

24. See Bava Mezia 32a-b.

25. Bava Mezia 32b. The distinction between idolatrous and monotheistic Gentiles, a linchpin of halakhic thought in the area of Jewish-Gentile relations, of course entails discrimination of another order. The topic lies, however, beyond my immediate ken.

26. See Arakhin 6a-6b.

27. See chapters 7–8, taking note of the unstated transition from 8:5 to 8:6. R. Broyde asserts that Rambam confined the *mizvah* of *zedakah* to giving to the poor. I do not find his argument fully convincing; and, in any event, that surely has not been the thrust of the halakhic tradition as a whole.

28. Bereshit Rabbah, 42:8. Other interpretations of the term *ha-ivri*, referring to descent from Ever or trans-river origins, are also cited by the midrash.

29. At which point divine intervention reversed the import of Bilam's declamations is unclear.

30. Bava Mezia 62a. The discussion here turns upon the quandary as it affects and confronts the parties. In this connection, questions have been raised about the possible role of a disinterested observer who has the flask in his possession.

31. Bava Mezia 33a; cf., with respect to a different situation, and with recourse to another prooftext, 30a.

32. Vayikra 19:17. In a note, R. Chavel comments that Ramban here possibly alludes to, and challenges, Rambam's more idealistic position, as formulated in *Sefer Ha-Mizvot, asei* 206; see also De'ot 6:3.

33. *Yoreh De'ah* 251:3. Surprisingly, the specific case of R. Akiva's scenario was codified by neither Rambam nor the *Shulhan Arukh*.

34. See Pesahim 21b and Ramban's catalogue of *mizvot* he contends Rambam had erroneously omitted; see his animadversions upon the *Sefer Ha-Mizvot, asei* 16. It should be stressed that in this context, the term, *"le'hahayoto,"* is not confined to literal life-saving but refers to general sustenance as well.

35. See, with respect to a clash between *kibbud av va-em* and other *mizvot*, Kiddushin 32a; and, more generally, that between *talmud* and *ma'aseh*, Mo'ed Katan, 9a–b. Obviously, application of this factor depends, in large measure, upon how possibility is defined and upon the ability and the readiness of the "others" to undertake the task in question.

36. See Horayot 13a, where, on the one hand, technical factors of one's formal status in the scale of *yohasin* is presented as a ground for priority, while, on the other hand, at bottom, personal spiritual qualities are assigned supremacy. Currently, the element of *yohasin* as a yardstick of triage is relatively neglected — whether because, as R. Moshe Feinstein held, its use is rather impractical in the modern reality, it was also no longer decisive, or for some other reason.

37. See Yoma 33a, Megillah 6b, and Menahot 64b. The priority evidently applies to both selection and sequence.

38. *Yoreh De'ah*, 258:9; see also *Siftei Kohen* 258:19.

39. See Bava Kamma 115a-b. The gemara in Bava Mezia 30a, does speak of possible exemption from *hashavat avedah* if *"shelo merubah mi-shel haveiro,"* implying that if the stakes were equal, one ought to engage in *hashavah*. This seems to contradict the gemara of 33a. Rishonim raised the issue and suggested various possible resolutions to reconcile. See various *hiddushim*, 30a, of Ramban, Rashba, Ritva, and Meiri.

40. *Hoshen Mishpat*, 264:1.

41. *Iggeret Ha-Kodesh* ch. 16. The same point was made, in the moderate tones of a medieval Provencal commentary and without the *Ba'al Ha-Tanya's* moralizing passion, in *Hiddushei Rabbeinu Avraham min Ha-Har*, Nedarim 80b, ed. R. M. Y. Blau (New York, 1962), p. 167.

42. Gezelah Va-Avedah 6:11. The formulation invites some question as to whether Rambam refers solely to exclusive lifelong pursuit or even to more limited involvement.

43. Hilkhot Mattenot Aniyyim 9:3. See Bava Batra 8b-9a.

44. See his *She'elot U'Teshuvot*, sec. 5, for the specific case to which I allude. The better known general formulation appears in sec. 128; see R. Broyde's discussion of that text in this volume. I would only add that his assertion that the Gra disagreed with Maharik seems a bit far-reaching. The Gra only states, with respect to the source cited by Maharik, "*ve-eyno mukhrah.*"

45. See Rambam, Shevu'ot 2:1–4, and Ran, Nedarim 2a.

46. Shevu'ot 11:1 and 12:2. Unlike many other Rishonim, Rambam regarded the use of a properly administered *shevu'ah* very positively, and not as a mere occasional necessity.

47. Berakhot 63a. As recourse to the last verse cited should indicate amply, the counsel of this *beraita* raises important questions. These, however, cannot be discussed fully here.

48. *Torat Ha-Adam*, in *Kitvei Ha-Ramban*, ed. R. C. B. Chavel (Jerusalem, 1963), 2:104. My citation here is grounded on the assumption that, in the incident discussed, the issue turned on leaving in the middle of the *shiur*. However, alongside this interpretation, Ramban suggests an alternative view, that the problem was one of the continued presence of *kohanim*, despite the intrusion of a defiling cadaver. *Prima facie*, the prospect of continued presence does not appear to constitute a viable option, as the prohibition with respect to a *kohen* is clear-cut and, depending on a number of variables, probably *mi-de'oraita*, and is presumably not overridden by the prospect of hearing a *shiur*. Be that as it may, in any event, the position that the first issue was open to subjective preferential resolution was certainly entertained by some Rishonim. See Ramban here and the *sugya* in Ketubbot 17a, and Rishonim *ad locum*.

Chapter 5

Beyond the Pale?
Reflections Regarding Contemporary Relations with Non-Orthodox Jews*

Readers familiar with the Orthodox Forum's publications, monitoring their direction and annually awaiting the most recent harvest, may marvel somewhat at the choice of this year's topic. There is no question regarding its relevance and importance, both perpetual and contemporary, but the sense of *déja vu* is unmistakable. "Theme: The Relationship of Orthodox Jews with Believing Jews of Other Religious Ideologies and Non-Believing Jews." Hadn't that, in effect, they seem to recall, some vividly and many faintly, been the substantive focus of the 1992 volume on *Jewish Tradition and the Nontraditional Jew*?[1] True, almost a score of years have since elapsed; and granted that within a rapidly changing social and philosophic scene, each historical context colors discourse with the nuances of its own perspective; but must basic hashkafic issues be examined afresh once every decade and a half? Are the medieval analogues cited in that volume — laxity in the performance of basic *mizvot* such as *tefillin* or *mezuzot*, or widespread sexual promiscuity — less instructive today than in still recent memory? And does not the debate over *Austritt*, which tore German Orthodoxy asunder in nineteenth-century controversy,[2] clearly anticipate, in 2010 as in 1990, current dilemmas? And, quite apart from the historical record, haven't the analyses of core principled elements, such as *tokhahah* or the dialectic tension between *ahavat Yisrael* or the obverse, remained largely stable? And so, we rightly ask ourselves, with

Rabbi Yehoshua, מה חידוש היה בבית המדרש היום, "What novel teaching was there at the study hall today"(Hagigah 3a)?

In reply, I could suggest that even over a brief span, innovative factors can affect the course of thought materially; and that, in our case, among these we could single out the diffusion of postmodernism and the quest for heightened spirituality. Of possibly greater import is the fact that the respective volumes do not share identical subjects in the first place. As its title, formulated in the singular, clearly indicates, the earlier volume concentrated upon the relation to an individual deviant; and, while Dr. Judith Bleich's essay, "Rabbinic Responses to Nonobservance in the Modern Era," correctly focused upon the shift from responding to personal malfeasance to confronting the challenge of freshly reared and organized movements and ideologies, the bulk of the volume maintains its personal emphasis.

Of more critical significance, however, is a further distinction, extending well beyond what may strike some as a nitpicking attempt to carve out space for some freshly minted wares. I refer to the limelight riveted upon belief,[3] as opposed to observance — and, hence, upon the heretic as contrasted with the renegade. This topic *per se* deconstructs into two distinct units. At one plane, we perceive rejection of details of consensual theological doctrine, whether developed in the course of historical and collective assent, or whether forged in the crucible of animated and often acrimonious debate by authoritative theologians. Admittedly, Jewish equivalents of the councils of Nicea or Trent are not readily identifiable, but, in a lower key, they may be discerned.

At a second plane, there are those who, not content with tilting swords with the Rambam over the catechetical weight of a specific codicil, question the very notion of Jewish dogma — either to the point of denying its historical existence or by asserting that it lacks all normative halakhic force. This position is most familiarly identified with Mendelssohn, who affirmed it quite unequivocally; but it was subsequently adopted by many in the early stages of the Reform movement who, for obvious reasons, so long as they still claimed allegiance to the halakhic canon, preferred to denigrate potentially divisive doctrinal elements while focusing upon ritual and ethical implementation; and it even gained credence among some avowed adherents of tradition who, in the similar interests of communal unity, preferred to be denominated as Orthoprax rather than Orthodox.

In actual fact, however, this position constitutes a skewed misrepresentation both of what had been and of what could have been. It is, of course, true that dogma occupies a less prominent station in *Yahadut* than in Christianity — particularly, if the basis of comparison is Lutheran "justification by faith." It is, further, equally true that we encounter in Hazal little of systematic theology, whose efflorescence gained momentum only after Rav Saadyah Gaon and the Rambam. But there is also little of systematic morality in Hazal, and Spinoza's *Ethics* was as alien to their spirit as Luther's *Ninety-Five Theses*. Would anyone therefore deign to assert that the ethical dimension did not constitute an authentic and integral facet of *Yahadut*? It is of course arguable that Rav Yitzhak's midrashic comment, cited by Rashi in his opening remark,

לא היה צריך להתחיל את התורה אלא מהחדש הזה לכם שהיא מצוה ראשונה שנצטוו בה ישראל ומה טעם פתח בבראשית?

The Torah should have commenced with the verse "This month shall be unto you the first of months" (Shemot 12:1), which is the first commandment given to Israel. What is the reason, then, that it commences with the creation? (Bereshit 1:1, s.v. *be-reshit*)

as well as the rejoinder that Bereshit was included as a forensic weapon to fend off polemical Gentile attacks upon Jewish possession of Eretz Yisrael, clearly imply that Torah constitutes a purely legal codex, sans hashkafic and dogmatic components. However, at bottom, the discussion is confined, hypothetically, to what might have been rather than to what there is; it relates, primarily, to cosmology and historical narrative rather than to theology; Rav Yitzhak presumably relied upon alternate sources, written or oral, to posit cardinal doctrinal truths; and, in any event, it is problematic to base so radical a thesis[4] upon this Aggadic riposte, which, furthermore, some Rishonim[5] challenged. There is no dearth of dogmatic formulations, and this normative force is reflected in declarations that whoever fails to subscribe to them is to be barred from the world to come.[6]

Moreover, *Yahadut* could not have been imagined otherwise. Speaking of religion generally, Whitehead[7] observed that some conception of the nature and the history of the world within which it is manifested and of what exists beyond it constitutes one of its indispensable components. How much truer, however, is the statement of *Yahadut*, a historical religion not only in the sense that it was rooted in revelation in history, but also in the sense that the assumption and affirmation of certain historical events constituted a critical aspect of the woof and warp of Jewish living. Consequently, the content of the corpus of belief and its place within personal religious experience is, for us, *shelomei emunei Yisrael*, a major concern.

The precise halakhic status of belief is shrouded in controversy. The Rambam,[8] largely followed by the *Sefer Ha-Hinnukh*,[9] enumerated three separate *mizvot* regarding conviction of the most cardinal of dogmas — the existence of the *Ribbono shel Olam*. On the other hand, the Geonic author of *Halakhot Gedolot* omitted all such commandments from his count, as did Rabbi Eliezer of Metz in his *Sefer Yere'im*. In all likelihood, however, the omission is best ascribed, as the Ramban (who was himself ambivalent on the issue) contended, to the view that the duty to acknowledge authority cannot itself emanate by its own fiat, rather than to rejection of the norm of belief *per se*:

> והנראה מדעתו של בעל ההלכות שאין מנין תרי"ג מצות אלא גזירותיו יתעלה שגזר
> עלינו לעשות או מנענו שלא נעשה אבל האמונה במציאותו יתעלה... הוא העיקר
> והשורש שממנו נולדו המצות לא ימנה בחשבונן.

> It appears that the view of the author of the *Halakhot Gedolot* is that the enumeration of the 613 commandments is limited to decrees that He issued as calls to action or prohibitions proscribing action, but the belief in His existence, may His name be extolled ... is the foundation and root from which the commandments stem and is thus excluded from their enumeration. [10]

As for the Rambam, just how far he extended his position is graphically illustrated by a passage in which he relates to the full range of the obligatory tenets expounded in his list of thirteen principles, rather than to belief in God alone. As a coda to that list, he avers:

וכאשר יהיו קיימים לאדם כל היסודות הללו ואמונתו בהם אמתית, הרי הוא נכנס בכלל ישראל וחובה לאהבו ולחמול עליו וכל מה שצוה ה' אותנו זה על זה מן האהבה והאחוה, ואפילו עשה מה שיכול להיות מן העבירות מחמת תאותו והתגברות יצרו הרע, הרי הוא נענש לפי גודל מריו ויש לו חלק, והוא מפושעי ישראל. וכאשר יפקפק אדם ביסוד מאלו היסודות הרי זה יצא מן הכלל וכפר בעיקר ונקרא מין ואפיקורוס וקוצץ בנטיעות.

When all these foundations are established in a person and his belief in them is true, he is included among the community of Israel and one is required to love him and to show compassion upon him and all that God commanded us interpersonally, of love and brotherhood; even if the other has sinned out of temptation or by being overcome by his evil inclination, he is punished in accordance with the severity of his defiance, but he has a share [in the world to come], and he is considered among the sinners of Israel. But when a person casts aspersions upon one of these foundations, he has left the community and denied the essential principle, and he is called a heretic and one who uproots the foundational teachings. [11]

The centuries that followed spawned some amelioration of these assertions, with both the primacy of belief and details of some of the tenets to which the Rambam referred undergoing challenge.[12] But the place of belief as an essential component of our tradition remained secure. The blandishment of Tennyson's faith that lies "in honest doubt," with the prospect that it holds out for spiritual self-determination is, to many, appealing. The cadences of Torah are pitched, however, in other voices:

וידעת היום והשבת אל לבבך כי ה' הוא הא-לקים בשמים ממעל ועל הארץ מתחת אין עוד.

תמים תהיה עם ה' א-לקיך.

Know therefore this day and keep in mind that the Lord alone is God in heaven above and on earth below (Devarim 4:39).

You must be wholehearted with the Lord your God. [13]

The implications of recognition of the importance of belief for the projected discussion at this Forum should be self-evident. Virtually by definition, the focus upon this aspect is more charged than delineation of the details of practical observance, inasmuch as it deals with the content of faith rather than with the degree of personal or communal commitment to it. Hence, with respect to the issues apparently on our table, dogmatic fealty is a two-edged sword. On the one hand, given the topic's importance, concern lest the purity and integrity of *hashkafah* be diluted or contaminated as a result of contact with nonbelievers, or that heretical or even quasi-heretical groups or ideas may be accorded a nuance of legitimizing recognition, is understandably acute. For many, that concern militates for sharp separation. On the other hand, precisely in view of the gravity of the subject, the sense of responsibility to safeguard Torah from spurious interpretation and to ensure maximal dissemination of *amittah shel Torah* is likewise greatly enhanced. Hence it is arguable that, if we can reasonably ensure protection of our own turf — a critical condition — our cause may stand to gain from interactive contact and discourse; and this, not only as a result of the self-knowledge which can spring out of contrast and differentiation —

כשושנה בין החוחים כן רעיתי בין הבנות כתפוח בעצי היער כן דודי בין הבנים –

Like a lily [rose] among thorns, so is my darling among the maidens.
Like an apple tree among trees of the forest, so is my beloved among
the maidens (Shir Ha-Shirim 2:2–3) —

but out of possible enrichment, in the proper climate, of some of our own insights and perceptions.

I trust that I have adequately explained why I feel we are not treading water, not simply reconstructing a burnished rerun of half-forgotten discourse from which we wipe accumulated dust. That, however, is by no means my primary task. I have been charged with dealing with the issues currently at hand, with noting what presently exists and what can and what should exist if we mobilize the energy, the capacity, and, above all, the will, to bring it into being; and it is to that mandate that I now turn.

Let me open with an anecdote. In the course of his stay in Eretz Yisrael in the summer of 1935, the Rav visited the secular kibbutz of Kinneret. His host proffered some fruit, which the Rav naturally but politely declined. Sensing the reason for the refusal to partake of the offering, the kibbutznik observed that he presumes that it was grounded in concerns about *kashrut*; whereupon he proceeded to inform his thunderstruck guest that the local kitchen was absolutely kosher. When asked for the cause of this anomaly, he narrated the following story. Rav Kook once spent a Shabbat at the kibbutz, and he of course brought his own food. He ate each *se'udah* with the group, including participation in the *moza'ei Shabbat* fireside *kumsitz*. Upon taking leave of his hosts, he thanked them graciously and concluded with a brief wish. "I hope that next time I'll be able to eat together with you." Sure enough, the *haverim* voted to introduce *kashrut* in their public *hadar okhel*.

I am not so Pollyannish as to imagine that such a scenario could be repeated routinely. Rav Kooks are few and far between, and the response to the force of his personality also is not too common. Nor do I pretend that I would or could have emulated him, letting my yearning for fraternity overwhelm my concern about *tevel* and *orlah*. And I don't recall whether, relying upon the information to which he had become privy, the Rav ate. My point relates to an entirely different continuum. Given the currently prevalent winds in our camp — or, for that matter, in that of our adversaries — let us assume that I, and my comrades, would have abstained. But to the accompaniment of which sentiment? How many would have felt and expressed Rav Kook's pain? And how deeply? Would we truly yearn for that "next time," consumed by candid regret that it seems to be constantly becoming increasingly remote? And even if we sense that, under present circumstances, we have little choice but to confine ourselves inexorably behind barriers we have jointly constructed, could we at least fully internalize Beruriah's response to the iniquity which had infiltrated and possibly enveloped Rabbi Mayer, herself, and her community:

הנהו בריוני דהוו בשבבותיה דר"מ והוו קא מצערו ליה טובא הוה קא בעי רבי מאיר
רחמי עלייהו כי היכי דלימותו אמרה ליה ברוריא דביתהו מאי דעתך משום דכתיב

יתמו חטאים מי כתיב חוטאים חטאים כתיב ועוד שפיל לסיפיה דקרא ורשעים עוד
אינם כיון דיתמו חטאים ורשעים עוד אינם אלא בעי רחמי עלייהו דלהדרו בתשובה
ורשעים עוד אינם.

There were once some highwaymen in the neighborhood of Rabbi
Mayer who caused him a great deal of trouble. Rabbi Mayer accordingly prayed that they should die. His wife Beruriah said to him: How
do you make out [that such a prayer should be permitted]? Because
it is written "Let *hatta'im* cease"? Is it written "*hote'im*"? It is written
"*hatta'im*!" Further, look at the end of the verse: "And let the wicked
men be no more." Since the sins will cease, there will be no more
wicked men! Rather pray for them that they should repent, and there
will be no more wicked. [14]

The gemara thence concludes with the report that Rabbi Mayer followed
his wife's prescription, and it was indeed effective. That is, sadly, frequently
not the case. But do we pine for it and do we lament our limitations?

Before we choose a course of action, we must effect a change of
mindset and a change of heart. We must, at the very least, reduce the
level and the scope of mutual demonization. So long as communal leaders
are viewed, respectively, as nothing but power-hungry iconoclasts or as
benighted obscurantists, we shall, collectively, pay a heavy price. Unless
— and until — we develop a propensity for mutual respect, acknowledging that there may be mediocrities and charlatans in various camps, but
steadfastly refusing to tar indiscriminately, both the interests of *klal Yisrael*
and the integrity of *Reb Yisrael* will be adversely affected. Unquestionably,
where the most basic elements of our religious faith and existence are at
stake — the totality of our relation to Torah, or critical aspects of that relation regarding the content of *emunot ve-de'ot*, the character of Halakhah,
the substance of *Tanakh,* and the contours of our commitment, as *ovdei
Hashem* — confronted by heterodox denominations, passions naturally
and justifiably run high. History has amply demonstrated that internecine
religious strife is often the most bitter, as combatants are animated by a
sense of engagement in the encounter of the children of light with the
children of darkness. For us, however, as Jews committed to the entirety
of Torah, let vitriolic antagonism not prevail, routinely and consistently, as

the sole or even as the dominant passion. Let us therefore be intent upon monitoring our motivation, with an eye to ensuring that if indeed we have been charged to enter the lists of fraternal strife, literal or figurative, we do so impelled by devotion and responsibility, but animated by the hope and the prospect of binding reconciliation.[15]

This martial imagery and some of its associations bear an attitudinal message relevant to significant facets of our personal and collective life. They do not, however, relate directly to the specific topic targeted for this conference. Participants are not being asked to consider whether and how to combat rival constituencies, but rather, whether and how to coordinate and cooperate with them in a positive spirit, well beyond an uneasy truce which is only galvanized into heightened unity by the impact of crises rocking our national boat. It is precisely at this juncture that the question of mindset confronts us. Many, in the most deeply committed sectors of the Orthodox world, on these shores, as in *Eretz Ha-Kodesh*, harbor a profound distrust of competing camps and their leadership (often more so of the Reform and the Conservative movements than of the outright secular). Moreover, often in light of our resurgence, after sociological soothsayers had projected our impending collapse half a century ago, they extrapolate a continuation of this trend, paralleled by a corresponding decline of rival denominations, and they consequently find occasion for congratulatory triumphalism. I certainly share in the joy over the growth in *talmud Torah* in so much of our Orthodox world, of whatever stripe. And yet, we ask ourselves, at a time when, as Rav Michel Feinstein zt"l observed pithily, "Half of *klal Yisrael* knows nothing of *shema Yisrael*," may we simply crow on our laurels? And does anyone imagine that if every non-Orthodox temple were to shut down forthwith, that on the morrow the membership would flock, en masse, to the nearest *shul* or *shtibel*? If indeed temple attendance and affiliation are waning, and on the assumption that the absentees are beyond the reach of our own message, is there not, beyond competition, as much cause for dismay as for gratification? If we are concerned, as we ought to be, about the future spiritual destiny of our siblings, and if we are convinced that, in certain areas, a measure of comity could enhance it, might the option not be at least worthy of consideration?

Lest anyone jump to fallacious conclusions, let me clarify. I am not in favor of untrammeled cooperation, let alone consolidation, merging, or agglomeration. I am not advocating joint rabbinical boards or similar initiatives which, for decades, obsessively traumatized or mesmerized many on the American Jewish scene. As *shomerei ha-dat* and *mahzikei ha-dat*, we have a sacred duty to protect and enhance the purity and integrity of Torah as we received it from our masters and as we are committed to transmitting to our successors. Beyond a certain point, no sheer quantitative gain can justify dilution or distortion; and, beyond a certain point, a blended structure is in danger of encountering just such a reality. Where and when they felt that the critical line might be transversed, *gedolei Yisrael* have resisted latitudinarian initiatives in the past and they shall presumably continue to do so in the future.

It should be clear, however, that this assertion complements its predecessor and in no way contravenes it. My focus is, again, on the mindset. How do we, personally and communally, perceive our relation to apparent adversaries, and how do we envision ourselves? Is ours a dual commitment — not, *has ve-shalom*, to two Torot, but to multiple aspects of our unitary Torah, through which our historical community realizes its manifest destiny as ממלכת כהנים וגוי קדוש, "a kingdom of priests and a sacred nation?" Or is ours a monochromatic bond, all our efforts being single-mindedly directed, theoretically and practically, to the integrated realization of one overriding goal? Of course, in a sense, the whole of Torah is oriented — as, in a broader sense, is the religious life in its entirety — to creating an ideal world, one in which, as *ein od milvado* in the transcendental sphere, so in the terrestrial. Beyond doubt, we should all strive to pursue the counsel of the mishnah, וכל מעשיך יהיו לשם שמים, "Let all your deeds be for the sake of Heaven."[16] However, action "for the sake of Heaven" is itself multifaceted; and, as Rav Haym Volozhiner recognized,[17] it is self-evident that, in another sense, *yesh od milvado*, as a palpable reality, to be perceived and confronted. And it is to that plane that we need to address ourselves. To take a simple concrete example, numerous *pesukim* incorporate the message of לה׳ הארץ ומלאה, "The earth and all its plenitude is Hashem's," even as they concurrently assert that this self-same earth has been granted to man, entitled to partake of it and entrusted with nurturing and developing it. Moreover, in this latter capacity, he is commanded to share the terrestrial plenty with his Master's divine treasury, on the one hand, and with the deprived and the disenfranchised, on the other — all of this, within the compass of a single and very partial department of human life.

How, at this diversified plane, do we relate to our specific problem? Confronted with the dual conclusion of the encomium to Jerusalem in Tehillim (122) — למען אחי ורעי אדברה נא שלום בך "For the sake of my kin and friends, I pray for your well-being" and למען בית ה׳ א-לקינו אבקשה טוב לך "For the sake of the house of the Lord our God, I seek your good," do we feel exclusive responsibility to the latter goal, relating to the first only when it in no way competes with the second — or, better still, when the two reinforce each other mutually? Or do we acknowledge a genuinely dual commitment — advancing both components in tandem wherever feasible, striving to coordinate divided effort where it is not, and recognizing candidly that the interests of the two may conflict, as each diverts attention and resources from the other? How genuine and significant a value are the interests, material and spiritual, of אחי ורעי, "my kin and friends," to us? In situations of conflict, do we cut the Gordian knot by affirming that those to whom the welfare of בית ה׳ א-לקינו, "the house of the Lord our God," is of little or no interest are, in effect, disbarred from the community of אחיך or עמיתך, "spiritual comrades and brethren," so that we, in turn, assign sparse value to their concerns?[18]

Our ultimate aspirations are, in theory, reasonably clear — and they are greedy, relating not only to "believing Jews of other religious ideologies and non-believing Jews," but to humanity as a whole. We yearn, at the eschatological plane, for a reality in which the world at large — the social as well as, in a sense, the cosmic — is suffused with pervasive faith, experiential as well as conceptual, and committed to acknowledgment of epiphanous *malkhut shamayim*. We make no attempt to conceal this undemocratic vision. On the contrary, we trumpet it forth, passionately. It is central to the *berakhah* of *malkhuyot* on Rosh Hashanah:

מלוך על כל העולם כולו בכבודך והנשא על כל הארץ ביקרך והופע בהדר גאון עוזך על
כל יושבי תבל ארצך וידע כל פעול כי אתה פעלתו ויבין כל יצור כי אתה יצרתו ויאמר
כל אשר נשמה באפו ה' א-לקי ישראל מלך ומלכותו בכל משלה

Reign over the entire universe in Your glory; be exalted over all the
world in Your splendor, reveal Yourself in the majestic grandeur of
Your strength over all the dwellers of Your inhabited world. Let everything that has been made know that You are its Maker, let everything
that has been molded understand that You are its Molder, and let
everything with a life's breath in its nostrils proclaim, "The Lord God
of Israel is King, and His majesty rules over everything."

But it is not reserved for rare festive prayers, occupying, as it does, an
equally dominant place in the weekly recital of *nishmat* —

כי כל פה לך יודה וכל לשון לך תשבע וכל ברך לך תכרע וכל קומה לפניך תשתחוה וכל
לבבות ייראוך וכל קרב וכליות יזמרו לשמך –

For every mouth shall offer thanks to You, every tongue shall swear
loyalty to You, every knee shall bend to You, all who stand erect shall
bow down before You, all hearts shall fear You, and every innermost
part shall sing praise to Your name — [19]

and, perhaps even more significantly, in the presumably humbler context
of the thrice-daily avowal of *alenu*:

לתקן עולם במלכות ש-די וכל בני בשר יקראו בשמך להפנות אליך כל רשעי ארץ יכירו
וידעו כל יושבי תבל כי לך תכרע כל ברך תשבע כל לשון לפניך ה' א-לוקינו יכרעו ויפולו
ולכבוד שמך יקר יתנו ויקבלו כולם את עול מלכותך ותמלוך עליהם מהרה לעולם ועד.

To perfect the universe through the Almighty's sovereignty, and all
flesh shall call out in Your name, to turn all the earth's wicked toward
You, that all the world's inhabitants shall recognize and know You,
that every knee shall bend, every tongue shall swear, before You,
Lord our God, shall they bend and prostrate, and to the honor of
Your name shall they call out glory, and they shall all accept the yoke
of Your sovereignty, and You shall reign over them speedily for all
eternity.

In envisioning this catholic prospect, a Jew of any stripe may be typically content, to think of the biblical millennium, as prophesied by Mikhah and Yeshayahu, jointly:

והלכו עמים רבים ואמרו לכו ונעלה אל הר ה' אל בית א-לקי יעקב ויורנו מדרכיו ונלכה באורחתיו כי מציון תצא תורה ודבר ה' מירושלם.

And the many peoples shall go and say, "Come, let us go up to the Mount of the Lord, to the House of the God of Jacob, that He may instruct us in His ways, and that we may walk in His paths," for instruction shall come forth from Zion, the word of the Lord from Jerusalem. (Yeshayahu 2:3)

The Orthodox Jew — and this is where the greed lies — almost invariably thinks solely of the ways and paths of our theological persuasion and halakhic tradition.

The aspiration is, then, both clear and enthralling. The implication for our present discourse is presumably equally clear. If we are charged with ennobling the universal human spirit, at the plane of *bein adam la'havero* and, concurrently, enthroning *Malko shel olam*, at that of *bein adam la-Makom*, how much more pressing should be our normative duty to *Knesset Yisrael*, in light of our personal and collective kinship and of its unique chosenness. Consequently, that duty should constitute a significant facet of our deliberations concerning our relation to spiritual "other." Does it? Surely, the impression prevalent among both interested laymen and professional historians is that discussion has focused upon the impact upon and within our own Orthodox ranks, with an eye to maintaining viability and vigor; to sustaining the provenance and the integrity of our tradition and its values; to containing the power and the influence of adversarial forces, present and future. Given the urgency and the potency of dangers and pressures, the emphasis upon coping with an agenda ranging from survival through continuity and striving for efflorescence, is fully understandable. But is it sufficient? And is it sufficiently balanced?

The aspiration for *tikkun* is, I repeat, clear and enthralling. I fear, however, that its implication for our issue is, in many respects, less consistently enthralling, for this scenario evidently relegates the epoch between the present and the Messianic era to a period of *teshuvah*. This process in no way demeans it. Its creative and purgative aspect, conjoined with the quest for grace and regeneration, renders *teshuvah*, at the personal plane, and, *a fortiori*, in the public sphere, as one of the most challenging and dramatic of developments. Its role as the defining characteristic in a lengthy process of transition does, however, complicate matters considerably — at time, in ways and in respects which may undermine *teshuvah* proper.

This concern bears directly upon our immediate issue of relationship to the non-Orthodox. For one thing, the modern liberal soul often recoils at the substance and tone of its presumed relationship to rivals, rejecting not only the attitude often encountered in circles close to Mercaz Harav, that the renegade is, deep down, a *homo religiosus* encased in a secular shell, but also being perturbed by the view of the "other" as so much prey waiting to be ensnared in a transmuting net. Moreover, the traditional community may find itself caught in a dilemma. On the one hand, it strives to imprint its stamp upon the Jewish world in its entirety. On the other, it recognizes that, inasmuch as the process of *teshuvah* is, by definition, fundamentally spiritual, recourse to non-spiritual means may have counterproductive repercussions, which may dilute or defile the desired process. The exertion of excessive pressure, the assumption of an aura of omniscient superiority, the appeal to unspiritual motivation — all may serve to debase content and foment resistance.

The difficulties are real and the road probably lengthy and tortuous. Nevertheless, our commitment to the vision and our aspiration to contribute to its realization should constitute an aspect of our spiritual reality and ambition. I confess that in surveying these lines, I am troubled by traces of pretentious grandiloquence, if not downright bombast. Yet I do indeed submit that our overview of our issues cannot be confined to the local and contemporary, much less to confrontation between the RCA, the RA, and the CCAR. I see no satisfactory serious alternative to, minimally, raising fundamental concerns and at least familiarizing ourselves, across a broad canvas, with primary problems and sketching possible options and directions, which transcend current hot-button issues and domestic resolutions.

That task, itself, is greatly complicated by a diverse set of significant variables. Among these may be obviously included: (1) the nature and degree, as regards both content and motivation, of deviation; (2) its socio-historical content — personal or collective, within a Gentile or a Jewish, and, particularly, theocratically oriented, halakhic state; (3) the nature of the playing field, with which camp in dominance; (4) how viable are various initiatives, and what kind of response are they likely to elicit, in the Orthodox community, or in others? (5) apart from narrowly religious or theological ramifications, what might be possible national or social repurcussions? (6) What is the prevailing climate and level of commitment to Torah, both practical and conceptual, in circumstances under consideration? (7) Are we authorized to pursue compromise directions, be it even in the interest of axiological and spiritual expediency; and if so, when is it desirable?[20]

I refer to these factors as variables, clearly implying that, individually and collectively speaking, they ought to have some bearing upon the course of decision and direction. I regard this view as almost self-evident. Regretfully, I recognize that other *bnei Torah* may object to such flexibility, advocating instead a more consistent and narrowly formulated approach, replete with sharply defined and, in all likelihood, tougher directives. I do not for a moment question either the sincerity or the viability of alternate positions. But אין לדיין אלא מה שעיניו רואות, "a judge can only be guided by that which his eyes see." I can relate to our cardinal issues only as I perceive them. Having stated my position, and with a watchful eye upon these variables and under which circumstances they should be assigned their respective weights, I proceed to outline the major challenges and possible courses.

I believe we can single out two primary areas, which both overlap and impact upon each other but which may also be viewed as separate components of our relationship to the "others." The first concerns attitude and evaluation — not only our collective perception, but how we presume, in light of classic sources and traditions, that they are regarded celestially. The second relates to our own interaction, if any, with the non-Orthodox — of what scope and of which character.

As to the former, we turn instinctively to Scriptural expressions of divine affection or wrath. From the Rambam's perspective, these will probably not shed much light on our dilemma, inasmuch as he neutralizes their literal meaning, given its anthropomorphic character.[21] That view has not taken root as the mainstream tradition, neither among the philosophical community nor among the populace. Nonetheless, even along a broader front, to our dismay, this source provides relatively little guidance, inasmuch as, in light of the variables, prophetic expressions are often dramatically opposed, so that only a self-serving evaluation of the status of a given period could shed much meaningful light upon the fitting relation to it. Chapters in Tehillim, saturated with vehement hatred and containing liturgical pleas for the destruction of enemies, are presumably more relevant. We should bear in mind, however, that these generally constitute a defensive response to life-threatening personal danger, rather than a chapter in public conflict.[22] Moreover, for most of us, these *perakim* can offer meager direction. We are not, spiritually and psychologically, sufficiently pure to be able to harbor such a level of negative emotion.

We will probably get clearer guidance by turning to Hazal, among whom Rabbi Mayer and Rabbi Yehudah, each armed with a supporting prooftext, were apparently divided on this issue:

בנים אתם לה' א-לקיכם בזמן שאתם נוהגים מנהג בנים אתם קרוים בנים, אין אתם נוהגים מנהג בנים אין אתם קרוים בנים דברי ר' יהודה רבי מאיר אומר בין כך ובין כך אתם קרוים בנים, שנאמר בנים סכלים המה ואומר בנים לא אמון בם ואומר זרע מרעים בנים משחיתים ואומר והיה במקום אשר יאמר להם לא עמי אתם יאמר להם בני א-ל חי.

"You are sons to the Lord your God"; when you behave as sons you are designated sons; if you do not behave as sons, you are not designated sons; this is Rabbi Yehudah's view. Rabbi Mayer said: in both cases you are called sons, for it is said, "They are sottish children" (Yirmiyahu 4:22), and it is also said, "They are children in whom there is no faith" (Devarim 32:20); and it is also said, "A seed of evil-doers, sons that deal corruptly" (Yeshayahu 1:4), and it is said, "And it shall come to pass that, in the place where it was said unto them 'Ye are not my people,' it shall be said unto them, 'Ye are the sons of the living God'" (Hoshea 2:1).[23]

Elsewhere we hear of an analogous debate between a Sadducee and Rav Hanina, with the latter evidently inclined to Rabbi Mayer's position:

אמר ליה ההוא צדוקי לר' חנינא השתא ברי טמאים אתון (פירש"י: "ודאי טמאים אתון ואין שכינה ביניכם שורה בטומאה) דכתיב טומאתה בשוליה אמר ליה תא חזי מה כתיב בהו השוכן אתם בתוך טומאתם אפילו בזמן שהן טמאין שכינה שרויה ביניהן.

A certain Sadducee said to Rav Hanina: now you are surely impure [Rashi explains: You are surely impure and the Divine Presence dwells not in impurity], for it is written, "Her filthiness [impurity] was in her skirts" (Ekhah 1:9). He answered: come and see what it is written concerning them: "That dwells with them in the midst of their impurity" (Vayikra 16:16), i.e., even at the time when they are impure, the Divine Presence is among them.[24]

These texts refer to the divine relation to *klal Yisrael* — the collective beneficiary of the special, and, up to a point, reciprocal — bond, inherent in its covenantal link to the *Ribbono shel Olam*. However, elsewhere, a similar chord is struck at the personal plane. Commenting upon the affirmation of grace and commiseration, as a sequel to *ma'aseh ha-egel* and subsequent pardon, Rabbi Mayer notes:

וחנתי את אשר אחון אע"פ שאינו הגון ורחמתי את אשר ארחם אע"פ שאינו הגון.

And I will bestow grace on whom I will bestow grace, although he may not deserve it, and I shall have pity upon whom I shall have pity, although he may not deserve it.[25]

And elsewhere, in yet another connection and an even more striking vein, the same context is depicted as the basis for a dialogue between Mosheh Rabbenu and the *Ribbono shel Olam* concerning, again, the status of the wicked and their disposition:

דתניא כשעלה משה למרום מצאו להקב"ה שיושב וכותב ארך אפים אמר לפניו רבונו של עולם ארך אפים לצדיקים אמר לו אף לרשעים א"ל רשעים יאבדו א"ל השתא חזית מאי דמבעי לך כשחטאו ישראל אמר לו לא כך אמרת לי ארך אפים לצדיקים אמר לפניו רבש"ע לא כך אמרת לי אף לרשעים והיינו דכתיב יגדל נא כח ה' כאשר דברת לאמר.

When Mosheh ascended on high, he found the Holy One, blessed be

He, sitting and writing "long-suffering." Said he to Him, "Sovereign of the Universe! Long-suffering to the righteous?" He replied, "Even to the wicked!" He urged, "Let the wicked perish!" "See now what thou desirest," was His answer. "When Israel sinned," He said to him, "didst thou not urge Me, [Let Thy] long-suffering be for the righteous [only]?" "Sovereign of the Universe!" said he, "but didst Thou not assure me, Even to the wicked!" Hence it is written, "And now, I beseech thee, let the power of my Lord be great, according as thou hast spoken, saying."[26]

In a relatively minor key, the issue also surfaces in a marginal, albeit, familiar halakhic context. We recall that *tefillat Kol Nidrei* opens with a preceding plea for dispensation to join in prayer with sinners. The source of this *minhag* is a passage in the Mordekhai in Yoma who, in turn, bases it upon a gemara in Keritut, the gist of which is that the inclusion of miscreants within the structure of a *ta'anit* is one of its integral aspects:

אמר ר' שמעון חסידא כל תענית שאין בו מפושעי ישראל אינו תענית שהרי חלבנה
ריחה רע ומנאה הכתוב בין סמני הקטורת.

Said Rabbi Simon Hasida, any fast in which no sinners of Israel participate is no fast, for behold the odor of *galbanum* is unpleasant and yet it was included among the spices for the incense.[27]

As is common in numerous hashkafic debates, no definitive *psak* determines its resolution. Speaking out of my own experience, however, I can attest to the fact that, toward the conclusion of *Kol Nidrei*, while reciting the *pasuk* of ונסלח לכל עדת בני ישראל ולגר הגר בתוכם כי לכל העם בשגגה, "The whole Israelite community and the stranger residing among them shall be forgiven, for it happened to the entire people through error" (Bamidbar 15:26), I have consciously thought that *le'khol*, the entire, should include Shulamit Aloni. This notion may strike some as an illegitimate intrusion of subjective predilection upon a holy text and a sacred moment. I cannot agree. In areas that have been left open, we have a moral and halakhic right — possibly, a moral and halakhic duty — to take a stand; and in such cases we are entitled to include personal proclivity as a component of that stand. All the more so when the preponderance of Hazal's explicit dicta on the issue can be mustered in our support.

This is not to deny that we encounter in Hazal some stridently harsh statements regarding ideological apostates. Indeed, as the Rambam, previously cited, stated, the non-Orthodox heretical lapse in belief is regarded more seriously than breach in observance; and the sequence concerning punitive levels in the gemara in Rosh Hashanah[28] clearly reflects this priority. By way of exemplification, one might cite a *beraita* with respect to *avelut* upon the death of an apostate:

כל הפורש מדרכי צבור אין מתעסקין עמו בכל דבר אחיהם וקרוביהן לובשין לבנים
ומתעטפין לבנים ואוכלין ושותין ושמחין שנאבד שונאו של מקום שנאמר הלא משנאיך
ה' אשנא ובתקוממיך אתקוטט תכלית שנאה שנאתים לאויבים היו לי.

Regarding he who separates himself from the ways of the community, none involves himself in his care; the brethren and relatives wear white and wrap themselves in white; they eat, drink, and celebrate, for an enemy of God has been eliminated, for the verse states, "O Lord, You know I hate those who hate You, and loathe Your adversaries. I feel a perfect hatred toward them, I count them my enemies" (Tehillim 139:21–22).[29]

We note, however, that this procedure, precisely because it is so severely punitive, is reserved, in light of the source cited, for *mesan'ekha*, Your adversaries, those who are not merely non-observant but who radiate and generate animosity to the *Ribbono shel Olam* — who have, in effect, severed themselves totally from the world of Jewish living. The parameters of the term are open to flexible judgment, so that its application to a given individual or group is most unlikely. Moreover, the normative demand to judge leniently — assuming that it applies to ordinary interpersonal relations and is not confined to the judicial process[30] — militates our recognition of the positive aspects of non-believers' lives and focusing upon them, as well as upon evaluating specific components charitably.

In effect, we are brought back, albeit in a different sense, to the mind-set. We cannot give our ideological rivals that of which they are most desirous — the inherent equalization of religious and secular ethics, on the one hand, and, in the mode of *elu va-elu*, the recognition of Reform and Conservative Judaism as full-scale versions of Torah, on a par with traditional *mesorah*. Such legitimization would emasculate the epicenter of Orthodoxy. But there is no essential barrier to a fairer and more generous perception of the movements' respective leaderships and of their adherents. We can certainly affirm — I hope I can make the point without condescension — that merit can inhere in the virtue of "others;" that many of our Reform and Conservative brethren sincerely seek the *Ribbono shel Olam*; and that their quest has worth.

The attitudinal element is significant in its own right; but it also bears upon the aspect of interaction, to which we now turn. In this connection, we might best dwell primarily upon three components. The first concerns the prospect of joint pursuit of common Jewish goals — social, political, and spiritual, with an eye to advancing a collective aim or ameliorating mutual pain rather than impinging upon each other. The second relates precisely to such impact, and it subdivides into two: supportive enhancement and adversarial antagonism, respectively. Within the contemporary context of our discourse, the first issue should presumably present no problem. It is warranted by both collective national responsibility and rudimentary sensibility, and it is supported by amply publicized precedent — the struggle over Soviet Jewry, marshalling support for the State of Israel, legislative contretemps over *shehitah*, and efforts on behalf of sensitizing *hesed shel emet* treatment of death and bereavement, to name just a few. Moreover, such cooperation bears the imprimatur of the Rav zt"l, who consistently advocated unified stands on matters of external import, *kelappei huz*, wherein the full range of the religious spectrum participates, as an emissary to the non-Jewish world or to our indigenous community, in an attempt to push the common envelope, but not on internal matters, *kelappei penim*, which, in light of crucial ideological differences, are not susceptible to agreed resolution or even compromise.[31]

Nevertheless, I am occasionally startled to discover that even palpably positive initiatives may be opposed if hatred — at times, vitriolic — rears its ugly head, and fear lest any credit whatsoever might redound to rival groups, overshadowing and possibly eviscerating basic human and Jewish instincts. I recall vividly a telephone conversation with a former *talmid* who was applying for a position of *rabbanut* in upstate New York. He was to be interviewed the next day and, in preparation, simulated anticipated questions and possible responses. He had been given to understand that the issue of intramural relations — to wit, how he would relate to other denominations — would probably rank high on the list, and he was calling me for advice on how to field it. Upon further inquiry, it turned out that the specific issue — which had apparently generated some debate in the *kehillah* — related to Yom Hashoah and whether he would favor a joint or separate convocation. Shocked, I responded that, as far as I knew, the Nazis had not differentiated. Could we? In my stupefaction, I realized that we had an educational charge to fulfill.

The second area, in both of its aspects, admittedly requires greater caution, but here too we need to monitor — and on occasion modify — our stock responses. At issue is the advisability of extending assistance — manpower, material, moral, spiritual — to non-Orthodox movements, thus enhancing their stature and entrenching their position within the Jewish world, on the one hand, but also intensifying their commitment to *avodat Hashem,* on the other. The question is deceptively simple, but the answer quite complex. In our world, there are those who subscribe to the thesis that under no circumstances is it permissible or advisable to advance the cause of deviationists, and they have no compunction about striving to present what they see as a convincing and vociferous case for their position. For them, the answer to our question is as straightforward as the query. However, I find this view wholly untenable, on moral, national, and, quite frequently, halakhic grounds. As I have had occasion to stress in various contexts, non-Orthodox movements often provide a modicum of religious guidance, of access to Jewish knowledge and values, of spiritual direction and content. Moreover, they provide it for many beyond our own pale and reach. In such situations, the contribution to Jewish life is real and meaningful. Can anyone assert, as our critics claim we hold, that it makes no difference whether one is an atheist or a Reform Jew? Worse still, some insist upon ascribing to us a preference for the former.[32] But can any responsible Orthodox Jew, genuinely and responsibly concerned about either national viability or spiritual vigor, confirm this charge? And, were he confronted with such a choice with respect to a son or a daughter, is it conceivable that he would opt for atheism? Admittedly, in certain contexts, when power and authority within the public arena are at stake, and when an Orthodox alternative is readily available, some benefit may redound to us by the weakening of competition. But that is precisely what complicates the answer to a simple question. Weighing the respective significance of various components of our personal spiritual regimen — and, beyond that, the possible conflict between the needs of some individuals against public priorities, is never easy — particularly, when דברים העומדים ברומו של עולם, "manners of the utmost significance," are at stake. The religious interests of both *Reb Yisrael* and *klal Yisrael* challenge us to respond to their dual call upon us. Assuredly, however, there are many situations in which the cause of *Yahadut,* and the attempt, both duty and desire, to hasten the advent of ביום ההוא, "On that day," militate assisting movements with which we have sharp disagreements. Myopia may only impede it.

The dilemma may be illustrated through a practice which has gained ground in segments of the modern Orthodox world in recent years, in both North America and England — and, perhaps for precisely that reason, has surfaced as a problem. I refer to the organized mutual learning of Jewish — and generally, traditional — texts and problems, within joint or denominational settings, at the same session, or as successive presentations within a series. The advantages are clear. Ordinarily, regardless of who is holding forth, most of the audience will gain Torah knowledge and spiritual insight. We can, likewise, anticipate a rise in solidarity and fraternity. Moreover, in many such communities, refusal to participate will often be ascribed to a blend of fear, fuelled by insecurity, and supercilious arrogance, rather than to pristine insularity; it will be interpreted as an expression of demonization rather than as an assertion of perceived radical incompatibility, and the overall impression will hardly score points for our image. Finally, abstention will leave the entire playing field at the disposal of the heterodox; so, what have we gained?[33]

Two things. We have averted — or, at least, believe we have deferred — the hobgoblin of parity and have made it unequivocally clear that we regard ourselves as the only genuine alternative in town. Second, we have avoided the exposure of some of our constituency to winds of strange doctrine and to their evangels.

These are no small pickings. But so may that be true of a possibly exorbitant price — and hence, the dilemma. In all likelihood, the most effective response should be differential. The attitudinal stance of the speakers, the prevailing ideological climate, the social venue, the degree of implicit parity, the texts to be discussed, the religious and intellectual maturity of the audience — all require careful consideration in assessing the likely impact and the relevant risk-benefit ratio. And of course, we are confronted by the principled halakhic and hashkafic issue of how gains and losses are to be weighed with regard to the various alternatives. How do we measure qualitative versus quantitative factors? Who may be affected and to what extent? Above all, we must give thought to the menu of topics. Generally speaking, questions of science and religion, for instance, are preferable to debate over biblical criticism or psychoanalysis of the pillars of *mesorah*. It is not my purpose here, however, to assign report cards, but rather to suggest that in certain areas the optimal approach is differential; hence it will probably require more thoughtful and sensitive attention than blanket stonewalling. The practice of *nekiye ha-daat she-bi'Yerushalayim*, who cautiously refused to sit, at a *bet din* or as dinner guests,[34] with unfamiliar faces, is far more difficult to emulate in our context than in theirs.

This course is commended — and to some extent mandated — from various perspectives, both collective and personal. As to the former, it is rooted in two major values. Sanctification of the public square is, first and foremost, an aspect of the *mizvah* of *kiddush ha-Shem*, in the broader sense of ונקדשתי בתוך בני ישראל, "That I may be sanctified in the midst of the people of Israel," as referring to suffusing our communal and national scene with a profound awareness of our sacral character.[35] In a parallel vein, it is also conceived as a duty deriving from the paradigm of Avraham Avinu, on the one hand, and from the *mizvah* of *ahavat Hashem*, on the other:

ד"א ואהבת את ה' א-לקיך אהבהו על כל הבריות כאברהם אביך כענין שנאמר ואת
הנפש אשר עשו בחרן והלא אם מתכנסים כל באי העולם לבראות יתוש אחד ולהכניס
בו נשמה אינן יכולים לבראותו ומה ת"ל אשר עשו בחרן אלא מלמד שהיה אברהם
אבינו מגיירם ומכניסם תחת כנפי השכינה.

An alternate explanation: "And you shall love the Lord your God,"
make him beloved to all His creations, like your patriarch Avraham, as
the verse states, "And the persons they had made in Haran" (Bereshit
12:5), yet even if all the men of the world would gather together, they
could not create a single gnat and breathe a soul into it. Thus what does
the verse teach when it states, "That they made in Haran?" Rather, it
teaches that our patriarch Avraham would convert them and bring
them under the wings of the Divine Presence.[36]

Straddling our dual duty, personal and collective, we are enjoined to be
engaged by the quasi-legal and wholly ethical and religious concept of
arevut. Multifaceted on theoretical grounds as in application, it bespeaks
both liability for the sins of others and a corresponding charge to nurture
their spiritual welfare. On the one hand, we are responsible for the religious well-being of both the community and its members וכשלו איש באחיו
איש בעון אחיו מלמד שכל ישראל ערבים זה בזה, "'And they shall stumble one upon
another,' one because of the iniquity of the other, this teaches us that all
of Israel are guarantors one for another;"[37] and on the other, we have not,
halakhically, discharged our duty to perform a given *mizvah* so long as we
have not sought to enable the parallel performance of others — and this,
both as a dimension of our normative commitment to that *mizvah* and as
an element in *gemilut hasadim* toward them.[38] If we are bound to return a
lost object to its owner, is it conceivable that we remain wholly indifferent
with respect to his spiritual welfare? אבדת גופו מניין תלמוד לומר והשבתו לו "From
whence do we know [that one must save his neighbor from] the loss of
himself? From the verse, 'And you shall restore him to himself'"[39] — and,
we might add, על אחת כמה וכמה, *a fortiori*.

This responsibility is, admittedly, perhaps palliated somewhat if
the distressed individual has no interest in being succored.[40] As, on the
Rambam's view, one is exempt from *hashavat avedah* if the owner of the
lost object is apathetic, and even the cause for its loss, so presumably

with respect to spiritual guidance. Even this situation, however, cannot be asserted with any degree of certitude, since it may be readily contended that the analogy does not hold water — and this for at least two possible distinctions. First, as regards property, the owner's mastery of the object differs, from a religious perspective, from that over his spiritual self — or, for that matter, over his physical self.[41] Second, as regards the rescuer's responsibility vis-à-vis his endangered fellow, it is patently both broader in scope and, qualitatively, more intensive, in relation to his self than to his belongings. Hence, whatever the attitude of the threatened other, we, for our part, are possibly not relieved of our own charge.

On some views, such relief might be justified by self-inflicted spiritual recalcitrance. Addressing himself, for instance, to the need to prevent consumption of proscribed foods by their thief, Rabban Shimon ben Gamliel declares, הלעיטהו לרשע וימות, To wit, roughly: "Present it to the transgressor and let him bear the consequences."[42] However, this seemingly apathetic formulation aroused the amazement of a leading seventeenth-century *posek*, the author of *Havot Yair*,[43] and has subsequently undergone much qualification and modification, with some authorities rejecting it as a minority view. The fact that, in the whole of Shas, it appears only in an isolated instance is noteworthy and apparently supports this conjecture. Be this as it may, our commitment to providing spiritual guidance and preventing wanton violation remains firm.

This position having been asserted, there remains another aspect of our relation to the non-Orthodox: a major quotient of principled opposition to the very quest for any measure of accommodation with deviationists — with respect to various specific areas, for some, and as the pervasive and defining characteristic of our overarching relationship with the heterodox, for others. In many respects — particularly as regards core questions of faith and belief, of normative lifestyle and the sources of authority, whether formal or consensual — this situation is inevitable. These are, after all, the gut issues which define us, respectively; and I am certainly by no means in favor of shedding or diluting our commitment or identity. Much of what divides us lies beyond negotiation, and, whether with regret or resolve, we need for the foreseeable future to acknowledge this fact. Negotiations regarding the prospects of the use of a revised *ketubbah* or of joint recognition of an agreed upon *bet din* to be charged with authority over issues of marriage and divorce were initiated in good faith during the mid-1950s by the halakhic leadership of the R.C.A. and of the R.A. Nevertheless, despite the absence of acrimony, they produced nothing but the bittersweet fruit of missed opportunity. However, there exist matters of controversy of a more flexible nature, with respect to which both policy and its implementation may be subject to meaningful latitude. With regard to these, a measure of description and analysis may be helpful in formulating our own inclinations and in clarifying them to others. I harbor no illusion that this will, in and of itself, effect reconciliation and usher in the millennium. But even if it only helps improve the current climate, paving the way for a better tomorrow, *dayyenu*.

The central issue confronting us — at once the most pragmatic and the most passionately experienced — concerns the exercise of power in the context of religious controversy. Typically, one side may envision itself as an angel guardian, protecting and advancing cherished values, while another sees itself, passionately, as the aggrieved victim of discrimination; and vice versa. And both may be right. In practice, many of these issues impinge most directly and most immediately upon individuals; but, as the roots are likely to be collective, I shall attempt to focus briefly upon these — to deal, that is, with aspects, explicit or implicit, of the theory and conduct of the historical *kehillah*, with the contemporary scene in Israel or in the Diaspora, and, *a fortiori*, with a possible future theocratic community.

As a point of departure, we need to note a fundamental distinction. Unquestionably, there are numerous avenues through which an ideological community can harness its control of elements of the power structure of its base in order to impose its will upon constituents, so as to safeguard the perceived collective character of that entity, in accordance with political or spiritual goals. It may impose direct monetary or physical sanctions, ranging from incarceration to execution. In the economic sphere, it can utilize direct subvention or tax incentives favoring adherents, to the detriment or neglect of dissidents. On the legal front it can limit access or recourse to the system and disbar some from participation in certain processes.

Such initiatives are, essentially, largely discriminatory in nature, and hence understandably objectionable to liberal sensibility. There is, however, no denying that, historically, many were adopted by, among others, our traditional community, and some (as, indeed, is the case with many modern and presumably democratic societies as well) are of the woof and warp of the halakhic corpus.

Generally confining, these sanctions are often grounded in exclusion — at times, perhaps even expulsion — from the halakhic community, through classification under the rubric of one of a complex of kindred categories, such as *mumar, rasha,* or אינו עושה מעשה עמך, "he who does not act as befits Your people;"[44] or, conversely, through the lack of the characteristics requisite for definition as אח, רע, or בן ברית. Generically, they entail prioritizing the sustenance or safeguarding the integrity of *bet Hashem* — in the broader or narrower sense of the concept — over the welfare and aspirations of the individual. In this respect, this mode is out of sync with much of the modern temper, which is wholly at peace with penalty administered by the state and its agencies in response to deviant conduct, but only where *lèse majesté* of flesh and blood is concerned, not with recalcitrant conscience-driven positions invoked against מלך מלכי המלכים.[45]

It is not to my present purpose to rationalize this practice or to "justify the ways of God to man" within the context and against the background of modern democratic theory and practice. I dealt with some of the central issues in some early essays;[46] and, some strange attempts to cross-breed *Yahadut* and postmodernism notwithstanding, find little cause for recasting or revising my basic formulations. My task here is rather to survey whether and to what extent the premises latent in what I have briefly outlined should dictate our response to the question to which I have been asked to address myself.

The relevance of the nature and scope of the imposed standards touches precisely upon the distinction I wish to stress. Some of the positions espoused by the Orthodox community and its leadership, which breed resentment among its opponents, are not, strictly speaking "theirs," at all. Rather, they constitute application of halakhic norms to concrete situations. Disqualification of *parshiyot* of *tefillin* written by a Reform *sofer* is, indeed, discriminatory. But the decision to enact it is no recent innovation of Hungarian rabbis — or of their current Israeli or American counterparts — desperately fending Neological encroachments. It is nothing more than the implementation of the Rambam's dictum — based, in turn, upon Talmudic sources — that only כל שמוזהר על הקשירה ומאמין בה הוא שכותב "Only one who is commanded regarding the tying and believes in it may write,"[47] which leaves little, if any, latitude for *poskim*, even should they prefer leniency. Likewise, determination of who is to be authorized to engage in *siddur* Kiddushin or Gittin must be made with an eye to the gemara's admonition,

> כל שאינו יודע בטיב גיטין וקידושין לא יהא לו עסק עמהם,

> He who does not know the particulars of divorce and betrothal should have no business with them,

which, as the example cited clearly indicates, sets a high standard of mastery:

> א״ל רב יימר לרב אשי... אפילו לא שמיע ליה הא דרב הונא אמר שמואל?

> Rav Yemar asked Rav Ashi... Even if he is ignorant of this ruling of Rav Huna in Shemuel's name?

that is, must he know that we accept the view of Rabbi Yose, that Kiddushin in which the declaration of הרי את מקודשת לי כדת משה וישראל is inferred contextually but not verbalized are valid?

> א״ל אין הכי נמי

And the concluding response is — indeed, if he is ignorant of this, he cannot qualify.[48]

Some have sought to qualify these limitations by invoking concepts which mitigate the responsibility of the disbarred, by invoking concepts which shift the blame to others. He or she may be categorized as the victim of his upbringing,[49] of his passions, which, it is contended, should be evaluated more liberally,[50] or as merely a party to a collective apostasy.[51] However, these concepts, while possibly valid in themselves, and certainly are very much in line with much contemporary moral theory, are of little relevance for the issue under discussion. They can be significant with regard to the mitigation of personal fault but of no import when the issue is one of objective competence or commitment.[52] Would we routinely entrust the construction or maintenance of a complex reactor to a well-intentioned but barely trained technician?

On the other hand, in certain situations our course of action may very well be determined by public policy factors or axiological considerations, when pure Halakhah would admit some leeway. The optimal degree of centralization with respect to *kashrut* or *mikva'ot* is not subject to categorical halakhic fiat; and Halakhah as a whole clearly acknowledges the existence of *devar ha-reshut* and the legitimacy of including relatively extraneous elements, which nevertheless have spiritual consequences, in the process of decision. Moreover, we are not so ethereal as to reject wholly any truck with patently pragmatic or, if you will, political factors. In such cases, however, the subjective factor in the formulation or exposition of policy will be far more significant.

I presume it would be a bit naïve to expect that our non-Orthodox opponents will be wholly convinced or mollified by this distinction. Even should they appreciate it, some resentment over what they often perceive as marginalizing discrimination and unfair delegitimization — particularly, in the ranks of the Conservatives — would probably persist. Nevertheless, it is to be hoped that the rancor would be palliated and residual accusative temper ameliorated. While we would not anticipate unqualified acceptance of our own position, we could hope that other camps would at least understand us better, and consequently respect us more, if they regarded us as spiritually motivated rather than as power-hungry autocrats. The climate of discourse and the quality, both civil and religious, of discussion, purged of some acrimony, could then be improved significantly, as regards both למען אחי ורעי "For the sake of my brethren and

kin" and למען בית ה' א-לקינו "for the sake of the house of the Lord our God,"
in the broader senses of these terms.[53]

Of no less importance is the value inherent in our own awareness
of the distinction. Without necessarily conceding any of our positions
in either category, recognition of difference could potentially issue in
critically fairer assessment of how and why we structure the process of
collective decision. In a climate which increasingly values transparency,
we could better our standing in this respect, possibly both improving
the quality of decision proper and attaining greater and more charitable
appreciation of its nuances. It would also clarify somewhat when we could
be conciliatory and when intransigent, altering, for instance, our recourse
to concern about the slippery slope — a concern which is unquestionably
rooted in Hazal[54] but whose application in our modern context requires
careful crafting.

I reiterate that, unquestionably, the issues which divide us from the
non-Orthodox are substantive and substantial, and I harbor no illusion
about easy or early resolution of our conflicts. Much of what is preached
and professed by many beyond the pale of Orthodox belief as being gospel
truth, ranging from claimed historical facticity to meta-historical vision,
regarding the secular as well as the sacred, is regarded by *maʾaminim bnei
maʾaminim* as nothing short of *kefirah*. Much of what is extracted from
Scripture or ingested into it is shot through with *apikorsut*. Above all, the
composite portrait of the *Ribbono shel Olam* often presented, by critical
scholarship, as the biblical and/or Jewish perception of deity is, for us,
blasphemous *hiruf ve-gidduf*. Of all this we are painfully aware; and of all
this we are perforce on our guard. Nevertheless, I submit that if we are in
earnest about our concern regarding אחי ורעי, my brethren and kin, and
honest about the role of ירושלם הבנויה כעיר שחברה לה יחדו, "Jerusalem, built
up, a city knit together" (Tehillim 122:23), we should recognize the value
of such resolution and strive, in the interest of both national and spiritual
welfare, to internalize it as such. Wasn't the conjunction of these aspirations crucial to the climactic vision of Sinai? And was it not part of what
Ruth, incisively imagined by Keats as sad-heartedly, "sick for home, / She
stood in tears amid the alien corn," at the Rubicon of personal destiny,

intuited as essential to the molding and enhancement of permanent Jewish commitment?

Postscript

When this paper was initially presented to the Orthodox Forum last spring, it was subtitled: "An Overview Regarding Relationships with Non-Orthodox Jews." Taken literally, this description augured, to say the least, a sweeping and indeed pretentious undertaking. It presumably was to include a historical survey and analysis of how relationships have in actual fact developed, without limitations grounded in geographic, historical, or cultural context. The historical playing field was apparently to have been multiple sectors of religious existence, personal and collective; while covering the full range of Orthodox Jewry and its contrasting constituency, only negatively defined, of indiscriminate non-Orthodox Jews. Contemporaneously, the paper was, evidently, to study and describe the current sociological and ideological status of the respective groups, and, finally, to posit, prospectively, a recommended agenda and modality.

It was a tall order — excessively so; and I marvel and regret that I did not realize this fact fully at the time. In presenting this revised version now, more aptly and modestly subtitled, "Reflections Regarding Contemporary Relationships with Non-Orthodox Jews," I have dealt with both the numerator and the denominator. That is, I have both increased the relevant material and reduced the menu to more modest proportions. In effectuating the latter, I relied somewhat upon this Forum's mandate, whose introductory paragraph, geared to describing the aim of this Forum, spoke of coming to grips with "the question of how the Orthodox community addresses the Conservative and Reform communities to the additional question of how to address the growing secular Jewish community. This issue mirrors some of the aspects of the Israeli phenomenon and contains some uniquely American elements." As any reader can judge, however, my presentation has fallen well short of realizing this more limited aim, even at the level of an overview, particularly as regards its scope.

I have largely omitted treatment of secular Jewishness, in part because of lack of space and my personal limitations, and in part because while one can of course speak of secular Jewry and the spiritual orientation of nonobservant and non-believing Jews, secular Judaism, as such, is an oxymoron, as secular Anglicanism would be. This downsized essay is, then, centered upon the present scene, discussed against the background of past experience. It draws upon halakhic categories and their application, while yet clearly falling short of a full-blown Torah discourse, and it focuses upon a summary exposition of the direction I believe ought to be pursued, circumstances permitting. I have also, despite close to four decades of residence in *Eretz Ha-Kodesh*, paid relatively limited attention to the Israeli scene, which would require full treatment on its own.

I find this omission regrettable, but in closing I wish to assure the reader that the limitations were not the result of oversight. I simply feel that while much of my discussion is pertinent to the gamut of contexts billed in the introduction, much does not, since the differences between the respective confrontations are significant. One cannot equate a Reform movement, which explicitly rejects any formal fealty to Halakhah, with the Conservative, which, despite recent highly deplorable shifts to the left, continues to nurture a self-image of halakhic commitment. Despite our profound difference from "believing Jews of other religious ideologies," they obviously cannot rightly be denominated as secular. Likewise, the Israeli scene, particularly, as viewed from the vantage point of a *yeshivat hesder,* differs markedly from the Diaspora, the reality of common danger significantly heightening the sense of *berit goral.* When a *dati* and a *hiloni* have sat in a tank jointly, their common safety and respective futures often inextricably intertwined, the reality of their relation is perceived, intuitively and existentially, in light of their very special situation.

Hence, rather than lump disparate issues under a common umbrella, I have focused upon a narrower spectrum, and I leave it to the reader to invite comparison or stress dissonance. For the lacunae, I beg indulgence — ‏ועוד חזון למועד‎.

Notes

* The editors would like to thank Rabbi Dov Karoll for providing translations of many of the primary texts in this chapter.

1. (Northvale, N.J. 1992). I should add, however, that irrespective of possible duplication in the choice of topic, the cast of contributors has changed markedly.

2. This chapter in German Jewish history has been widely studied and is the subject of a considerable literature. For our purposes, a recent book which combines detailed attention to this topic with analysis of its broader context — Adam S. Ferziger, *Exclusion and Hierarchy: Orthodoxy, Nonobservance, and the Emergence of Modern Jewish Identity* (Philadelphia, 2005) — is most helpful. One need not adopt the book's theses — foremost among which is the assertion that in the modern era, the Orthodox community did not content itself with classifying outsiders but, in effect, built a new identity and molded fresh categories — in order to benefit from this study.

3. Coleridge rightly insisted upon radically differentiating faith from belief. Here I have largely ignored the distinction, however, since it is not very relevant to my topic.

4. Mendelssohn's position was in all likelihood oriented to his specific Jewish background and agenda. Beyond this, however, it probably reflects the pallid character of the Enlightenment. Recently, this position has been energetically pressed by Marc Shapiro, but it can hardly be defined as a variant of avowed Orthodoxy.

5. See, e.g., Ramban and Rabbenu Bahye, *ad locum*.

6. See Sanhedrin 90a.

7. See Alfred North Whitehead, *Religion in the Making* (New York, 1927), pp. 191–193.

8. See *Sefer Ha-Mizvot, Asei*, 1–2; *Lo Ta'aseh*, 1; and Hilkhot Yesodei Ha-Torah, 1:1–7. It is noteworthy that the Rambam evidently rejects agnosticism as well as atheism.

9. *Mizvot*, 1–2. The *Hinnukh* diverges from the Rambam, however, with respect to some details of the content of belief. For instance, whereas the Rambam focused upon abstract metaphysical aspects of divine existence and providence, the *Hinnukh* includes belief in concrete historical events:

להאמין שיש לעולם א-לוה א-לוה אחד ... וכי הוא הוציאנו מארץ מצרים ונתן לנו את התורה.

To believe that the world has one God... and that He took us out of Egypt and gave us the Torah (*mizvah* 25).

10. השגות הרמב"ן על ספר המצות להרמב"ם, מצות עשה, א'.

11. *Perush Ha-Mishnayot*, Rav Kapah's edition, Sanhedrin, Introduction to *Helek*, s.v. *ve-kha'asher*, pp. 144–145.

12. Probably the best-known is the critique of Rav Yosef Albo's *Sefer Ha-Ikkarim*, but he was certainly not alone.

13. Devarim 18:13. As to the substance of this *temimut*, Rishonim disagreed. The Ramban, Devarim, 18:13, gave it a religious cast, inasmuch as we were commanded, in a sacrificial vein, to ignore knowledge, true though it might be, emanating from other

entities, albeit recourse to that knowledge would enable us to avert prospective debacles. The Rambam, Avodat Kokhavim, 11:16, defined it in cognitive terms as a need to affirm and acknowledge that all forms of superstition and witchcraft are utter nonsense.

14. Berakhot 10a. Strictly, and grammatically, speaking, the *pasuk* contains no deviation. The term חטאים, as punctuated with a *dagesh* in the *tet*, is the plural of the *nomen agentis* of חַטָא, "sinner," and not of חֵטְא, "sin." Nevertheless, as in many midrashic texts, even a minor irregularity suffices as the basis for homiletical comment.

15. This course may very well be mandated by the normative thrust of *ahavat Yisrael*. Quite independently of that, however, its benefits — spiritual, ethical, and social — are self-evident, even from a universal perspective.

16. Avot, 2:12. See Rambam, *Shemonah Perakim*, chs. 4–5, and Hilkhot De'ot 3:3.

17. See *Nefesh Ha-Haym*, III.

18. For a recent example, see, הרב מנחם אדלר, בינה ודעת, הלכות מחללי שבת בזמננו (ירושלים) תשס"ח. Interestingly, while the volume is grounded upon rigorous premises and pervaded by them, the author — apparently recognizing that, in the modern context, his conclusions and counsel are often untenable — frequently suggests consulting a *posek*, who could relate to the concrete situation as it arises and presumably could find grounds for leniency.

19. As an aside, it might be of interest to note, parenthetically, that, for the Rav, the recitation of *nishmat* was the climax of the *haggadah* during the *seder*; and, together with סדר עבודת יום הכיפורים, a highlight of his overall *avodat Hashem*.

20. In this connection, it might be noteworthy to cite a comment attributed to the late Lubavitcher Rebbe, that the problem with the Conservatives is not so much that they compromise, as that they regard it as a principle.

21. See *Guide*, 1:60ff.

22. Cf. C. S. Lewis, *Reflections on the Psalms* (London, 1958), ch. 3, "The Cursings." While written from an explicitly Christian point of view — and hence not wholly palatable for a Jewish reader — the chapter contains some valuable insights.

23. Kiddushin 36a.

24. Yoma 56b–57a.

25. Berakhot 7a.

26. Sanhedrin 111a–b. This conjectured exchange may also serve as an explanation for the repetition of the tetragrammaton after the pardon in *Ki Tissa* and its single mention in *Shlah*.

27. Mordekhai, Yoma, 725, paraphrasing Keritut 6b.

28. See 17a–18a.

29. Evel Rabbati (= Semahot), 2:10. It is noteworthy that the "celebration" is confined to brethren and relatives, with parents evidently excluded. I presume that such a gesture is more than they could be asked to bear.

30. See Rashi, Vayikra 19:15, who cites from the Sifra two views regarding the identity of the referent in the *mizvah* of בצדק תשפט עמיתך.

    As to the definition of הפורש מדרכי ציבור, Rashi, Sanhedrin 47a, s.v. *mi-darkei* (in an analogous connection, regarding the license for a *kohen* to defile himself in order to bury his father) explains, כגון מומר. The Rambam, however, defines him as one who, while not sinful, dissociates himself from *klal Yisrael*: אף על פי שלא עבר עבירות אלא נבדל מעדת ישראל ואינו עושה מצות בכללן ולא נכנס בצרתן, "Though he violates no transgressions, simply the fact that he separates himself from the community of Israel, does not perform *mizvot* in their midst and does not participate in their travails" (Teshuva 3:11). The Rambam's view was adopted, but also expanded, by the Mehabber. See *Yoreh De'ah*, 344:8. See also Rosh Hashanah 17a, where Rashi states that the term encompasses a range of heretics.

31. Several years ago Michael Rosenak wrote of the Rav's position in this connection and focused on this distinction. In doing so, he discussed a passage in חמש דרשות which sharpened the difference between the two realms, and, to some extent, denigrated the spiritual aspect of the non-Orthodox world. Rosenak saw this as the Rav's fundamental attitude. At the time, I wrote him, objecting that the passage, enunciated in a highly partisan address at a Mizrachi convention, was grossly atypical, as anyone who knew and observed the Rav, including his direct relations with non-Orthodox circles, generally marked by dignity and respect, could readily attest; and that it was both inaccurate and unfair to relegate the work of a generation to the sidelines on the basis of a single brief passage. I also pointed out to him that he was basing his remarks upon a faulty English translation of a faulty Hebrew translation of the original Yiddish. Nevertheless, he held his ground. For the passage in question, see *The Rav Speaks* (a translation of *Hamesh Drashot*) (Toras Horav Foundation, 2002), pp. 43–47. It is true that the Rav was perturbed by what he rightly perceived as the tendentious and disingenuous substance of some *teshuvot* written by Conservative rabbis. I might add that I, myself, encountered something of this directly in working on a *responsum* intended to waive the ban on Gentile wine, which had been referred to the Rav — who then turned it over to me — by one of its Conservative opponents. But that is still a far cry from Rosenak's cavil.

32. See, e.g., Nathan Rotenstreich, "Secularism and Religion in Israel," *Judaism*, 15:3 (1966), 273–283; and my response, in "Religion and State: The Case for Interaction," *Judaism*, 15:4 (1966), 410–411, reprinted in *Leaves of Faith* Volume II, 28.

33. Cf. *Iggerot Mosheh*, *Yoreh De'ah*, 1:139 and 2:106–107; and note the comment thereon in Marc B. Shapiro, *Saul Lieberman and the Orthodox* (Scranton, Pa., 2006), pp. 21–22, with regard to teaching in a Conservative *talmud Torah*. It should be noted, however, that Rav Moshe's *heter* relates to the personal license of the teacher, whereas our discussion refers to the systemic public square.

34. See Sanhedrin 23a. One of the Gerer rabbei'im is reported to have commented

— perhaps, half in jest — that he would sit with adversaries but insisted upon knowing who they were.

    At some level, the issue arises with respect to the venue of publication as well,
but, obviously, to a far lesser degree.

35. In a limited vein, the Rambam cites three distinct aspects of the *mizvah*; see Yesodei
Ha-Torah 5, *passim*. Above and beyond all three, however, is the overarching sense
most consonant with פשוטו של מקרא, i.e., enhancing the sacral quality of His divine
name(s). See Seforno, Vayikra 22:22.

36. Sifre, Va'ethanan, on Devarim 6:4. The portrait of Avraham as a great proselytizer is
of course familiar from other *midrashim*; but the link with *ahavah* is telling.

37. Shevuot 39a.

38. See Sotah 37a and Rashi, Rosh Hashanah 29a, s.v. קמ"ל.

39. Sanhedrin 73a.

40. See Bava Mezia 31a; for the discussion concerning *avedah mida'at*. The Tur, *Hoshen
Mishpat*, 260, assumes that in such a case ownership ceases as the object becomes
hefker. However, the Rambam, Gezelah Va-Avedah 12:11, holds that ownership
remains intact, and only the *mizvah* of returning the *avedah* is nullified.

41. The notion that a person is *not* master of his own being, while anathema to secular
modernists, is of course a linchpin of classical religious thought. It served to negate
a possible legal right to sell oneself, and, from Plato to Spenser, as a rationale (unlike
Camus) for rejecting suicide.

42. Bava Kamma 69a. The final word in the original of this dictum is *ve-yamut* — literally, "and let him die." However, as I presume that if the thief's life were actually in
danger, as he consumed his loot, one would certainly be duty-bound to save him, I
have preferred to translate generically. The only "death" in question is that which is
the just dessert of the sin.

43. See Resp. 142. For a recent survey of the formula and its qualifications, see R. J. David
Bleich, "The Case of the Poisoned Sandwich," *Tradition* (Fall 2008), 58–86.

44. These terms, each divisible into subcategories, all relate to non- or anti-halakhic
content and are listed here in descending order of severity. The first denotes apostasy,
the second entails violation of certain kinds of prohibition, and the third, failure
to maintain a halakhic regimen, flexibly defined for various applications. The term
אינו עושה מעשה עמך is more marginal than the others cited here. Moreover, its practical
definition is relative to the area of its application. A single narrow aberrant violation
does not, *per se*, place the deviant beyond the pale. See Bava Mezia 48b, *Tosafot*, s.v.
be-oseh; and cf. ibid., 62a.

45. It has been widely suggested that recourse to coercion is the litmus test serving as the
Rubicon dividing the premodern *kehillah* from its successor; see, e.g., Ferziger, ch. 3.
This assertion obviously invites a question as to whether this development entails an
attitudinal shift or just the loss of requisite power.

46. See, particularly, "Religion and State: The Case for Interaction," *Judaism*, 15:4 (Fall 1966), pp. 387–411; and *Judaism*, 16:2 (Summer 1967), pp. 226–227. Reprinted in *Leaves of Faith*, Volume II (Jersey City, 2004, 1–32).

47. Tefillin 1:13.

48. Kiddushin 6a.

49. See Shabbat 68b and Rambam, Mamrim 3:1–3.

50. See Sanhedrin 26b, and *Tosafot*, s.v. *he-hashud*.

51. See Ramban, Bamidbar, 15:22–30. I am inclined to think that a close reading of the Ramban's text does not necessarily yield a radical distinction between collective and individual apostasy, with respect to their gravity and possible pardon. Even if one does read this into the Ramban, the scope of the distinction is, as I have noted, limited.

52. An analogy may be noted between this formulation and the question — debated by, *inter alia,* Kant vs. the Utilitarians — as to whether ethical and/or religious virtue is to be defined by subjective input and intent or by objective output and result. And indeed, some link exists, since, well before Kant, the matter had been treated in the world of Halakhah, within which it figures prominently.

    Anecdotally, the following incident may be illustrative. At a meeting held some years ago between the staff of an Israeli yeshivah and a group of Conservative leaders, Dr. Schorsch cited the text of the mishnah in Menahot (110a), אחד המרבה ואחד הממעיט ובלבד שיכוון ליבו לשמים, "Whether one offers much or one offers little, as long as one directs his mind toward Heaven," as a guideline for choice of a *posek*, on the basis of goodwill and intent, rather than upon the range of knowledge. Whereupon an observer questioned whether he employed parallel criteria in selecting a doctor.

53. It should be stressed, however, that the history of dogmatic and doctrinal religious conflict is replete with illustrations of the thesis that tension — and, at time, persecution — is most intense when at issue are what to an outsider appear to be mere nuances, the very proximity sharpening the mutual threat.

    דמינה מחריב בה דלא מינה לא מחריב בה.

    Its own kind destroys it, while a different kind does not destroy it (Zevahim 3a).

54. Many Rabbinic ordinances, classified as *gezerot*, are rooted in the fear that neutral A may lead to undesirable B. However, Hazal established a general principle that גזירה לגזירה לא עבדינן; i.e., we don't proscribe neutral C out of concern that it will lead to neutral A, and thence to B. See Bezah 3a.

Chapter 6

Law and Spirituality: Defining the Terms

Spirituality, as concept and reality, revolves around three distinct elements. In one sense, it denominates a kind — or, if you will, a level — of existence. In a primitive context, this might crudely refer to a physical essence, albeit more rarefied than gross carnal being. In a more sophisticated vein, it bears metaphysical import.[1] At the highest plane, it is of course identified with the *Ribbono shel Olam*. He is, Himself, pure spirit, אין לו דמות הגוף ואין לו גוף, "He has not semblance of a body nor is He corporeal," and not subject to the vicissitudes of matter:

> וכל הדברים האלו אינן מצויין אלא לגופים האפלים השפלים שוכני בתי חומר אשר בעפר יסודם אבל הוא ברוך הוא יתברך ויתרומם על כל זה.

> All these states exist in physical beings that are of obscure and mean condition, dwelling in houses of clay, whose foundation is in the dust. Infinitely blessed and exalted above all this, is God, blessed be He (Rambam, Hilkhot Yesodei Ha-Torah, 1:12).

Moreover, He is a source from which emanates a derivative spirit, as it were, such as "dove-like sat'st brooding on the vast abyss, and mad'st it pregnant:"[2] ורוח א-לקים מרחפת על פני המים, "the spirit of God hovered over the face of the waters." At a second, categorically inferior, plane, it denotes a plethora of immaterial entities, differently conceived in various cultural traditions. These, for us, may be angelic שהמלאכים אינם גוף וגויה אלא צורות נפרדות זו מזו, "the angels are nevertheless not corporeal and have no gravity-like bodies which have weight," (Yesodei Ha-Torah 2:3) or demonic: והגוף הזה, says Ramban of a demon, הוא רוחני יטוס לדקותו וקלותו באש ובאויר, "The body [of these demonic creatures of two elements] is of a spiritual nature; on account of its delicacy and lightness it can fly through fire and air" (Vayikra 17:7). But whatever the moral state, the metaphysical state is purely spiritual.

At yet another plane, however, we encounter spirituality within the context of the physical. In a very limited sense, it has even been taken by some to include the animal world. The term, רוח הבהמה, "the spirit of the beast," is of course familiar from the *pasuk* in Kohelet; and Ramban, in particular, took pains to stress the significance of this aspect as a spiritual category, and not merely as a reference to one of the four elements, in Aristotelian terms, or to a molecular entity, in modern usage. Rambam had totally dissociated the human spirit from the animal, emphasizing that the terms, נפש ורוח, "soul and spirit," have totally different referents with respect to both:

ואינה הנפש המצויה לכל נפש חיה שבה אוכל ושותה ומוליד ומרגיש ומהרהר אלא
הדעה שהיא צורת הנפש ובצורת הנפש הכתוב מדבר בצלמנו כדמותנו ופעמים רבות
תקרא זאת הצורה נפש ורוח ולפיכך צריך להזהר בשמות, שלא יטעה אדם בהן וכל
שם ושם ילמד מעניינו.

Nor does it [i.e. the human "form"] refer to the vital principle in every animal by which it eats, drinks, reproduces, feels, and broods. It is the intellect which is the human soul's specific form. And to this specific form of the soul, the Scriptural phrase, "in our image, after our likeness" alludes. This form is frequently called soul and spirit. One must therefore, in order to avoid mistakes, pay special attention to the meaning of these terms which, in each case, has to be ascertained from the context (Rambam, Hilkhot Yesodei Ha-Torah, 4:8).

Ramban, by contrast, taking note, *inter alia*, of the capacity for feeling and reflection cited but discounted by Rambam, repeatedly insists upon recognizing a common factor. Thus, he explains that the pre-Noahide prohibition against carnal consumption was grounded upon concern for the bestial *nefesh*:

כי אין לבעל נפש שיאכל נפש כי הנפשות כולן לא-ל הנה, כנפש האדם וכנפש הבהמה
לו הנה, ומקרה אחד להם כמות זה כן מות זה ורוח אחד לכל ועל הדרך היוני שיראוהו

חוקריו מן השכל הפועל התנוצץ זיו וזוהר צח מאד ובהיר וממנו יצא ניצוץ נפש הבהמה
והנה היא נפש גמורה בצד מן הפנים ולכך יש בה דעת לברוח מן הנזק וללכת אחרי
הנאות לה והיכר ברגילים ואהבה להם כאהבת הכלבים לבעליהן והיכר מופלא באנשי
בית בעליהם וכן ליונים דעת והכרה.

One creature possessed of a soul is not to eat another creature with a
soul, for all souls belong to God. The soul of man, just as the soul of the
animal, are all His, "even one thing befalleth them; as the one dieth,
so dieth the other; yea, they have all one breath" (Kohelet 3:19). Now
in the opinion of the Greek philosopher [Aristotle], as interpreted by
those who scrutinize his words, it was out of the Active Intellect that
there emitted a very fine and bright flash and glitter of light, from
which came forth the spark which is the soul of the animal. It is thus in
a certain sense a real soul. It therefore has sufficient understanding to
avoid harm, and to seek its welfare, and a sense of recognition towards
those with whom it is familiar, and love towards them, just as dogs love
their masters, having a wonderful sense of recognition of the people of
their households, and as, similarly, pigeons have a sense of knowledge
and recognition (Vayikra 17:11).

Nevertheless, Ramban obviously assumed the uniqueness of the human
spirit, singularly derived from divine aspiration — ויפח באפיו נשמת חיים,
"He breathed into his nostrils the breath of life;"[3] and it is upon man — in
Browning's phrase, "half angel and half dust, and all a passion and a wild
desire" — that the conception of physically based metaphysical spirituality centers.[4] Within our own tradition no less than in that of religious
humanism, in general, the themes of man's dual origin and dual nature
— whether dichotomized or integrated, in conflict or in harmony — are
both common and central, almost to the point of being platitudinous; and,
asserted or assumed, they seem to posit spirituality as the defining quality
of human existence.

From spirituality as fact we move, second, to spirituality — here,
purely human — as attitude and approach. We are, of course, all bound
by physical limitations, impelled by instinctual drives, and constrained
by socioeconomic needs. Montaigne's trenchant observation, put in the
mouth of Raymond Sebonde, that man aspires for the stars and all the

while cannot rise from his toilet seat, is universally applicable; and Hazal,[5] we recall, took note of Pharaoh's arrogant folly in pretending otherwise. However, the balance between astral aspiration and anal bondage may be variously struck. Individuals and societies can establish priorities. They can succumb to the weakness of the flesh, the appetite for affluence, or the lust for power, or they may seek to transcend them. A spiritual life, in this sense, is one which seeks to maximize spiritual achievement and to advance the distinctly human aspect of personal and communal existence — of man as *zelem E-lohim*, "the human face divine;" of man as a moral and intellectual being, of man as a creative *ruah memallela*, "spirit which speaks," capable of esthetic perception and expression. For secular moralists, the issue is simply one of the quality of mundane life — although for them, too, existence *sub specie aeternitatis* is a value. From a religious perspective, the priority of *hayyei olam* over *hayyei shaah* is a crucial aspect of the spiritual agenda.

Thirdly, spirituality denotes a mode of experience and activity, a quality of personality which finds expression not only in what is pursued, but how. In part, it relates to perception, to the degree of supra-materiala being ascribed to observed reality. Thus, the mythological view of nature — fauns, satyrs, maenads, and all — is more spiritual than the scientific. Analogously, Carlyle's theory of history is more spiritual than Marx's; the Rabad's view of the afterlife less spiritual than Rambam's. Even more critically, anthropomorphism — particularly, insofar as it relates to corporeality rather than to emotions — is not only theologically repugnant but spiritually deficient.

Primarily, however, at issue is sensibility and expression. A spiritual person is one who not only perceives reality as spiritual, but experiences it as such. He is one who relates himself and his situation to the world of pure spirit — transcendental, in religious terms, or cultural and/or national, secularly conceived;[6] and who can give his sense of that relation a given cast. That cast encompasses a cluster of elements: ethereality, vitalism, dynamism, inwardness, feeling, personal expression, imagination. The emphasis is experiential and, hence, significantly subjective. Beyond the inner sense, and the inner voice, we may also note — and this factor has attained increased popularity in current parlance — the mode of its expression. What is intended is not necessarily verbalization but, rather, more physical means of rendering the spiritual — dance, song, vehicles of exuberance, passion, and enthusiasm; not quite the Dionysiac, but in that general vein. In this respect, the Romantics' preference for music over visual art, or the Baal Ha-Tanya's grading a *niggun* without words above one with a text (although he regarded "a *niggun* without a *niggun*" as loftier still) may be viewed as reflecting spiritual sensibility.

Given this account of spirituality, we are confronted with the question of its relation to the halakhic linchpin of our religious world — and, hence, derivatively, of its relation to ourselves. As regards the first two senses of the term, with respect to which the spiritual is juxtaposed with the material, there is, of course, no problem. There have undoubtedly been schools of thought that have perceived both the cosmos and man in more purely spiritual terms than *Yahadut*, ascribing, mystically or philosophically, an almost ethereal character to the whole of reality, and virtually denying the empirical. And there are certainly cultures which, far more than our own, have denigrated the material, as either, in Plato's terms, metaphysically flaccid, or, with Augustine, as a *massa perditionis*, corrupt and corrupting. The central tradition of *hashkafah* has never gone this far. As the leading modern figures, in particular, have emphasized, it has adopted neither pole of James' familiar dichotomy, world-acceptance or world-rejection, and has opted, instead, for world-redemption. Nevertheless, the fundamental affirmation of spirit, as fact and value, is central to traditional Jewish thought; and whatever controversies have flared over the degree of centrality — and they have been significant — have arisen within the parameters of clearly accepted spiritual priority.

If we have a problem, it obtains with respect to our third aspect — the spirituality of sensibility and expression. *Prima facie*, here, too, there is no conflict. We rightly regard the focus upon inwardness as endemic to any meaningful religion, and it was clearly and succinctly articulated by Hazal: רחמנא ליבא בעי, "The Merciful One desires the heart."[7] Further, the purgation envisioned in the familiar midrash as the *telos* of *mizvot*, לא ניתנו המצות אלא כדי לצרף את הבריות, "The precepts were given only that man might be refined by them,"[8] is unquestionably spiritual. Beyond this, we can also heartily espouse the spirituality of exuberance. Rambam, regarded by classical *maskilim* as the paragon of restrained rationalism, was emphatic on this point. After describing the festivities of *simhat bet ha-sho'evah*, he concludes Hilkhot Lulav with a ringing affirmation regarding the performance of *mizvot* in general:

> השמחה שישמח אדם בעשיית המצוה ובאהבת הא־ל שצוה בהן עבודה גדולה היא וכל
> המונע עצמו משמחה זו ראוי להפרע ממנו שנאמר תחת אשר לא עבדת את ה' א־לקיך
> בשמחה ובטוב לבב[9] וכל המגיס דעתו וחולק כבוד לעצמו ומתכבד בעיניו במקומות
> אלו חוטא ושוטה ועל זה הזהיר שלמה ואמר אל תתהדר לפני מלך וכל המשפיל עצמו
> ומקל גופו במקומות אלו הוא הגדול המכובד העובד מאהבה וכן דוד מלך ישראל אמר
> ונקלותי עוד מזאת והייתי שפל בעיני ואין הגדולה והכבוד אלא לשמוח לפני ה' שנאמר
> והמלך דוד מפזז ומכרכר לפני ה' וגו'.

Rejoicing in the fulfillment of a commandment and in love for God who had prescribed the commandment is a supreme act of divine worship. One who refrains from participation in such rejoicing deserves to be punished, as it is written, "Because you did not serve the Lord thy God with joyfulness, and with gladness of heart" (Devarim 28:47).[9] If one is arrogant and stands on his own dignity and thinks only of self-aggrandizement on such occasions, he is both a sinner and a fool. It was this that Solomon had in mind when he uttered the words, "Glorify not thyself in the presence of the King," (Mishlei 25:6). Contrariwise, one who humbles and makes light of himself on such occasions, achieves greatness and honor, for he serves the Lord out of sheer love. This is the sentiment expressed by David, king of Israel, when he said, "And I will be yet more vile than this, and will be base in mine own sight (II Shemuel 6:22)." True greatness and honor are achieved only by rejoicing before the Lord, as it is said, "King David leaping and dancing before the Lord, etc. (II Shemuel 6:16)" (Hilkhot Lulav 8:15).

The statement stands opposed not only to the patrician critique of Mikhal,[10] royal daughter and wife, but to Appolonian restraint, or Philistine decorum, in general.

And yet we do have a problem — one which, moreover, we ignore at our peril. It may perhaps best be delineated by noting elements frequently regarded as opposed to spirituality. The spiritual is often contrasted with the material, the formal, and the intellectual[11] — all three being viewed as relatively external when compared to, in Hamlet's phrase, "that within which passeth show." Yet all three figure prominently within the halakhic order. Even pietists who trumpet the priority of *hovot ha-levavot* acknowledge the critical role of *hovot ha-evarim*. Technical *shiurim* abound in numerous areas:

כל מדת חכמים[12] כן היא בארבעים סאה טובל בארבעים סאה חסר קורטוב אינו יכול לטבול בהן.

All the standards of the Sages are such. In [a bath of] forty *se'ah* [for instance] one may perform ritual immersion; in [a bath of] forty *se'ah* minus one *kortob* one may not perform ritual immersion (Ketubbot 104a).

And, finally, the central, almost anomalous, place assigned to *talmud Torah* hardly requires evidential prooftexts.

The potential for attenuated spirituality clearly exists, then. Our adversaries have, of course, gone further, contending that this potential has indeed been realized. From non-Jewish and from Jewish sources, the charge has been leveled since, at least, the dawn of Christianity. The critique of Pharisaism touched upon duplicity and insincerity, but at its heart — in the Pauline version, particularly — lay the broadside attack upon legalism and the juxtaposition of letter and spirit. The theme, commingled in Protestant writings with the opposition of faith and works, has reverberated since, with some contending that the lapse of Halakhic Judaism is not accidental but endemic. In the modern period, this criticism has been particularly honed by existentialists. For Dostoevsky's spokeswoman in "Notes from the Underground" as for Buber, programmed religion inevitably stultifies spirituality. For Berdyaev,[13] these stand opposed, by definition, inasmuch as normative service implies the servitude which he regards as anathema to the spiritual life.

These charges are familiar, and they have served as the focus of considerable polemic. Our concern, however, is not with what we say to our adversaries — we certainly are not inclined to dance to their fiddle — but with what we say to the *Ribbono shel Olam* or to ourselves. For the antinomy is real and the tension immanent. Apart from the material, formal, and intellectual factors already cited, other divisive elements might be mentioned. As Rambam[14] noted, law is formulated with reference to the public; spirituality, by contrast, is highly personal. In a related vein, law is, by definition, normative, and, hence, objective, while the spiritual is presumably subjective, and more contextually oriented. Above all, while Halakhah may be perceived as constraint — it establishes a floor for the religious life and both provides a basis and points a direction for progress towards the attainment of values, moral and religious — it may also be seen as imposing a ceiling; as clipping the wings of soaring aspiration. This sense is perhaps most keenly felt within the modern context. The backdrop of much current spirituality is, after all, Romanticism; and the Romantics were, both deeply subjective — art was, for them, not so much descriptive mimesis as self-expression — and, as T.E. Hulme[15] complained, persistently expansive.

Given the dichotomy, our message and our challenge is clear. We shall abandon neither the normative nor the experiential pole. On the one hand, as committed Jews, we have neither the right nor the desire to reject Halakhah. We know that it is the fountainhead of collective *Yahadut* — initiating with שם שם לו חק ומשפט, "There He made for them a statute and an ordinance" at Marah,[16] and culminating in the covenantal commitment at Sinai and Arvot Moav. It is the essence of national existence within our homeland — ראה למדתי אתכם חקים ומשפטים כאשר צוני ה' אלקי לעשות כן בקרב הארץ אשר אתם באים שמה לרשתה, "Behold I have taught you statutes and ordinances, even as the Lord my God commanded me, that ye should do so in the midst of the land whither ye go in to possess it" — and not only there. It is, equally, the linchpin of personal *avodat Hashem*. אי אתה בן חורין להיבטל הימנה, "you are not free to withdraw from it" — but even if one were, there is no inclination. A Jew certainly experiences the *Ribbono shel Olam* as Creator and Redeemer, ה' צורי וגואלי; but, first and foremost, he encounters Him as ultimate Commander, before whom he stands in servile bondage; with respect to whom, בטל רצונך מפני רצונו, "Nullify your will before His will" is the *alpha* and *omega* of religious existence. In full-throated song we wholeheartedly pronounce אנא עבדא דקודשא בריך הוא, "I am a servant of the Holy One, Blessed is He." We are not abashed by the contrast between sonship and servitude prevalent in much Christian theology; and we are not tempted by the sirens holding out the promise of secularized humanistic Judaism, *à la* Erich Fromm's *Ye Shall Be as Gods*. We implore *Avinu Malkenu*, or plead אם כבנים אם כעבדים, "whether as children or as servants," in one breath. And we know full well that it is זו ה' דבר הלכה, "the word of God is the law" which links us, with bonds of love and awe, to our Master, and it is that which grants us ultimate freedom: אין לך בן חורין אלא מי שעוסק בתורה, "There is no freer man than one who engages in the study of the Torah."

On the other hand, we dare not, and we may not, forgo spirituality, as either value or mode. Its significance is dual. First, it ennobles and purifies human personality, as such, a quality to be admired even irrespective of specifically religious ramifications. This point was vividly brought home to me some years back when one of the Rothschilds, wholly devoid of halakhic commitment, came to visit the Rav. I asked him later how the visit had gone, and he responded, "You know, he is a spiritual person;" and I noted that this was meaningful to him.

Second, it brings a person closer to the *Ribbono shel Olam* — and, hence, to His service. As a religiously oriented individual enhances his spirituality, he becomes increasingly sensitized to the presence of *Shekhinah*; and we recall that a constant sense of that presence, שויתי ה' לנגדי תמיד, "I place God before me constantly," was posited by the Rema, in the very opening codicil of *Shulkhan Arukh Orah Haym*, as an overarching principle of religious existence, כלל גדול בתורה ובמעלות הצדיקים אשר הולכים לפני האלקים, "a major principle of the Torah and among the attributes of the righteous that walk with the Lord."

What is needed, clearly, is balance; and it is that which, within the parameters of tradition, has been sought. As might have been anticipated, *a priori*, it has historically been variously formulated, within different movements or cultures and by different masters; and, at times, there has been alternation, with the pendulum swinging between relative pietism and legalism. Some of this variety has been traced by my late brother-in-law, Professor Yitzchak Twersky zt"l,[17] and, most fully — albeit, by and large, from a less traditional perspective — in the two volumes, *Jewish Spirituality*, in the series on *World Spirituality*;[18] and much will surely be amplified by forthcoming papers at this Forum. The point is that we need not be surprised. On so critical an issue, should we expect, ought we prefer, uniformity? What we should seek is assurance that whatever emphasis is predicated be determined not by the weakness of the second-ary factor, tepid religious experience or shallow normative consciousness, but by the strength of the dominant.

What we need, however, is more than balance, with its connotation of respective checks and equilibrium. We need mutual, genuinely reciprocal, fructification. On the one hand, the spiritual is to inform and enrich the material and the intellectual. To this end, we need to have recourse to two elements. First, we have to develop our own selves as spiritual beings. To the extent that we are sensitive, generally, we shall enhance the capac-ity for being sensitive, religiously. Shallowness and aridity in one area leave their mark along the whole front. Secondly, we can harness specific halakhic categories. Quantitativeness is, as the Rav[19] stressed, an intrinsic feature of halakhic existence. This element is natural and understand-able. It manifests itself, in part, in a concern for *shiurim*, proper units of time and space; and, in part, in awareness of the number and/or duration of *mizvah* performances. This aspect is fundamentally highly positive — although at times one finds that fretting over requisite qualification may, regrettably, drain attention from the interactive religious character of the act. However, it needs to be counterbalanced, on purely halakhic grounds, by the qualitative dimension, by awareness of not only how much we do or how many *shittot* we consider, but of how we do, as regards both the motivation and the character of performance.

To take a relatively narrow example, we might note the gemara in Yoma with respect to *keri'at shema*: הקורא את שמע לא ירמוז בעיניו ולא יקרוץ בשפתותיו ולא יורה באצבעותיו, "He who reads the Shema may neither blink with his eyes, nor gesticulate with his lips, nor point with his fingers") — this being subsumed, as the Rif explains, under the rubric of the guideline cited in the *sugya* subsequently, ודברת בם עשה אותן קבע ואל תעשם עראי, "'And you shall speak of them,' — do them seriously and not casually." Moreover, on the basis of the Yerushalmi,[20] Ramban[21] expands the requirement for *keva* to Berakhot, generally, this view being subsequently codified in *Shulkhan Arukh*;[22] and the concept of focused concentration can surely be applied to *mizvot* at large. To take broader categories, the qualities of *ahavah* and *yirah*, normatively obligatory at all times, should, if woven into the fabric of a halakhic performance, enrich its substance.

Ramban held that the Torah itself had assigned a specific *mizvah* to the task of qualitative enhancement. Rambam, it will be recalled, interpreted ולעבדו בכל לבבכם, "serve Him with all your heart," as referring to daily *tefillah*. Ramban, however, held that this obligation was only *mi-de'rabbanan*. Hence, he offers an alternative, and far more comprehensive, interpretation of the phrase and of the norm:

> ועיקר הכתוב ולעבדו בכל לבבכם מצות עשה שתהיה כל עבודתנו לא-ל יתעלה בכל לבבנו כלומר בכוונה רצויה שלימה לשמו ובאין ההרהור רע לא שנעשה המצות בלא כונה או על הספק אולי יש בהם תועלת כענין ואהבת את ה' א-לקיך בכל לבבך ובכל נפשך ובכל מאדך שהמצוה היא לאהוב את ה' בכל לב ולב ושנסתכן באהבתו בנפשנו ובממונינו.

The essential meaning of the Scriptural phrase, "to serve Him with all your heart," is the positive commandment that every one of our acts of divine service be performed absolutely wholeheartedly, i.e., with the necessary full intent to perform it for the sake of His name, and without any negative thought; not that we perform the commandments without proper intentionality, or only on the chance that they may bring some benefit — in the spirit of the commandment "You shall love the Lord your God with all your heart, soul and possessions" means that the commandment is to love God with the totality of our hearts, and that we should be prepared to risk our lives and possessions on account of the love for Him. (*Sefer Ha-Mizvot*, Commentary to *asei* 5)

I do not know to what extent the *kavvanah* demanded by Ramban coincides with intentions and mindsets familiar from his own subsequent mystical tradition. But it is the overall thrust which, for our purposes, is crucial.

Other Rishonim lacked this fulcrum. Unquestionably, however, the burden of this passage is consensual. It is, after all, implicit in the demand for *ahavah*, which ought presumably suffuse our total standing as *ovdei Hashem*. In this connection, it is important to emphasize that the contribution of spirituality to our service of God is not confined, *ad hoc*, to moments of *mizvah* performance. It pervades our entire existence — as persons, generally, and as religious beings, specifically. The reinforcement of our spiritual aspect enhances the realization of ויהי האדם לנפש חיה, "and man became a living soul" — rendered by Onkelos as רוח ממללא, "spirit which speaks" — in the wake of ויפח באפיו נשמת חיים, "He breathed into his nostrils the breath of life;" and this realization is the basis of our standing before our Master. I presume few are today capable or desirous of striving for the spiritual level which Ramban placed at the apex of *mizvah* performance:

> והעוזבים כל עניני העולם הזה ואינם משגיחים עליו כאלו אינם בעלי גוף וכל מחשבתם
> וכוונתם בבוראם בלבד כענין באליהו בהדבק נפשם בשם הנכבד יחיו לעד בגופם
> ובנפשם כנראה בכתוב באליהו וכידוע ממנו בקבלה.

> But those who abandon altogether the concerns of this world and pay no attention to it, acting as if they themselves were not creatures of physical being, and all their thoughts and intentions are directed only to their Creator, just as was the case of Eliyahu, [these people] on account of their soul cleaving to the Glorious Name will live forever in body and soul, as is evidenced in Scripture concerning Eliyahu and as is known of him in tradition... (Vayikra 18:4).

Rightly or wrongly, this otherworldly strain does not resonate well with modern readers, of almost every ilk. But acknowledgement of the fact that spirituality, as a quality of soul, is likely to bring even the average person closer to the *Ribbono shel Olam* can and ought to be widespread.

Conversely, Halakhah enriches spirituality; and this, in at least two major respects. First, its prescribed forms and technicalities, while undoubtedly constraining, and meant to constrain, in one sense, are liberating in another. With respect to many *mizvot* mandated procedure frees the individual from groping for means to flesh out a ritual initiative, and enables him to pour all of his spiritual energies into the religious experience proper.

As a case in point, we may briefly examine prayer. Votaries of spirituality complain frequently about the standardized text of the *siddur* and lament the devaluation which has occurred, historically, in the institution of voluntary *tefillat nedavah* or in the impetus toward innovative *hiddush davar* in compulsory prayer. The lament is understandable. In some cases, standardization does indeed undermine the inwardness which constitutes the essence of prayer, and this tendency surely needs to be resisted. There is, however, another side to the coin. With reference to Rabbi Eliezer's statement in the mishnah in Berakhot, העושה תפלתו קבע אין תפלתו תחנונים, "One who makes his prayers rote; his prayers do not constitute pleas," the gemara seeks to define *keva*; and, *inter alia*, cites the joint response of Rabbah and Rav Yosef: כל שאינו יכול לחדש בה דבר, "Whoever is not able to insert something fresh in it." This is, presumably, a manifesto for spirituality in *tefillah*. Yet, the gemara immediately cites Rav Zeira's comment: אנא יכילנא לחדושי בה מילתא ומסתפינא דלמא מטרידנא, "I can insert something fresh, but I am afraid to do so for fear I should become preoccupied") — presumably, not only as a biographical tidbit, but as a general caveat and guideline. Rambam's formulation that uniformity in *berakhot* was instituted in order that:

שיהיו ערוכות בפי הכל וילמדו אותן ותהיה תפלת אלו העלגים תפלה שלימה כתפלת בעלי הלשון הצחה,

an orderly form would be in everyone's mouth, so that all should learn the standardized prayer, and thus the prayer of those who were not expert in speech would be as perfect as that of those who had command of a chaste style (Hilkhot Tefillah 1:4),

is relevant not only as concerns those who can barely express themselves but, equally, with respect to anyone who has difficulty in formulating and experiencing simultaneously.

And the same may be suggested, *mutatis mutandis*, with respect to some other *mizvot*. How much spiritual energy would be wasted every *seder* night, if one had to improvise the evening's structure and content, even if it were done in advance? How much distraction from the experiential substance of *yom teru'ah* would ensue if we had to invent anew the texts and themes of the day's prayers and *teki'ot* every Rosh Hashanah? The Halakhah has entitled us by confronting us with the existent and demanding that we cope with its challenges.

Secondly, however, the contribution of Halakhah to spirituality extends beyond the removal of barriers or the diversion of energy from one task to another. It consists, primarily, in a positive and substantive vein, in bonding ourselves to its Author, in deepening and intensifying our relation to the *Ribbono shel Olam*. Encounter with Him and His will in every area, almost at every step; attention riveted upon understanding and implementing His directives; awareness of His pervasive presence in all walks of life; the constant challenge to free, and yet obedient, decision — all of these impact significantly upon our religious being and upon our link to *Shekhinah*. That link, in turn, impacts profoundly upon our total spiritual life.

Admittedly, however, while this interactive reciprocal fructification exists at the general plane, its realization at the personal level requires some effort. The key is an awareness, in-depth awareness, of one critical point. We have spoken of the confrontation and possible conflict of law and spirituality in general terms; and, indeed, in the abstract, the specter of legalism looms large. However, as committed Jews, we do not regard the issue abstractly, and we do not deal with *a* legal system. We deal with *devar Hashem*, with divine will as expressed in ordinances and incorporated in *the* legal order of Halakhah. When this fact is fully absorbed and integrated, we sense that we do not just encounter a codex but a vivifying presence; that vitalism and dynamism derive from clinging to our Commander and Legislator — ואתם הדבקים בה' א-לקיכם חיים כלכם היום, "You who cleave to God your Lord, you are all living today;" that He, and, derivatively, His revealed will, is the wellspring of effervescence, מקור מים חיים, "the source of living waters;" and that, consequently, divine law and human spirituality can interact positively within our own selves. However, where this conviction is jaded, and awareness of the transcendental character of *halakhah* superficial, the sense of conflict may penetrate.

Of course, recognition of the uniqueness of Halakhah as *devar Hashem* does not necessarily assure the strain of interactive balance I would encourage. If illustration be necessary, I might cite — on the authority of a person whose veracity I consider unimpeachable — a story concerning a certain *adam gadol*. On one of the *yamim noraim*, he (out of deference, I omit his identity) noticed that one of his sons stood for *Shemoneh Esreh* considerably longer than he had. He approached him, and asked to see his *mahzor*. Upon leafing through it, he observed laconically: "Strange, we both have the identical text, and yet it takes you so much longer." I have the highest regard for the person in question — *kotano avah mimotnai*; but the story is chilling. Without this recognition, the problem is greatly exacerbated, however.

The Rav zt"l was keenly — and, at times, painfully — aware of this problem. The awareness is already very much in evidence in *Ish Ha-Halakhah*. He knew fully the critique leveled at the world of Brisk — particularly, in Y.L. Perez's "Bein Shnei Harim" — as being coldly aspiritual; and, in a work idealizing its tradition, he takes up the cudgels in response.

> האם משולל הוא איש ההלכה כל אותה התפארת של החוויה הדתית הגועשת והסוערת
> הבוערת בלבת אש קודש, שאיש הדת האכסטטי רגיל בה?...הפועם רגש של כמיהה
> ועריגה לה' בנשמתו של איש ההלכה?

Is halakhic man devoid of the splendor of that raging and tempestuous sacred, religious experience that so typifies the ecstatic *homo religiosus*? ... Is it possible for halakhic man to achieve such emotional exaltation that all his thought and senses ache and pine for the living God?

And his reply is unequivocal:

> איש ההלכה מוכשר וראוי להתמכר לחוויה דתית נאדרה בקודש, על כל צביונה
> ושיכלולה. ברם ההתלהבות הדתית הכבירה באה אליו אחרי ההכרה, אחרי שרכש לו
> כבר ידיעה בעולם האידיאלי של ההלכה ובבואתו בעולם הריאלי. ומתוך שחוויה זו באה
> אחרי ביקורת חריפה והסתכלות עמוקה וחודרת, הרי היא גדולה ביותר.[23]

Halakhic man is worthy and fit to devote himself to a majestic religious experience in all its uniqueness, with all its delicate shades and
hues. However, for him such a powerful, exalted experience only follows upon cognition, only occurs after he has acquired knowledge of
the *a priori*, ideal halakhah and its reflected image in the real world.
But since this experience occurs after rigorous criticism and profound
penetrating reflection, it is that much more intensive.[24]

Educationally, however, this sequential approach seems neither feasible
nor desirable. It is, at best, suited for only an elite coterie.[25] Subsequently,
in any event, as his pedagogic experience expanded, some of the Rav's
early confidence waned and gave way to a sharper sense of the difficulties involved as well as to a measure of frustration. His basic faith in the
interaction of Halakhah and spirituality, and his personal quest to attain
and to inculcate it, never wavered. But he recognized increasingly that the
path was tortuous and that if the goal were to be attained, significant effort
would need to be invested.

I have discussed, primarily, the possibly corrosive impact of halakhic
living upon spirituality, and of the need to address the issue. We need,
however, to be no less sensitive to the reverse — the dangers posed by
a bent for spirituality upon full Torah commitment. These dangers are
multiple. First, there is the possibility that a thirst for the spiritual will
issue in disdain for what is perceived to be non-spiritual. The latter might
be "pure" *talmud Torah*, dismissed either out of anti-intellectualism, or
out of passionate moral and religious fervor. In this connection, one
of course recalls the polemical preface to *Hovot Ha-Levavot* — parts
of which, incidentally, Reb Haym Brisker did not hesitate to brand as
apikorsut.[26] Or it might be rote and shallow performance of *mizvot*. The
outcry against *mizvat anashim melumadah* has, of course, been the staple
of pietists and moralists throughout the generations; and, in the modern
era, it has united the *mussar* movement and *Hasidut*. However, its impact
may be a two-edged sword. At the personal level, it may inspire more
spiritual observance; or, it may, contrarily, lead one to abandon observance entirely, inasmuch as technical performance is deemed meaningless
anyway. And, at the interpersonal plane, it may lead to demeaning the

ordinary Jew, routinely but tepidly enacting his halakhic commitment. There is, to be sure, a democratic streak in certain spiritual movements — in Romanticism, generally, and in *Hasidut*, particularly: appreciation, if not idealization, of the child, the untutored, even the simpleton, and their naïve faith. However, these may also engender an aristocracy of their own. Rousseau's or Chateaubriand's admiration for the primitive and their contempt of the *bourgeois* were two sides of the same coin.

We, as committed Jews, cannot, however, dismiss "mere" observance. Quite apart from the mystical quality ascribed to a *mizvah* by the *Nefesh Ha-Haym*, the impact upon the personal Jew and his modicum of *avodat Hashem* remains significant. Back in the nineteen-sixties, Professor Twersky addressed a student body at Yeshiva University and argued that, if forced to choose between Mendelssohn's adogmatic ritual observance and Buber's non-halakhic spirituality, he would opt for the former. At the time, I challenged this thesis, contending that a ritual act, wholly devoid of a faith infrastructure,[27] entailed neither a *ma'aseh mizvah* nor a *kiyyum mizvah*. I abide by that position; but, if we are dealing not with adogmatic observance but with superficial, and yet belief-based, action, we cannot delegitimize it.

A second danger, already noted *en passant*, pertains to attitudes toward the material. As secularism serves as a leveling ideology in one vein — it recognizes no ultimate difference between times, places, persons, or objects — so spirituality can democratize in another. Where the focus upon spiritual essence is exaggerated, the danger of minimizing material halakhic status increases. This is of particular relevance with respect to the land of Israel. One recalls the stir raised here a decade ago by remarks attributed to the Lubavitcher Rebbe, that while *olotekha u-shelamekha* could only be offered in the *bet ha-mikdash, aliyotekha u-shelemutekha* could be attained universally.

Somewhat akin to this factor, lurks a third danger — perhaps best noted by reference to the *issur* of *shehutei huz*. The prohibition against slaughtering and offering sacrifices anywhere but in *mikdash* appears in the Torah twice — but in very different contexts and, presumably, with different import. In Re'eh, in accordance with a dominant motif of that *parshah*, it is related to enshrining *bet ha-behirah*, wherever it may be, as the unique locus of sacrificial worship:

> השמר לך פן תעלה עלתיך בכל מקום אשר תראה. כי אם במקום אשר יבחר ה׳ באחד שבטיך שם תעלה עלתיך ושם תעשה כל אשר אנכי מצוך.

Take heed that you do not offer your burnt offerings at every place that you see; but at the place which the Lord will choose in one of your tribes, there you shall offer your burnt offerings, and there you shall do all that I am commanding you (Devarim 12:13–14).

That status would be impaired by diversification and the existence of competing centers; hence, evidently, the proscription.[28] In Aharei Mot, on the other hand, *shehitat huz* is forbidden in order to avoid continued drift to the worship of alien spiritual entities; ולא יזבחו עוד את זבחיהם לשעירים אשר הם זנים אחריהם, "They shall no longer sacrifice their sacrifices unto the satyrs, after whom they go astray" (Vayikra 17:7). That heretofore prevalent practice verging upon idolatry is henceforth interdicted.[29]

Spirituality, analogously, poses a potential threat on both fronts. First, its creative and dynamic aspect may exert a centrifugal thrust, issuing in alternative modes of religious experience and expression which, if insufficiently integrated, may rival normative categories. Secondly, the spiritual impulse may be adulterated, religion becoming tinged with superstition or vestigial magic, spirituality degenerating into spiritualism or its equivalent.

Finally, alongside the religious, there looms a moral danger. Excessive spirituality, possibly tinged by otherworldliness, may lead to averting one's gaze from mere material suffering. We are, of course, enjoined to emulate the *Ribbono shel Olam,* המגביהי לשבת, המשפילי לראות בשמים ובארץ, "Who is enthroned on high yet deigns to look down upon heaven and earth;" but the lesson of Rav Yohanan's familiar observation כל מקום שאתה מוצא גבורתו של הקב״ה אתה מוצא ענוותנותו, "Wherever you find the greatness of the Holy One, Blessed be He, there you find His humility" (Megillah 31a), can be all too easily lost. And inordinate spirituality may accelerate that loss.

I regard none of this as cause for discarding spirituality. It remains an indispensable component of the religious life. These are, however, reasons for nurturing and honing it carefully; and, together with the caveats against arid legalism, constitute an overriding challenge for optimal personal realization in the quest for integrated *avodat Hashem*. If we had to decide between pallid normative observance and non-halakhic spiritual dynamism we would, as commanded beings, unhesitatingly, albeit regretfully, opt for the former. But does anyone imagine that the *Ribbono shel Olam* confronts us with such a cruel choice? Our aim, duty and aspiration both, is the conjunction of spiritualized Halakhah and disciplined spirituality; the fusion which enables us to realize the poetry and prose of ideal Jewish existence.

The topic of this paper, as well as of this conference, is, in every sense, timeless. Yet it bears, additionally, a clear immediate relevance, in light of the recent upsurge in spirituality within the Western world, generally, and our own Jewish sector, particularly. I take it this was a factor in the choice of the topic and, hence, that, in conclusion, I should presumably address myself — with specific reference to the Jewish scene — to the current scene somewhat. I must confess that I cannot claim extensive intimate contact with the phenomenon, but I trust that I can nonetheless address myself to several significant issues regarding it.

The most palpable manifestation of this movement, in public perception, is exuberance and enthusiasm — particularly, within the context of prayer. Songfests, midnight dancing, Carlebach *kabbalat Shabbat* — these are among the hallmarks. In seeking to assess this development, I am convinced that, on the whole, its effect has been salutary — especially in the lay community. The verve and the excitement felt by many in the course of more visibly "soul"-oriented *tefillah* stand in marked contrast to the pallor and desiccation which characterized many *batei knesset* a decade ago. Carping critics sometimes object that the vibrant hour of *kabbalat Shabbat* is, for many, merely a faddish island within an otherwise tepid and possibly "yuppie" existence. Possibly. I have no way of judging; and who has designated me to evaluate the depth of other people's sincerity? Be this as it may, an island is also not to be lightly dismissed; and, beyond that, I find it difficult to believe that the interlude leaves no imprint upon the totality of personal spirituality.

When I gave vent to this evaluation in Jerusalem recently, some listeners responded with a measure of surprise. "*Et tu, Brute?*" They needn't. In a talk before a group of *rabbanim* close to twenty years ago, entitled, by way of adaptation, "Spirit and Spirituality," I stressed the need for a much greater injection of *ruah* — within our educational institutions, particularly. Again, in an address before the Educators Council of America in 1985 — subsequently disseminated by the Israel Koschitzky Virtual Bet Midrash of Yeshivat Har Etzion [and published as the final chapter of *By His Light*] — I stated: "I spoke before about a passionate concern for Torah. The key, indeed, is the passion — passion which is important in its own right as a component of *avodat Hashem*, and passion which holds the key to the development of other components.... In order to attain that, we, as educators, should be ready to sacrifice — and even sacrifice considerably — a measure of objective intellectual accomplishment." I have since recurred to this theme, periodically; so I feel perfectly consistent in asserting that, for the bulk of the purveyors and participants of current spirituality, the net religious result is indeed positive.

There are, however, several reservations — some, major. First, as regards the perception of spirituality. We are all in favor of enthusiasm and would find it difficult to believe that, in the age of Locke and Shaftesbury, the term had negative associations. However, we must beware of conditioning our definition or conception of spirituality upon enthusiasm and its external expression. Does anyone question the spirituality of George Fox and his quietist Quakers? Is Byron more spiritual than Wordsworth — the Wordsworth who defined poetry as "emotion recollected in tranquility;" he who taught us to approve "the depth and not the tumult of the soul;" he who could attest, in concluding the "Ode on the Intimation of Immortality," "To me the meanest flower that blows can give / Thoughts that do often lie too deep for tears?" On the contrary, nothing is more unspiritual than confining the world of the spirit to its outward expression, to *Sturm und Drang* at any level. Was not this part of the message of the famous counsel of Carlyle, the patron-saint of Victorian spirituality, "Close thy Byron, open thy Goethe?"

Second, the question of the balance of innovation and tradition needs to be carefully considered. I am not certain as to whether or how far the

Rema's dictum, ואל ישנה אדם ממנהג העיר אפילו בניגונים או בפיוטים שאומרים שם, "A person should not deviate from the local custom — even in the matter of the particular tunes or liturgical poems that are traditionally recited there" (*Orah Haym* 619:1) applies to ordinary daily or Shabbat prayer. After all, the Rema waited until Hilkhot Yom Ha-Kippurim to pronounce it. But the issue as such, relating not only to the *niggunim* but to the overall atmosphere of *tefillah* and its locus, needs to be confronted, judiciously and sensitively.

The more critical concerns lie, however, beyond the purview of the practical aspects of conduct in the *bet ha-knesset*, and touch upon major cruces, especially as they impinge upon the *dati le-umi* Torah community. By way of example, in one of the more "spiritual" *yeshivot hesder*, the assembled *zibbur* burst into dance in the midst of *tefillat Yom Kippur*. It was subsequently explained that — and the rationale is even more per-turbing than the event — inasmuch as they dance on Simhat Torah, why differentiate. Clearly, whoever can offer such a rationale has no idea of the genuine import of Yom Kippur — and probably also has no idea of the import of Simhat Torah. Surely, he has erased from his consciousness the gemara's explanation for the omission of *hallel* on *yamim noraim*:

אמר רבי אבהו אמרו מלאכי השרת לפני הקב"ה רבש"ע מפני מה אין ישראל אומרים שירה לפניך בר"ה וביום הכפורים אמר להם אפשר מלך יושב על כסא דין וספרי חיים וספרי מתים פתוחין לפניו וישראל אומרים שירה.

R. Abbahu stated: The ministering angels said in the Presence of the Holy One, blessed be He: Sovereign of the Universe, why should Israel not chant hymns of praise before Thee on New Year and the Day of Atonement? He replied to them: Is it possible that the King should be sitting on the throne of justice with the books of life and death open before Him, and Israel should chant hymns of praise? (Rosh Hashanah 32b).

In this instance, not the halakhic calendar but personal inclination dic-tated the day's mood.

Even more seriously, misguided spirituality distorts *talmud Torah*. In another yeshivah, students are encouraged to adopt, as do their masters, quasi-mystical interpretations for apparent halakhic discussions in the gemara. And this, in the name of a presumably spiritual quest for *pen-imiyut ha-Torah*. Spatial metaphors regarding what is higher, deeper, or inner are used congenially to suggest a greater degree of truth, value, or sanctity which the method presumes to attain. The spiritual impulse in this connection is dual. Spiritually, advocates of Rambam's rejection of literal anthropomorphism admire it for two reasons. First, it issues in a purer conception of divinity, as opposed to grosser renderings. Quite apart from the result, however, there is a strain of spirituality in the process. A metaphorical or allegorical reading is not so fettered or shackled by the text, and relatively untrammeled imagination can be brought to bear upon its explication. Here, too, analogously, both elements are at work. A *penimi* analysis of שנים אוחזין בטלית or שור שנגח את הפרה enables one to soar far above the dull sublunary sphere of garments and cattle to a firmament of celestial reality. Second, the liberating enterprise, *per se*, by dint of its very nature, provides an exhilarating stimulus. For those who countenance the validity of these insights, *ashrei ha-maamin*. But those of us who were trained to deal with halakhic *realia* in their own terms, are chagrined by the harnessing of misconceived spirituality, in order, literally, לגלות פנים בתורה שלא כהלכה, "to produce an interpretation of Torah that is contrary to *halakhah*."

Most serious, however, are the dangers which lurk in a relatively abstract realm. Religious spirituality expresses itself, primarily, in two areas. The first, at which we have already glanced, is that of forms of worship and modes of expression. The second is focus upon the nature and degree of adhesion and linkage to the transcendental order, in general, and to the *Ribbono shel Olam*, in particular. In its more extreme form, this tendency is reflected in various mystical traditions, particularly Oriental ones. In a lesser vein, however, it remains a significant component of more moderate religious outlooks.

Per se, the aspiration for linkage is of course positive, provided that awareness of the absolute chasm separating man from his Creator is not jaded. Where the sense of the "wholly other" is eroded, the striving for fusion can become highly dangerous, even more so from a Jewish perspective than from a Christian one. The Gaon's critique of the *Tanya*, in this respect, is familiar; and it is paralleled by Barth's rejection of Schleiermacher's Romantic theology. The natural bent of spirituality in religion very often expresses itself, however, precisely in diminishing the sense of chasm and engendering a feeling of familiarity. Of many of its votaries, particularly in the current vogue, one might invoke the gemara's rhetorical query, ?חברותא כלפי שמיא "Can one behave familiarly with Heaven?" (Berakhot 34a)

In seeking to trace the roots of our current spiritual vogue, we should no doubt look, in part, to some universal factors, inasmuch as the phenomenon extends beyond our borders. However, if we should focus upon insular sources, particularly within the *dati le'umi* community here in Israel, unquestionably the figure of Rav Kook[30] would loom prominently. His personality and his writings have left an indelible imprint upon that community, and reinvigorated spirituality is surely part of his patrimony, as it was central to his life and works; and for this we are all in his debt. Some would contend that he is also, unwittingly, responsible for some of the excesses. I do not feel qualified to judge; but it is a fact that those whom I would regard as having gone overboard regard themselves as his progeny. Be this as it may, it is essential that we grasp the seriousness of this issue.

We are not just dealing with some moot theological abstraction. At issue is the character of man's relation to the *Ribbono shel Olam*. Much of what now passes for spirituality implicitly presses for the demotion of *yirah* in the interest of *ahavah*. C.S. Lewis has somewhere observed that most people don't want a Father in Heaven, but rather a Grandfather. Some would prefer a mate. This, for traditional *Yahadut*, is critical. This is hardly the place to examine this crucial issue in depth, but one point needs to be clarified emphatically. To be sure, Hazal decried the inferiority of *avodah mi-yirah*, but never *yirah* itself. As a motive for the religious life and the performance of *mizvot* in general, love is pre-eminent; but as an integral component of the inner religious life, as one aspect of man's experience of God and his relation to Him, fear or awe takes its place alongside love. The selfsame Rambam who, in the concluding chapter of *Sefer Madda* denigrates *avodah mi-yirah*, posits reverential awe in the second chapter of that treatise as a positive commandment; and he goes so far as to state that *ahavah* and *yirah* can jointly spring from the same contemplative experience. Indeed, one might suggest, without paradox, that one could fulfill the *mizvah* of *yirah*, impelled by *ahavah*.

It is entirely possible that, even as specific *mizvot*, love is superior to fear or even awe; and this is perhaps suggested by Ramban's[31] celebrated explanation of why *asei doheh lo ta'aseh,* "a positive commandment overrides a negative one," or by Rambam's[32] statement that practical *mizvot* were intended to engender *yirah* and the philosophic knowledge communicated by the Torah to instill *ahavah*. However, the place of *yirah* as a cardinal aspect of our normative religious life is beyond question. It constituted the central motif of *ma'amad har Sinai*; in Hazal, religious commitment is generally denominated *yirat shamayim*; and we say daily, וייחד לבבנו לאהבה וליראה את שמך, "unite our hearts to love and fear Your name."

I'm afraid, however, that votaries of current spirituality often tend to erode the status of *yirah*; and, together with it, the status of the very essence of *Yahadut: kabbalat ol malkhut shamayim* and *kabbalat ol mizvot.* In Israel today, in certain circles much is heard of *hit'habberut*, as linkage, but little of *hit'hayyevut*, as obligation. Only recently, I heard of the Bar Mizvah of the son of a local spiritually inclined rabbi, at which the homiletic parlance was suffused with linkage and self-realization but nary a word about yoke or bondage. Or to take a published example, what is one to make of the following affirmation by Rav Shagar, regarded as bearing affinity to current spiritual circles:

האמונה בהלכה, כמו גם אמונת חכמים בהקשר זה, אינה נובעת בהכרח מכך שיש לי
הוכחה שהם היו החכמים הכי חכמים. מקורה בסוג של אינטימיות – התורה והיהדות
זה אני! הבחירה שלי בעצמי היא בחירה בתורה, במסורת. לא לחינם הביעו חכמים
במדרשים רבים את אהבתם לתורה במטאפורות הלקוחות מחיי איש ואשתו. הכרה זו,
שבפי חז"ל נקראת קבלת עול מלכות שמים נותנת את האופציה למגע עם האין-סוף,
בהיותה מוחלטת וראשונית.

Belief in the Halakhah, like the belief in the Sages in this connection, does not necessarily derive from being sure that these sages were the wisest. Rather, its source is a kind of intimacy: Torah and Judaism

— this is I! My choice of myself *is* the choice of Torah, of tradition. Not for nought did the Sages, in so many *midrashim*, express their love of Torah through the metaphor of conjugal life. This realization — which the sages term "the acceptance of the yoke of Heaven" — affords the possibility of contact with the Infinite, in that it is absolute and primal.[33]

And to think that this exercise in narcissism is to be equated with *kabbalat ol malkhut shamayim*!

Still more worrisome — hopefully atypical, but still a chilling straw in the wind — I found a conversation to which I was recently privy. Towards the end of a wedding of a *hatan* from a markedly spiritual yeshivah — during which the dancing proceeded with admirable gusto — I overheard one of his peers confidently reassure another:

בעצם, אתה לא צריך לקנא בא-לקים, מפני שאתה הוא. רק החלק שבנו שעושה רע
איננו א-לקים; אשר לכל השאר, אתה הוא.

Actually, you don't have to envy God, because *you are He*. Only the part of us that does evil is not God. As for the rest, you are He!

I may not be quoting verbatim, but the citation is close to that; and the substance of the remarks is utterly accurate. I was confronted by the obvious question: Was there any connection between the gusto and the blasphemy, no less grievous for being innocent? I am convinced that there is no necessary link, but cannot be certain about specific cases; and this leaves room not only for thought but for concern.

We are confronted, then, with significant difficulties. The benefits of the current wave of spirituality are many and diverse; and, if such matters can be quantified, I repeat that, on balance, they outweigh the reverses even within our own Orthodox camp. However, some of its manifestations — particularly, ideological flotsam and jetsam — are truly worrisome; and with these we need to cope.

This brings us, finally, back to our primary problem: How to attain optimal fusion of divine law and human spirituality, committed to both while eschewing neither. We live by the serene faith that it can be done. We refuse to believe that we are doomed to choose between arid formalism and unbridled sensibility. We reject both Leibowitz and Buber. But that faith needs to be energized, and to that end, we need to harness effort and commitment. The apocryphal remark attributed to an anonymous *hasid*, מתנגדים דאוונען נישט – אין צײַט; חסידים דאוונען נישט – נישט אין צײַט "*Mitnaggedim* pray not — but on time; Hasidim pray — but not on time") — is both facile and tendentious. It is also false. It is our mission to assure that legists and spiritualists both pray — on time.

Notes

1. See Edwyn Bevan, *Symbolism and Belief* (Boston: Beacon Press, 1957) [the Gifford Lectures of 1937], pp. 151–60.
2. *Paradise Lost*, 1:21–2, based on Hagigah 15a, כיונה המרחפת על בניה ואינה נוגעת "Like a dove that hovers over her brood but does not touch them."
3. See Ramban, Bereshit 1:28 and 2:7.
4. In this connection, extensive discussions of the nuanced differences of נפש, רוח, נשמה, particularly in light of Kabbalah, are, of course, relevant.
5. See Tanhuma, Shemot 7:15.
6. The general editors of the series of volumes, *World Spirituality*, published over the last fifteen years, shy away from a clear definition of the term. However, in the preface printed at the beginning of each volume, they present, "as a working hypothesis," the following: "The series focuses on that inner dimension of the person called by certain traditions 'the spirit.' This spiritual core is the deepest center of the person. It is here that the person is open to the transcendent dimension; it is here that the person experiences ultimate reality." The concluding statement gives the term a purely religious cast; and, indeed, the series is subtitled, "An Encyclopedic History of the Religious Quest." I can appreciate this inclination but I feel that, on the subjective plane, aspects of spirituality may also manifest themselves within a secular context.
7. Sanhedrin 106b. Our text reads הקב"ה instead of רחמנא but Rashi appears to have had רחמנא, and, when cited, this is the prevalent text.
8. Bereshit Rabbah, 44:1; familiarized by Rambam, *Guide* 3.26, and Ramban, Devarim 22:6.
9. The ordinary, and more literal, interpretation of the *pasuk* explains בשמחה ובטוב לבב, "with joyfulness and with gladness of heart," as referring to a situation during which there had been no *avodat Hashem* whatsoever. Rambam — followed by Rabbenu Bahye, *ad locum*, takes it to denote a mode of service.
10. The gravity of her remark is underscored by Hazal's statement that her subsequent barrenness was its punishment; see Sanhedrin 21a. However, Ralbag, II Shemuel, 6:20,

suggests a more rational interpretation — i.e., that David's passion for her waned as a result of the incident.

11. Of course, spirituality may assume an intellectual cast, contemplative or even discursive, in the form of *amor Dei intellectualis* or in the quest for knowing God, in accordance with David's counsel to Shlomo — ודע את א-לקי אבי, "Know the God of my father;" and, in our world, the two very different and yet related examples of Rambam and Habad spring to mind. Nevertheless, broadly speaking, spirituality is often associated with more conative and emotional modes of experience.

12. The term, מדת חכמים, "standards of the Sages," with reference to the specific example of *mikveh*, may suggest that the requirement of forty *se'ah*, for a person who can be fully immersed in less, is only *mi-de'rabbanan*, as apparently assumed by the Me'iri — Mikva'ot 2:1, 7:1; but cf. 1:7 — and possibly the Rosh, Hilkhot Mikva'ot, the end of sec. 1. The principle enunciated certainly applies *mi-de'oraita*, however.

13. See, particularly, his *Slavery and Freedom, passim*.

14. See *Guide* 3:34.

15. See his essay, "Romanticism and Classicism"; reprinted in *Criticism: The Major Texts*, ed. W.J. Bate (New York: Harcourt, Brace, 1952), pp. 564–73.

16. Shemot 15:25. Rashi, following the gemara in Sanhedrin 56b — with respect to the general concept, although the details vary — explains that the *mizvot* commanded at Marah were an earnest of subsequent Torah, part of which was revealed earlier. However, Ramban, *ad locum*, contends that, *al derekh ha-peshat*, the *hok u-mishpat* in question were civil and moral ordinances, אינם חקי התורה והמשפטים אבל הנהגות ויישובי המדינות, "The expression does not refer to the statutes and ordinances of the Torah, but rather to the customs and ways of civilized society."

17. See his essay, "Talmudists, Philosophers, Kabbalists: The Quest for Spirituality in the Sixteenth Century," in *Jewish Thought in the Sixteenth Century*, ed. Bernard Dov Cooperman (Cambridge, MA: Harvard University Press, 1983), pp. 431–59; and, in a broader vein, "Religion and Law," in *Religion in a Religious Age*, ed. S.D. Goitein (Cambridge, MA: Association for Jewish Studies, 1974), pp. 69–82.

18. Vols. 13–14 in the series, ed. Arthur Green (New York: Crossroads, 1986–1987).

19. See 54–56 'עמ ,(ט"תשל :ירושלים) איש ההלכה – גלוי ונסתר.

20. See Berakhot 2:5; זאת אומרת שאסור לעשות מלאכה בשעה שיברך, "This means that it is forbidden to do work at the time one recites the blessings [of *Shema*]."

21. See *Milhamot Hashem*, Berakhot 9a (in the Rif).

22. See *Orah Haym*, 183:12, 191:3.

23. איש ההלכה – גלוי ונסתר, עמ' 74.

24. *Halakhic Man*, trans. Lawrence Kaplan (Philadelphia: Jewish Publication Society, 1983), pp. 82–3.

25. The question of broad application hovers over the essay, generally, but especially so with respect to this point.

26. This was related to me by the Rav.
27. Whether indeed Mendelssohn went so far in his rejection of any normative duty to believe, I do not here presume to ascertain. The discussion at the time was predicated upon the assumption that this was the case.
28. The incessant and unsuccessful battle (רק הבמות לא סרו, "only from the high altars they did not desist") against local altars during the period of *bayit rishon* presumably revolved around this issue.
29. This point is reflected in a comment which appears in Vayikra Rabbah, *ad locum*, to the effect that *korbanot* were to serve as a means of weaning the community away from idolatry:

> לפי שהיו ישראל להוטים אחר עבודת כוכבים במצרים והיו מביאים קרבניהם לשעירם...והיו מקריבין קרבניהם באיסור במה ופורעניות באות עליהם אמר הקב"ה יהיו מקריבין לפני בכל עת קרבנותיהן באהל מועד והן נפרשים מעבודת כוכבים והם ניצולים.

> Because Israel were passionate followers after idolatry in Egypt and used to bring their sacrifices to the satyrs…and they used to offer their sacrifices in the forbidden high places, on account of which punishments used to come upon them, the Holy One, blessed be He said: "Let them offer their sacrifices to me at all times in the Tent of Meeting, and thus they will be separated from idolatry and be saved from punishment," (22:8).

The phrase, באיסור במה (in the forbidden high places) is puzzling, but I presume that it, too, refers to the *issur* of Avodah Zarah. It might be noted that this text was cited by the Maharam Al Askar, as a possible source for Rambam's rationale for *korbanot* in his *Guide*, 3:32, 3:46. See *She'elot U'Teshuvot Maharam Al Askar*, sec. 117, p. 302.

30. A recent collection of essays surveying various aspects of Rav Kook's thought was entitled, *Rabbi Avraham Isaac Kook and Jewish Spirituality*, ed. Lawrence Kaplan and David Shatz (New York: New York University Press, 1995). See, especially, the essays by Jerome I. Gellman, "Poetry of Spirituality," and Norman Lamm, "Harmonism, Novelty, and the Sacred in the Teachings of Rav Kook."

31. See his comment on Shemot 20:8:

> ולכן מצות עשה גדולה ממצות לא תעשה כמו שאהבה גדולה מהיראה כי המקיים ועושה בגופו ובממונו רצון אדוניו הוא גדול מהנשמר מעשות הרע בעיניו.

> It is for this reason that a positive commandment is greater than a negative commandment, just as love is greater than fear, for he who fulfills and observes the will of his Master with his body and his possessions is greater than he who guards himself from doing that which is not pleasing to Him.

It is noteworthy that the discussion is placed within the context of, and with reference to, the categories of servitude.

32. See *Guide*, 3:52.
33. Cited from an extensive interview with him, published in *De'ot*, 3 (February, 1999; שבט, תשנ"ט), p. 12.

Chapter 7

Contemporary Impediments to *Yirat Shamayim*

Other participants in this year's Orthodox Forum colloquium have been assigned the stimulating and inspiring task of coping with one of the most central and august aspects of the religious life, in general, and of *Yahadut*, in particular: *yirat shamayim*.[1] Theirs is the analysis of content, both denotative and connotative; the nice perception of nuances, carefully honed and delineated; the definition of the phenomenon *per se* as well as the description of its interactive relation to proximate concepts; the limning of its own contours and the determination of its position within the broader spiritual landscape.

Mine is, alas, a sorrier lot. I have been charged with the survey and analysis of impediments to the attainment of this lofty goal — presumably, of such as exert this influence perennially as well as those which are characteristic of the contemporary context. I am not, however, complaining. Would that this were, at the practical plane, a non-topic. Would that adherence to familial and communal spiritual patrimony were the order of the day and deviant defection from the traditions of *Knesset Yisrael*, a rare exception. However, one need not be steeped in sociology to perceive how tragically different is our current reality. Even unencumbered by statistics, any knowledgeable observer, residing בתוך עמי, "within my [own] people," is painfully aware of the magnitude of the problem and its ramifications, whether in Israel or the Diaspora. Ignoring the issue would thus constitute irresponsible pretense, and its confrontation becomes a matter of duty — painful, but duty nonetheless.

Moreover, at issue is not only possible desertion but, equally, the impact upon dilution and desiccation of religious experience of those firmly entrenched within the fold. And here, I find myself in excellent company. Students of Rav Mosheh Haym Luzatto's classic, *Messilat Yesharim*,[2] will recall that his discussion of the qualities of *zehirut* and *zerizut* — of care and alacrity, respectively — is capped by a survey of the elements which impede the optimal attainment of these virtues and of the need to avoid these. Ramhal could, in turn, have looked for precedent, amongst Rishonim, to that premier blend of *musar*, pietism, and philosophy, Rabbenu Bahye's *Hovot Ha-Levavot*,[3] which follows a similar procedure with respect to its topics.

Finally, my charge does entail a modicum of definition, however cursory and rudimentary, after all. Obviously, we can hardly identify and analyze impediments without some elucidation of what is being impeded. Hence, in our case, this self-evident proposition impels a preliminary discussion of the meaning of *yirat shamayim*. Broadly speaking, the term admits of three distinct senses. At one plane, it denotes a specific *mizvah* — catalogued as such in familiar *pesukim*: את ה' א-לקיך תירא ואתו תעבד ובשמו תשבע — "Hashem, your God, you shall fear, Him you shall serve, and by His name you shall swear." Or again: את ה' א-לקיך תירא אתו תעבד ובו תדבק ובשמו תשבע — "Hashem, your God, you shall fear, Him you shall serve, unto Him you shall cleave, and by His name you shall swear;"[4] enumerated amongst the list of *taryag* [613 commandments]; defined with reference to content and characteristics, and contradistinguished from parallel norms, such as the commandments to emulate the *Ribbono shel Olam*, to love Him, and to serve Him. והמצוה הד', the Rambam predicates, היא שצונו להאמין יראתו ולהפחד ממנו ולא נהיה ככופרים ההולכים בשרירות לבם ובקרי אבל נירא ביראת ענשו בכל עת וזהו אמרו את ה' א-לקיך תירא.

> And the fourth [positive] commandment is, that He has commanded us to affirm His awesomeness, and to fear Him, and we shall not be as infidels who pursue their hearts' desires wantonly. Rather, we shall fear His retribution at all times; and this is the import of "Hashem, your God, you shall fear."[5]

At a second plane, the term refers to the impetus motivating overall religious experience and observance. In this sense, *yirah* is posited as an alternative to *ahavah*; and it is generally perceived as an inferior alternative, love being deemed as preferable to fear or even awe as an incentive to the religious life. Thus, while in dealing with love and fear as specific *mizvot*, the Rambam in no way grades them, but simply postulates, האֵ-ל הנכבד והנורא הזה מצוה לאהבה וליראה אותו — "This august and awesome God, we are commanded to love and fear"[6] — when, in the concluding chapter of *Sefer Madda*, he discusses their respective roles as energizing and moving worship he emphatically endorses *avodah me-ahavah*, "service out of love" as the prime and desired mover, and relegates *avodah mi-yirah* to the religiously unsophisticated and uninitiated.[7] The invidious comparison, we note, has its roots in Hazal. It appears, for instance, with regard to different levels of *teshuvah*;[8] and, in a personal vein, is the focus of discussion concerning the quality of Iyov's and Avraham's service of God.[9]

At yet a third plane, *yirat shamayim* does not merely denote the impetus to religious being but, rather, refers, comprehensively, to its overarching scope — to a life of faith, service, and obedience, actualized in accordance with divine will. Thus, Rav Yohanan cites Rabbi Elazar's sweeping assertion, אין לו להקב"ה בעולמו אלא יראת שמים בלבד — "In this world, the *Kadosh Barukh Hu* has only *yirat shamayim*,"[10] the gamut of specific norms certainly not being excluded. Similarly, the statement that הכל בידי שמים חוץ מיראת שמים — "All is in the hands of Heaven, but for *yirat shamayim*"[11] — obviously embraces the totality of religious observance as beyond the pale of deterministic fiat. Indeed, the Rambam went so far as to postulate that the exclusion refers to the totality of freely willed human activity, even palpably neutral choices being presumably weighed in the light of spiritual alternatives, and with an eye to possible ramifications:

וכל מעשה בני האדם בכלל יראת שמים הם וסוף כל דבר ודבר ממעשה בני האדם בא לידי מצוה או עבירה

The entire range of human activity is included within *yirat shamayim*, as, ultimately, each and every human act entails [an aspect of] *mizvah* or *averah*. [12]

Hence, in dealing with impediments to *yirat shamayim*, we shall need to approach the topic from a multiplanar perspective. That perspective is also in order with reference to the historical period under consideration. The formulation of my specific topic, "Contemporary Impediments to *Yirat Shamayim*," was obviously grounded with an eye to the modern era. And this, I presume, for two possible reasons. First, it is the scene within which we live and work — and, hence, of greatest interest and relevance to ourselves. Second, the formulation was probably also based on the supposition that the phenomenon was particularly prevalent in the modern world, so much more secularly oriented than the preceding Renaissance, medieval, or classical periods. The issue is therefore more pressing, and the need to cope with it especially challenging and urgent.

The factual assumption is, obviously, a virtual truism. The assertion of man at the expense of God (to invert a phrase once coined to encapsulate Jonathan Edwards' thought) characteristic of much modern culture and the concomitant emphasis upon the attainment of personal gratification within the temporal world, as that within which, in Wordsworth's terms, "we find our happiness or not at all," has palpably and radically altered the context of religious existence and influenced the conditions for its realization. Moreover, the post-Emancipation emergence of most of Jewry into the mainstream of general — and, particularly, Western — culture, has changed the character and direction of much of *klal Yisrael*, specifically, and therefore has impacted upon both its disaffected and committed components. Hence, the pursuit of *yirat shamayim* and the barriers to its achievements have assumed a more acute dimension.

These observations border, again, on the platitudinous. And yet, we need beware of exaggeration. Impediments to religious faith, sensibility, and lifestyle were not patented by Voltaire or Comte, by Spinoza or Y.L. Gordon. They are inbred within human nature, inherent within patterns of culture, the primary categories familiar from time immemorial. They are endemic to the fabric of the soul, part and parcel of כי יצר לב האדם רע מנעריו — "For the desire of his heart is evil from his youth,"[13] or of Kohelet's observation, אשר עשה הא-לקים את האדם ישר והמה בקשו חשבונות רבים — "God made man upright, but they have sought out many complexities,"[14] on the

one hand; and to דרך ברייתו של אדם להיות נמלך בדעותיו ובמעשיו אחר ריעיו וחבריו
ונוהג כמנהג אנשי מדינתו — "It is natural for man to be drawn, with respect to
his traits and actions, after his friends and peers, and to conduct himself in
accordance with local practice,"[15] and we need no exposure to Augustine
or Aristotle to acknowledge these facts.

Indeed, the course of danger has been clearly anticipated and
described by the Torah. Within the exposition of the significance of the
mizvah of *zizit*, we encounter a *pasuk*, familiar from our recitation of *keriat*
shema: והיה לכם לציצת וראיתם אתו וזכרתם את כל מצות ה' ועשיתם אתם ולא תתרו אחרי
לבבכם ואחרי עיניכם אשר אתם זנים אחריהם — "It shall constitute *zizit* for you, and
you shall see it, and you shall remember all of Hashem's commandments,
and you shall not stray after your heart and after your eyes after whom
you fornicate."[16] The Rambam, followed by the *Sefer Ha-Hinnukh* and the
Semag, read the conclusion of the *pasuk*, upon which he comments, as a
negative imperative:

> ועל ענין זה הזהירה תורה, ונאמר בה ולא תתורו אחרי לבבכם ואחרי עיניכם אשר אתם
> זנים כלומר לא ימשך כל אחד מכם אחרי דעתו הקצרה וידמה שמחשבתו משגת האמת

> And with respect to this matter, the Torah has admonished us, as is
> stated in it, "And you shall not stray after your heart and after your
> eyes after whom you fornicate." To wit, that each of you should not
> be drawn after his own limited understanding and imagine that his
> thought has attained the truth;[17]

and he enumerated it, accordingly, within the list of *mizvot lo taaseh*.

His predecessor, Rav Saadya Gaon, had not included it in his list,
and it has been reasonably suggested[18] that he interpreted the reference
to possible straying as a rationale for *zizit*, in light of pitfalls it helps avoid,
rather than as an independent admonition.[19] On either reading, however,
the anticipatory concern over a lapse in commitment is evident.

With an eye to a point I suggested earlier, I believe the concern
here expressed is not confined to apostasy or the abjuration of halakhic
commitment, fundamentally and comprehensively. There are, of course,
contexts, which admonish against such extreme developments, aptly rep-
resented by a *pasuk* familiar from the *parshah* of *shema*: השמרו לכם פן יפתה

לבבכם וסרתם ועבדתם אלהים אחרים והשתחויתם להם — "Beware for yourselves lest your heart be diverted and you shall deviate and worship other gods and prostrate yourselves before them."[20] To my mind, this is not the case, however, with respect to our *pasuk*. It includes, rather, impact upon the quality of religious life — attrition which erodes the vitality of faith and observance, allure which saps content and conviction. It includes, that is, the gamut of contemporary impediments under our consideration.

Of particular note is a second exegetical detail. Rashi, possibly on the basis of a midrash, explains: העין רואה והלב חומד והגוף עושה את העבירה — "The eye sees, and the heart desires, and the body enacts the transgression."[21] According to this interpretation, the *pasuk* deals with a single continuum, visual allure tempting the viewer into passional desire — and, thence, possibly into halakhic violation. However, the gemara in Berakhot cites a different view:

> דתניא אחרי לבבכם זו מינות וכן הוא אומר אמר נבל בלבו אין א-לקים אחרי עיניכם
> זה הרהור עבירה שנאמר ויאמר שמשון אל אביו אותה קח לי כי היא ישרה בעיני אתם
> זונים זה הרהור עבודה זרה וכן הוא אומר ויזנו אחרי הבעלים.

> "After your heart" — this [refers to] heresy, as is written, The knave says in his heart, There is no God. "After your eyes" — this [refers to] sinful [sexual] rumination, as is written, And Shimshon said to his father, take her unto me, for she has found favor in my eyes. "You fornicate" — this refers to idolatrous rumination, as is written, "And they fornicate after the Baalim."[22]

This is likewise paralleled by a comment of the Sifre,[23] *ad locum* (presumably, the gemara's source), albeit with a different exemplifying prooftext.

On this reading, the *pasuk* does not deal with sequential phrases of a single failure, but, rather, with multiple dangers, relating to varied areas of religious life and different wellsprings of religious lapse.[24] The Ramban adopted this interpretation, with slight modification, but localized it:

> ואמר ולא תתורו אחרי לבבכם, להזהיר ממנה שלא יטעו בה...זו האפיקורסות...שלא
> יהרהרו מן התכלת באפיקורסות או בעבודת גלולים, אבל יהיה לכם הכל לציצית
> וראיתם אותו וזכרתם.

> And it states, "And you shall not stray after your heart," as referring
> to heresy, to forewarn us with regard to it…that the *tekhelet* should
> not induce heretical or idolatrous thought, but, rather, that it should
> be all as fringes which you will see and be stirred to remembrance."[25]

Surprisingly, the Ramban understands that the projected danger is not that
of general religious failure, but, rather, that which might, prospectively,
derive from the *tekhelet*. To these strings — given their unique character,
to which the Ramban addresses himself earlier, as the fusion of all colors
(much as physical science regards white light today), as endowed with
profound teleological significance, and out of its azure affinity with sea,
sky, and the *kisei ha-kavod*[26] — one might attach problematic mystical and
metaphysical qualities, associated with pagan culture; and it is against this
tendency that the Torah forewarns.

It is a strikingly original interpretation, but one which, for our purposes, largely eviscerates the *pasuk* as a relevant source. Given the more
conventional understandings of the gemara and the Sifre, however, we are
here introduced to the psychological and existential patterns which will
help us classify impediments to *yirat shamayim*; to ideological wanderlust
and passional concupiscence, respectively. I assume, for our purposes,
that the terms, *hirhurei averah* or *zenut*, need not be understood in their
narrower senses, as denoting thoughts of fornication or sexual license, but
can be read as referring to libidinous lust, generally — or, even beyond
that, to material desire, which competes with the committed religious life,
distracts a person from its realization, and distances him from the Creator.
At one plane, the Jew, as *homo religiosus*, is confronted by the allure of
material gratification, by the beck and call of the flotilla of sirens of the
order of *hayyei sha'ah*, the realm of temporal bliss. These vary greatly.
They of course include carnal experience in the narrow sense of the term,
the satisfaction of physical needs and aspiration, in response to urges,
both bestial and human, at the level of need, comfort, or luxury. However,
they also include less visceral elements, more social or passional than
appetitive — power, status, opulence, leisure — as well as the blend of
the carnal and the passional typified by sexuality. At a second plane, the

aspiring Jew encounters obstacles more closely related to the quest for *hayyei olam*, whether the attraction of alternate religions, enticing by dint of ritual pageantry or social provenance, or the impact of ideology and speculation which poses philosophic difficulty.

These are the archetypal impediments, material and spiritual, to the optimal attainment of *yirat shamayim*. To these may be added elements, such as esthetic pleasure, especially music, which straddle both realms. Taken collectively or even independently, these are formidable dangers under the best of circumstances. However, each unquestionably has been reinforced within the modern context. On the material side, the concern with creature comfort, and the faith — at least, within the West — that it could be significantly attained, have increased measurably; and the scientific and technological revolution, animated by Bacon's conviction that "knowledge is power" and the relative mastery of nature as the fruits which that revolution has wrought, are self-evident as agents of that concern.

That revolution, more than welcome *per se*, has, however, exerted an ancillary negative impact upon instinctive religious sensibility. Religious existence is significantly interwoven with a sense of dependence. At the philosophic and theological plane, it manifests itself in the Rambam's assertion that only divine existence is independent, in contrast with all else: שכל הנמצאים צריכין לו והוא ברוך הוא אינו צריך להם ולא לאחד מהם — "For all existent [entities] need Him, and He, blessed be He, does not need them or any of them."[27] Existentially and psychologically, it expresses itself in a sense, alternately, of need and reliance. Emphasis upon this factor is frequently related with Schleiermacher, who almost identifies religion with absolute dependence, but antecedents are plentiful, and roots in our tradition are clear. The Maharal, for instance, in explaining why *tefillah* is denominated *avodah*, dwells upon its link to dependence:

אבל התפלה מורה שהאדם נתלה בו יתברך...שכל ענין התפלה שהוא מתפלל אל השם יתברך לפי שהוא צריך אל השם יתברך נתלה בו ית׳ ואין קיום לו בעצמו כי אם בו יתברך ולכך מתפלל אליו על כל צרכו

But prayer indicates that man is dependent upon Him, blessed be He... For the whole substance of prayer is that he [i.e., the *mitpallel*] prays to Hashem, blessed be He, because he needs Him and is dependent upon Him, and has no independent personal existence but through Him, blessed be He. Therefore He prays to Him with respect to all his need.[28]

He, in turn, may very well have looked to a familiar *pasuk* in Tehillim:

הנה כעיני עבדים אל יד אדוניהם כעיני שפחה אל יד גברתה, כן עינינו אל ה' א-לקינו עד שיחננו

Behold, as the eyes of servants unto the hand of their masters, as the eyes of a maidservant unto the hand of her mistress, so our eyes are unto Hashem, our God, until He will grace us.[29]

At the human plane, Dostoevsky's Grand Inquisitor could have opted for rejecting the trade-off of liberty for economic security. Vis-à-vis the *Ribbono shel Olam*, however, the basic human condition — and *a fortiori*, the basic Jewish condition — is defined by the terms of a servitude which holds man in bondage to his Master and Provider.

Scientific progress, has, however, eroded the sense — and, from a certain point of view, possibly also the reality — of human dependence. As Bonhoeffer noted, "The world which has attained to a realization of itself and of the laws which govern its existence is so sure of itself that we become frightened."[30] In an admittedly lesser vein, according to some Rishonim, a similar problem arose millennia ago, and spiritual leadership took steps to cope with it. The gemara in Pesahim, citing a passage from the Tosefta, states that among the initiatives undertaken by Hizkiyahu which earned the approbation of contemporary Torah scholars was the banning of medical books. The gemara gives no reason, but Rashi explains:

לפי שלא היה לבם נכנע על חולים אלא מתרפאין מיד

Because their heart was not subdued over the sick, as they were cured immediately.[31]

The Rambam went out of his way to criticize and even ridicule this attitude;[32] and we are inclined to agree with him, as I presume few if any today would readily assent to abandoning state-of-the-art medical care, when available. However, the basic religious issue is real, and positive as we may be about the humanitarian benefits of science, we cannot but lament the concomitant illusion of self-reliance and the vitiation of the sense of dependence.

The erosion of this sense is, in part, endemic to the modern scene as a whole — a function of the infrastructure which, in industrialized societies, enables even the poor to reap some benefits of a system which confers upon them, in areas such as health and sanitation, benefits of which the Croesuses of two centuries ago could barely dream. For many, however — particularly, in the West — the process is often both accelerated and exacerbated by affluence. I have neither the inclination nor the right to indulge in railing against the pitfalls of opulence. Nevertheless, without risking the hypocrisy of such moralizing, one can simply note the obvious fact that the amenities afforded by affluence as well as the self-image buttressed by it, may often reduce one's reliance upon divine sustenance. The theme recurs in Sefer Devarim, whether as anticipatory admonition — פֶּן תֹּאכַל וְשָׂבַעְתָּ...וְרָם לְבָבֶךָ וְשָׁכַחְתָּ אֶת ה' אֱ-לֹקֶיךָ — "Lest you eat and be sated...and your heart shall then be uplifted, and you shall forget Hashem, your God"[33] — or, as prophetically retrospective narrative: וַיִּשְׁמַן יְשֻׁרוּן וַיִּבְעָט, "And Yeshurun waxed fat, and rebelled."[34] And it appears, enunciated by a suppliant anxious to avert spiritual lapse, in the penultimate chapter of Mishlei: רֵאשׁ וָעֹשֶׁר אַל תִּתֶּן לִי...פֶּן אֶשְׂבַּע וְכִחַשְׁתִּי וְאָמַרְתִּי מִי ה' — "Give me neither poverty nor riches...Lest I be sated and abjure, and say 'Who is Hashem?'"[35] The scenario I am herewith discussing, does not, again, necessarily deal with outright apostasy or religious defection. The prospect of attrition induced or stimulated by material prosperity is, in its own right, grave enough. Optimally, in *tefillah*, even the wealthiest are suffused by a sense of need, as the archetype of תַּחֲנוּנִים יְדַבֶּר רָשׁ, "A pauper pleads,"[36] prescriptive as well as descriptive, characterizes their prayer no less than that of the indigent. That reality requires, however, an exercise of will and imagination not always readily attainable.

The extension and amelioration of life has been accompanied, moreover, by a change in outlook and sensibility. Other-worldliness which could be expressed to the strains of a danse macabre while a plague decimated

Europe, has been largely supplanted by affirmation. Bentham's identification of happiness and the good with the pursuit of pleasure has not gone without serious challenge; but, at the popular plane, utilitarian ethics are inlaid to an extent unthinkable in medieval culture. For all the levity and the traces of ribaldry in some of the *Canterbury Tales*, and despite Arnold's complaint over the lack of "high seriousness of noble purpose," Chaucer could conclude with a prayerful epilogue, in which he expresses the hope that he will attain divine forgiveness for "my giltes, and namely of my translacions and enditinges of worldly vanities, the which I revoke in my retraccions."[37] Two centuries later, Sir Philip Sidney, his career as an Elizabethan courtier notwithstanding, could open his final sonnet with the exhortation, "Leave me, O love which reachest but to dust,/And thou my mind aspire to higher things;" and conclude it with a parting assertion: "Then farewell, world; thy uttermost I see;/Eternal Love, maintain thy life in me."[38] Modern counterparts would strike a very different note.

The possible impact of this change upon the level and quality of *yirat shamayim* should be obvious. It may be sharply exemplified by reference to remarks of Rabbenu Bahye ben Asher. Under the rubric of *yirah* in his compendium, *Kad Ha-Kemah*, he addresses himself to the relation between Kohelet's initial nihilistic assessment that all is *havel havalim*, "vanity of vanities," with the concluding affirmation, סוף דבר הכל נשמע את הא־לקים ירא ואת מצותיו שמור כי זה כל האדם — "In sum, when all has been considered; Fear God and observe His commandments, for that is the whole of man;" and he comments למדך בזה כי לא תתכן היראה זולתי אם יהביל ויבזה ענייני העולם הזה — "This is to instruct you, that *yirah* is inconceivable unless one condemns and despises the matters of this world."[39] Few modernists would accept this sweeping assertion *in toto*. Precisely for that reason, however, it is, for our purposes, noteworthy.

The change in the philosophic climate is even more marked; and here we confront not only issues concerning the quality of *yirat shamayim* within the context of commitment but the loss of religious identity, ranging from "honest doubt" to secularization and apostasy. Arnold's contrast between a culture in which "The Sea of Faith/Was once, too, at the full," and his own context, of which he asserts, "And we are here, as on a darkling plain/Swept with confused alarms of struggle and flight/Where ignorant armies clash by night,"[40] is, in its lament over the loss of certitude, both familiar and typical.

Here, too, the impact of science has been crucial; and this, in several respects. At one level, it has often challenged the verities of Torah across a broad front, particularly with regard to factual issues. Harnessing the methodology and claims of various disciplines — physical, historical, and linguistic — its practitioners and advocates have often sought to cast a pall over the integrity and veracity of sacral texts and classic tradition; and while much of the battle was fought in earlier centuries, from Spinoza to Spencer, and has, to an extent, subsided, its echoes are still part of the current scene.

The influence of scientism has, however, extended beyond factual assertion and has encroached upon sensibility. As cultural historians have not tired of noting, as Dante's neat three-story geocentric cosmos has given way to modern conceptions, the prospect of the tyranny of Tennyson's "hundred million years and hundred million spheres," often arousing more stupor than wonder, has, quite apart from issues concerning the age of the universe, undermined the sense of man's worth and of his relation to ultimate reality. And this has often affected *yirat shamayim* directly. Confronting a universe supposed by Einstein to be thirty-five billion light years in diameter, it is difficult to experience the sense of direct *amidah lifnei ha-Melekh*, of standing directly before the *Ribbono shel Olam*, so essential to *yirah*.

In a third vein, the scientific approach has imprinted upon the minds of many a kind of practical empiricism, whereby the canons of judgment are identified, be it subliminally, with palpable proof, logical or sensual. In principle, such a mindset is inimical, if not antithetical, to *emunah*, as is manifest from a passage in Bava Batra. The gemara narrates that, in the course of a homiletic discourse, Rav Yohanan projected that, at some future juncture, the *Ribbono shel Olam* would bring huge precious stones and place them in the gates of Jerusalem. The size seeming to him fantastic, a student ridiculed him. Subsequently, the latter embarked on a voyage, in the course of which he encountered angels hewing precious stones of the predicted size; and upon inquiring as to their destination, he was informed that they were to be positioned at the gates of Jerusalem. Upon his return, he approached his master and exclaimed: דרוש רבי לך נאה לדרוש כאשר אמרת כן ראיתי — "Hold forth, my rav! It is befitting for you to hold forth! Just as you stated, I have seen." Whereupon Rav Yohanan responded: ריקא אלמלא ראית לא האמנת מלגלג על דברי חכמים אתה — "Scoundrel! Had you not seen, you would not have believed. You ridicule the words of the sages."[41] While *Yahadut* does not foster fideism, it clearly rejects positivism. It is precisely that, however, which many modernists, even such as to whom the philosophic nomenclature may be totally foreign, imbibe from the passive and symbiotic absorption of prestigious scientific premises and habits. Hence, in this respect too, scientism may impede *yirat shamayim*.

The potential straying "after your heart" is not confined, classically or contemporaneously, to sciences, however. The *minut* in question may also derive from humanistic culture — indeed, more directly so. The possible ravages of philosophy, as decried by variegated pietists, are too familiar to require elaboration; but, in our connection, we may nevertheless single out two distinct dangers to *yirat shamayim*. The first is full-fledged *minut* proper, raising the banner of skeptical inquiry as a point of departure and, at times, adopting heretical or agnostic theses at conclusion. At this level, the upshot may be total defection. Absenting that, however, there still lurks the lesser danger of spiritual or emotional desiccation, inhibiting profound religious experience, whether out of an erosion in the capacity for awe and wonder — that "cold philosophy" of which Keats lamented that it "will clip an Angel's wings/Conquer all mysteries by rule and line/ Empty the haunted air, and gnomed mine/Unweave a rainbow"[42] — or whether the restraint it often preaches brakes all powerful spiritual experience. As regards the last point, literature — particularly, "the literature of power" — presumably poses no problem and should even serve to compensate. Obviously, however, authors have their own agendas, explicit or implicit, which may not coincide with a Torah *hashkafah*; and literary imagination is often currently harnessed for the production of so much which is both religiously and morally deleterious.

At the heart of the contemporary accretion to both *aharei levavkhem* and *aharei enekhem* lie two distinct and yet related factors. The first is the homocentric character of much modern culture — even of its religious component. At one plane, we are witness to an overwhelming emphasis upon human welfare and desire, however defined, as the *telos* of the good life. At another, liberal doctrine ensconces man — preferably, individual man — as the arbiter of moral and theological truth, in the face of traditional authority. Quite apart from the specifics of a particular contretemps, the concomitant defiance may be inconsonant with fostering the humility so critical to meaningful *yirat shamayim*. This tendency is greatly exacerbated by the thrust of postmodern theory and practice. While its character may intensify certain modes of religion, the subjectivist bias encourages a heterodox *elu va-elu* which leads to an unbounded doctrinal no man's land, devoid of dogmatic content or commitment. *Yirat shamayim*, however, demands both.

The second factor is that which the *mizvah* of *zizit* is explicitly intended to counteract. The Torah explains that it is geared to inculcating remembrance of the entire complex — וזכרתם את כל מצות ה' ועשיתם אתם — "And you shall remember all the *mizvot* of Hashem and implement them."[43] The implication that the spiritual dragon to be confronted is obliviousness is clear. The Torah addresses itself to this issue in various contexts, through both normative admonition and narrative rebuke: השמר לך פן תשכח את ה' א-לקיך — "Beware, lest you forget Hashem, your God," at one pole, and צור ילדך תשי ותשכח א-ל מחללך — "The Rock who begot you, you ignored, and forgot God who bore you,"[44] at another. The topic has, however, a distinctly current dimension. Secular modern culture does not so much rebel against the *Ribbono shel Olam* as it ignores Him. Its model is not Hazal's portrait of Nimrod — so called, they suggest, because יודע רבונו ומתכוין למרוד בו — "He knows his Master and [yet] intends to rebel against Him;"[45] nor Aeschylus' Prometheus, nor Milton's Satan. It is, rather, that of less heroic and less magisterial figures, engrossed in serenely, perhaps complacently, conducting their affairs, without reference to divine order. "*Je n'ai pas besoin de cette hypothèse*," replied Laplace when asked why he had omitted God from his treatise, *Mécanique Celeste*. For religious modernists who do not, of course, wholly omit, the core besetting sin is היסח הדעת, obliviousness[46] — not that which, Heaven forfend, denies heretically, but such as is content with feeble fulfillment of the Rema's opening codicil in *Shulhan Arukh*: שויתי ה' לנגדי תמיד הוא כלל גדול בתורה ובמעלות הצדיקים אשר הולכים לפני הא-לקים — "'I have always set Hashem before me' — this is a grand principle regarding Torah and the levels of the righteous who walk before God."[47] The feebleness *per se* constitutes, however, a serious impediment to *yirat shamayim*.

I have focused upon spiritual impediments — in part, because of personal orientation and predilection, and, in part, because I regard them as the most critical. Unquestionably, however, one can note others as well, of a more sociological character. Just how attractive the world of *yirat shamayim* is — culturally, ethically, even, to a point, esthetically — may impact significantly. How young people, in particular, are treated by family, teachers, peers, or the general community; the nature of the interpersonal stimuli and/or provocation to which they are exposed; the *kiruv* of embrace without conquest, the degree of understanding and empathy they encounter on their religious odyssey — all may exert profound influence upon the course of their experience and development.[48] None of this can or should be denied. At the extreme, these may make the difference between sustaining or abandoning commitment. However, even where basic identity does not hang in the balance, here too, the quality and level of Torah existence frequently does. "If one is angry at the *hazzan*," runs a Yiddish adage, "one does not answer *amen*."

Hazal were well aware of this element; and they counseled accordingly: לעולם תהא שמאל דוחה וימין מקרבת לא כאלישע שדחפו לגחזי בשתי ידיו — "One should always distance [a disciple] with the left and draw [him] near with the right, unlike Elisha who pushed Gehazi with both hands."[49] Moreover, I was once struck by the addendum of a *mashgiah* of one of the preeminent haredi *yeshivot ketanot*, to the effect that, given our prevalent cultural climate and rising student expectations, the guideline should be amended to dictate two-handed *kiruv*.

I freely acknowledge the relevance of these factors; and any attempt to cope with religious attrition at the public plane must clearly take them into serious consideration. However, they raise a host of halakhic, educational and communal issues which lie, I believe, beyond my present mandate and, to some extent, possibly, beyond my expertise. I return, therefore, to my more narrowly defined area of primarily personal confrontation.

In this connection, with an eye to both the narrower and the broader senses of *yirat shamayim*, we may distinguish between four separate levels of contemporary impediments to its attainment. The most comprehensive is emotional atrophy, the inability to feel deeply and sensitively about almost anything — especially, of a spiritual nature; the personality of a lotus-eater of sorts, unruffled and uninspired, marked by lassitude and insouciance, issuing in, or bred by, radical ennui.

At a second level, we may note an individual fully capable of powerful emotion, both positive and negative, but tone deaf to the quintessence of *yirat shamayim*: reverence. He may love and hate, he may aspire and labor, he may even admire and appreciate — but all under a low ceiling. If he is pragmatically oriented, and if he believes sufficiently in the cardinal tenets of natural religion, the existence of God and reward and punishment, he may attain *yirat ha-onesh*, the fear of retribution. But if he lacks the capacity for reverence, for anything or anyone, he is, with respect to the higher strains of *yirat ha-romemut*, the "awe of majesty," a spiritual cripple.

One rung higher, we can encounter a person endowed with the capacity for reverence, but lacking the ability or the desire to perceive its unique content within the context of the divine and transcendental. Awed by the grandeur of human creativity, cosmic mystery, or, like Kant, by the moral law, he is nonetheless insensitive to *sui generis* response to *sui generis* reality. He does not fully appreciate the import of *yihud Hashem*, in its qualitative sense, and, hence, does not apprehend the sense of the singularly numinous. Finally, within our own community, there exist those who, whether floundering or assertively self-assured, may be religiously motivated in universal terms, but not attuned to the particularistic context of *Yahadut*, not sufficiently convinced that *Mosheh emet ve-torato emet*, "Mosheh is true, and his Torah true." Whereas the previous class is marked by taints of idolatry, these decline or defect, tinged by skepticism or agnosticism.

Modes of response to these levels, and strategies capable of coping with them, obviously vary. One cannot compare a loyal but superficially complacent votary with a troubled and teetering soul, perhaps anxiously seeking to find God and to believe in Him, but riven by philosophic doubt and unable to make the leap of faith. Attitudes need to differ, the means to vary, and in counseling individuals or groups, we clearly take this into account. However, if a general comment may nonetheless be advanced, across the board, we need to pay special attention to the spiritual — or, if you will, the experiential — dimension. It is not that we have over-intellectualized faith. It is, rather, if such a term exists, that we have under-emotionalized it. Oblivious to Coleridge's crucial distinction, we have often been satisfied to identify it with belief. I trust that I shall not be misunderstood. I am deeply committed to serious *talmud Torah*, crucially important *per se*, as both a major aspect of *avodat Hashem* and a means to its enhancement. The sense that בראתי יצר הרע ובראתי לו תורה תבלין — "I have created an evil desire, and I have created Torah as its antidote,"[50] ascribed to the *Ribbono shel Olam*, is, for me, not just an authoritative dictum but an existential axiom. *U-le'ovdo zeh talmud* — "To serve Him — this refers to [Torah] study."[51] Its value and effectiveness is, however, very much a function of its experiential character; and that, in turn, depends, in no small measure, upon its emotional quotient. Ambivalence and shallowness flourish when *devekut* has withered or passion has waned.

We are particularly challenged by a simple fact — upon reflection, perhaps obvious, and yet, in a sense, singular and incongruous. I introduce it on a semi-homiletic note. With respect to the commandment to love God, *be-khol levavekha*, the mishnah, noting the use of *levav* as opposed to *lev*, observes: בכל לבבך בשני יצריך ביצר הטוב וביצר הרע — "With your whole heart, with both the good and the evil desires."[52] Its intent is clear. Even potentially destructive and aggressive energies, properly sublimated and channeled, can be harnessed into service as an element in the soul's quest for *ahavat Hashem*. Analogously, the admonition against being misled by straying after *levavkhem*, may be equally inclusive, urging us to beware not only of what tempts our darker visage but of what appeals to the child of light in us, as well; of what may be grounded in positive virtue and yet, in sum, may affect *yirat shamayim* adversely, nonetheless. Paradoxically, at times we sow gentle breezes and reap the whirlwind.

The phenomenon is manifest in a number of areas — and this, with respect to values which may either clash with *yirat shamayim* or compete with it. A case in point, at the most fundamental level, is the premium upon the development of personality. We — more the *ben Torah* in us, than the modernist — are not content with training our children or ourselves to bring our faculties to bear upon coping with the quandaries of life and its vicissitudes. We strive to mold the self, proper — to maximize ability, to extract and exploit the potential immanent, by divine gift, in our inner core. We share the Greek passion for *paideia*, as an educational and civic ideal — and this, out of religious aspiration, as an end in itself, rather than merely as a means to inculcate or improve the capacity for dealing with issues. *Baalei ha-mussar* speak incessantly of the responsibility to build *kohot ha-nefesh* [traits of the soul], beyond activating or energizing them; and this emphasis is an integral part of our authentic collective tradition.

Moreover, we encourage, as part of this process, a stress upon dynamism and vibrancy: man as agent — *gavra* in contrast with object — *hefza*. This is reflected in the extraordinary emphasis upon will as the epicenter of the self; and, in the tradition of the Rambam, free will, postulated as both experienced reality and desideratum, and not just as a dogmatic tenet. Free will is the linchpin of the entire halakhic universe, the basis of the normative demand which confronts the Jew or Jewess at every turn. The exercise of choice, with respect to a plethora of minutiæ is central as both means and end. In the process of energizing consciousness, we mold it. Not for us is the immolation of the will idealized in certain mystical traditions. The capacity for choice, is, to us, a quintessential aspect of that humanity which enables us to serve the *Ribbono shel Olam* and submit to Him.

And yet, *alyah ve-koz bah*. The course may boomerang. The capacity for chosen spiritual aspiration may issue, instead, in vaulting secular ambition. The more powerful the personality, the graver the potential for rebellion, the stronger the passion for independence, the greater the reluctance to submit. The *kabbalat ol malkhut shamayim* of the docile may be less attractive or even significant, but it is probably more secure.

Moreover, an energized but undirected or misdirected will is a dangerous loose cannon. This prospect is graphically reflected in a remarkable passage in Yirmiyahu. In the wake of a passage full of dire prognosis, it is anticipated that *Knesset Yisrael* will respond by inquiring how or why it has incurred divine wrath; and the *navi* is instructed, speaking on behalf of God, to expound the causes:

והיה כי תגיד לעם הזה את כל הדברים האלה ואמרו אליך על מה על־ה׳ עלינו את כל הרעה הגדולה הזאת ומה עוננו ומה חטאתנו אשר חטאנו לה׳ א‑לקינו. ואמרת אליהם על אשר עזבו אבותיכם אותי נאם ה׳ וילכו אחרי אלהים אחרים ויעבדום וישתחוו להם ואותי עזבו ואת תורתי לא שמרו

And it shall come to pass, when you will tell this people all these matters, and they shall say to you: "Wherefore has Hashem pronounced all this great evil against us? What is our iniquity and what the sin that we have committed against Hashem, our God?" And you shall say to them: "Because your fathers have forsaken Me, speaks Hashem, and they have pursued strange gods, and they have worshipped them and bowed to them, and Me they have forsaken and disobeyed my Torah."

This brief catalogue — including idolatry, the abandonment of God, and the obliviousness to Torah — would seem reason enough. And yet, the *navi* continues, there is a further overshadowing surfeit:

ואתם הרעתם לעשות מאבותיכם והנכם הלכים איש אחרי שררות לבו הרע לבלתי שמע אלי.

And you have done worse than your forefathers, each directed by the inclination of his evil heart, so that you didn't listen to Me.[53]

Arbitrary will, evidently conceived as not merely the perpetrator of specific sins but, rather, as the dynamic engine of rebelliousness impelling to sin, is placed beyond idolatry and the rejection of Torah, *in toto*.

Much the same message is projected in an earlier context, at the personal plane. Within the context of his farewell address, Mosheh Rabbenu anticipates a prospective rebel whose self-assured response to threatened punishment will be insouciance:

שלום יהיה לי כי בשררות לבי אלך

Peace will be with me, as I shall pursue the inclination of my heart.[54]

The imprecations anticipated for him in the subsequent *pesukim* attest boldly to the gravity with which the Torah regards a life governed by *sherirut lev*. Hence, inasmuch as the stronger the "heart," the greater the potential for just such a life, the bolstering of personality and of will, as its dynamic principle, engenders the risk of enabling rebelliousness. This is not to imply that such a result is inevitable. Properly channeled, a rich personality can be invaluable towards both sustaining fundamental fidelity and enhancing the quality of religious experience, its reverential component included. As the semantics of the adjective "strong-willed" attest, the danger is there, however, and it suffices to warrant the inclusion of our cherished development of personality and its volitional powers as a possible impediment to the advancement of *yirat shamayim*.

In a kindred vein, a similar scenario may be envisioned with respect to the intellectual sphere. Here, too, we deal with abilities much valued by ourselves, in the Torah world no less than in the academic. Even those who do not subscribe to Rambam's equation of *zelem E-lokim* with intelligent *daʾat*,[55] accord it a central place in the definition of humanity and recognize its contribution to religious existence. Explaining the position of the plea for *daʾat* as the first of the petitional Berakhot in *shemoneh esreh*, the Yerushalmi observes: אם אין דיעה תפלה מניין — "If there is no reason, whence prayer?"[56] Hence, the overriding emphasis upon study as a value, and the development of the capacity and the desire to study as central to spiritual growth.

Moreover, this emphasis is not confined to passive learning and the accumulation of knowledge. It includes the ability, so plaintively sought in the *berakhah* preceding *keriat shema*, *le'havin u-le'haskil*, "to understand and to perceive."[57] Almost inevitably — particularly, in the modern context — this entails inculcating and encouraging a modicum of critical perspective, as regards both the reading of texts and the analysis of concepts, which, in turn, fosters a measure of independence.

Here, too, then, we risk encounter with a golem who may turn upon his creator and/or mentor; with forces which, once unleashed, may reduce an educator to the role of the sorcerer's apprentice. As the primeval serpent well knew — and this was crucial to his temptations, as appealing to spiritual pride, no less than to sensual appetite — *da'at* opens access to knowledge, and knowledge is power, not only in Bacon's sense, as enabling a measure of human mastery over man's natural environment, but as providing and possibly encouraging spiritual autonomy. That autonomy is, however, precisely what possibly distances man from the Creator, undermining *yirat shamayim* at its root.

Within the modern context, the phenomenon is all too familiar, probably requiring no explanatory exemplification. Nevertheless, I cite one incident which has stuck in my memory. Addressing a Mizrahi audience in the fifties, the Rav zt"l almost waxed lyrical as he sang the praises of critical analysis as a central aspect of the process of *lomdut*; expounding how, upon encountering an opinion of, say, Rabbenu Tam, the aspiring *lamdan* is not content with integrating the material, but confronts Rabbenu Tam with the need for a supportive rationale, etc. Then, evidently intuiting whence this trend could lead, he raised his voice, and, interceding, exclaimed:

רבותי, ציהט נישט קיין פאלשע מסקנות!

Gentlemen, don't draw any false conclusions!

He did not amplify and he did not qualify, but the brief interposition put the concern with maintaining the tensile balance between different and potentially conflicting values into bold relief. It is a concern which any surveyor of current impediments to *yirat shamayim* inevitably shares.

The same pattern is evident in yet a third realm — the moral. Morality, natural or revealed, is central to our *Weltanschauung*, and its organic integration with the world of faith a primary tenet. It relates to the Scriptural description of the *Ribbono shel Olam* — א־ל אמונה ואין עול צדיק וישר

הוא — "A God of fidelity without iniquity, righteous and upright is He."[58] And, at the human plane, it constitutes a prime *telos* of personal growth and educational effort. Moreover, in this area, we are not content with assuring response to normative charges. We seek to mold ethical sensibility — a feeling for both justice and mercy, a sense of tragedy, compassion for suffering and deprivation. Yet, this very sensibility and its attendant scruples may make it difficult to understand, or to come to terms with, details or even whole areas of Halakhah which, *prima facie*, may be jarring, as inconsistent with it.

Similar considerations are germane with respect to an ethic of a different character. I have previously touched upon the issue of excessive worldliness, and noted its negative impact upon spirituality, in general, and *yirat shamayim*, in particular. The perennial question of how to relate to the world bears, however, a more fundamental aspect; and, at that plane, we — certainly, those of us with some modernist inclination — are basically positive. Despite significant nuanced differences, both the Rav and Rav Kook, the twin polestars of our *hashkafah*, shared this perception. The Rav, in particular, distanced himself from the polarities of James's categories of world-acceptance and world-rejection, and insisted upon world-redemption. That, too, however, is grounded in fundamental affirmation. We categorically reject Augustine's view of the natural order as *massa perditionis*, regarding that conception as inconsonant with the declaration,

וירא א-לקים את כל אשר עשה והנה טוב מאד

And God surveyed all that He had made and, behold, it was very good[59]

— that evaluation remaining valid even after human lapse into sin. Our admiration for the *Kad Ha-Kemah* notwithstanding, we certainly do not share its author's contention that meaningful *yirat shamayim* can only be attained by disengagement from the temporal world and refusal to ascribe any value to it.

Involvement we do not treat as a neutral option but as a sacred challenge, as part of our duty to discharge the universal mandate of *le'ovdah u-le'shomrah*, to advance the divine goal — לא תהו בראה לשבת יצרה — "He created it [i.e., the world] not as a waste; He formed it to be inhabited."[60] And we both heed and take heart from the authoritative voice of the Rambam: שאין ראוי לאדם שיעסוק כל ימיו אלא בדברי חכמה ובישובו של עולם — "It is not fitting for a man to engage all his days in anything but matters of wisdom and the development of the world."[61] Yet, here again, this charge, so appealing to us, ideologically and psychologically, may open the door to the excesses of worldliness, inviting the lament of Wordsworth's familiar sonnet: "The world is too much with us; late and soon, / Getting and spending, we lay waste our powers; / Little we see in Nature that is ours." That we assuredly reject. No Jew could accept the sonnet's subsequent preference for being "a pagan, suckled in a creed outworn." But the concern over the loss of spirituality — "We have given our hearts away, a sordid boon!" — we surely share.[62]

In one sense or another, the foregoing quartet can be subsumed under the comprehensive rubric of religious humanism; and what has been said of each component, with reference to our commitment and the relevant caveats regarding the respective concerns, might be stated with an eye to the category as a whole. *Yahadut* is, in one sense, profoundly humanistic. This quality is reflected in at least three distinct areas. Perhaps foremost among them is the esteem accorded man, whether considered independently, as expressed in the doctrine of *zelem E-lokim*, or as regards his position within the created cosmic order. Second, we note the centrality accorded human needs and aspirations within the core halakhic corpus. Finally, the sensitivity to human welfare is manifested in the criterion for defining exigencies which warrant deviation from that corpus. "*Ha lamadta*," as the Rambam explains with regard to *pikuah nefesh* overriding Shabbat,

שאין משפטי התורה נקמה בעולם אלא רחמים וחסד ושלום בעולם

Hence, you have learned that the ordinances of the Torah are not [meant to serve] vengeance in the world, but, rather, [to serve] mercy, lovingkindness, and peace in the world.[63]

And yet, that humanism, fraught with possibly dangerous overreaching, is guarded. Esteem is tempered by the contrast of frailty bordering on nothingness with transcendental majesty and power; and the danger of anthropomorphism is proactively anticipated by the preventive prohibition against graven images. Regard for human welfare, for its part, is constantly pitched within the context of man's servitude to God. And so the axiological balance is struck, charting a course subsequent generations would do well to follow.

We need to note, additionally, however, another recent impediment, regarded by its devotees not as a dilution of *avodat Hashem* but as its optimal realization; one which does not challenge basic commitment to Torah and *mizvot* but undercuts the specific strain of *yirah*, in favor of an overriding and almost exclusive concern with *ahavat shamayim*. As previously noted, the priority of *ahavah* to *yirah* as the motive force of the religious life is grounded in Hazal; and it is conceivable that some Rishonim held that this superiority obtains even when we deal with the two as independent *mizvot*. However, at times, the relative neglect of *yirah* stems from the human psyche more than from textual and theological sources. The sense of proximity and warmth and the desire for it — in part, the basis of *ahavah* and, in part, its product — is far more comforting and reassuring than the sense of distance and recoil experienced in *yirah*; hence, the gap in emotional appeal. Many, C.S. Lewis has somewhere noted, do not want a Father in Heaven, but rather a Grandfather in Heaven. Oblivious to Hazal's critique of חברותא כלפי שמים, "familiarity with respect to Heaven,"[64] they are, in Carlyle's phrase, "at ease in Zion."

The phenomenon has numerous manifestations, ranging from great leniency with respect to halakhic issues concerning utterance of divine names or Berakhot to pronouncements regarding the respective identities of God and man which, to say the least, border on the blasphemous. Perhaps the most prominent, however, is the trend towards neo-Hasidic modes of worship, focused upon a quest for spirituality to which the strains of *ahavah* are most conducive. As I have written in a previous Forum volume,[65] I do not regard this quest as problematic *per se*; and, properly channeled and balanced, it can be quite positive. However, in the absence of such balance — and it is to such absence that we are often witness — the negative impact upon *yirat shamayim* can be grave.

Given the data, we — individually and communally, as *ovdei Hashem* and as spiritual mentors — are confronted with a serious dilemma. If values to which we adhere and attitudes we advocate contribute to the contemporary impeding of *yirat shamayim*, ought we change course or, at least, reduce the degree of our advocacy? Perhaps, one reflects, we need to reexamine and reorient our *hashkafah*; or, falling short of that, acknowledge that, while we continue to regard it as valid and deeply Jewish, it is possibly insufficiently suited to meeting the challenge of contemporary conditions, intellectual and social.

Self-evidently, the upshot of such a possible assessment can, *a priori*, move us in one of two antithetical directions. One option, perhaps not so much focused on the values I have noted as with an eye to the impact upon practical halakhic observance, is to challenge the thrust of this paper — and, in a sense, of this conference. We have posited *yirat shamayim* as a major desideratum and, hence, have sought avenues to enhance and encourage it. We have not, by and large, correspondingly explored possible negative religious fallout. It is sometimes contended, however, that the persistent pursuit of such a sublime but abstract ideal may undercut halakhic commitment, as punctilious attention to minutiæ may be disdained as paltry in comparison with lofty and comprehensive goals. Consequently, it is argued, religious stability and fidelity is better served by greater stress upon observance, even at the expense, conscious and subconscious, of concomitant diminution of harping upon *yirat shamayim*.

I acknowledge that this prospect is indeed possible, and, moreover, that it has, at times, materialized. Nevertheless, such a contention, while well-motivated, is, from our standpoint, essentially misguided. It is grounded upon a Christian, and possibly antinomian, conception of the composite spiritual self and of the character of the halakhic order. *Yahadut* is not content with a self-image which assigns a premium to law, to the neglect of spirituality. It contends that, fundamentally and ultimately, the spiritual cause proper is advanced by normative response and discipline. Admittedly, it doesn't always work out as such, but that is part of our abiding faith: פקודי ה' ישרים משמחי לב — "The commandments of Hashem are right, rejoicing the heart;" לא נתנו המצות אלא לצרף בהן את הבריות — "*Mizvot* were but given in order to purge [human] creatures."[66] Whatever our perception of local pitfalls, any grand spiritual strategy grounded upon the opposition of the harmony between catharsis and discipline is, from a Torah standpoint, objectionable.

The alternate reassessment, the possibility that cherished humanistic directions should be toned down in the interests of promoting *yirat shamayim* raises fewer issues of principle, but the prospect of the need for it is painful to contemplate; hence, the sustained hope and even faith that it can be averted. On this point, no one who knows me needs to be told where my predisposition lies. The values in question are such as I have imbibed from childhood; which during the span of over half a century, I have sought to internalize and disseminate. My instincts and aspirations, as both a striving *oved Hashem* and as a *mehannekh*, are all very much in favor of retaining these emphases; and, as I survey the educational and sociological landscape, in Israel as well as in the Diaspora, I sense that the need for them has magnified rather than lessened.

And yet, there is a proviso. Ever mindful of Hazal's priority, *yirat het'o kodemet le'hokhmato*,[67] both temporally and axiologically, we need to insure the proper balance between the components I have cited and the overarching ideal, both normative and experiential, of dominant *yirat shamayim*. It shall profit us little, as individuals or as a Torah community, if we build worlds but dilute the *unum necessarium*.

Ideally, therefore, we ought opt for sustaining and enriching our multifaceted spiritual and cultural heritage, while concurrently taking heed that it flourish within the context of abiding and pervasive *yirat shamayim*. If I may invert Carlyle's comment upon the quest for happiness, we shall maintain the denominator but seek to increase the numerator.

We shall persist in our adherence to religious humanism, but in a spirit of utter humility, never lapsing into the mode of apotheosis which Toynbee rightly criticized as the fatal flaw and besetting sin of Greek culture. We shall be faithful to the spirit of the whole of the eighth *tehillah* — to the query of מה אנוש כי תזכרנו ובן אדם כי תפקדנו — "What is man that

You are mindful of him, and the son of man that You think of him?" and the concluding declaration, ה' אדנינו מה אדיר שמך בכל הארץ — "Hashem, our Lord, how mighty is Your name throughout the earth," no less than the intervening catalogue regarding human majesty and dominion: ותחסרהו מעט מאלהים...כל שתה תחת רגליו — "You have made him barely lower than the angels... You have put all under his feet."[68] We shall preach the dignity of man, but ever mindful, as were the great Renaissance humanists, of the potential for evil inherent in freedom and of the need to maximize striving towards realizing his sanctity.

We shall persist in cultivating moral sensibility, but with the profound sense that where we encounter difficult terrain, after we have walked the extra mile, we humbly but thoroughly submit to divine norm and wisdom. That is the gist of the crucial test of the *akedah*, the conjunction of responsive *hinneni* with tremulous fear and trembling.[69] Recognizing that Avraham was commanded to sacrifice his judgment as well as his son, we note it was only this total readiness which earned him the designation of *yarei*:

כי עתה ידעתי כי ירא א-לקים אתה ולא חשכת את בנך את יחידך ממני

> For now I know that you are a God-fearer, inasmuch as you have not withheld your son, your only son, from Me.[70]

We shall continue to shy away from the perception of life, and of the world within which it is realized, as largely an interminable minefield; viewing it, instead, as an arena of opportunity — in Keats' celebrated phrase, "a vale of soul-making." Hence, we shall encourage and celebrate human creativity, while constantly internalizing and instilling the awareness of its source: וזכרת את ה' א-לקיך כי הוא הנתן לך כח לעשות חיל — "And you shall remember Hashem, your Lord, for it is He that gives you the strength to accomplish."[71] We shall drill home the message that success does not negate dependence, and that total self-reliance is a snare and a delusion. טוב לחסות בה' — "It is good" — morally, psychologically, and, above all, religiously — "to rely upon Hashem."[72]

Further, we shall not denigrate *yirah* in the interest of spiritual ease

and psychological comfort. Rather, we shall live and act out of the profound sense that fear and joy, tremor and love, are, vis-à-vis the *Ribbono
shel Olam*, intertwined and reciprocally fructifying. This sense was one of
the linchpins of the Rav's religious thought and experience; and, as such,
its ample and nuanced elucidation served as one of the foci of *U'vikashtem
Mi-sham*. Moreover, it has been developed with reference to another spiritual quality — in certain respects, quite distinct from *ahavah*, and yet, in
others, closely allied with it, so that it provides a measure of analogy: joy.
שמחה מיט יראה געפלאכטן אין איינעם — *mori verabbi*, Rav Hutner zt"l, was
wont to sing on Purim, אחוץ ביי איז נישטא ביי קיינעם.[73] One might entertain
some question regarding the claim to exclusiveness, but the genuineness
of this fusion within Torah is beyond doubt. And it was well formulated
by one of the Rosh Yeshiva's polestars, Rav Avraham Eliyah Kaplan:

> היראה לא צער היא, לא כאב, לא דאגת תמרורים. ומשל למה היא דומה? לרטט יראתו
> של אב על בנו הקטן האהוב לו, בשעה שהוא מורכב על כתפו והוא רוקד עמו ושוחק
> לפניו, להיות נזהר בו שלא יפול. יש כאן שמחה שאין דומה לה, עונג שאין דומה לו.
> והיראה הנעימה כרוכה על עקבם.

> *Yirah* is neither anxiety, nor pain, nor bitter worry. What does it
> resemble? The tingle of the concern of a father for his beloved young
> son while he carries him on his shoulders, dances with him and plays
> with him, to be careful of him lest he fall. You have here incomparable
> joy, incomparable gratification. And pleasurable concern is entwined
> with them.[74]

The semi-frolic conjured up in the description may seem exaggerated. But
the basic theme is essentially sound. It is a clear reflection of the conjunction implied in twin *pesukim*: עבדו את ה' ביראה; עבדו את ה' בשמחה — "Serve
Hashem with fear;" "Serve Hashem with joy."[75]

Finally, we shall of course persist in immersing ourselves in serious
talmud Torah, and revel in the dialectic of passive absorption and energetic
creativity therein. We shall do so, however, pervaded with Hazal's sense
that its worth and even legitimacy is conditioned upon its conjunction
with *yirat shamayim*, serving not only as a prelude and context but as a
suffusive concomitant component:

מה להלן באימה וביראה וברתת ובזיע אף כאן באימה וביראה וברתת ובזיע

Just as there [i.e., at Sinai], with trembling and fear, with tremor and trepidation, so here [the process of learning Torah] too.[76]

Sans *yirah*, on their view, Torah study may be not only worthless but inimical.[77]

It is a tall order: a large agenda, and an equally large proviso. *Yirat shamayim* is a key value in its own right and the key to so much else. The wisdom — and, to an extent, the right — of maintaining a rich and variegated spiritual and cultural life is, in great measure, conditioned upon the quotient of awe and awareness of divine presence which suffuses it. At the educational plane, perhaps a differential approach to programming should be more seriously considered, with the ability to maintain an appropriate level of *yirat shamayim* a central variable. At the personal and communal plane, we pray daily for divine assistance in neutralizing impediments to *yirat shamayim*. May we do our share, that we may be worthy of His.

Notes

1. This paper focuses upon my assigned topic with reference to the specific context of Jewry, and accordingly utilizes much halakhic material. The core issues are, however, by no means insular, and I trust that much of the discussion, *mutatis mutandis*, has universal bearing as well.
2. See chaps. 5 and 9, respectively.
3. See, e.g., 2:6, 4:7, 7:7.
4. Devarim 6:13 and 10:20.
5. *Sefer Ha-Mizvot, asei*, 4.
6. Yesodei Ha-Torah, 2:1.
7. See Teshuvah, 10:1–2, 5–6.
8. See Yoma 86b.
9. See Sotah 27b, 31a.
10. Shabbat 31b.
11. Ketubbot 30a.
12. *Teshuvot Ha-Rambam*, ed. Y. Blau (Jerusalem, 1960), sec. 436 p. 715.
13. Bereshit 8:21. I find some difficulty in translating *yezer*, which I have rendered as "desire." J.P.S. has "imagination" while Artscroll, similarly, renders "imagery." These, however, miss the passional and/or moral element, so prevalent in Hazal's use,

entirely. The Septuagint has *dianoia* while the Vulgate, analogously, has *cogitatio*. These, however, strike me as too intellectualistic. I have therefore preferred "desire," to be understood as the capacity to will rather than as a specific wish.

14. 7:29. The term חשבונות, which I have translated as "complexities," may also have ethical connotations of an element of deviousness.

15. Deòt, 6:1.

16. Bamidbar 15:39. In other contexts, the verb, תור, is neutral, denoting exploration. However, here it clearly implies spiritual deviation, and I have translated it accordingly. The last term in the *pasuk*, זנים, can have narrow literal meaning, regarding lascivious sexual behavior — more specifically, adultery; see Yevamot 61b — or broader metaphorical import. I have rendered it more literally, but with the intent that metaphor should be read into the translation.

17. Avodat Kokhavim, 2:3.

18. See Rav Y.F. Perlow's remarks in *Sefer Ha-Mizvot Le'Rav Sa'adya Gaon*, 2:6b.

19. Regarding similar interpretations of such a construction in other contexts, see the Rambam's *Sefer Ha-Mizvot*, Shoresh 5, and the Ramban's comments thereon.

20. Devarim 11:16. The apostasy anticipated in this *pasuk* is not quite identical with the modern sense of the term, abandonment of faith, as dual allegiance was, in biblical times, much more common, although not, as Eliyahu's challenge amply attests, a legitimate halakhic option.

21. Bamidbar 15:39, s.v. *ve-lo*. For possible antecedents, see the texts cited in *Torah Shelemah, ad locum*; Yerushalmi, Berakhot, 1:5.

22. Berakhot 12b.

23. Sifre, Shelah, ch. 9, on Bamidbar 15:39. Commenting on this text, the Netziv notes:

> אין לפרש שלא יהיה מין ממש שהרי כבר כתיב וזכרתם את כל מצות ה' קלות וחמורות אף כי
> עון מינות...אבל לפי הפשט ה"פ שלא ילמדו דברים הבאים לידי מינות המושכים את האדם ...
> וכל לימוד הפילוסופיא וחקירה בדברים המסוכנים נקרא בשם זה.

> This should not be taken to refer to outright heresy, for the verse has already stated, "And you shall remember all the *mizvot* of God" — minor and major — which surely encompasses heresy.... Rather, the proper interpretation is that you should not study matters which may lead to heresy, which draw man's heart away. And all study of philosophy and delving into dangerous matters is included in this category. (*Emek Ha-Netziv ad locum.*)

24. The interpretation of the *pasuk* may be intertwined with a specific halakhic issue, as to whether it contains a single injunction, with two alternate details, or a pair of independent prohibitions. The Behag, in his list of personal *mizvot*, only cites *aharei levavkhem*, and this has invited some discussion amongst Aharonim as to whether two *issurim* might have been counted. See *Hakdamat Sefer Halakhot Gedolot*, in *Sefer Halakhot Gedolot*, ed. N.Z. Hildesheimer (Jerusalem, 1987), pp. 45–46, and the notes thereon. However, the question may also depend on premises concerning

the principles which govern the count of *mizvot*. See the Rambam's *Sefer Ha-Mizvot, Shoresh* 9. In this connection, note that the Rambam cites both *aharei eineikhem* and *aharei levavkhem*, and yet only enumerates a single injunction.

25. Bamidbar 15:39, s.v. *ve-amar*.
26. See Menahot 43b.
27. Yesodei Ha-Torah, 1:3.
28. *Netivot Olam*, *"Netiv Ha-Avodah,"* ch. 3. The link between servitude and service, as two senses of *avodah*, is pervasive in this *netiv*, and implicit in this passage.
29. Tehillim 123:2.
30. Dietrich Bonhoeffer, *Letters and Papers from Prison* (London: Collins, Fontana Books, 1959), p. 107.
31. Pesahim 56a, s.v. *ve-ganaz*.
32. See his *Perush Ha-Mishnayot*, Pesahim, 4:10. Ordinarily, this commentary is of course confined to the mishnah. However, the Rambam states that the issue is so crucial and the view under discussion, [i.e., Rashi's], so grievously erroneous, that he cannot but denounce it.
33. Devarim 8:12,14; and cf. ibid, 6:10–12.
34. Ibid, 32:15.
35. Mishlei, 30:8–9. Cf. *Mesillat Yesharim*, ch. 1.
36. Ibid, 18:23. At the level of *peshat*, the *pasuk* is of course commenting upon ordinary interpersonal discourse. Hazal, however, applied it to *tefillah*, as well. See Devarim Rabbah, 2:3.
37. The epilogue, entitled under the heading, "here taketh the makere of this book his leve," follows the *Tales* and, in standard editions, is printed after them. Its sincerity has been much debated; but even if it be read as lip service, which I doubt, it stands as a sign of the times.
38. "Astrophel and Stella," sonnet 110.
39. S.v. *yirah, Kitvei Rabbenu Bahye*, ed. Rabbi C.B. Chavel (Jerusalem, 1970), pp. 192–93.
40. "Dover Beach."
41. Bava Batra 75a.
42. "Lamia," 2:234–37.
43. Bamidbar 15:39.
44. Devarim 8:11 and 32:18, respectively.
45. Rashi, Bereshit 10:9.
46. In halakhic nomenclature, this term has a fairly defined meaning, denoting a situation in which a datum is left untended, unattended, and out of mind, for whatever reason. Thus, one is enjoined from *hesah ha-da'at* with respect to *tefillin* while wearing them. Or, even more rigorously, sacral food, such as *terumah* or *kodshim*, which is the subject of *hesah ha-da'at*, may not subsequently be eaten; and a parallel standard disqualifies a red heifer from serving as a *parah adumah* if it has been similarly

ignored. In our context, however, I use the term in its broader attitudinal sense, as
insouciance grounded in distance, the absence of attention reflecting, if not disdain,
at least a lack of relation or need.

47. *Orah Haym*, 1:1. The *pasuk* cited is from Tehillim 16:5.

48. These issues have been discussed extensively in a recent book by Faranak Margolese,
    Off the Derech (Jerusalem, 2005).

49. Sotah 47a. Gehazi, whom Hazal regarded very negatively — see Sanhedrin 90a and
    107b — is a more extreme example, but the principle has broad application. The depth
    of Hazal's feelings on the issue may be gauged from their readiness to single out Elisha
    for criticism.

50. Kiddushin 30b.

51. Sifre, Ekev, sec. 5, on Devarim 11:13. The remark is paralleled by adjacent comments
    which posit *korbanot* or *tefillah* as the referents of *avodah*.

52. Berakhot 54a.

53. Yirmiyahu 16:10–12.

54. Devarim 29:18. It is noteworthy that no modifying adjective appears here, willfulness
    as such being excoriated.

55. See his *Guide*, 1:12.

56. Yerushalmi Berakhot 4:4.

57. The phrase also recurs in the Rambam's characterization of Talmud; see Talmud
    Torah, 1:11.

58. Devarim 32:4.

59. Bereshit 1:31.

60. Bereshit 2:15 and Yeshayahu 45:18, respectively.

61. Gezelah Va-Avedah, 6:11.

62. Some have suggested — in certain respects, not without justification — that this facet
    is more acute in Israel than in the Diaspora, inasmuch as ideals of national service
    and visions of historical destiny compete with more narrowly religious commitments.
    On this view, the potential inherent in presence in *eretz ha-kodesh* and its proximity
    to *Shekhinah* may, for some, be counterbalanced by other factors. I believe that this
    is indeed the case; but the topic and its possible ramifications require fuller treatment
    than I can give here.

63. Shabbat 2:3.

64. Berakhot 34a.

65. See my contribution, "Law and Spirituality: Defining the Terms," in *Jewish Spirituality
    and Divine Law*, eds. A. Mintz and L. Schiffman (New York: Ktav, 2005), reprinted as
    chapter 6 in this volume, 175–202.

66. Tehillim 19:9, and Bereshit Rabbah, 44:1, respectively. Cf. Rambam, *Guide*, 3:26;
    Ramban, Devarim, 22:6; and Maharal, *Tiferet Yisrael*, ch. 7, who, in contrast with the
    Ramban's moral thrust, casts the purgation in question in largely metaphysical terms.

67. Avot 3:9. The mishnah speaks of *yirat het* rather than *yirat shamayim*. The relation between the terms requires exploration, although, at times, they appear to be used interchangeably; see, e.g., Shabbat 31b. This issue lies beyond my present scope, however. It is noteworthy that the mishnah is not content with asserting that, while the wisdom will flourish, the religious dimension will be deficient. It states that the wisdom itself will, in due time, decay.

68. Tehillim 8:5–10. The intermediate description could be read as part of the question, i.e., the Psalmist marvels why, given the relative insignificance of man, he has been so graced. Even on this reading, however, the admiration for man's station is manifest.

69. The word, *hinneni*, appears in the text before the reason for God's call has been specified. In light of the sequel, however, it can be understood as total readiness nonetheless.

70. Bereshit 22:12. The relevant issues are self-evident and they have spawned a substantial literature. I content myself with calling attention to a particularly stimulating and incisive chapter in Emil Fackenheim, *Encounters between Judaism and Modern Philosophy* (Northvale, N.J., 1994), ch. 2.

71. Devarim 8:18.

72. Tehillim 118:8.

73. "Joy and *yirah*, intertwined as one / Other than by Jews is found in no one." The text was composed at a relatively early stage, but was printed in פחד "בעל למרן הזכרון ספר יצחק" זצ"ל (ירושלים, תשד"מ) קב-ג.

74. בעקבות היראה: דברי מחשבה (ירושלים תש"ך), יב.

75. Tehillim 2:10 and 100:2, respectively. Of course, the specific manifestations of the two qualities may, and often should, vary, depending on circumstances or temperaments; see the comments in *Midrash Shohar Tov*, p. 100. However, the encompassing conjunction is a fundamental value.

76. Berakhot 22a. The question of the proper mindset for Torah study is highly interesting and important, but requires further treatment than I can give here.

77. See, particularly, Yoma 72b and the comments of Rabbenu Bahye on Devarim 30:15.

Chapter 8

Formulating Responses in an Egalitarian Age:
An Overview

This year's Orthodox Forum, convened under the rubric, "Formulating Responses in an Egalitarian Age," stands in marked contrast to its recent predecessors. They generally dealt with phenomena whose value and whose place in the world of tradition is clearly acknowledged, but whose specific Jewish character, as well as their relation to other elements, required analysis and definition. No one questions the importance of spirituality as a universal category or its concomitant position within *Yahadut*. Similarly, we all recognize the immanent character of toleration and its limits as an issue to be confronted and explored. Discussion of the conceptual approach to Jewish learning, more of an "insider topic," focused upon an area which is not only relevant to Jewish life but stands at its epicenter. Elucidation of the perception and parameters of authority is endemic to our understanding of any religious community. In all of these instances, we found ourselves coping with spiritual and intellectual problems whose resolution, inherently and *a priori*, would be part of any agenda to formulate a serious and comprehensive *hashkafah*.

If my antennae not deceive me, I sense that this is not quite our situation this year. Both the heading proper and some of the accompanying material convey the impression that we are confronted by a phenomenon, ideology and movement both, which somehow casts a pall over our world and its values; which is inimical to the traditional order and constitutes a potential threat to its stability and viability; which has a subversive and

corrosive impact upon the ideational content and the institutional fabric
of Orthodox Jewish life.

Conjoined to the first, one notes a second difference. Forum discussion has, generally, been just that — the exchange of knowledge and ideas
related to selected major themes, governed and coordinated in accordance
with a freely chosen agenda. "Response" takes some of the edge off the
internal dynamic and largely presupposes a stance vis-à-vis some external stimulus. That stance may of course be positive or negative, affirmative appreciation or heated rejoinder; but it is, in either case, somewhat
imposed. And what is most to our purpose, it may be manifested in two
distinct areas: discourse and action. At the theoretical plane, we shall
forge an ideological response by engaging in familiar intellectual dialogue.
In addition, however, we shall evidently strive to suggest and develop a
pragmatic and possibly programmatic response, as we assess the present impact of egalitarianism upon Jewish life and seek to influence their
prospective interaction. Response at that plane may of course vary markedly, and may include condescendingly benign stonewalling, vehemently
combative opposition, or empathetic openness on the road to reorienta-
tion and reappraisal. Whatever one's position, however, whether adamant
rejection or progressive adaptation, we shall find ourselves entering the
lists more than is our wont. The "free play of the mind," so admired by
Arnold, will, in all likelihood, be conjoined to the formulation of policy as
well as the mapping of strategy. Personally, together with Professor Stone,
I have been charged with focusing upon two questions. The first reads:
"How do we distinguish between ordinary halakhic processes responding
to new stimuli and calls for direct revision of a divinely inspired, permanently fixed, Torah?" This question can conceivably be understood in two
distinct senses. We may distinguish between two entities, creatively, by
establishing difference and relating variously to them, whether through
the innovation of whole categories or through the introduction of nuanced
criteria which transmute superficial similarity into a distinction with a
difference. Where others see no reason for differentiation, even when they
note disparate characteristics, a fertile mind will seize upon previously

unappreciated dissimilarity as a basis for apprehending contrast and for acting on that apprehension.

Alternatively, we may distinguish, passively, when categories and parameters are already well-defined but we must yet address ourselves to the task of recognizing under which rubric to classify a given entity — and this, not by drawing the conceptual lines of the class but, rather, by examining the content and contours of the unit. Here, we engage primarily in observation and perception, as we strive to discern the character of a phenomenon and to fasten upon its definitive qualities. Distinguishing in both senses is, of course, standard intellectual fare, the bread-and-butter of denizens of the *bet hamidrash* — and not only of the Brisker strain. They are, however, clearly different, and I should presumably clarify which is the mandate which has been thrust upon me — or, whether, perhaps, both are included. I do not pretend to plumb the depths of authorial intent, but I hazard the assumption that the question posed relates to distinguishing in the latter sense. Presumably, a committed Jew understands how to relate differentially, in attitude and in practice, to initiatives which seek to implement Torah, on the one hand, or to eviscerate it, on the other. He may not be familiar with the wording of the ninth of the Rambam's thirteen *ikkarim* —

והיסוד התשיעי הבטול, והוא שזו תורת משה לא תבטל ולא תבוא תורה מאת ה' זולתה ולא יתוסף בה ולא יגרע ממנה לא בכתוב ולא בפירוש אמר לא תוסף עליו ולא תגרע ממנו

And the ninth principle is that of [non] nullification; that is, that this Torah of Mosheh will not be nullified, and there will not come in its place a substitute Torah from God; there will be nothing added, nor diminished, from it, not in writing and not in explanation, as it says, "do not add to it or detract from it" —

or, its equivalent in *Mishneh Torah;*[1] and he may not have a catechetical mindset altogether. But, his ignorance of theology notwithstanding, he knows in his guts what has been the backbone of Jewish faith.[2] That faith in the abiding character of Torah as binding is the core of *emunah*, simple or sophisticated. There is, of course, discussion in Hazal as to whether any

element of Torah can be preempted, whether יש כח ביד חכמים לעקור דבר מן
התורה, "it is in the power of the Rabbis to uproot a biblical matter." This
should mislead no one, however. At no point does the gemara, Bavli or
Yerushalmi,[3] entertain the possibility that whole sections of the Torah
can be nullified — in order to relieve societal needs, to conform to the
Zeitgeist, or even to stimulate religious experience. Such a contention does
not even qualify, halakhically, as error, worthy of requiring an expiatory
sacrifice:

> אין בית דין חייבין עד שיורו בדבר שאין הצדוקין מודין בו אבל בדבר שהצדוקין מודין
> בו פטורין מאי טעמא זיל קרי בי רב הוא.

> The Court is not liable [for a sin offering] until they adjudicate a
> matter that the Sadducees do not concede; but as to a matter [ruling]
> to which [even] the Sadducees accept, they are exempt. What is the
> reason? Such [a point] is known to every school child.[4]

The discussion rather centers upon the limited authority to prescribe regulations with respect to detail which, in certain circumstances, will lead
to practical conclusions different from those mandated by primal Torah
regulations. At a theoretical plane, the situation is different with respect to
interpretations of Hazal and, *a fortiori*, of later links in the *mesorah*. The
Rambam held that, in this area, direct revision by properly constituted
authority was indeed a legitimate and viable possibility:

> בית דין גדול שדרשו באחת מן המדות כפי מה שנראה בעיניהם שהדין כך ודנו דין
> ועמד אחריהם בית דין אחר ונראה לו טעם אחר לסתור אותו הרי זה סותר ודן כפי מה
> שנראה בעיניו שנאמר אל השופט אשר יהיה בימים ההם אינך חייב ללכת אלא אחר
> בית דין שבדורך.

> The Great Court, which interpreted the Torah casuistically with one
> of the [received] methods [of interpretation] as it seems to them; and
> they ruled accordingly, and later another court arose and it saw reason
> to contradict [the interpretation of the first court] it may contradict
> and judge as it sees fit, as it says "To the judge who will be in those
> days" — you are obligated to follow the court which [exists] in your
> generation.[5]

But the committed Jew, instinctively and intuitively, knows how steadfast has been the historical fealty of *Knesset Yisrael* to Hazal; and, if he knows of this *pesak* of the Rambam at all, rightly senses that, inasmuch as the right to revise is restricted to a later Sanhedrin, its exercise is of millennial moment, of no immediate practical application. Distinction in the first sense, seems, therefore, fairly clear. Questions will obviously arise with respect to detail, but the broad outlines should be almost self-evident; and I doubt that it is to this task that we have assembled to address ourselves. Perceiving difference is, however, a subtler and trickier undertaking. While grosser contrasts pose no challenge, nicer nuances very often do. I know of no litmus test, simple or comprehensive, which could invariably give us satisfactory guidance, nor can I conceive of one. Primary general directions can, however, be pointed; and this, by analogy to a similar dilemma.

With respect to problematic prophecy, the Torah itself hypothesizes a quandary: וכי תאמר בלבבך איכה נדע את הדבר אשר לא דברו ה'?, "And if you will say in your heart — how will we know that which God did not speak?" And it goes on to posit a definitive criterion: אשר ידבר הנביא בשם ה' ולא יהיה הדבר ולא יבא הוא הדבר אשר לא דברו ה' בזדון דברו הנביא לא תגור ממנו, "That which the prophet will speak in God's name and that [predicted] event does not occur, that is the thing God did not speak; with malice that prophet has spoken, and do not fear him."[6] This test relates to the substance of the prophecy. That being the case, however, it only covers a limited class of situations. As Rashi noted:

ואם תאמר זו במתנבא על העתידות הרי שבא ואמר עשו כך וכך ומפי הקדוש ברוך הוא
אני אומר כבר נצטוו שאם בא להדיחך מאחת מכל המצות לא תשמע לו אלא אם כן
מומחה הוא לך שהוא צדיק גמור כגון אליהו בהר הכרמל שהקריב בבמה בשעת איסור
הבמות כדי לגדור את ישראל הכל לפי צורך שעה וסייג הפרצה לכך נאמר אליו תשמעון.

And if you say: this is so of one who prophesies concerning the future. What if he [the prophet] comes and says do such and such and from the Holy One, Blessed Is He I speak, they [i.e., his listeners] have already been commanded that if he comes to subvert one from [observing] any of the *mizvot*, do not listen to him, unless he is known to you as completely righteous, such as Eliyahu on Mt. Carmel who offered a sacrifice as the time when altars [other than that of the Temple] were forbidden, in order to correct Israel, all according to the need of the time, and to fill the gap [in observance]. Therefore it says, "Harken unto him."[7]

The solution which Rashi offers, focused upon the personality of the prophet, is grounded upon the conclusion of a brief discussion in the gemara:

היכא דמוחזק שאני דאי לא תימא הכי אברהם בהר המוריה היכי שמע ליה יצחק אליהו בהר הכרמל היכי סמכי עליה ועבדי שחוטי חוץ אלא היכא דמוחזק שאני.

Those cases in which he is recognized are different, for if you will not say so, Avraham at Mt. Moriah, how did Isaac obey him; Eliyahu on Mt. Carmel, how did [the Jews] rely on him to offer sacrifices [outside the Temple]; but where he is recognized [the case] is different.[8]

The gemara does not specify with regard to which qualities one is to be validated as *muhzak*. As we saw, Rashi's comment on the *pasuk* singles out piety, "that he is totally righteous." The Ramban is critical of this emphasis:

וזה איננו נכון בעיני שאין ההמחאה שהוא צדיק גמור אלא שהוא נביא אמת מוחזק לכל במה שהקדים לאמר עתידות ובאו והוא האות שלו כמו שהזכיר בפרשה הזו או המופת שעשה בפנינו וזאת חזקת הנביאים.

This seems to me incorrect. The ratification is not to the effect that he is totally righteous but, rather, that he is a true prophet, recognized by all, inasmuch as he has foretold future events which have then occurred; and this is his sign as is mentioned in this section, or if he performed a wonder in our presence. And this is, [generally], the certification of prophets.[9]

On his view, it is the veracity of past prophecy which is crucial. And indeed, in his *perush* on the gemara, Rashi cites two areas: שהוא צדיק ונביא אמת, "That he is a righteous and a true prophet."[10] The individual upon whom one relies to the point of accepting his authoritative decision to deviate temporarily from a halakhic norm must both be marked, generally, by saintly religious character and, specifically, have a track record as a prophet. This dual focus is distinctively relevant for the Rambam. Given his view that a prophet cannot merely be a vehicle for conveying messages, and his insistence upon the highest standards of moral rectitude, intellectual excellence, and religious intensity and depth as preconditions for prophecy, there is great coincidence between the personal and the functional aspects of the *muhzak*. Signs and wonders are not a sufficient condition to establish one's status as a prophet or to require others to heed his message:

ולא כל העושה אות ומופת מאמינים לו שהוא נביא אלא אדם שהיינו יודעים בו
מתחלתו שהוא ראוי לנבואה בחכמתו ובמעשיו שנתעלה בהן על כל בני גילו והיה מהלך
בדרכי הנבואה בקדושתה ובפרישותה ואחר כך בא ועשה אות ומופת ואמר שהא-ל
שלחו מצוה לשמוע ממנו שנאמר אליו תשמעון ואפשר שיעשה אות ומופת ואינו נביא
וזה האות יש לו דברים בגו ואף על פי כן מצוה לשמוע לו הואיל ואדם גדול וחכם וראוי
לנבואה הוא מעמידים אותו על חזקתו... ובדברים האלו וכיוצא בהן נאמר הנסתרות
לה' א-לקינו והנגלות לנו ולבנינו ונאמר כי האדם יראה לעינים וה' יראה ללבב.

Only a person of whom we knew beforehand, by his wisdom and his actions, in which he transcended all his peers, and he conducted himself in the ways of prophecy, and its sanctity and asceticism, who then came and performed a sign and a wonder, and stated that God sent him — with regard to him we are commanded to listen as it is written "Harken unto him." And it is possible that a sign or a wonder is performed by someone who is not a prophet, the signs having some arcane basis. Nevertheless, we are commanded to listen to him, inasmuch as he is a great and wise person, and qualified for prophecy, we predicate his legitimacy... With regards to these matters and the like we are commanded, "The secret things belong to the Lord our God, but those things that are revealed belong to us and to our children," and it is written, "For man looks on the outward appearance but the Lord looks on the heart."[11]

The acceptance of *nevu'ah* is grounded upon recognition of the *navi*. For the Rambam, this is true of response to all claims to prophecy; but it is doubly crucial when, as in the instances cited in the gemara in Sanhedrin, one is confronted by prophecy which is innovative and, in a sense, even deviationist. The same may be posited with regard to our question. "How do we distinguish between ordinary halakhic processes responding to

new stimuli, and calls for direct revision of a divinely inspired, permanently fixed Torah?" In two ways. At one plane, we test the substance of
suggested innovations. The halakhic universe was not created yesterday.
It has a long history, in the course of which methodology was refined,
canons of interpretation established, modes of evidence limned, a corpus
of relevant sources and their hierarchy defined. Some of these were set
down formally, as, for instance, the thirteen *middot* of the Torat Kohanim
or the thirty-two of Rabbi Eliezer ben Rabbi Yossi Hagelili. Other elements, more fluid in nature, evolved more flexibly; but these, too, within
certain parameters. Knowledge of where the frontiers lie and sensitivity
to their violation is, partly, acquired through theoretical formulation and
analysis. Primarily, however, it is imbibed through reverential immersion
in the tradition, whether through existential relation to its texts or, better
still, through immediate exposure to its current masters. The aphorism
גדולה שמושה... יותר מלימודה, "Its apprenticeship is greater then its study"[12]
is not confined to *pesak*. It is, however, surely crucial with respect to that
sensitive area — as regards the examination of *pesakim* no less than their
formulation.

The second test concerns the *posek* — and this, with reference to both
his learning and his spiritual persona. Unquestionably, some *pesakim* of
Rav Moshe Feinstein or Rav Shlomo Zalman Auerbach zt"l (not all of
which found their way into print), had they come from Rabbi X or Y,
would have raised eyebrows and possibly incited protest. Is this discriminatory? Superficially, yes; in a deeper sense, categorically not. With regard
to such giants, one knows that a decision issues out of a mastery of the halakhic corpus, imbedded in their bones no less than in their heads; that is
anchored in a nuanced intuition of the halakhic process and of how it bal-
ances normative mandates with human needs. Primarily, one knows that
it issues from a person of profound faith and abiding belief in the absolute
truth of Torah; one of overriding responsibility to the halakhic tradition
and its texts; one in whom the interpretation of Halakhah and its implementation unfolds within a context of pure submissive קבלת עול מלכות שמים,
"Acceptance of the yoke of the kingdom of heaven" and קבלת עול מצוות,
"Acceptance of the yoke of *mizvot*." One can securely respond affirmatively,

אליו תשמעון, "Listen to him," when one is fully confident of both the modality and the motivation of any innovative initiative. Without casting any personal aspersions, this dual test is not met by promulgators of clarion calls for "direct revision" of basic halakhic norms. Substantively, these often do not spring out of the tradition and its processes but contravene them — at times, in the name of progressive revelation, explicitly pressing for a drastic restructuring of the whole halakhic order, and not just for rescinding particular directives. Moreover, their impact is not cushioned by assuaging reassurance about the motivation. The calls, while at times issuing from persons fundamentally committed to the truth of Torah, and whose sincerity I have no desire to challenge, are nevertheless often fuelled by extraneous concerns and the felt need — admittedly, perhaps moral and religious, no less than societal — to conform to current philosophic vogue. At the very least, one is left with unease about the ideological and axiological basis of the balance between the permanent and the contemporary. Indeed, מוחזק שאני – שהוא צדיק ונביא אמת, "*Muhzak* (recognized) is different — that he is a righteous and a true prophet." At this juncture, the reader may very well ask: All is well and good, but what has this to do with egalitarianism? The modality of evaluation is presumably relevant to any problematic phenomenon. Indeed, I confess I am slightly perplexed myself. Could not the litmus tests suggested for distinguishing between varied responses in an egalitarian age be equally applicable to responses formulated in an agnostic or hedonistic age? Perhaps, I answer, what is anticipated is not a set of guidelines for distinguishing between others' responses, but, rather, a response of my own to egalitarianism which should, in some way, allow for adopting some of its contentions, through the *modus operandi* of ordinary halakhic processes, while yet steering clear of heresy. And yet, the question persists. Could not the same criteria, to be presumably postulated on this score — consistency with acknowledged methodology, consonance with the authoritative corpus, concern for values as well as norms — likewise direct any traditional response to hedonism? They certainly could. If, nonetheless, our assignment confronts us as it does, I suspect it is because we are, collectively, attracted, philosophically and pragmatically, by egalitarianism while sybaritic libertinism leaves us cold. We leave *carpe diem* to the Latins, but in the Declaration of Human Rights we find universal moral import. Hence, in this area, the critical task of winnowing the chaff from the wheat, when we consider that here may be wheat worthy of Menahot, assumes significant dimensions. We are therefore called upon to define, however briefly, our relation to contemporary egalitarianism, at the level of cardinal tenets and basic *hashkafah*. As I perceive it, egalitarian thought is characterized by three major themes, although these need not appear in conjunction. The first, and most fundamental, is the metaphysical uniformity of man. For secularists, this conception is virtually axiomatic, deriving from the nature of their total world-view.

Secularism is a leveling force. Metaphysically, it regards, and must regard, all places, all times, all objects, and all persons as inherently of a piece, as there is no basis and no source for radical differentiation. Disparity can only be functional and artificial, of a purely secondary order. For the religious egalitarian, uniformity is not *a priori* necessary, but he assumes its existence nonetheless as an article of faith, faith in the catholic brotherhood of man under the impartial fatherhood of God.

A second, less pervasive, theme, familiar from other contexts as well, is that of moral relativism. Radically expressed, this would entail the rejection of any ethical absolute whatsoever. In a more moderate vein, it would deny the concept of natural law, reduce mores to social convention, and leave, at most, a few overarching virtues such as love or justice, as ultimate values. Closely related, third, is the assertion of personal autonomy, with the individual firmly ensconced as the primary, if not the sole, arbiter of right and wrong. These basic philosophic premises militate, at the social and political plane, against preferential status for any person or priority for any ethos. They are the linchpins of an ideology which translates, in practice, into movement toward their implementation through pressure for social and political changes. Some of these changes are separable as independent initiatives, each with its local impetus. They are much reinforced, however, by a comprehensive systematic conceptual framework, whose adherents — over and above their concern with the pragmatic ramifications of perceived inequality and their quest for universal entitlement

— regard the bare fact of discrimination, regardless of its utilitarian consequences, as an outrageous spiritual abomination.

While egalitarianism is not exclusively, reciprocally, and inextricably bound to these premises — one could certainly conceive of an absolute, divinely revealed system which should be egalitarian in character and content — the presently prevalent strain is, I believe, very much grounded in them. If we ask ourselves where does *Yahadut* stand with regard to them, the answer is self-evident. Recognition of the uniqueness of man is central to our religious humanism; but so is the sense of metaphysical distinction. It inheres in the concept of *kedushah* — of place, time, object, and, above all, of *Knesset Yisrael*. That *kedushat Yisrael* is grounded in chosenness, the fusion of privilege and responsibility which underlies Jewish distinctiveness; and, it is, from our perspective, decidedly metaphysical. Even if one should side with those who contend, in the face of assorted *midrashim* that *behirat Yisrael* was not, *ab initio*, part of a providential scenario but, rather, the fruit of historical development, we nevertheless acknowledge that the choice, having been determined, broke fresh ground and created a distinctive level of intrinsic metaphysical status. Moreover, there are additional levels of *kedushah* within *Knesset Yisrael* proper, particular chosenness having been accorded *shevet Levi* and *kohanim*; and while merit can, for certain purposes, supersede them, ממזר תלמיד חכם קודם לכהן גדול עם הארץ, "A bastard who is a scholar takes precedence over a high priest who is an ignoramus,"[13] the categories are very much part of the halakhic order. Premises concerning ethical and religious relativism or ultimate personal autonomy are, if anything, even less palatable. Normative absolutes are the essence of Torah and our status as commanded spiritual beings the bedrock of our relation to the *Ribbono shel Olam*. Consequently, in relating to egalitarian ideology, there is no alternative to clearly recognizing and candidly asserting that, as a system, it is, for us, wholly untenable. However we may view certain specific initiatives, we cannot countenance the philosophic framework. In practice, where halakhically feasible and axiologically desirable, nuanced revisions, in the direction of either stringency or latitude, may lie in store. The frontiers of what, in this area, the Torah world regards, attitudinally and pragmatically, as acceptable or even preferable, may be tested anew, as the substantive significance of modes of conduct and our collective relation to them is altered contextually. Ideologically, however, we cannot encounter egalitarianism on its turf but, regardless of what is currently politically correct, must rather confront it with our own truth. Where it exists, we may note and even stress our own affinity with certain universal elements and egalitarian values; and we should explain the nature of *behirat Yisrael* and its demands. But we have neither the right nor the desire — nor, for that matter, the ability — to sweep cardinal tenets under the rug. Halakhah does not regard every inequality as an inequity.[14] I believe that this account of our stance and mindset is reasonably accurate.

I would, concurrently, submit, however, that it is possibly too one-sided. Unquestionably, total egalitarianism — radical and comprehensive, ideology as well as lifestyle — constitutes a philosophy and an ethic we categorically abjure. It strikes at the heart of cardinal tenets regarding the given reality and the ideal desideratum of personal Torah life and of communal Jewish polity. However, as a component of our spiritual universe, the motif of אני בריה וחברי בריה, "I am a creature and my fellow is a creature" (Berakhot 17a) strikes a responsive chord; and this, not only because we are humanly sensitive to דמעת העשקים ואין להם מנחם, "the tears of the oppressed, lacking all comforter" (Kohelet 4:10) — the outcry of the disadvantaged, disenfranchised, and discriminated against — but because, at some plane, the prospect of the brotherhood of man under the fatherland of God resonates, beyond our ethical consciousness, in our religious sensibility. Hence, rather than dismiss the egalitarian impulse cavalierly, we need — striking a balance between the universal and the particularistic, between hierarchy and leveling — to assess its place within our overall *hashkafah*.

Still, our fundamental stance should be clear, to ourselves and to our audience. In discussions of the issue, one occasionally catches traces of an attitude which accepts egalitarianism as an ultimate desideratum and, then, confronted with its apparent inconsonance and inconsistency with halakhic data, strives to find modes of innovation or improvisation which might enable its implementation within the constraints of Torah.

There may, indeed, be areas of Halakhah — the tragedy-ridden reality of *mamzerut* is a prime instance — which, in practice, *poskim* seek to circumscribe and even circumvent. Egalitarianism, as a whole, is not, however, among them; and our relation to its cardinal issues ought not be tainted by apologetics.

In one area, the principled hashkafic rejection of egalitarian ideology admittedly leaves us open, morally and politically, to the charge of egocentric inconsistency. Since the Emancipation, Western Jews have traditionally pressed for full civil and political rights. That pressure has, in large measure, been fuelled by egalitarian impulses and theory; and, to some, it seems palpably unfair that Jews should not seek to enlarge the bounds of others' equality. The argument is not without appeal, but it is fundamentally specious. Despite the often aggressive claims of its proponents, equality need be neither total nor comprehensive. The rejection of one criterion does not militate for the abandonment of all. The extent to which moral standards ought to be translated into legal sanctions has of course been widely debated. In dealing with it, however, we can hardly resolve the issue by equating the right to vote or to attend a university with the right to terminate incipient fetal life. Similarly, within the Jewish community, affinity with the civil rights movement does not entail the social acceptance of the rupture of Jewish identity often attendant upon intermarriage.

The issue is exacerbated by a comparison of the respective American and Israeli scenes. How would we relate, we might be asked, to a local equivalent of *hok ha-shevut*, which would admit Christians indiscriminately but impose barriers before Jews, Moslems, or atheists? As the answer is self-evident, we stand exposed to the sarcasm of Macaulay's lampooning representation of a particularist's assertion that others are duty-bound to tolerate him as he is right and they are wrong, while the reverse does not obtain. Some might suggest that the gap in consistency could be reduced if Diaspora Jews would forgo some of their entitlement; but as this is a most unlikely prospect, we must look to more salient considerations. Probably the most relevant is the conventional argument that weight needs to be assigned to self-definition. The United States is, socially, a predominantly Christian country but is not formally so, while Israel was conceived and founded as a Jewish state. Hence, as applied to *hok ha-shevut*, for instance, every prospective Jewish *oleh*, while not yet a citizen of *medinat Yisrael*, is already a member of *Knesset Yisrael*; and, thus, is admitted to the national home of the Jewish polity, as a returning American expatriate need not apply for a "green card." On this reading, we presumably would not cavil at an Indonesian immigration law which would be tilted in favor of Moslems. The contention is valid, and it obviates many specific objections. I doubt, however, that it answers all; and I think we should recognize that it is entirely conceivable that the conjunction of the pursuit of certain interests in the Diaspora with adherence to the principle of chosenness and to ethnic identity in Israel may indeed issue in a measure of disparity to which we need to be sensitive.

If we noted a mix of the theoretical and the pragmatic in dealing with our first question, it is even more marked as we relate to the second: "How should we respond to changes in society which are motivated by a combination of both positive factors of equal respect for all persons as a manifestation of *zelem E-lohim* and negative factors (tolerance of sexual practices beyond halakhic norms)?" Any serious answer must take into consideration two kinds of factors. There are, first, issues of principle. To what extent are we obligated or permitted, halakhically and morally, to stake out a position, ranging from revulsion to support, with respect to such changes? Second, there are matters of interests — not, I trust, material and personal, but spiritual and communal. What impact will a given stance, or its absence, have upon the moral climate of our environment — upon our institutions, upon our youth, upon ourselves? And of course we need to wrestle with these concerns with an eye to a more general dilemma, regarding the balance of principle and interests. To what extent do we have the right or the duty to sharpen or modify what might have been our optimal response in light of possible fallout? I am not so naïve as to reject this factor entirely, but determination of how much weight should be assigned to it requires careful deliberation. In part, these issues would obviously confront us even if we were dealing with change impelled by purely negative or wholly positive factors. With respect to them, too, we would have to weigh, apart from the content of response, whether to respond at all — and if so, in which vein. We can distinguish between at least three strains of response. There is, first, attitude and sensibility. Even when we in no way enter the lists for or against a given phenomenon, we may still, personally and intimately, react to it, with recoil or enthusiasm. Secondly, we may engage it, verbally and forensically, with individual or collective expressions of encouragement or opposition. Finally, we may encounter it actively by seeking to direct the course of events, as regards both society and state, whether through initiatives in the private sector or by promoting governmental involvement to advance or inhibit a particular change. And all of this, again, with respect to monochromatic change.

Unquestionably, however, the situation is more complex when we confront a mixed impulse, and, in answering the question posed to me, I shall try to bear this factor in mind. Whether, confronted by an egalitarianism twinned to a non-judgmental moral stance, we shall respond at all, will surely depend on how much we care, and on how we prioritize our energies and resources. That we ought to care can, I hope, be taken for granted — at the very least, at the level of personal reaction; and this, not only because our own community may become infected, but out of concern for the possible contamination of the broader society *per se*. The insularity of much of the Torah world in this respect is an educational disaster. Abortion on demand is a moral abomination, whoever the fetus may be. We have much to learn from the late Lubavitcher Rebbe, who took up the cudgels for a modicum of prayer in the public schools.

Unquestionably, we shall be far more concerned if and when our own are involved — caring about Israel more than elsewhere, and about Diaspora Jewish communities more than about their ambience. We are not so universalistic as to disregard national ties; and modern history has amply demonstrated that felt ethnicism generates more concern than abstract pronouncements about global fraternity. Insouciance is, however, out of the question.

To care, morally, is, in all likelihood, to judge. I am not at all certain that those who advocate a non-judgmental stance practice what they preach. They tend to be quite intolerant of intolerance — i.e., of the violation of what they regard as a value; and if they are indeed non-judgmental about homosexuality or abortion, it is because they regard these as morally neutral. *Yahadut*, however, does not preach ethical distance at all. As a system, grounded in Halakhah and general morality, it rejects, as previously noted, the relativism upon which much of the abdication of judgment rests; and, hence, it clearly encourages the individual Jew or Jewess to adopt a position vis-à-vis developments in the surrounding world.

An attitudinal response is, then, certainly in order. One might of course question whether this should translate into personal judgment, with respect to an individual or a group. On the one hand, the *pasuk* enjoins, בצדק תשפט עמיתך, "Judge your fellow justly."[15] The Torat Kohanim, cited by Rashi, offers two explanations of this charge, addressed to authorized judges or to the ordinary person, respectively:

שלא יהיה אחד מדבר כל צורכו ואחד אתה אומר לו קצר בדבריך שלא יהיה אחד עומד
ואחד יושב...דבר אחד בצדק תשפט עמיתך הוי דן את כל האדם לכף זכות.

"That one should not speak as long as he needs, and to the other you [the judge] say abridge your words, or that one [party] stands and the other sits…. Another explanation: judge your neighbor righteously; judge all men favorably."[16]

The latter charge, considerably amplified in a *sugya* in Shabbat and Avot De-Rabbi Natan, and emphasized by the *She'iltot*,[17] need not relate to anything expressed to one's fellow; it may simply include private evaluation. It does, however, make allowance for judgment, even if it mandates its quality and perspective. On the other hand, Hillel's equally familiar dictum, ואל תדין את חבירך עד שתגיע למקומו, "Do not judge your friend until you stand in his place,"[18] appears to discourage judgment altogether. However, it should be obvious that this counsel, too, does not advocate the acceptance of alternative mores. It rather urges empathy and humility in perceiving and interpreting how and why deviation from normative conduct has occurred. We are all familiar with the exchange between Rabbi Mayer and Beruriah:

הנהו בריוני דהוו בשבבותיה דרבי מאיר והוו קא מצערו ליה טובא הוה קא בעי רבי
מאיר רחמי עלויהו כי היכי דלימותו אמרה ליה ברוריא דביתהו מאי דעתך משום דכתיב
יתמו חטאים מי כתיב חוטאים חטאים כתיב.

There were thugs who lived in R' Mayer's neighborhood who greatly
disturbed him; R' Mayer prayed that they should die. His wife Beruriah
said to him, "Why is this your opinion — because [the verse says] 'sinners should be destroyed.' Does it say sinners (written plene)? No, it
says 'sin should be destroyed.'"[19]

And I assume most would today be inclined to adopt her softer position,
sparing personal criticism even with respect to changes we might find
objectionable. That, too, however, is a far cry from what the movers of
such changes seek.

As to the substance of response, we need to pay particular attention
to the mixed roots of the changes under consideration. In this respect, we
are confronted by a quality endemic to much of modern culture. It has
often been remarked that while, in medieval and Renaissance literature,
one could tell the saints from the sinners without a scorecard, the modern
scene is far murkier. Shakespeare has been highly praised for the creative
diversity which could humanize an Iago as well as a Desdemona, but even
in his plays we are hard put to find a whisky priest or a Raskolnikov.
This spiritual chiaroscuro confronts us with a challenge. The Hazon Ish
is reputed to have asked, how could one expect meaningful dialogue
between the secular and the religious communities when the same act is
valued by the former as an expression of love and classified by the latter
under *hayvei keritut*.

Nevertheless, at the conceptual plane, the challenge ought not be
insuperable. Avoiding the genetic fallacy, we may, in the spirit of the fabled
angelic missive of the *Kuzari*, appreciate motives while decrying results:
כונתך רצויה בעיני הא-לוה אבל מעשך אינו רצוי, "Your intentions are desirable in
God's eyes but your actions are not."[20] Moreover, we may distinguish
between various strains of the motivation proper. By way of precedent,
in this respect, one might cite a remarkable gemara. Addressing himself
to the narrative regarding the daughters of Lot, who had intoxicated their

father and then had sexual relations with him, Rabbi Hiyyah bar Abba in the name of Rabbi Yehoshua ben Korhah derives a striking moral: "A person should always leap at [the opportunity to fulfill] a *mizvah*.

לעולם יקדים אדם לדבר מצוה שבשביל לילה אחת שקדמתה בכירה לצעירה קדמתה ארבעה דורות לישראל עובד ישי דוד ושלמה ואילו צעירה עד רחבעם דכתיב ושם אמו נעמה העמונית.

As a result of the one night that [Lot's] elder daughter preceded the younger daughter, [the older daughter's descendants] preceded to enter the Jewish people by four generations — Oved, Yishai, David and Shlomo — while [the descendants of the younger one] delayed until Rehavam as it says "his mother's name was Na'amah the Ammonite."[21]

Whether, from a technical standpoint, this sexual liaison was, to a non-Jew, halakhically proscribed as incest, was debated in another gemara,[22] and the Rambam and the Meiri differed as to the *pesak*.[23] But that the entire scenario of duped sexuality was reprehensible seems reasonably clear. Several lines earlier, the selfsame Rabbi Hiyyah bar Abba contrasts the relative modesty of the younger daughter who, unlike her elder sister, in naming her child, concealed Lot's paternity; and Rashi, analogously, castigates the latter for having initiated the *zenut* (fornication).[24] And yet, on the assumption that the motivation was, at least in part — there was an altruistic aspect of rehabilitating a scorched world, but, surely, a selfish moment as well — admirable, Hazal could appreciate the positive component, and speak of a *devar mizvah* in this context, to boot. Even at the attitudinal plane, however, such a discriminating approach should no doubt be implemented with selective care — depending, in large measure, on the weight of the positive and negative elements, respectively.

I have little difficulty in applying it to the Hazon Ish's case of a wedded couple which does not observe *taharat ha-mishpahah*. I am not only unwilling but unable, however, to react similarly to romantic love which issues in intermarriage. The magnitude of the transgression, as both a violation of a basic halakhic norm and as a general apostasy, בה' בגדו כי בנים זרים ילדו, "They betrayed God, as they gave birth to foreign children" (Hoshea 5:7), is such that it effectively overshadows everything else. Yet, the basic principle of axiological discrimination should be borne in mind.

This last distinction is of relevance to the specific question confronting me. The term "changes in society" has two distinct, albeit linked, referents — one, sociological, the other, ideological; and they differ in motivation no less than in content. In practice, abortion may be impelled by convenience or distress. The theoretical claim to a right to abort, in contrast, is probably fuelled by philosophic assumptions regarding personal autonomy. The homosexual is driven by a psycho-physiological urge, his advocates by a socio-cultural manifesto. And, of course, the specific gravity of the sociological trends themselves varies widely. We can hardly regard intermarriage and gay unions equally. In ferreting wheat from chaff, we need to observe which is the grain at hand, and steer our course accordingly.

These considerations relate to response as attitude. To them, in dealing with verbal and with active response, must obviously be added pragmatic factors. These focus upon results — the fallout of acquiescence, of affirmation, of antagonism, or any blend of the three. Clearly, decisions regarding such responses will entail a plethora of specific judgments, but the overall thrust of planning response should, almost *a priori*, be manifest. We are guided by two primary concerns: a) commitment to the cause of *avodat Hashem* and its advance; b) sensitivity to human personality and its welfare.

The need to assess how best to promote each of these, separately and jointly, and what kind of balance to strike when they are in apparent conflict, is the alpha and omega of any meaningful and effective spiritual strategy — whether in private counseling, in educational endeavor, in institutional initiative, or in communal enterprise.

These twin concerns are distinct, and yet, reciprocally intertwined; and this, in several senses. First, sensitivity to those whom we challenge enhances the prospect that they will heed our message. When Hazal counseled, לעולם תהא שמאל דוחה וימין מקרבת לא כאלישע שדחפו לגחזי בשתי ידיו ולא כיהושע בן פרחיה שדחפו לאחד מתלמידיו בשתי ידיו, "always, even as the left hand rejects, let the right hand attract, and not as Elisha, who thrust away Gehazi with both hands, nor like R. Yehoshua ben Perahiah, who thrust away one of his disciples with both hands,"[25] they were not only concerned with the value of respecting an interlocutor's dignity, but with the prospect of enhancing his sanctity. Secondly and conversely, appreciation of *zelem E-lohim* — or, at another plane, of personal *kedushat Yisrael* — is itself part of the world of *avodat Hashem* we are striving to enhance.

And yet, divergence and even conflict there will probably be, and we need, thirdly, to give thought to optimal balance. I do not think, for a moment, that a single answer is in order. We may lean towards one orientation or another, but the exigencies of a given historical reality must always be considered. Whichever concern is in relative neglect requires special counterbalancing sustenance. This formula almost assures a kind of perennial unpopularity, but it is what spiritual responsibility demands. How such an approach will reflect itself in a response to the current trends of egalitarianism should probably be better determined by those much closer than myself to the vortex of this ideology and its manifestations.

My own assessment is that within the hard core of the Torah world, the human aspect requires greater emphasis than it is currently receiving, while the reverse is true of the broader Jewish community. But I may be wrong. With respect to both venues, however, we should be careful to embrace both values, even as the educational and tactical nuances shift; and we should not compromise authenticity in the quest for acceptability. The maintenance of standards should take precedence over the enhancement of rating.

In determining policy in this area, axiological considerations should certainly be primary. Nevertheless, they do not stand alone. Some place in the planning of response, with an eye to particular present historical circumstances — what F. H. Bradley called, "my station and its duties" — will obviously be accorded purely tactical factors. Of these, several familiar elements may be singled out for special mention.

The first — most directly related to the *mizvah* of reproachful *tokhahah*, but pregnant with far broader ramifications — concerns likely reaction to a prospective initiative. We recall Rabbi Elazar ben Rabbi Shimon's directive:

כשם שמצוה על אדם לומר דבר הנשמע כך מצוה על אדם שלא לומר דבר שאינו נשמע
רבי אבא אומר חובה שנאמר אל תוכח לץ פן ישנאך הוכח לחכם ויאהבך.

Just as it is a *mizvah* to say something which will be heeded, so it is a
mizvah to refrain from saying something which will not be heeded:
R' Abba says "it is obligatory, as it says 'Don't rebuke a fool [scoffer?]
lest he hate you; rebuke the wise and he will love you.'"[26]

But we also recall the qualification of many Rishonim who asserted that,
at the public plane, this counsel could not always be heeded, as it had to be
balanced by the need to stake out Torah positions and sustain principles.

In a related vein, we will obviously need to evaluate how a given
course, heeded or not, will inhibit problematic "egalitarian" trends —
and at what cost. Consider the worst: intermarriage. Unquestionably, as
the non-Orthodox community realized belatedly, this plague needs to
be confronted, first and foremost, educationally; and this, not only by
an ethnocentric appeal for Jewish continuity but by inculcating a positive sense of the meaning of chosenness and the uniqueness of *kedushat
Yisrael*. Concurrently, however, some will advocate severe social sanctions
in the hope that prospective ostracism will serve as an effective deterrent.
I take no issue with this, on principle. An individual who has crossed the
line should not be surprised to find himself beyond the pale; and, as I have
indicated, I do not view this as an issue with regard to which respect for
the underlying involvement of *zelem E-lohim* should counterbalance the
gravity of the deviation. Several years ago, a group of Orthodox rabbis
floated a suggestion that, given the scope of the phenomenon, the view
of those who "marry out" as pariahs should be ameliorated, so that they
could continue to feel and function as members of the Jewish community,
with all that this could imply for their own and their children's future. In
short order, the suggestion evoked vehement protests — in part, on the
grounds that its proponents were too soft on the phenomenon, and, in
part, out of concern that a more understanding attitude would dilute the
deterrent effect of the traditionally tougher stance. The first contention
certainly deserves to be weighed on its merits; but, as to the second, both

the current force of deterrence and the cost, human as well as Jewish, at which it is attained, requires assessment.

In considering the last point, a partial analogy might be helpful. Rabbenu Gershom was asked whether a *kohen*, who had converted to Christianity and then repented, should be stripped of his prerogatives. The discussion in his *teshuvah* revolves, in part, around the formal halakhic questions — much debated by earlier Geonim and subsequent Rishonim, on the basis of a *sugya* in Menahot[27] — as to whether a person who had worshipped Avodah Zarah, perhaps even under duress,[28] could perform *avodah* for the *Ribbono shel Olam*, and as to whether the sanctity of *kehunah* is vitiated by apostasy.[29]

Rabbenu Gershom argues for leniency with regard to these issues; but then adds further elements to his decision:

> הילכך אין לנו ראיה לא מן המקרא ולא מן המשנה לפוסלו אלא שיש לסייע מן המקרא
> וממשנה שלא לפוסלו דכתיב ולא תונו איש את עמיתו באונאת דברים הכתוב מדבר
> כיצד אם היה בעל תשובה לא יאמר לו זכור מעשיך הראשונים ואם תאמר לא יעלה
> לדוכן ולא יקרא בתורה תחילה אין לך אונאה מזו ועוד נמצאת אתה מרפה ידיהם
> של בעלי תשובה ולא נכון לעשות כן דאמר ר' יוחנן כל האומר מנשה אין לו חלק לעולם
> הבא מרפה ידיהם של בעלי תשובה.

Therefore, we have no proof from Scripture or the Mishnah to invalidate him; on the contrary, we have proofs from Scripture and Mishna not to invalidate him as it says 'one shall not oppress his compatriot.' With regard to verbal oppression the verse is speaking. How? If he [a person] is *a ba'al teshuvah* one should not say to him remember your earlier deeds. And if one will say, this priest should not go up to the [platform] and he should [not be called first to the Torah] there is no greater oppression than this. Moreover, one [undermines] *ba'alei teshuvah*, and it is not proper to do so, as R' Yohanan said 'whoever says Menasheh has no portion in the world to come undermines *ba'alei teshuvah*."[30]

This concern, lest the *kohen* be affronted, on the one hand, and with possibly discouraging recantation, on the other, introduces a new dimension to the discussion; and it is one which may have wider application. We should of course note that the *kohen* in question may have converted in a climate of intimidation, if not of outright duress, in the first place; and, most critically, that he has repented. These elements are generally absent in the contemporary case of intermarriage. Nevertheless, at least as a basis of comparison with respect to the weight assigned to deterrence, the analogy may be instructive.

Thirdly, at a totally different level, we need to consider what has popularly become known as "the slippery slope" — the concern that acceptance of certain innovations, even if they are halakhically tenable, may invite pressures for further progressive change, resulting, incrementally, in the erosion of traditional sensibility or even outright halakhic violation. This issue has been raised most vigorously with respect to various initiatives concerning the role of women. Within the Torah world and the rabbinic establishment, response to these has been widely divergent. Some have contended that whatever the *Shulhan Arukh* does not proscribe could be regarded with favor. Others have rejected this premise as a general approach; and they have further resisted any innovation, particularly if fuelled by feminist ideology, on the grounds that it might lead to further demands or trigger a domino effect And, there is, of course, a spectrum of intermediate responses. Here again, we need to maintain a dual watch. The concern about the slippery slope is, in principle, both legitimate and genuine. It is firmly rooted in Hazal, who anchored many *gezerot* upon it, as graphically illustrated in the Rambam's explanation as to the basis of the prohibition against fowl cooked with milk:

אבל אם אמר בשר העוף מותר מן התורה ואנו נאסור אותו ונודיע לעם שהוא גזרה
שלא יבא מן הדבר חורבה ויאמרו העוף מותר מפני שלא נתפרש כך החיה מותרת
שהרי לא נתפרשה ויבא אחר לומר אף בשר בהמה מותרת חוץ מן העז ויבא אחר לומר
אף בשר העז מותר בחלב פרה או הכבשה שלא נאמר אלא אמו שהיא מינו ויבא אחר
לומר אף בחלב העז שאינה אמו מותר שלא נאמר אלא אמו לפיכך נאסור כל בשר בחלב
אפילו בשר עוף אין זה מוסיף אלא עושה סייג לתורה וכן כל כיוצא בזה.

But if it [i.e., the court] says: "The meat of the fowl is permitted by the Torah, and we shall forbid it; and we shall inform the people that this is a Rabbinic [precautionary] injunction, so that no deleterious effects derive therefrom, [as would occur] if they were [inclined] to say — fowl meat is permitted, because it is not explicitly prohibited, so the flesh of a wild animal is permitted because it is not explicitly forbidden; and someone else will also say even the flesh of a [domestic] animal is permitted except for the flesh of a goat; and someone also will say even the meat of a goat is permitted with the milk of a cow or a sheep, as only the [goat's] mother is explicitly prohibited; and someone else will say that even with the milk of any goat but the mother it is permitted, as only the mother's is explicitly prohibited; therefore we shall prohibit even the fowl meat, it [i.e. the court] is not adding [to the Torah] but making a fence around the Torah, and so it is with similar matters.[31]

In this case, one encounters outright *de-oraita* violation early in the chain. The principle is in force, however, even when that is not the case. Yet, in applying the principle, two factors need to be weighed. We shall have to evaluate, first, the likely course of events. How truly slippery is the slope? What innovation is likely, and how likely, to generate which kind of pressures? Second, we shall need to examine at what cost — whether in the form of possible alienation of certain constituencies or in the impairment or dilution of the quality of spiritual life — the presumed security of an ultra-conservative stance is being attained. This last factor will itself require dual consideration, as we strive both to perceive the prospects of various alternative scenarios on the ground and to determine how much weight to assign this particular concern.

As for myself, I presume that, with respect to both the women's issues, specifically, and the fear of the slippery slope, generally, I find myself somewhere in the middle — enthusiastically supportive of some changes, resistant to others, and ambivalent about many; but I take it that this is not the venue for dealing with the details of various agendas. I feel strongly, however, in conclusion, that none of us can be content with a middling position with regard to a corollary issue. If we cannot countenance egalitarianism as a total ideology, and we cannot rally behind its comprehensive platform, we need to labor to assure that its positive component, respect for *zelem E-lohim*, be properly internalized and inculcated.

The formulation of my question notwithstanding, that concept does not mandate, for us, "equal respect for all persons." It demands that all, equally, be regarded with respect, but its quality may differ. We subscribe to both parts of Rabbi Akiva's familiar formulation.

At one plane, חביב אדם שנברא בצלם, "Beloved is man because he was created in His image"; additionally, however, חביבין ישראל שנקראו בנים למקום, "Beloved is Israel who are called the children [of God]."[32] And what is true of affection, translates into esteem. While a balance between the ethnic and the universal is variously struck in some of our most fundamental and familiar sources — in *pesukei de'zimrah*, for instance, in one sense, and, most notably, in the opening of *shema*, in another — that balance is often insufficiently appreciated and inculcated within our Torah community.

Its neglect is, however, spiritually unconscionable and pragmatically foolhardy. We need to ascertain that, as we insist that the universal element not effectively neutralize the particularistic, we be equally insistent that the reverse not occur. If our response to the egalitarian manifesto is resistant, we are charged with the moral, religious, and educational responsibility to find compensatory means to assure that Ben Azzai's overarching principle, זה ספר תולדות אדם, זה כלל גדול מזה, "'This is the book of the generations of man' — this is a greater rule than this one,"[33] attain — in our homes, in our schools, in our hearts — the position it deserves. That we owe not just to the other — in Milton's phrase, "the human face divine." That we owe to the *Ribbono shel Olam*, and to ourselves.

Notes

1. See Teshuvah 3:8.
2. *Perush Ha-Mishnayot*, preface to ch. 10 of Sanhedrin, tr. Rav Y. D. Kapah (Jerusalem, 1965), p. 144. In his notes, Rav Kapah addresses a parallel text from *Mishneh Torah*, Melakhim 11:6, which due to censorship, has been omitted from most of the printed editions.
3. See Yevamot 89b-90b, and Gittin 4:2, respectively.
4. Horayot 4a; cf. Sanhedrin 33b.
5. Mamrim 2:1. Inasmuch as the Rambam does not qualify, as he does in the next

halakhah, that only a greater *bet din* is authorized to reverse its predecessor's decision, it seems clear that even a lesser one is entitled to do so.

6. Devarim 18:21–22.
7. *Ad locum*, 18:22.
8. Sanhedrin 89b.
9. Devarim 18:21.
10. Sanhedrin 89b, s.v. *heikha*.
11. Yesodei Ha-Torah, 7:7; and cf. ch. 8, *passim*, and 10:1–3.
12. Berakhot 7b; and cf. *Tosafot*, Ketubbot 17a, s.v. *mevattelin*.
13. Horayot 13a.
14. To the trio of themes previously cited might be added: the quest for parity within relationships. This has particularly come to the fore in the context of feminism, with respect to marriage. The issue is important, but here I have largely skirted it; inasmuch as I believe that feminism is qualitatively different from other manifestations of egalitarianism cited. Conceptually, its claims are less radical and more limited in scope. Practically, despite some confrontations with the prevailing social order, generally, and the world of Halakhah, specifically, its challenge to tradition is hardly of a piece with intermarriage or abortion, and should be dealt with independently. Neither the challenge nor the response to it revolves around levels of *kedushah* or personal autonomy, although, admittedly, some conceptual links and certain operational alliances do exist. I am inclined to think that the linkage is greater within the broader sociological context than within our specific Jewish community. I grant, however, that this assessment — with respect to the American scene, largely the perception of an outsider — is open to challenge. In any event, the fuller treatment the issue deserves lies beyond my present scope.
15. Vayikra 19:15.
16. Kedoshim, 7:4:4; cited in part by Rashi Vayikra 19:15 s.v. *be-zedek*.
17. Shabbat 127a-b, *A.d.R.N.*, 8:7–8, and *She'iltot De-Rabbi Ahai Gaon, She'ilta* 40, respectively.
18. Avot, 2:4.
19. Berakhot 10a. Of course, at the level of pure *peshat*, the word *hatta'im*, with the *dagesh* in the *tet*, is the *nomen agentis* for sinners. The *derash* relates to the use of this unusual form which resembles the plural of sins.
20. "Introduction" in Yehudah Even Shemuel's translation. Of course, as reflected in the concluding coda, part of the thrust of the work is the undermining of this thesis, by way of stressing the need for conjoined action and intention.
21. Bava Kamma 38b, Nazir 23b, Horayot 10b.
22. See Sanhedrin 58b.
23. Issurei Bi'ah 14:10 and *Bet Ha-Behirah*, Sanhedrin 58b, respectively.
24. See the gemarot previously cited and Rashi, Bereshit 19:33, respectively. The Ramban

(Bereshit 19:32), however, focusing upon their longing for progeny — and, probably, upon midrashic statement — takes a much more positive view of their motivation, and even of the initiative proper: "And perhaps [it might be suggested] that they said let us do that deed which is appropriate for us, and perhaps God will have mercy and we will give birth to a male and a female, and the world will be preserved through them, as 'the world will be built on kindness' (Tehillim 89:3). Not for naught did God save us. And behold that they were modest, and did not wish to say to their father that he should marry them, even though Noahides are permitted to marry their daughters. Perhaps (the act) was most repulsive in the eyes of the generation and it had not been done ever (*me'olam*).

25. Sotah 47a.
26. Yevamot 65b.
27. See Menahot 109a, and *Tosafot*, s.v. *lo*; *Tosafot*, Sotah 39a, s.v. *ve-khi*; *Shibbolei Ha-Leket*, sec. 33; Rambam, Nesi'at Kappayim, 15:3.
28. *Bet Yosef*, *Orah Haym*, 128, assumed that the controversy was confined to a *kohen* who had converted willingly, but that if the conversion was coerced, all would agree that his status as a *kohen* remained intact; and, in *Shulhan Arukh*, *O.H.*, 128:37, he decided accordingly. However, as noted in *Bedek Ha-Bayit*'s comment on the *Bet Yosef*, the Rambam clearly appears to have disqualified even in the case of duress.
29. These are two separate factors. The first would only disqualify the *kohen* from *nesi'at kappayim*, the second from priority in *keriat ha-Torah*, as well.
30. Cited in *Mahzor Vitry*, sec. 125.
31. Mamrim 2:9.
32. Avot 3:14.
33. Torat Kohanim, Kedoshim 7:4:12.

Chapter 9

Reflections upon *Birkot Ha-Torah*

Not surprisingly, few texts are as pregnant with concepts central to the definition of a yeshivah and its goals as *birkot ha-Torah*. Within the space of several lines — recited either prior to daily Torah study or before and after *keriat ha-Torah* in public — are encapsulated a number of major themes which express aspects of the traditional Jewish conception of *talmud Torah*, in particular, and of the religious life, generally. In seeking to understand the nature and aspirations of our own yeshiva, it behooves us, therefore, to reflect, however cursorily, upon the substance of these Berakhot.

At the outset, we are confronted by the question of the nature of the Berakhot, and how, with respect to their origin and obligation, they are to be classified. At one level, this entails determining whether they have been mandated *mi-deʾoraita* or *mi-deʾrabbanan* — an issue which was debated by Rishonim, with the Ramban insisting that they had been prescribed by the Torah while the Rambam evidently held that, like most Berakhot, they were of Rabbinic origin.[1] At a second level, however, irrespective of origin, the character of the Berakhot is at issue. That, in turn, may very well hinge upon textual factors; and this in two respects, one more general, and the other, quite specific.

With regard to personal *birkot ha-Torah*, the gemara (Berakhot 11b) cites three different Berakhot recited by three Amoraim, and then concludes: "Hence," i.e., in order to encompass the various themes included in the respective formulations, "Let us recite all of them;" and such is, of course, our familiar practice. It should be noted, however, that, *prima facie*, the texts point in different directions. The first, "*Asher kiddeshanu be-mizvotav ve-zivvanu la'asok be-divrei Torah*," is framed as a *birkat ha-mizvah*, cut from the same cloth as similar assertions recited prior to lighting candles or eating in a *sukkah*. The second, "*Ve-ha'arev na Hashem Elokeinu et divrei Toratekha be-finu*," is a petitionary plea for learning characterized by pervasive sweetness and light. The last, "*Asher bahar banu mi-kol ha-ammim ve-natan lanu et Torato*," is a paean of thanksgiving for collective chosenness manifested through the revelation of Torah to *Knesset Yisrael*.

Given this variety, one naturally asks what is the normative core of the obligation to recite *birkot ha-Torah*. The question may very well be out of court, as it is entirely conceivable that the obligation is multifaceted. Nevertheless, the quest — particularly, with respect to a possible *de'oraita* dimension — persists. Rav Haym Soloveitchik (Brisker), in a novellum preserved both through oral tradition and in a volume of his son, Rav Yitzhak Zev (*Hiddushei Maran Riz Halevi*, p. 10), contended that the obligation did not derive from the fact that Torah study was a *mizvah* prior to whose performance a *berakhah* must be recited. It related, rather, to Torah *per se*, qua object, as a gift which the *Ribbono shel Olam*, with munificent grace, had conferred upon us, irrespective of the command to study it.

In support of this contention — which, of course, consorts better with the latter Berakhot, but which he, evidently, advanced even with regard to the first — Reb Haym adduced several proofs. First, although the *Mehabber* in *Shulhan Arukh* (O.H. 589:6) accepted the view that women should not recite a *berakhah* prior to performing a *mizvah* from which they have been exempt, he nevertheless simply states, "Women recite *birkat ha-Torah*" (O.H. 47:14; cf. Rosh Hashanah 33a, *Tosafot*, s.v. *ha*). This can be easily understood if the *berakhah* is over the object of Torah rather than over the *mizvah* to study it. Similarly, the argument is buttressed by the institution of Berakhot around *keriat ha-Torah*, although there is presumably no independent *mizvah* to read in public. Conversely, the *Mehabber* (O.H. 47:4; see also the source in *Sefer Ha-Agur*, *Tefillah*, 2) sets down that if a person meditates upon Torah matters without articulating them, he should not recite a *berakhah*, although he is patently fulfilling the *mizvah*.

Perhaps the most trenchant proof in support of Reb Haym's thesis was offered by Rav Aryeh Pomoranchik, in his *Emek Berakhah* (p. 5). The gemara (Berakhot 11b) cites views that a *berakhah* should be recited only when certain tracts of Torah are studied, to the possible exclusion of Midrash, Mishnah, or Talmud. These are obviously mainstays of Torah study; hence, the apparent inference that the *berakhah* relates to Torah *per se* — and, therefore, conceivably confined to its Scriptural epicenter.

These arguments can be rebutted. It may be rejoined, for instance, that women, too, albeit in a more limited vein, are obligated to study Torah; that *keriat ha-Torah* is an independent institution, invested with its own *sui generis* structure, unrelated to our topic; that no Berakhot are recited in performing *mizvot*, such as the love of God or one's fellow, which are not manifested by objective expression; and that the gemara concludes that study of any aspect of Torah requires a *berakhah* precisely because it rejected Reb Haym's contention. Nevertheless, halakhic arguments aside, the thesis is amply supported by a simple textual point. Both in the Bavli (Berakhot 21b) and in the Yerushalmi (Berakhot 7:1), *birkot ha-Torah* are treated as of a piece with those over food, before and after — *birkot ha-nehenin* and *birkat ha-mazon*, respectively. Obviously, the analogy only holds insofar as Torah qua object is the focus. It is, of course, arguable that the gemara is confined to the last Berakhot or their equivalent, but that "*la'asok be-divrei Torah*" is an ordinary *birkat ha-mizvah*. Nevertheless, the cogency of the core concept is clearly implicit in the gemara's comparison.

The validity of this thesis, even with regard to the first *berakhah*, presumably depends — at least, up to a point — upon a textual factor. The prevalent Ashkenazi version reads "*la'asok be-divrei Torah*," "to engage in Torah matters," thus focusing upon the activity, presumably normative, of Torah study. However, Sephardim generally accept the reading — found in basic Geonic sources, the Rif and the Rambam, and even among some *hakhmei Ashkenaz* — "*al divrei Torah*," "over Torah matters," which posits Torah itself at the heart of the *berakhah*, and thus sets it apart from the ordinary *birkat ha-mizvah*. Nevertheless, the Ashkenazi formulation, too, bespeaks uniqueness. The verb employed is not *li'lmod*, "to study," but *la'asok*, the term generally used to denominate commerce. What is envisioned is clearly not merely an act, or even a series of acts, but an enterprise. Even for the ordinary individual, belabored by the demands of a secular career, Torah is ideally defined as a calling. For the layman, too, it is, in a very real sense, to be a vocation, with all that the concept implies, quantitatively and qualitatively, in terms of aspiration and commitment. Commenting on the *pasuk*, "*Im be-hukkotai telekhu*," "If ye walk in my statutes," Hazal state (Sifra, Behukkotai, 2):

> יכול אילו המצות, כשהוא אומר ואת מצותי תשמרו ועשיתם אותם הרי מצות אמורות,
> הא מה אני מקיים אם בחקותי תלכו להיות עמילים בתורה.

> Can this refer to *mizvot*? When it says, "And ye shall keep my commandments and do them," *mizvot* have already been cited. So how am I to understand, "If ye walk in my statutes?" That you are to be laboring in Torah.

"To be laboring in Torah" — that is the demand and the expectation; and it is to that commitment that *birkot ha-Torah* relate.

The emphasis upon committed effort is further sharpened — indeed, radically so — by another textual variant. We, Ashkenazim and Sephardim alike, conclude the second *berakhah* by addressing "*ha-Melammed Torah le-ammo Yisrael*," "He who teaches Torah to His people, Israel." This is also the coda cited in most editions of the Rambam's *Mishneh Torah* (Hilkhot Tefillah 7:10). In a responsum (*Teshuvot Ha-Rambam*, ed. J. Blau, sec. 182, p. 333), however, he rejects this formulation categorically: "But whoever concludes '*ha-Melammed Torah*' errs, for God does not teach it to us, but, rather, has commanded us to study and to teach it. And this is grounded upon a principle of our faith — to wit, that the enactment of *mizvot* is in our hands, not by divine compulsion to perform or neglect them." The critique is a ringing assertion of human freedom, and, as such, refers to the full range of spiritual experience. Nevertheless, given the specific thrust of *li'hyot amelim ba-Torah*, it is particularly apt with respect to this most critical and sensitive sphere.

The Rambam's version has not, of course, gained acceptance. The spirit which animated it, however, has had a broad and profound influence, especially as regards *talmud Torah*. I am reminded, in this connection, of an anecdote — I presume it has numerous analogues — told to me by the Rav's mother, Rebbetzin Pesia Soloveitchik z"l — about an ordinary laborer in the town of Pruzhan, who, upon being blessed by well-wishers that he should become a great *talmid hakham* by virtue of miraculous *gilluy Eliyahu*, demurred with the rejoinder that he would be most appreciative of supernal assistance in any other area, but as to growth in Torah, he aspired to attain that on his own.

However Torah study be denominated, the conjunction of the first two *birkot ha-Torah* — indeed, on *Tosafot*'s view (Berakhot 46a, s.v. *kol*), they are components of a single *berakhah* — is striking, in one sense, and so typically Jewish in another. The first focuses upon Torah study as a normative duty, the second relates to it as a prospective joy. The conjunction reflects our overarching attitude to *talmud Torah*, in particular, and to *avodat Hashem*, in general. On the one hand, we learn because we must. No category is more central to *Yahadut* than *mizvah*. A Jew exists as a *mezuvveh* — as a called and commanded being. He acts in response to duty, irrespective of inclination. We have been collectively defined as servants of God, "*avadai hem;*" and to serve is to discharge one's task, regardless of desire or gratification. What the Rambam (Hilkhot Kelei Ha-Mikdash 3:1), on the basis of the Sifra, stated with respect to *Leviyim* —

ומצות עשה להיות הלוים פנויין ומוכנין לעבודת המקדש בין רצו בין שלא רצו שנאמר ועבד הלוי הוא את עבודת אהל מועד

And it is a positive commandment that *Leviyim* be ready and directed for the service of *mikdash*, whether they want to or not, as it is stated, 'But the *Leviyim* alone shall do the service of the tent of meeting' —

is true, analogously, of every Jew. So, we should, and would, learn Torah, even if it did not attract or inspire us, even if we were not "turned on" in the slightest.

Obviously, however, we do want to be inspired — and much more. Our commitment to obligation and the moral law is no less fervent than

Kant's, and we could subscribe to the substance of Wordsworth's "Ode to Duty." But we do not share the Kantian polarization of duty and inclination or the idealization of inner struggle as the basis, if not the definition, of moral existence. We acknowledge that "Who is a hero? He who conquers his will" (Avot 4:1); but the notion that moral and spiritual greatness is conditional upon the exercise of heroism is wholly foreign to us. Correspondingly, we categorically reject the persistent Christian antithesis of law and love. In sum, *Yahadut* is law and law and law. It is, also, love and love and love.

So, we should, and would, learn Torah — as we would fulfill other *mizvot* — even if it were, to our palate, castor oil. We aspire, however, to experience it as milk and honey; and it is for that level of gratification, at once spiritual and visceral, that we pray in imploring "*ve-ha'arev na.*" The fusion of duty and joy, obligation and gratification, commitment and fulfillment, is central to our view of *avodat Hashem*; and it receives special emphasis with respect to *talmud Torah*. "Oh how I love Thy law! It is my meditation all the day" (Tehillim 119:97). In describing it, Hazal (Eruvin 54b) resorted to metaphors of elemental passionate experience — an infant sucking at his mother's breast, bride and groom on their wedding night:

אמר רבי שמואל בר נחמני: מאי דכתיב אילת אהבים ויעלת חן וג' למה נמשלו דברי
תורה לאילת? לומר לך: מה אילה רחמה צר, וחביבה על בועלה כל שעה ושעה כשעה
ראשונה – אף דברי תורה חביבין על לומדיהן כל שעה ושעה כשעה ראשונה. ויעלת
חן – שמעלת חן על לומדיה. דדיה ירוך בכל עת, למה נמשלו דברי תורה כדד? מה דד
זה, כל זמן שהתינוק ממשמש בו מוצא בו חלב – אף דברי תורה, כל זמן שאדם הוגה
בהן – מוצא בהן טעם.

R. Samuel bar Nahmani expounded: With reference to the Scriptural text (Mishlei 5), "Loving hind and a graceful roe etc.," why were the words of the Torah compared to a hind? To tell you that as the hind has a narrow womb and is loved by its mate at all times as at the first hour of their meeting, so it is with the words of the Torah. They are loved by those who study them at all times as at the hour when they first made their acquaintance. "And a graceful roe"? Because the Torah bestows grace upon those who study it. "Her breasts will satisfy thee at all times." Why were the words of the Torah compared to a breast? As with a breast, however often the child sucks it so often does he find milk in it, so it is with the words of the Torah. As often a man studies them so often does he find relish in them.

The conjunction of the first two *birkot ha-Torah* — all the more so, if they are, truly, a single *berakhah* — is, then, a remarkable testament to the inextricable intertwining of norm and yearning at the center of Jewish existence and experience.

If this concept (of the intertwining of norm and yearning) is elucidated through the substance and sequence of entire Berakhot, others are expressed via specific phrases or even a single word; and, of these, several may be noted. One is the term *"lishmah"* with which — in most current readings, although not, *inter alia*, the Rambam's — the body of *"ve-ha'arev na"* concludes. The thrust of the word is itself multifaceted. At one plane, it relates to the motivation of Torah study — as, by the same token, of other *mizvot*. *Lishmah* defines the ideal of serving the *Ribbono shel Olam* for His sake rather than for our own; in order to enhance the Kingdom of Heaven rather than for the pursuit of adventitious reward. In this vein, as the Rambam (Hilkhot Teshuva 10:2–5), in particular, emphasized, it is integrally related to the *mizvah* of *ahavat Hashem*, the call to love the *Ribbono shel Olam* with our whole being, and to serve Him accordingly. (On the Ramban's view, the concept is also related to a kindred *mizvah*, *"le'ovdo be-khol levavkhem"* — to serve Him with all your heart. See his animadversion upon the Rambam's *Sefer Ha-Mizvot*, Asei 5.)

At a second plane, however, the term is more narrowly focused. It posits Torah knowledge as an independent value (to the extent that, within a religious context, any value can be independent). It utterly rejects, for instance, the perception of the study of gemara as pseudo-philosophy; and, as Rav Haym Volozhiner so vigorously contended, even cavils at reducing *talmud Torah* to the instrumental role of inducing religious experience or commitment. Our faith in Torah, all Torah, properly studied, as illuminating and ennobling is, of course, profound and abiding; and the emphasis upon relating it to the whole of the spiritual life is beyond question. Yet,

Torah study cannot be animated solely by such ancillary concerns, however worthwhile — not if we wish to be included among "those who know Your name and who study Your Torah for its own sake." That appellation is reserved for those for whom the bare fact that a text or an idea is *devar Hashem* is reason enough for its study.

Moving from the personal to the public arena, we encounter two additional themes in the *berakhah* recited at the conclusion of *keriat ha-Torah*. The phrase, "*ve-hayyei olam nata be-tokhenu*" — "And eternal life He has implanted within us," has been diversely interpreted. The Tur (O.H. 139) sees it in juxtaposition to the preceding phrase "Who gave us the Torah of truth") and explains:

פי' תורת אמת היא תורה שבכתב וחיי עולם נטע בתוכנו היא תורה שבע"פ דכתיב דברי
חכמים כדרבונות וכמסמרות נטועים.

To wit: "The Torah of truth" refers to the written Torah, and, "And eternal life He has implanted within us," to the oral Torah, as it is written (Kohelet 12:11), "The words of the wise are as goads and as nails well fastened."

The conclusion, alludes to a gemara in Hagigah (3b) which takes the word *netu'im* (i.e. well fastened) in the literal sense of "planted," and, in this vein, amplifies the organic metaphor in order to expound the efflorescence and diversity of Torah:

נטועים, מה נטיעה זו פרה ורבה – אף דברי תורה פרין ורבין. בעלי אספות – אלו תלמידי
חכמים שיושבין אספות אספות ועוסקין בתורה, הללו מטמאין והללו מטהרין, הללו
אוסרין והללו מתירין, הללו פוסלין והללו מכשירין. שמא יאמר אדם: היאך אני למד
תורה מעתה? תלמוד לומר: כולם נתנו מרעה אחד – א-ל אחד נתנן, פרנס אחד אמרן,
מפי אדון כל המעשים ברוך הוא, דכתיב וידבר אלקים את כל הדברים האלה.

"Well planted:" just as a plant grows and increases, so the words of the Torah grow and increase. "The masters of assemblies:" these are the disciples of the wise, who sit in manifold assemblies and occupy themselves with the Torah, some pronouncing impure and others pronouncing pure, some prohibiting and others permitting, some disqualifying and others declaring fit. Should a man say: How in these circumstances shall I learn Torah? Therefore the text says: "All of them are given from one Shepherd." One God gave them; one leader uttered them from the mouth of the Lord of all creation, blessed be He; for it is written: "And God spoke all these words."

The organic element is endemic to the world of *Torah she-be'al peh*, generally, to which the gemara and the Tur relate. Unlike written Torah, clearly defined and wholly delimited, it is marked by growth and development. These qualities are especially characteristic, however, of the yeshivah world, within which *hiddush*, the capacity for creative innovation, is held in such high regard. The organic moment is doubly significant. First, it lends a vitalistic cast to Torah learning, to be marked, ideally, by both verve and imagination. Secondly, it deepens the basis of normative commitment by investing submission to the authority of Halakhah with an open-ended character. Historicists and Conservative ideologues champion development as a liberating factor, freeing an adapting present from the onerous shackles of a fossilized past. Properly perceived, however, it is no less an obligating factor, imposing, in effect, boundless commitment. As such, it is, most aptly, the vehicle of the covenantal relation of *na'aseh ve-nishma*, "We shall implement and heed." As the *Bet Halevi* noted (*Bet Halevi al Derush U'Mili De-Aggadta*, Jerusalem, 5707, p. 121, Parashat Yitro, s.v. *ve-attah*; see also p. 130):

אבל תורה שבע"פ הרי אין לה סוף וקצבה ובכל דור ודור מתחדשים חדושי דינים
והלכות.... ועל כוונה זו אמרו ישראל אז נעשה ונשמע, דנעשה קאי שקיבלו עליהם
לעשות כל האמור להם אז, ונשמע קאי על להבא דקיבלו על עצמם לשמוע עוד לדברי
החכמים שבכל דור ודור כל מה שיתגלה אח"כ בחידושי התורה.

But *Torah she-be'al peh* has no bound or limit, and in every generation new laws and *halakhot* are innovated... And it is with this intention that Israel then said, *Na'asseh ve-nishma*, as the import of *na'asseh* is that they took upon themselves to do all that they were told then, while *ve-nishma* refers to the future, that they took upon themselves to heed, further, the words of the sages of every generation, all that would be discovered subsequently as Torah novellae.

The Ra'avyah (I:168) interprets *"ve-hayyei olam nata be-tokhenu"* in a wholly different vein. He cites and rejects the view that it refers to Torah, and presents, alternatively, his own explanation. *Birkot ha-Torah*, he suggests, relate to both Torah and other themes:

דמקצת קאי אתורה ומקצת קאי אישראל ואשאר מצות, כגון וחיי עולם נטע בתוכנו
דקאי אשאר מצות וגמילות חסדים שישראל עוסקים בהם תדיר ואנו מודים להקב"ה
על שניהם.

Part refers to Torah and part refers to Israel and other *mizvot*, such as, "And eternal life He has implanted within us," which refers to other *mizvot* and to *gemilut hasadim*, in which Jews are always engaged, and we thank God for both.

The import of the passage is striking. However, an obvious question arises. Granted that "other *mizvot* and *gemilut hasadim*" are important, but why are they cited in a *berakhah* over Torah? Oughtn't Hazal rather have instituted a *birkat ha-hesed*, to be recited prior to visiting the sick or attending a funeral? The answer is equally obvious. Torah which is divorced from other *mizvot*, which is devoid of meaningful relation to *hesed*, is inherently flawed. Torah is, optimally, *Torat hesed*, an organic whole within which both orders are integrally fused. Hence, the component of *gemilut hasadim* is included in *birkat ha-Torah*, under the rubric of *hayyei olam*.

In conclusion, quite apart from their content, a word about the role which *Hazal* ascribed to *birkot ha-Torah*. With reference to the *pesukim* in Yirmiyahu (9:11–12),

מי האיש החכם ויבן את זאת ואשר דבר פי ה' אליו ויגדה על מה אבדה הארץ נצתה
כמדבר מבלי עבר. ויאמר ה' על עזבם את תורתי אשר נתתי לפניהם ולא שמעו בקולי
ולא הלכו בה,

Who is the wise man, that he may understand this, and who is he to whom the mouth of the Lord hath spoken, that he may declare it? Wherefore is the land perished and laid waste like a wilderness, so that none passeth through it? And the Lord saith: Because they have forsaken my law which I set before them, and have not hearkened to my voice, neither walked thereto,

Rav comments (Nedarim 81a): "Are not 'they have forsaken my law' and 'they have not hearkened to my voice' the same? Rav states: It means that they did not say a *berakhah* prior to learning Torah.'"

To learn Torah without a preceding *berakhah* does not merely constitute failure to fulfill a particular *halakhah*. It entails — and here, we return to our point of departure — missing the essence of Torah itself. Learning without praise, thanksgiving, and petitionary aspiration is learning which fails to realize the joy and the marvel, the awe and the wonder, of *talmud Torah*. To learn with insouciance or indifference, or even with presumed dispassionate objectivity grounded in intellectual curiosity, is to reduce *devar Hashem* to an academic discipline. Hence, as the Rav stressed (see his *Shiurim Le'Zekher Abba Mari z"l* [Jerusalem, 5745], pp. 1–2), on the basis of the Rambam, *talmud Torah* sans Berakhot does not merely miss out on a *mizvah*; it constitutes a positive violation. In effect, such learning disregards, perhaps even implicitly denies, the unique character of Torah; small wonder, then, that there is an *issur*.

This theme is complemented by an elaboration of the Maharal (see the introduction to *Tiferet Yisrael*; and cf. *Turei Zahav*, O.H. 47:1). Addressing himself to the gemara in Nedarim, he asks how is it conceivable that Rav could have interpreted the *pasuk* as ascribing the decimation of the land to the failure to recite *birkot ha-Torah* when *nevi'im* repeatedly saw it as caused by the most heinous of sins — idolatry, fornication, and murder? He responds that, unquestionably, it was over these that the country was punished. Rav, however, sought to confront another question: If, as *Hazal* assumed, people then engaged in Torah study, how could they have become so degenerate and dissolute? Where was the illuminating and ennobling influence of Torah study — "For its light stimulates regeneration?" With respect to this query, Rav responds that those who fail to utter *birkot ha-Torah*, who, therefore, implicitly approach learning without tremulous awe, relegating confrontation with the divine word to the exercise of rational inquiry, are impervious to that light. Only when Torah is perceived as it is and related to as such, does genuine and pervasive spiritual illumination occur.

By the same token, this sense of Torah's uniqueness is the spirit in which we, who do recite *birkot ha-Torah* — suffused by the duty to persist, brimming with prayerful anticipation of joy, filled with humble gratitude for having been singled out as the chosen recipients of the *Ribbono shel Olam's* own Torah, — approach it. Above all, overwhelmed by the sheer marvel. In the words of the Tur (O.H. 47; the final phrase alludes to Mishlei 8:30):

ויכוין בברכתו על מעמד הר סיני אשר בחר בנו מכל העמים וקרבנו לפני הר סיני והשמיענו דבריו מתוך האש ונתן לנו את תורתו הקדושה שהיא בית חיינו כלי חמדתו שהיה משתעשע בה בכל יום.

And, in his *berakhah*, one should think of the convocation at Sinai, that He chose us from among all the nations; brought us near to Mount Sinai and made us hear His words out of the fire, and gave us His sacred Torah which is the base of our lives — His precious vessel with which He reveled daily.

It is with this intent, with an eye to these aspirations, out of souls yearning for their realization, that a yeshivah is conceived. Beyond conception lies fulfillment; beyond the dream, implementation. Toward these, we labor with might and main. For *siyyata di-shemaya*, for divine assistance in their achievement, we bless and pray, with humility and hope.

Note

1. See Ramban's list of *mizvot asei* which he held had been omitted by the Rambam in the latter's *Sefer Ha-Mizvot* (printed after the section on *mizvot asei*), no. 15. For fuller discussions, see *Sha'agat Aryeh*, 24–25, and, especially, *Torat Refael, Orah Haym*, 1.

Chapter 10

To Double Business Bound: Reflections on the Divided Life of *Ovdei Hashem*

I

And, like a man to double business bound,
I stand in pause where I shall first begin,
And both neglect.[1]

דר' שמעון בן יוחי אמר אילו הוינא קאים על טורא דסיני בשעתא דאיתיהיבת אורייתא
לישראל הוינא מתבע קומי רחמנא דאיתברי להדין לבר נשא תרין פומין חד דיהוי לעי
באורייתא וחד דיתעביד בה כל צורכוי.

R. Shimon ben Yohai asserted: "Had I stood at Mount Sinai at the time
that Torah was given to Israel, I would have demanded that a person
be given two mouths: one with which to learn Torah, and the other
with which to manage all other matters."[2]

Prima facie, these two passages, the first put by the world's premier dra-
matist into the mouth of Claudius, whom Hamlet denominated "thou
incestuous, murd'rous, damned Dane," the other expressing the fervent
spirituality of the saintly avatar of mystical *avodat Hashem*, do not admit
of the faintest comparison. Quite apart from their antithetically contrasted
authorship, their motivation and substance differ no less than the sources.
Claudius, contemplating his role in engineering his brother's murder,
while groping for prayer and pardon, is immobilized by an admixture of
ambivalence and tormenting guilt. "Pray can I not, / My stronger guilt

defeats my strong intent." And so, radical self-knowledge trumps incipient guilt.

Patently, none of this, *le'havdil*, has any bearing upon Rashbi's provisional plea. He is rather impelled by the concern, and possibly, pain, generated by the inherent limits of personal and universal insufficiency. *Ars longa, vita brevis* — היום קצר והמלאכה מרובה. "The day is brief, and the labor plentiful" (Avot 2:15). The prospect of defeat he envisions is not grounded in indecisiveness, let alone in indolence or guilt, but rather in the magnitude of the spiritual challenge, as well as in the limits and ravages of time. "Where, alack," Shakespeare lamented in one of the variations on the theme in his *Sonnets*, "Shall Time's best jewel from Time's chest lie hid?" (65). Moreover, as to Rashbi's response to his dual charge, he, of course, neglects nothing.

Nevertheless, comparison, be it in the shadow of dissociation, is meaningful, after all, as in reading the texts jointly we encounter not only tangency but coincidence. The depth of Shakespeare's psychological insight and the magic of his verbal deftness have enabled him to encapsulate within the dramatic parameters of several lines of gripping soliloquy the essence of a fundamental facet of the human condition: the quandary of double business. Succinctly stated, the problem, for many if not most, inheres in the parcelization of effort and responsibility — indeed, of life itself. The day is brief and the *melakhah* — delineated in the mishnah in the singular but clearly relating to a plural phenomemon — is *merubbah*, not only in terms of quantitative scope, but, in light of its being, qualitatively, diffuse. The scarcity of wherewithal — in time, energy, resources — to attain all that one needs to get done or that one wants to get done generates a need to divide the available means, often leaving no area fully entitled. The process of prioritization — particularly, if pursued on a grand scale — may then result in bitterness, dilute the quality of life, and leave clouds of uncertainty hovering over personal existence.

Moreover, the issue touches upon the realization of ambition and the utilization of potential no less than upon the discharge of duty. Commenting upon the Torah's description of Avraham Avinu's death

— ויגוע וימת אברהם בשיבה טובה זקן ושבע — "And Avraham expired and died in gracious old age, elderly and satiated" (Bereshit 25:8) — the Ramban notes:

שראה כל משאלות לבו ושבע כל טובה ... ולא יתאוה שיחדשו בו הימים דבר ... והוא
ספור חסדי השם בצדיקים ומדה טובה בהם שלא יתאוו במותרות כענין שנאמר "תאות
לבו נתת לו", ולא כמו שנאמר בשאר האנשים "אוהב כסף לא ישבע כסף" ואמרו בו
"אין אדם יוצא מן העולם וחצי תאוותיו בידו יש בידו מנה מתאוה מאתים השיגה ידו
למאתים מתאוה לעשות ארבע מאות שנאמר אוהב כסף לא ישבע כסף".

He saw all his heart's wishes [realized], and was sated with bounty; and he had no desire that passing days should innovate anything for him… This is the story of Hashem's beneficence to the righteous and a proper quality that they possess — that they do not yearn for superfluities, as it is written, "His heart's desires You have granted him" (Tehillim 21:3). Unlike what is stated about most people, "A lover of money shall never have enough money" (Kohelet 5:9); and they [Hazal] said of them, "Upon leaving the world, a person has but satisfied half his desires. If he has one hundred units [of currency], he desires two hundred; if he has attained two hundred, he desires four hundred, as it is written, 'A lover of money shall never have enough money'" (Kohelet Rabbah 1:34).

The Ramban's description, so grossly inconsonant with the Faustian impetus of much modern Western culture, with its thirst for drinking life to the lees, exacerbates the dilemma, inasmuch as it enlarges the bounds of appetite without correspondingly increasing the reservoir from which the capacity for double business or double gratification can be drawn. Hence, the prospect of a shortfall can stimulate frustration, distort judgment, and immobilize decision.

The challenge of dual existence does not, of course, perturb all equally. Personality, commitment, and conscience are major variables. For a monist, however — and a denizen of a dank cave during a thirteen-year sojourn, such as Rashbi, should almost certainly be regarded as such — the pressures exerted by double business can be both pragmatically and spiritually formidable. All the more so, inasmuch as, while Claudius' simile may conceivably refer to a random occasion, in other contexts, as an existential dilemma, the phenomenon can be quite extensive in duration and quite disconcerting in impact. Whether the man to which he refers is "bound" in the sense of a destination to which he is headed, or whether, alternatively or additionally, in the sense of a linkage or bond that commits him legally or existentially, the duality as such may constitute a powerful challenge, stifling achievement and engendering frustration.

II

Human life had not quite commenced in this vein. At the dawn of creation, man and woman had been clearly defined and differentiated, each assigned a distinctive role in the process of propagation, and related to no other business.

> ויברא א-לקים את האדם בצלמו בצלם א-לקים ברא אתו זכר ונקבה ברא אתם. ויברך אתם א-לקים ויאמר להם א-לקים פרו ורבו ומלאו את הארץ וכבשה ורדו בדגת הים ובעוף השמים ובכל חיה הרמשת על הארץ.

> And God created the man in His image, in the divine image He created him; male and female He created them. And God blessed them and said to them, "Be fruitful and multiply, and fill the earth and conquer it, and lord over the fish of the sea, the fowl of the heavens, and over all living creatures which crawl over the face of the earth" (Bereshit 1:28).[3]

But, then again, in one admittedly puzzling respect, perhaps it had begun on this note, after all. Rashi, *ad locum*, refers us to Hazal's attempt to resolve the apparent contradiction between "and God created the man," and "male and female He created them," regarding which R. Yehudah suggests:

> בתחלה עלה במחשבה לבראות שנים ולבסוף נברא אחד.

> Initially, the plan had been to create two separate [beings]. Subsequently, however, only one was created.[4]

Rashi concludes by postulating a more literally oriented explanation:

ופשוטו של מקרא כאן הודיעך שנבראו שניהם בששי ולא פירש לך כיצד ברייתן ופירש
לך במקום אחר.

The *peshat* of the text, however, means that here we are only informed
that both were created on the sixth day. Nothing is said here, however,
as regards the mode and sequence of their creation, and that is elucidated elsewhere.[5]

According to the Aggadic reading, the question of the primal character of
the blueprint *homo sapiens* obviously arises: Was the latent initial intent
that there be a single persona with two destinies or two personae welded
by an extraneous link? The impact of these alternatives for our topic is
self-evident — and it serves as a point of departure for our discussion.

Whatever our disposition with respect to this issue, the early intrusion of double business may be perceived through other channels. At one
plane, we note the dichotomous metaphysical composition of human
nature — body and soul, spirit and matter, with all that this implies for
conduct and responsibility — or the grosser division of substance proper.
Speculating upon the course of the origins of humanity, the *midrash* attributes a dual approach to the *Ribbono shel Olam*:

אמר הקב"ה הרי אני בורא אותו בצלם ובדמות מן העליונים פרה ורבה מן התחתונים.

I shall create him, as regards image and form, as of the celestial [world],
but he shall propagate as of the bestial.[6]

As to function and duty, a trace of a possible dilemma is perhaps immanent in the second Biblical narrative of the creation of man. Unlike the
first, which focuses upon the experience of nature and the potential for
exploitation and hegemony, the second defines purposive human existence
in terms of charge and service. In this context, we note, from our perspective, a subtle shift. The need for implanting man within nature is implied,
early in the second chapter, as necessary to tend the newly created earth:
ואדם אין לעבד את האדמה — "There was no man to tend the earth" (Bereshit
2:5). Upon the realization of human creation, however, it turns out that his
role is defined more expansively (Bereshit 2:15): ויקח ה' א-לקים את האדם וינחהו

בגן עדן לעבדה ולשמרה. Not only to till and tend but to protect and conserve; not only *la'avod* but *le'ovdah u-le'shomrah*. To do double business.

Reference to this text invites the obvious retort, that this *pasuk* does not relate to double business at all, but entails, rather, a single, albeit not identical, task, performed with respect to different objects at various stages of development. This, in turn, raises the broader issue of the parameters and guidelines which, for our purposes, can direct us in defining and determining what constitutes the identity of an act as of a course of action and wherein need distinctiveness inhere in order that singularity be recognized.

The issue is germane to all walks of life and to a perceptive understanding of the niceties of any serious legal corpus. It has numerous conceptual and practical ramifications; and to the theoretically oriented Halakhist, in particular, it is the bread and butter of his endeavors. By dint of his engagement, that Halakhist is keenly aware that standards vary, as a function of the purpose and the area of discourse. In some, the key lies in the verb employed, in others, activity is defined with an eye to a complex of factors. For our present *telos*, we need to distinguish between formal and existential elements. Formally, students pursuing a doctoral program and hence writing dissertations in any given area are all part of a sociological pool, regardless of the area pursued, whether sacred or secular, humanistic or technological — and their relation to it. On the other hand, a *talmid* who reads *hiddushei Torah* and his peer who writes them are, linguistically, engaged in divergent activities, but, existentially, comrades in *talmud Torah*.

The business here under consideration, is, of course, spiritual; hence, its categories are limned by their relation to *avodat Hashem*. That area can itself be further divided and nuanced, to a significant degree; and, for certain purposes, this could be not only meaningful but essential. For ours, however, it would be largely redundant, and we shall, consequently, content ourselves with broader strokes — at times, lumping together under a single rubric what could have been readily differentiated, and, at others, contrarily, distinguishing what could have been easily fused.

III

This digression may strike us as remote from Rashbi and his lament over the need to divert time and energy from *talmud Torah* to the management of mundane affairs; and, in many respects, indeed it is. The dual role assigned to humanity in agricultural enterprise, insofar as both its interlocking facets relate to a single milieu, is no precursor to subsequent truly divided endeavor, assuredly not to the distinction between the radically distinguished realm of the sacred and the profane whose combined weight hung heavily on Rashbi's shoulders. And, yet, insofar as the psychological and spiritual difficulty in responding to multiple responsibility and variegated needs — whether in serving the *Ribbono shel Olam* or in servicing His creation, including that of the commanded agent — is concerned, both situations share much in common. Each entails tension, each is fraught with obstacles, each may generate frustration deriving from the inability to balance goals, and in each a person is seemingly doomed to only partial success — and, hence, to partial failure. As to the subsequent course of global history, if anything, the growth of culture and civilization issues in the proliferation, sometimes explosive and exponential, of possibilities, each with its particular onus and appeal.

The onus does not necessarily relate to concern over possible bad judgment, although the lurking prospect of error frequently compounds the anguish of choice. The pain can inhere in the need to choose at all — to forego desirable future gratification or to abjure sources of previous fulfillment. Moreover, anxiety may subsist even when one is convinced that he or she has chosen wisely. The maturing Matthew Arnold clearly sensed that he needed to leave the joys of his youthful romanticism aside and move on to a duller life of marriage, public service, and often prosaic responsibility. And yet the pain of transition, the desperate wish that he need abandon nothing in moving to the next phase, is palpable in so much of his verse, openly envious of peers who have not stayed the course — partly chosen, partly imposed — which is becoming his lot. "There thou art gone, and me thou leavest here, / Sole in these fields... / Fields where soft sheep from cages pull the hay, / Woods with anemonies in flower till May, / Know him a wanderer still; then why not me?"[7] Yet, despite the pangs, he, at most, looked back but did not seriously entertain the prospect of turning back. Abelard and Kierkegaard recognized that they needed to abandon Eloise and Regina, respectively. Yet, the acceptance and awareness were not devoid of anguish and regret. Our yeshivah world is wont to pronounce that the joy of the resolution of uncertainty — not so much in the course of pure *talmud Torah* as with regard to the determination of existential choice — is beyond compare. This assertion is, however, only true of certain situations — and then, often partially. Resolution can indeed usher in relief — but possibly at the cost often inherent in the process. Decision rarely proffers free lunches.

IV

Ought we, then, conclude that confrontation with double business inevitably entails a measure of anguish or even torment? Need we regard it as, in part, reflecting the character of human life as, in Hobbes' pungent phrase, "nasty, brutish, and short," and, in part, rendering it as such? Certainly not. Setting aside Claudius' description, which presumably refers to a humanly created dilemma, Rashbi's hypothetical demand raises an obvious question. Granted that he would have dared to press his request, and allowing for its justice (if *ma'amad Har Sinai* raises the level of obligation, oughtn't we have the right to ask for means for meeting it?), the fact remains that the *Ribbono shel Olam* patently decreed against the complaint; in all modesty, then, it behooves us to attempt to grasp the implicit rationale.

Several conjectures may be advanced, all premised on the assumption that Rashbi would not have deigned to challenge divine judgment. It may be suggested, first, that he acknowledged that the balance that was achieved between the spiritual and the material was optimal for the Jew, objectively speaking, and that it was surely subsumed under the primeval approval of the created universe — וירא א-לקים את כל אשר עשה והנה טוב מאד — "And God surveyed all that He had created, and it was very good" (Bereshit 1:31) — but he, personally, in light of subjective predilection, would have opted and pleaded for a more challenging alternative. Second, it may be contended that while the created human condition is admittedly not as pristine as it could have been, this should not be regarded as a purely negative concession to human fallibility and frailty. On the contrary, just as the inclusion of the evil inclination in the composite human spirit activates man religiously by exposing him to temptation, thus energizing the capacity for choice and the exercise of freedom, so with the structure of a single mouth. Its role — if you will, as the representative of *homo sapiens* in his entirety — its use to be divided among contrasting and, at times, conflicting forces — is to be perceived as among "the uses of adversity." It redounds to our benefit, precisely, because, once attained and sustained, ours is no longer "a fugitive and cloistered virtue, unexercised and unbreathed, that never sallies out and seeks her adversary, but slinks out of the race, where that immortal garland is to be run for, not without dust and heat" — deemed by Milton as unworthy of his encomium. We are now, rather, willing combatants: "Assuredly we bring not innocence into the world, we bring impurity much rather; that which purifies us is trial, and trial is by what is contrary."[8] These lines may strike some as sounding a Christian ring, but they clearly conform with elements deeply rooted — admittedly, not unanimously — in our own tradition.[9]

Third — and, to my inclination, preferably — the nature and impact of the dilemma of being "to double business bound" may turn on our own perception of the relation of the respective options. Is each business, at best, an obstacle course to stir the powers of volition and conscience, thus indirectly abetting human growth? Or can it be harnessed to contribute, in a direct sense, to the enhancement and realization of the very values with which it was competing for impetus and attention? With respect to the reciprocal dependence postulated by the mishnah in Avot (3:17) as defining the relation between Torah and flour — that is, *talmud Torah* and economic pursuits, respectively — ought not the quest for material means, when motivated by the desire to build an infrastructure which should facilitate *avodat Hashem*, be viewed as contributing to the realization of its supposedly contrasting goal?

In this sense, Rashbi's double business is not, ideologically and axiologically speaking, quite dual at all. Of course, at the pragmatic plane, initiatives may clash, schedules conflict, and priorities, short- or long-term, determined. And at that plane, almost a millennium later, Rabbenu Tam and his grand-nephew, Rabbenu Elhanan, were to disagree as to the primacy of *talmud Torah* vs. vocational *derekh eretz*.[10] And at that plane, a spiritual disciple of Rashbi may be anxious, after all, over being confronted by the distraction of double business and lapses into wishing that he had been among the *okhlei ha-man*, the consumers graced with celestial manna whose acquisition required no effort; among those of whom, in a debate cited in the Mekhilta, Rashbi asserted that, in a sense, they had been singularly privileged to have the gift of Torah bestowed upon them. R. Yehoshua had been fairly accepting in evaluating the life of double business and had apparently not regarded its impact upon commitment to Torah as particularly deleterious:

רבי יהושע אומר שונה אדם שתי הלכות בשחרית ושתים בערבית ועוסק במלאכתו כל היום מעלין עליו כאלו קיים כל התורה כולה.

R. Yehoshua asserts: "One can study two *halakhot* in the morning and two in the evening, and devote his whole day to his labor — and he would be regarded as one who had fulfilled the entire Torah."[11]

Rashbi, however, evidently focusing, characteristically, upon the demands imposed by serious *talmud Torah* and the responsibility attendant upon its exposition, infers, by contrast, that only those fortunate enough to be liberated from material worries are able and possibly authorized to pursue *talmud Torah* properly.

מכאן היה רבי שמעון בן יוחאי אומר לא נתנה תורה לדרוש אלא לאוכלי המן הא כיצד היה יושב ודורש ולא היה יודע מהיכן אוכל ושותה ומהיכן היה לובש ומתכסה הא לא נתנה תורה לדרוש אלא לאוכלי המן ושניים להם אוכלי תרומה.

R. Shimon ben Yohai inferred, thence, that the exposition of Torah was but granted to the consumers of manna. How is this [to be viewed]? Could one who knows not whence he shall derive sustenance to eat and drink or to dress and clothe himself expound [Torah properly]? Hence, it is to be concluded that] Torah was but granted to the consumers of manna and, secondarily, to the consumers of *terumah*.[12]

Rashbi does not, of course, advocate reducing the scope of one's Torah study in order thus better to manage mundane affairs. On the contrary, he implicitly counsels limiting general activity so as to improve the prospect for the mastery of Torah.[13] In any event, the controversy cited in the Mekhilta has significant implications. But insofar as common values inform both pursuits and mold an organically unified personality, duality will result in neither neglect nor resentment, and the lament will not be quite the same.

V

While I have dwelt upon a specific situation to exemplify the distinction I have presented, the principle as such cuts comprehensively to the core of Torah living. What is the mishnah's dictum, וכל מעשיך יהיו לשם שמים, "And all your acts should be for the sake of Heaven" (Avot 2:12), but a pithy encapsulation of the overarching fusion of unity in diversity, cited in the mishnah, and quite clearly ensconced by the Rambam in that role?

> נמצא המהלך בדרך זו כל ימיו כולן עובד את ה' תמיד אפילו בשעה שנושא ונותן ואפילו בשעה שבועל מפני שמחשבתו בכל כדי שימצא צרכיו, עד שיהיה גופו שלם לעבוד את ה'.

> The result is that if one pursues this course during his entire lifetime, that he serves God constantly, even while he is conducting a commercial transaction, and even while copulating, inasmuch as his thought throughout is that he care for his needs so that he shall be physically sound in order to serve God.[14]

It is presumably in this spirit — although in a different sense — that Kohelet's Scriptural approbation of duality should be understood. Pursuant to complementary counsels — אל תהי צדיק הרבה ואל תתחכם יותר למה תשומם, "Be not overly righteous nor overly wise; why destroy yourself?" and אל תרשע הרבה ואל תהי סכל למה תמות בלא עתך, "Be not overly sinful, nor be

foolish; why should you die prematurely?" — the next *pasuk* urges טוב אשר
תאחז בזה וגם מזה אל תנח את ידך כי ירא א-לקים יצא את כולם, "It is good that you
grasp the one nor release your hold upon the other, for a God-fearer will
discharge his duty to all."[15] It is palpably difficult to view this conclusion
as a recommendation for a joint commitment to moderate evil and virtue,
or as a compromise between the two. Is it only much evil which is to be
shunned, Hazal asked,[16] while a small quotient is acceptable? However the
answer is to be understood, I believe, the key lies in integrated diversity.

The concept is, of course, familiar from other contexts, for which
the relation between *talmud Torah* and *gemilut hasadim* may serve as an
instructive example. Both are listed in the mishnah in Pe'ah (1:1) as boundless. Hence, some clash, at the level of implementation, between these
greedy normative systems is inevitable, and Hazal, from that mishnah
down, took pain to define patterns of resolution. Yet, whatever one's *hashkafah* regarding optimal balance, no one assumes that this factor dictates
total bifurcation. We take the integration and the reciprocal fructification
for granted; and so, likewise, generally, with the relation between *talmud*
and *ma'aseh*. The point to be stressed here is that, *mutatis mutandis*, an
analogous relation obtains between the pure study and teaching of Torah
and advancing *yishuvo shel olam*.

VI

For a modern instance, reflecting the mindset and the values of the
yeshivah world, we might turn to a striking letter written to his wife by
a remarkable *gadol* and poignantly sensitive soul, R. Avraham Eliyahu
Kaplan. Reared in Lithuania and trained in its premier *yeshivot* at the turn
of the twentieth century, he subsequently moved to Germany, where he
headed the Hildesheimer Rabbinical Seminary. Acutely aware of some
of the deficiencies of religious education in both countries, he resolved
to revamp it; and to this end, he sought to focus upon teacher training.
In the process, he plunged into the nitty-gritty of establishing a quality
institution — raising funds, acquiring quarters, structuring a curriculum,
attracting students. In the letter, he enumerates and describes the pell-mell

of his multiple businesses; and then, suddenly, the *yeshivah bahur* in him comes to the fore, reminding him of his roots, as that *bahur's* inner voice reproaches him for reducing his commitment to them:

אולם מתוך כל רבוי העבודה הזה תשמע נפשי קול מדבר: והתורה מה תהא עליה? תורה זו שעמלת עליה על ימי נעוריך, שבזבזת לה את כל הגיגיך ושנעשתה לך למקור חיים וענג – האם תעזבנה עתה ונטשתה? זו תורה וזו שכרה?!!

But from the midst of this multifaceted labor, my soul hears a voice, speaking: "And what is to be of Torah? That Torah over which you labored throughout your youth, upon which you spent all your thoughts, and which became, for you, a source of life and gratification — will you now leave and desert it? Shall this be the *telos* of Torah and its reward?!"

True, his current activity is also geared to the study and dissemination of Torah — to young tyros who are setting out on their lifelong vocation, and will, thence, in turn, transmit what they have absorbed to their students. And yet,

אבל סוף סוף אין כאן מקום לכל אותו המקצע הרחב והנאור, הכביר והנשגב, אשר נקרא לו 'לומדות', אותו הטיול הנהדר בסירת מחשבתי על גלי ים התלמוד ומפרשיו – אכן צריך אדם להיות צדיק גמור וחסיד גדול בכדי שיוכל להקריב על מזבח התורה את התורה עצמה – לפרוש מן התורה בכדי לעבוד בעד התורה.

And yet, at bottom, there is no place here for that broad and illuminating subject, so lucid and majestic, which was called *lomdut*; that glorious excursion in my mind's dinghy on the waves of the sea of the Talmud and its commentaries. Indeed, a person must be a great *zaddik* and saint in order to be able to sacrifice Torah proper upon the altar of Torah; so as to leave Torah to labor on its behalf.[17]

Double business and unity of purpose, par excellence — at once passionate and majestic.

That was the gist of the letter and the quintessence of R. Avraham's Elyah's rich, albeit tragically brief, life. Not his alone, however. Looking retrospectively upon my own, I note, more clearly and more fully than when I heard the message articulated, the power and the consistency with which it was borne in upon me. That was the heart of the legacy I received at home, and, at bottom, it was common to my primary *morei derekh*, *rabbi muvhak*, the Rav zt"l; his brother, Rav Ahron zt"l; and the Rosh Yeshivah (as, with the definite article, he was known to *talmidim*), Rav Yitzchak Hutner zt"l. They differed on a range of issues regarding style, substance and priority in areas of Halakhah, *hashkafah* and public policy — although, fundamentally, less than many imagined. With respect to our issue, however, there was much substantive assent, concerning both the perception of the problem and the direction of its resolution.

A letter written by the Rosh Yeshivah — who, incidentally, in his early stages, was significantly influenced by the personality and ideology of R. Avraham Elyah — to a *talmid* who had lapsed into crisis upon leaving the yeshivah is typically instructive. The latter's lament had evidently been based on the perception of a secular career as entailing a "double life," and it induced a sharp and imaginative response:

אמנם מי למותר להגיד לך כי מעולם לא הייתי מסכים בשום אופן ל-"double life". ששוכר לו חדר בבית לחיות בו חיי תושב, ושוכר לו עוד חדר במלון לחיות בו חיי אורח, בודאי שיש לו double life, אבל מי ששוכר לו דירה בת שני חדרים יש לו broad life ואתה חביבי יקירי חלילה לך מלראות את עצמך בראי כפול של not double life... חיים כפולים.

> It is superfluous for me to tell you that I would never, under any circumstances, have agreed to a "double life." However, if one rents a room in a home in order to live there as a resident and rents an additional room in a hotel so as to live there as a guest, he indeed leads a double life. But if one rents a two-room apartment, he leads a broad life rather than a double life... And you, my dear cherished [one], far be it from you to see yourself via the dual mirror of a double life.[18]

This counsel is not quite identical with the affirmation of the possible need for votaries of Torah to offer it upon its own altar. Both assertions are, however, pervaded by the same harmonizing and animating spirit.

VII

Apropos of the sacrifice, as well as of the righteousness and saintliness deemed requisite for its implementation, a concluding observation is in order. The scenario depicted is one within which the *makriv* and the *korban* are, to a degree, coincident. The Torah which is being offered is, in one sense, a facet of personal existence and possession, what Hazal denominated as *torato dileh*, the learner's own Torah,[19] but it is that part of him which is consecrated to *malkhut shamayim*. Hence, in comparison with the remission of subjective mundane ambition, it is both less and more demanding. Less, insofar as one is offering what is already owned "by *hekdesh*," the divine treasury, and not fully his. More, insofar as to the spiritual committed soul, it is the most precious part of his being. The situation is quite different, however, in both directions, when the scope of the sacrifice is measurably wider; when a) it is not confined to periodic gestures but is manifested over the span of a lifetime, and when b) it entails the thwarting of ambition, natural but not necessarily sacral, related to the ego, if not the super-ego, in its quest for personal success.

Within our world, these are pangs particularly felt by the advocates and practitioners of "Torah and…." It is not so much the thirst for acclaim, strong as that often is. To be sure, Milton asserted that "Fame is the spur that the clear spirit doth raise / (That last infirmity of Noble mind) / To scorn delights, and live laborious days,"[20] and he knew, passionately, whereof he spoke. Keats aspired to be included among the English poets; and while he did not live to savor Arnold's verdict, "He is; he is with Shakespeare," the impetus of the hope was very much in evidence. But the lack or the loss of public acclaim — particularly, of the cheaper variety — is of relatively lesser import. Any creative aspirant of quality can serve as his own best critic and gauge the qualifications of his judges.

Beyond recognition, however, there lies a higher dimension — the quest for mastery and excellence, often accompanied by the competitive urge for preeminence. Presumably, a *ben Torah* who commits himself to double business is impelled by the conviction that the fusion may be personally rewarding and enriching, or that, with an eye for the needs of the public domain, it is generally valuable in molding leadership, or is, at the very least, the call of the hour.

Nevertheless, in all likelihood, he is also impelled by the desire for mastery *per se*; quite apart from recognition of his accomplishment, by the substantive attainment as such. In the event, however, there is, consequently, a price — at times, a perceptively grave price — to be paid. Breadth is purchased at the expense of comprehensiveness. Hazal's definition of a *talmid hakham*, ששואלין אותו הלכה בכל מקום, "one who can be questioned about all areas of Halakhah,"[21] is, for him, difficult to achieve, and the nuances of exposition increasingly elusive. The realization that while he has labored and achieved, "Tho much is taken, much abides;" that a crust of knowledge, levels of creativity, aggregates of elements of Torah strewn through basic sources, Scriptural or from the world of Hazal, and, beyond them, within Rishonim, Aharonim or *poskim*, are at the fingertips of some peers and/or colleagues, or even ensconced among the treasured reserves of others, while they have somehow eluded or passed him by, can be gnawing — at times, even depressing. As to the obverse, a parallel situation obtains. One may be a competent chemist or historian but not the preeminent, the gap between excellence and competence defying his attempt at bridging it. Lest I be misunderstood, it should be clear that this sentiment need not necessarily entail retrospective regret over the decision to pursue a chosen course, made in the past and subsequently dictating much of what followed. Even if one is genuinely convinced that he had pursued an optimal path — from both an objective Torah and spiritual standpoint, with reference to what F. H. Bradley called "my station and its duties," and his talents and circumstances, as well as what was, subjectively, the most gratifying and fulfilling scenario — he may regret his limitations without being in any way conscience-stricken.

Moreover, for our budding *lamdan*/scholar, the situation is further exacerbated by at least two local and contemporary factors. The first is the inordinately competitive climate of the major *yeshivot* on the Eastern European model, most of them oriented to nurturing and promoting *illuyim*.[22] The second is the more general shift, under the impact of the scientific revolution since the seventeenth century, in favor of the total mastery of a relatively narrow area as opposed to the development of Renaissance polymaths. Related to this attitudinal change is the expansion of an information explosion, all of which lessens the chance of multiple mastery of divergent or interdisciplinary fields, and raises the barriers to the development of competent candidates, capable and willing to cope with double businesses.

VIII

Unfortunately, these difficulties surface at a time when the need for such talents has magnified rather than diminished. Since the Emancipation and the *Haskalah*, the broad Torah world has paid a heavy price for the dichotomy typifying many of its leaders, fine *talmidei hakhamim* but divorced from the world around them. Furthermore, in many instances, they are divorced not by accident, but by design, often consciously trained to avoid all significant contact with that world and then handed the keys of the kingdom, authorized to pass judgment and determine policy for a society they have been educated to avert, whose pulse they don't feel, of whose existential language they are largely ignorant, and whose values they neither understand nor appreciate. Their accomplishments cannot be gainsaid, their stature is worthy of our respect; and far be it from me to strive for dilution of Torah knowledge and commitment in the service of national leadership. Would, however, that those in the Torah world, entrusted with double business, were more fully equipped to confront its challenges.

I certainly do not mean to suggest that the pattern of unified double business is, from a public standpoint, the sole legitimate or desirable model. Who would have wanted to alter one iota of that luminous fusion of *lomdut, zidkut*, sensitivity and insight which marked R. Shlomo Zalman Auerbach zt"l, through which he enriched and enlightened the broad Torah community? But on the other hand, ought we ignore, as blithely as much of the Torah world does, Hazal's dictum that only *talmidei hakhamim* versed in the range of the world's seventy languages[23] — or, in the

Rambam's formulation, ברוב הלשונות, "in the majority of languages" — qualified for membership in a Sanhedrin *gedolah*?[24]

Admittedly, to many, this prerequisite will have a highly technical ring, as regards both its substance, with nothing more than narrow linguistic facility intended, and its purpose — שלא תהא סנהדרין שומעת מפי המתורגמן, so that the members of the Sanhedrin, while hearing a case, will be able to adjudicate without recourse to interpreters (Makkot 6b). Surely, however, there is much to be said for a broader construction. Commenting upon the *pasuk*, לא תכירו פנים במשפט, "With respect to the judicial establishment, you will pay no regard to acquaintance" (Devarim 1:17), which, *prima facie*, may ordinarily be read as addressed to the *dayyanim*, demanding of them full impartiality, the Sifrei, *ad locum*, asserts that the admonition refers to those empowered to appoint *dayyanim*. In this sense, it prohibits all aspects of nepotism and simony, with general merit or formal halakhic regulations to be the sole basis for selection. Included in the catalogue of possible illegitimate choices is the factor of virtuosity in the knowledge of language: איש פלוני יודע בכל לשון אשיבנו דיין, "I shall appoint this person inasmuch as he knows all languages." Elaborating upon this motif, the Netziv, in his commentary *Emek Ha-Netziv*, *ad locum*, notes: בכל לשון והרי הוא משכיל בהויות העולם, "In all languages — hence, he is wise with respect to the realities of the world." In that context, the concern voiced relates to the prospect of harnessing this factor to malevolent ends. It should be clear, however, that the conception posited by the Netziv is no less relevant to the realization of positive ends. Even allowing for the distinction between the molding of the inner self and the structuring of the public square, the implicit definition of לשון as culture and sensibility has, therefore, significant implications for assessing and defining the role of unified double business in our communal and personal *avodat Hashem*.

The Rambam concludes his magnum opus, *Mishneh Torah*, with an apparent ringing rejection of life "to double business bound." Projecting the prospective character of the Messianic era and the source of its appeal to prophets and sages, he affirms:

ובאותו הזמן לא יהיה שם לא רעב ולא מלחמה ולא קנאה ותחרות שהטובה תהיה

מושפעת הרבה וכל המעדנים מצויין כעפר ולא יהיה עסק כל העולם אלא לדעת את
ה' בלבד.

And at that time, there shall be neither famine nor warfare, and neither envy nor competitiveness, as bounty will be widely conferred and
all delicacies as common as dust, and the entire world shall have no
business but to know God, exclusively.[25]

However, the fact that this scenario is relegated solely to the utopian mil-
lenarian setting reinforces our awareness of its current impracticality. As
an axiological manifesto, it is a clear statement that, even allowing for the
ascription of values and meaning to many secular careers, the choice of a
vocation is not immaterial, and that all factors being equal (are they ever?),
devotion to the study and, *a fortiori*,[26] the teaching of Torah is, personally
and publicly, optimal; as an implicit normative statement dictating how
a person ought to spend his or her "spare" time, its vision is pregnant
with contemporary relevance and captures our allegiance. This, however,
in the nature of what Hazal defined as *hilkheta li'meshihah*, a halakhic
standard to be implemented eschatologically.[27] As to the historical situation, what better instance of the dilemma posed by double business need
be sought than the Rambam's graphic account of the pressures exerted by
his medical duties at the royal harem, pressures which often left little time
for personal *talmud Torah*, but for Shabbat afternoon? And what more
ennobling manifestation of how the intensity of personality and the depth
of commitment enable transcending the force of necessity, or diffidence,
so that the confrontation does not issue in "both neglect" but in maximal
integration?

At bottom, our response to the quandary of double business is an
amalgam of pragmatic, moral, and religious elements. Practically, one
needs to develop the capacity for both decision and decisiveness — the
ability to judge incisively and effectively, to see life steadily and see it
whole, as well as the strength to act upon the decisions. Morally, we are
charged to adopt and to internalize Ben Zoma's counsel, itself an amalgam
of ethics and Torah, איזהו עשיר השמח בחלקו, "Wealthy is he who is satisfied
with his lot" (Avot 4:1), while yet suffused with an aspiration to ascend

spiritually at the personal plane, and to contribute to *yishuvo shel olam* by developing better mousetraps whose invention is stimulated by a measure of dissatisfaction with the older models as our part of the collective lot. Finally, in the more purely religious realm, an element often more associated with the East than with the West, but surely very deeply rooted in the tradition of Torah — acceptance. Acceptance of servitude, of the yoke of bondage to the *Ribbono shel Olam*, קבלת עול מלכות שמים; acceptance of the yoke of submission to the divine will, קבלת עול מצוות, as formulated in the corpus of Torah; and acceptance of whatever lot He has meted out to us, as the lodestar of life, divided and unified. For *ovdei Hashem*, in quest of gratifying holistic existence, in this triad inheres the *unum necessarium* for its attainment. I cannot agree with R. Nahman. Whether or not the entire world is to be perceived and experienced as an extremely narrow bridge, the accompanying assertion, possibly tinged with a touch of bravado, that the main thing is fearlessness, is wide of the mark. *Ve-ha'ikkar* is acceptance.

Notes

1. *Hamlet* 3:3:44–46.
2. Yerushalmi, Berakhot 1:2 and Shabbat 1:2.
3. For our purposes, I present this text as a normative assignment of duty. However, the *tannaim* disagreed on this issue, with R. Yohanan ben Nuri apparently interpreting it as a blessing; see Yevamot 65b. Cf. Bereshit 9:7, and Rashi and Ramban thereon.
4. Ketubbot 8a. This account, as Rashi notes, of course omits what a *peshat* reading regards as the final phase, i.e., separate creations. The concept of initial plans which were then modified at the plane of implementation raises obvious difficulties. It appears in various contexts; see Rashi, Bereshit 6:7; Eruvin 18a; *Tosafot*, Rosh Hashanah 27a, s.v. *ke-man*. Its elucidation lies beyond our scope here, however.
5. Bereshit 1:28, s.v. *zakhar*.
6. Bereshit Rabbah 14:3.
7. "Thyrsis." The "thou" who is addressed is a close friend, Arthur Hugh Clough, who had died several years before the composition of this elegy to him.
8. *Areopagitica*.
9. For a suggestive analogue, see Avodah Zarah 17a-b, where the gemara records a debate amongst *amoraim* with respect to a situation in which necessity compels undertaking an initiative requiring exposure to one of two temptations of differing degrees of

risk. For which is it preferable to opt? The text speaks, literally, of levels of reward for prospective successful resistance, but it appears likely that spiritual preference is included as a factor in the calculation as well.

10. See *Tosafot R. Yehudah He-Hasid*, Berakhot 35b, s.v. *ve-asafta*; *Tosafot Yeshanim*, Yoma 85b, s.v. *teshuvah*; and *Hagahot Maimuniyot*, Talmud Torah 3:2. The primacy ascribed by Rabbenu Tam to *derekh eretz* presumably refers to the expected quantitative division of time, rather than to axiological priority.

11. Mekhilta, on Shemot 16:4 (Va-yasa 2). Rashbi's position here parallels that which is cited in his name in Berakhot 35b, in opposition to that of R. Yishmael. Cf. also Menahot 99b. Irrespective of Rashbi's principled position, *per se*, the source of the inference cited here is surprising.

12. *Loc. cit.*

13. It is noteworthy that Rashbi only relates to לדרוש, which can mean either to explicate or to teach publicly. These are special tasks requiring particular skills and concentration.

14. De'ot, 3:3. Cf. *Shemonah Perakim*, chs. 4–5.

15. Kohelet 7:16–18.

16. See Shabbat 31b and Kohelet Rabbah, 7:17. The answers suggested in both texts are similar but not identical. The general thrust is the admonition against relaxation of effort to avoid sin and against acceptance of its habitual place in one's mindset and life simply because one has lapsed into it previously.

17. *Be-Ikvot Ha-Yir'ah* (Jerusalem, 5720), p. 200.

18. *Pahad Yizhak, Iggerot U'Mikhtavim* (Jerusalem, 5741), pp. 184–5. I am not fully certain as to whether the opening sentence relates to the *talmid* or to the Rosh Yeshivah.

19. See Kiddushin 32b.

20. "Lycidas," 70–72.

21. See Kiddushin 49b, Shabbat 114a, and Ta'anit 10b. With respect to these sources and the application of the term, *be-khol makom*, Rishonim (*ad locum*) discussed whether its intent is any place, with a small quotient sufficing, or every place.

22. This element, a prominent feature of the climate of some of the premier *yeshivot*, is of course problematic, inasmuch as it borders upon the thirst for fame, and should thus be regarded as a pursuit motivated by *she-lo li'shmah*, i.e., learning for personal adventitious gain rather than for its own sake. The gemara in Nedarim 62a explicitly rejects this aim as an improper incentive:

שלא יאמר אדם אקרא שיקראני רבי אשנה שאהיה זקן ואשב בישיבה אלא למוד מאהבה וסוף הכבוד לבוא.

(In this vein, see Sifrei, Devarim 6:5 and the Ramban's comments on that verse, as well as the Rambam, Hilkhot Teshuva 10:3–4.) However, human nature being what it is, this motive is all too common. I recall a comment once made to me by *mori ve-rabbi*, R. Hutner, in this connection. In surveying the current status of most *batei midrash*, he stated, with typical realism, that egotistical considerations impelled most of the *talmidim*. "As for *Torah li'shmah*, that was attained by perhaps three or four in a generation."

23. The number seventy appears in Hazal in numerous contexts as a thumbnail figure for the range of nations, cultures, and languages.

24. Sanhedrin 17a and Rambam, Hilkhot Sanhedrin 2:6, respectively. There is some debate as to whether this ability is a *sine qua non* or merely a preference; see *Kesef Mishneh* and *Sefer Ha-Mafte'ah* (in the Frankel edition, *ad locum*).

25. Hilkhot Melakhim 12:5. It is noteworthy that, in formulating this prognosis and in adducing a *pasuk* in its support, the Rambam speaks in universal terms —

ולא יהיה עסק כל העולם אלא לדעת את ה' בלבד ולפיכך יהיו חכמים גדולים ויודעים דברים הסתומים העמוקים וישיגו דעת בוראם כפי כח האדם שנאמר כי מלאה הארץ דעת את ה' כמים לים מכסים.

And the entire world shall have no business but to know God, exclusively. Therefore they will be great sages and know the hidden matters, grasping the knowledge of their Creator according to [full extent of] human knowledge, as the verse states (Yeshayahu 11:9), "The world will be filled with the knowledge of God as the waters cover the ocean bed."

However, the list of textual variants at the end of the Frankel edition cites some readings as, יהיו ישראל חכמים, the Jews will be. Cf. also Hilkhot Teshuva 8:2, whose narrower canvas does not contradict that of Hilkhot Melakhim but clearly differs from it.

26. See Bava Kamma 17a, Bava Mezia 85b, and Kohelet Rabbah 9:8.

27. See Sanhedrin 51b, Zevahim 45a.

Chapter 11

Diaspora Religious Zionism: Some Current Reflections

Matthew Arnold opened his critical essay on Wordsworth by citing Macaulay's observation, "after Wordsworth's death, when subscriptions were being collected to found a memorial of him, that ten years earlier more money could have been raised in Cambridge alone, to do honour to Wordsworth, than was now raised all through the country."[1] I very much hope that Diaspora religious Zionism is not in the throes of terminal demise but there is no denying that if this Forum had been convened half or a quarter of a century ago, the context would have been much livelier. Unquestionably, this movement — as a public and as a private phenomenon, institutionally and ideologically, qua political entity and in the form of a shared spiritual commitment — has seen more vibrant days. And yet, many of the relevant contemporary issues still cut to the heart of a Torah *hashkafah* (outlook), and remain worthy of note and incisive discourse.

Religious Zionism, tersely described and defined, is comprised of several components. In part, political movement, in part, both personal credo and public manifesto, it fuses the active and the contemplative. In all respects, however, it finds itself currently — in significant measure, in Israel, too, but to a greater measure, in the Diaspora- paradoxically, both embattled and dormant. The primary causes of both are dual. On the one hand, the fate of its religious element is but a local manifestation of the overall status and fortunes of Zionism in general. As the locus and the object of Zionist fervor, the State of Israel has been the victim of its own

successes. Once the threat to its existential security waned, and as the erst-
while David became increasingly perceived as a Goliath, concern for the
yishuv and for the welfare, physical or spiritual, of its inhabitants, lessened.
As an impetus for energizing the Jewish world, no fresh goal could even
approach the struggle for the founding of the state and the subsequent
nursing of its fledgling body politic and institutions. Moreover, whereas
the haredi world has a clearly focused agenda which it has pursued with
great intensity, much of the religious Zionist camp has encountered difficulty in the apportionment of effort and resources between religious
goals and more general Zionist aims.

In addition, as the dream metamorphosed into reality, a modicum
of disillusionment set in, fuelled, moreover, by an erosion in the ethical
status of Israeli society and a decline in its general idealism. At the same
time, specific Diaspora issues such as intermarriage and assimilation were
becoming exacerbated. Consequently, in many communities, Zionist
commitment, even amongst the strongly identified, Jewishly, became
jaded, as local and national interests competed for moral and material
support.[2]

Unfortunately, these trends did not spare the religious sector. In its
case, however, the adverse effects were compounded by a major additional
factor. The changes in the internal fabric of the general religious world
and of the Orthodox community, in particular, has impacted significantly
upon the strength, both relative and absolute, of its Zionist component.
If, at mid-century, Mizrachi and its adherents were a dominant presence
and Agudah was perceived, even by many of its supporters, as marginal,
the situation today is palpably and dramatically reversed. Moreover, at
issue is not just the matter of political clout. One senses a loss of vitality
and vibrancy in internal debate and discourse. A young acquaintance who
recently had occasion to survey religious Zionist publication of a generation ago was astounded by the richness and the level of the discourse,
as compared to the thinner fare to which he had become accustomed.[3]
Unfortunately, this decline is manifest in Israel as well, where a blend of
ideological rigor mortis has combined with obsessive concern with ter-
ritorial issues to paint the *dati-le'umi* (national religious) parties — at least,

for the time being — into a corner of isolation and political irrelevance. However, its impact is more keenly perceived around the world, where, due to physical and, hence, emotional, distance, the divisive debates over foreign policy which have generated much heat, as they have driven the Israeli polis asunder, have not registered abroad with equal resonance.

Small wonder that many Diaspora religious Zionists find themselves today weakened and possibly befuddled; perhaps asking themselves, as did Wordsworth, in the very different context, of his "Ode on the Intimations of Immortality,"

> Whither is fled the visionary gleam?
> Where is it now, the glory and the dream?

Moreover, beyond ideology, they are confronted by another issue — halakhic, philosophic, existential, and, perhaps acutely, pragmatic. Over all, looms the prospect of *aliyah* (immigrating to Israel). And it looms as a genuine option. Admittedly, to some extent, as, in recent years, with respect to France and Argentina, anti-Semitism continues to impact upon consideration of the issue. Broadly viewed, however, and relative to the sociohistorical course of the last century and a quarter, with respect to most contemporary Jewry, *aliyah* is more truly a matter of choice. Not, obviously, wholly free. Economic factors, for instance, still weigh heavily. And yet, choice has been considerably magnified. On the one hand, the gates of the Promised Land are open, and, on the other, the pressure to leave current host countries and enter through them has receded. Hence, judgment in the light of merit is more readily possible. At the public level, literal ascent to the promised rose-garden is, preeminently, all sweetness and light. At one plane, conceived en masse rather than in individual terms, it contributes to the service of national needs — social, political, economic, and security — as it fleshes out and intensifies the character of Eretz Yisrael as our homeland. At another, viewed from the perspective of classical secular Zionism, it ameliorates the Diaspora's Jewish problem. And, of course, beyond the pragmatic, *aliyah*, straddling the historical and the eschatological, constitutes a fulfillment of the divinely mandated providential commitment on the one hand:

הנני מביא אותם מארץ צפון וקבצתים מירכתי ארץ בם עור ופסח הרה וילדת יחדו
קהל גדול ישובו הנה. בבכי יבאו ובתחנונים אובילם אל נחלי מים בדרך ישר
לא יכשלו בה כי הייתי לישראל לאב ואפרים בכורי הוא

I will bring them from northern land and will gather them from the
ends of the earth, amongst them the blind and lame, the pregnant and
those who recently gave birth, en masse will they return here. They
will come crying, and with mercy I will direct them, guide them to
streams of water in a direct route by which they will not falter, since I
am a Father for Israel, and Ephraim is my firstborn (Yirmiyahu 31:7–8)

and of the realization of our own collective aspiration on the other:

בשוב ה' את שיבת ציון היינו כחולמים

When God brings back the returnees of Zion we will have been like
dreamers. (Tehillim 126:1)

And, while even at the public level, *aliyah* exacts a toll insofar as it may
entail a brain drain, as the exodus of the most highly motivated thins the
ranks of Diaspora Zionism, on the whole, the net result is clearly deemed
positive.

At the private level, however, *aliyah* is, palpably, very much a mixed
bag. Of the components of religious Zionism, it clearly offers the broadest opportunity, but, just as clearly, exacts the greatest toll. I trust that
the major relevant factors are well-known, but a summary catalogue may
nevertheless be helpful.

On the positive side of the ledger, the primary focus is, evidently,
upon spiritual elements — particularly, of a normative character. At least
four elements, bonding residence in Eretz Yisrael with the performance of
mizvot, may be identified. The first and most direct is the position of the
Ramban, widely trumpeted and popularized by Rav Zvi Yehudah Kook,
that the anticipation, at once promise and command, that we are to possess and settle Eretz Yisrael is to be enumerated amongst *taryag mizvot*
(613 commandments); and this, in two respects. Most fundamentally,
this *mizvah* is realized through the establishment and maintenance of the
hegemony of *Knesset Yisrael* in the promised land, which is not to be left

under the aegis of foreign rule, or as wilderness at the disposal of natural forces:

שנצטוינו לרשת הארץ אשר נתן הא-ל יתברך ויתעלה לאבותינו לאברהם ליצחק וליעקב ולא נעזבה ביד זולתינו מן האומות או לשממה.

Which is that we were commanded to inherit the land given by God, blessed be He to our forefathers, and that we should not abandon it to the hands of other nations or to desolation.[4]

In this vein, *vi-yeshavtem bah*, "and you should settle it," denotes *yishuv* as settlement — and, if necessary, conquest — as it affects the status of the land. Secondarily, however, the Ramban also subsumes *yeshivah*, mere physical residence — even in circumstances under which one's absence would in no way endanger national interests — as a personal fulfillment of the *mizvah*.[5]

While this element was included by the Ramban in a list of positive commandments whose omission by the Rambam he criticized, it is generally assumed, given the inclusion in *Mishneh Torah* of halakhot concerning the obligation to reside in Eretz Yisrael and the prohibition of leaving it,[6] that the Rambam would assent to the substance of the Ramban's position, the lack of formal enumeration notwithstanding. Be that as it may, no such gap exists with respect to a second factor: the status of the country as venue for the performance of many other *mizvot* — particularly, agriculturally related *mizvot ha-teluyot ba'aretz* (commandments specific to Eretz Yisrael).[7] This aspect is most sharply delineated in a gemara in Sotah — strikingly, with respect to Mosheh Rabbenu's aspiration to enter Eretz Yisrael and his passionate pleas in this connection:

דרש רבי שמלאי מפני מה נתאוה משה רבינו ליכנס לארץ ישראל וכי לאכול מפריה הוא צריך או לשבוע מטובה הוא צריך אלא כך אמר משה הרבה מצות נצטוו ישראל ואין מתקיימין אלא בארץ ישראל אכנס אני לארץ כדי שיתקיימו כולן על ידי אמר לו הקב"ה כלום אתה מבקש אלא לקבל שכר מעלה אני עליך כאילו עשיתם

Rabbi Simlai explicated: For what reason did Mosheh Rabbeinu long to enter the Land of Israel? Does he need to eat from its fruit or satiate himself by its abundance?! Rather, this is what Mosheh Rabbeinu said:

"The people of Israel were commanded numerous *mizvot* that can only be fulfilled in the Land of Israel. Let me enter the land so that I can fulfill them all." The Holy One, blessed be He, said to him: "What you seek is nothing but to receive the reward; I will consider it as if you have fulfilled them." (Sotah 14a)

The comment was subsequently cited by Rishonim[8] as a paradigm for the principle that one should actively seek out circumstances which will generate obligation, rather than rest content with its circumscription; but for our purposes it is precisely the specific application which is most immediately relevant.

A third factor returns us to the Ramban; and, this time, with reference to a frequently stated — and yet, surprisingly radical — position. Not content with linking certain *mizvot* with location, the Ramban contends that the halakhic regimen in its totality is geared to Eretz Yisrael which constitutes a metaphysical and yet natural habitat for its realization. Basing himself, in part, upon a comment of the Sifre that the *mizvot* of *tefillin* and *mezuzah* should be observed even in the Diaspora as a propaedeutic device for maintaining a mindset which should ensure their observance upon return to our native land, he notes that the remark apparently applies even to *hovot ha-guf*, personal, as opposed to agricultural, obligations;[9] and hence, he boldly draws the inference concerning the intrinsic bond between normative content and geographic context.[10]

This is, I repeat, a bold thesis, and one which, despite my enormous admiration and respect for the Ramban, I have great personal difficulty in digesting. Is it conceivable, we ask ourselves, that the *avodat Hashem* (serving God) and *kiyyum mizvot* (fulfillment of *mizvot*) of many *gedolei Yisrael, kedoshim hasidei elyon* (religious leaders, holy and of the highest piety), had only instrumental, but no intrinsic, value? And even if we circumscribe the comment to refer to specific acts but not to the totality of *avodah,* or if we suggest that the Ramban only delimits the rationale for Diaspora Halakhah but not its character, once commanded, does not this still demean the *tefillin* of the Rif or the Gra and diminish their significance?

And yet, in a milder version, the Ramban's position can be readily understood and fully appreciated. Without divesting Diaspora halakhic observance of intrinsic value, one could accept the notion that context and location affect the character and significance of an action, so that the identical *ma'aseh mizvah* (*mizvah* performance) could have incremental qualitative value when performed in *eretz ha-kodesh* (the Holy Land). Thus, it has been reported of *mori ve-rabbi* (my teacher and rabbi), Rav Y. Hutner zt"l, that, upon coming to Israel, after having worn *tefillin* en route, he was wont to put them on again, commenting: "Those had been *hutz la'aretz* (Diaspora) *tefillin*; now we shall put on Eretz Yisrael *tefillin*." And this increment is at the disposal of our prospective *oleh* with respect to each and every *mizvah*.

Finally, we note a fourth factor, more amorphous but no less significant than the preceding. Eretz Yisrael is conceived as a plane of paradoxical particular immanence — as a locus to which Hashem attends directly, with which He bonds, and in which, *mutatis mutandis*, He inheres. It is described, Scripturally, as, uniquely,

ארץ אשר ה' א-להיך דרש אתה תמיד עיני ה' א-להיך בה מרשית השנה ועד אחרית שנה

A land which the Lord your God constantly seeks out, the eyes of the Lord your God are upon it from the beginning to the end of the year. (Devarim 11:12)

Hence, Hazal could postulate that it is watered by the *Ribbono shel Olam* (Master of the Universe) directly, as opposed to the mediating agency employed vis-à-vis other countries:

ארץ ישראל משקה אותה הקב"ה בעצמו וכל העולם כולו ע"י שליח שנאמר הנותן מטר
על פני ארץ ושולח מים על פני חוצות

Eretz Yisrael is watered by the Holy One, blessed be He, Himself, and the whole world [is watered] through an emissary, as it says "He who gives rain upon the face of the land and sends water upon the face of the outskirts." (Ta'anit 10a)

And, halakhically, it is designated, in the mishnah,[11] as the most elementary and comprehensive of ten levels of the sanctity of *mikdash* (Temple), whose conceptual essence is encapsulated in the summary command-ment, ועשו לי מקדש ושכנתי בתוכם, "and they shall make a Temple for me and I will dwell amongst them."[12] Hence, quite apart from formal and/or technical *mizvah* performances, to live in Eretz Yisrael is, to subsist and suspire in the shade and in the shadow of the *Ribbono shel Olam*, over and above the norm prevalent in the Diaspora. To the sensitive religious soul, the implications for service and experience are self-evident.

These positive elements, signaling the religious significance of Eretz Yisrael and life within it, are complemented in classical texts by state-ments, some quite sharp, denigrating the Diaspora. Thus, at one plane, life in *huz la'aretz* is perceived as a spiritual vacuum of sorts, bonding with the *Ribbono shel Olam* being conditioned in some sense and to some extent, by location:

כל זמן שאתם בארץ כנען הריני לכם א-לוה אין אתם בארץ כנען [כביכול] איני לכם לא-לוה.

While you are in the Land of Canaan I am your Master; [when] you are not in the Land of Canaan [it is as if] I am not your Master.[13]

At another, emigration is described as tinged with idolatry — presumably, either because of the free choice of its environment *per se*:

כל המניח את ארץ ישראל בשעת שלום ויוצא כאילו עובד עבודת כוכבים;

Anyone who leaves Eretz Yisrael at a time of peace it is as if he is doing pagan worship;[14]

or, because subjection to pagan worshippers entails an element of subjuga-tion to their deities:

משאתם עובדים לעובדיהם כאלו אתם עובדים להם.

When you are subjugated to their worshippers it is as if you are wor-shipping their deities.[15]

The *ke'illu*, "as if," softens this formulation. It remains however, harsh indeed. But can anyone contend that it is wholly inconsonant with perceived reality?

This brief catalogue, comprised of elements directly and immediately related to the religious realm, hardly exhausts the attractions of *aliyah* and subsequent residence in the promised land. All that has been outlined heretofore could have confronted a prospective *oleh* several centuries ago no less than his contemporary counterpart. The current scene differs, however, markedly. Despite the momentous impact of the factors we have considered, they do not abide alone. At the very least, one additional major area which the modern religious Zionist — if he is truly that, not just an individual who is committed to both *Yahadut* and Zionism, but one in whom the two are thoroughly intertwined — will take into account, bears examination. I refer to the sociohistorical reality our prospect will encounter in Israel should he reach its shores. That reality is, itself, divisible into three components. There is, first, the vertical historical axis, bonding with the full range of Jewish existence, across the millennia, from our incipient national cradle to the epiphany of our meta-historical vision. Second, we note the horizontal social axis — particularly, as manifested by the demographic reality, or, as his Shunamite hostess told Elisha בתוך עמי אנכי ישבת — "I reside amongst my people" (II Melakhim 4:13) — life as part of an indigenous majority rather than of an alien minority, with all this crucial fact implies for the organic unity of state and society and for the organic unity of personal sensibility.

Finally, we encounter the more narrowly Zionist dimension. I have noted elsewhere, that one of the major cruces dividing Zionist from non-Zionist Orthodoxy, concerns, at its core, a theological issue: the division, as it were, of the historical drama between providential control and human initiative. Abstract and abstruse as the point may seem, the question of the legitimacy and scope of activism bears directly upon the appraisal of the re-entry of *Knesset Yisrael* as a national entity upon the universal arena. To the extent that a religious Jew identifies with dynamic activism, he will be attracted to religious Zionism. And he will be drawn to ascending to Eretz Yisrael, for that is where the action in this vein lies.

Even if truncated, this is an impressive list; and it invites some question concerning the limits of its impact. Why, then, one might naïvely ask, do so many sincere and committed religious Zionists persist in residing and laboring in the Diaspora?

As in parallel halakhic scenarios, the answer, in part, lies in ambivalence or rejection regarding a number of the aforementioned contentions, some of which may be dismissed as fallacious, tendentious, or both. Differential immanence may be denigrated as theologically primitive, and the grading of *mizvot* on the basis of some geographic scale likewise. The centrality accorded to *yeshivat Eretz Yisrael* by the Ramban may presumably be challenged in favor of the Rambam's — or, in a later era, Habad's — more arguably universal focus.

Alternatively, one may turn the halakhic argument on its head, contending, as did one of the *ba'alei ha-Tosafot*, that precisely because of the normative demands imposed by residence in Eretz Yisrael, the burden is more than one can bear, and we are consequently now exempt from it:

והיה אומר רבנו חיים דעכשיו אינו מצוה לדור בארץ ישראל כי יש כמה מצות התלויות
בארץ וכמה עונשין דאין אנו יכולין ליזהר בהם ולעמוד עליהם.

Rabbeinu Haym would say that at this time it is not a *mizvah* to live in Eretz Yisrael since there are some *mizvot* based on the Land and punishments [for violating them] and we are not able to take [sufficient] precautions [not to violate them] and to live up to [the challenge of] fulfilling them.[16]

And we bear in mind that in order to neutralize the impact of an argument it need not be rejected categorically as false; marginalizing it may suffice.

The halakhic discourse proper — in part, as expressed in commentaries on relevant Talmudic texts, but primarily concentrated within the corpus of *she'elot u'teshuvot* (halakhic responsa), wherein the issues were confronted and decision required formulation at the specific pragmatic plane — is multifaceted. The principal issues concern the basic normative obligation of *aliyah* — does it exist at all, and, if so, whether *mi-de'oraita* (biblical) or *mi-de'rabbanan* (rabbinic)? Second, to what extent, if any, can it be mitigated or overridden by circumstance?[17] For the most part, *poskim*, largely following the Ramban, were inclined to affirm a measure of obligation. There were, however, notable exceptions. Thus, Rav Shlomo Kluger[18] in the nineteenth century, and Rav Moshe Feinstein,[19] in the twentieth, both argued that if most observant Jews, including pious and saintly *kedoshim hasidei elyon*, scholarly *talmidei hakhamim* as well as the untutored, remained in the Diaspora, evidently their sojourn there entailed no clear violation.

As to mitigating factors, these varied in character and degree. Rav Yizhak de Leon, in his role as expositor and defender of the Rambam against the critique of the Ramban, contends that the *mizvah* was not enumerated by the Rambam because it had no contemporary application, as the norm is confined to periods of Jewish hegemony in Eretz Yisrael:

נראה לי כי מה שלא מנאה הרב הוא לפי שמצות ירושת הארץ וישיבתה לא נהגה רק בימי משה ויהושע ודוד וכל זמן שלא גלו מארצם אבל אחר שגלו מעל אדמתם אין מצוה זו נוהגת לדורות עד עת בוא המשיח.

> It seems to me that the rabbi did not enumerate it because the *mizvah* of inheriting the Land and settling it were applicable only in the days of Mosheh and Yehoshua and David and while they were still not exiled from their land, but after being exiled from their land this *mizvah* is not applicable to subsequent generations until the coming of the Messiah.[20]

The emphasis here is clearly upon teleology: will *aliyah*, manifested within a national context, advance the collective goal postulated in וירשתם אתה וישבתם בה? In an analogous and yet fundamentally different vein, the nineteenth-century *Avnei Nezer*[21] asserts that the impediment of foreign rule is too formidable a barrier for an individual *oleh* to surmount; hence, he is exempt from braving alien masters. Most qualifications focus, however, upon personal factors — security, whether en route or, in Eretz Yisrael, once reached; livelihood; halakhic observance. Obviously, if recognized, these factors require definition and the continued current relevance of previously granted license bears examination; and these, too, figure in many responsa.

In summary, despite the numerical preponderance of *poskim* who dwell upon the obligation of *aliyah*, it may be fairly stated that, while the

positive religious aspects of life in Eretz Yisrael, as previously summa-
rized, are clear and significant, and while these should militate a far greater
scope for religious *aliyah* than presently exists, there is enough qualification to enable many to refrain. In this sense, at the level of personal
existential decision, the halakhic debate remains for many inconclusive,
and those who desire dispensation may find a basis for it. As formulated
in the bottom line of the brief *teshuvah* of the fifteenth-century *Terumat
Ha-Deshen*:

לכן כל איש ישער בעצמו בהשגת גופו וממונו באיזה דרך יוכל לעמוד ביראת השם
ובשמור מצותיו כי זה כל האדם.

> Therefore each person should estimate, on his own, [about] how pre-
> pared he is physically and financially, and in what way he can maintain
> his fear of God and abidance to His commandments since "that is the
> essence of man."[22]

The statement focuses upon spiritual ramifications, but, on the view of
many *poskim*, that material elements bear consideration as well, its differential approach can be readily adapted.

In large measure, however, the impact of the pro-*aliyah* arguments
is not so much affected by their total denial as by their being counterbalanced, and possibly outweighed, by contrary considerations. Many Israelis
are wont to assume that the primary restraint upon *aliyah* among religious
Zionists derives from cleavage to the fleshpots of Egypt. This is a conve-
nient assumption, especially inasmuch as it enables its advocate to flatter
himself by basking in the reflected glory of his own comparative idealism.
It is, however, also simplistic. I have no doubt that it is indeed true of a
segment of the religious Diaspora community, and that, moreover, basic
economic factors — such as, for instance, the ability to purchase adequate
housing — enter into almost everyone's decision making. For the most
part, however, I believe that other factors, of a less materialistic or hedonistic cast, figure more prominently.

These include the quest for vocational self-fulfillment, with respect
to personal development, on the one hand, and potential contribution
to *yishuvo shel olam* (the development of the world), on the other. In a

parallel vein, many are wary about the educational climate in the *dati-le'umi* community in Israel, and bemoan the absence of certain desired options — say, the fusion of positive haredi passion for *lomdut* (conceptual Jewish learning) with serious readiness for secular profession — as well as the presence of radical ideology which brandishes a version of religious Zionism they find narrowly fanatic and excessively aggressive.

For many, more specifically personal elements play a key role. Ringing out the old and ringing in the new may be abstractly appealing. In practice, however, it may also be jarring. At one terminus, the prospect of being known as a greenhorn is perturbing. Grappling with the language, coping with a fresh culture, popular and high, finding oneself out of sync with icons and villains alike, bereft of instinctive linkage with the sports arena or with the concert hall, the fear of seeming a stranger in one's own presumed chosen bailiwick — all can be daunting. Worse yet, many are concerned about a cultural gap piggy-backed on a generational gap, opening a chasm between themselves and their children.

At the other terminus, some anticipate parting as not sweet sorrow but just plain sorrow. The problem is most acute vis-à-vis family — especially, of course, parents. Even if they are well, and, only middle-aged, still functioning vigorously, awareness of our prospective *oleh* that he will be depriving both his children and his parents of the bliss that he enjoys through contact and linkage with both, can induce both moral and psychological reservations. And of course, the matter is complicated even further if one entertains the possibility that declining parental health may necessitate direct assistance, so that one's planned emigration may deprive his elders not only of much deserved and cherished *nahat* (pride) but of much appreciated *shimmush* (caretaking) as well. To be sure, technology and telecommunication will help bridge the gap, but an e-mail or a computer photo is still no substitute for fondling a baby or enriching the mind of a teenager.

Many of these factors carry little normative weight, and, to the committed religious Zionist, should presumably be no match for Rabbi Simlai or the Ramban. Nevertheless, these are issues which touch upon quintessential and existential concerns, and, collectively, they serve as a phalanx which can formidably inhibit the readiness for *aliyah*. Moreover, many are dissatisfied with certain aspects of the quality of current Israeli social and religious life; and not everyone responds favorably to Elie Schweid's mantra, that if you find fault with Israeli life, rather than maintaining a self-serving distance, you should feel bound to enter the lists in order to improve it. Add to this the normal quotient of inertia plus the instinctive fear of an unknown future, and the current limited scope of *aliyah* becomes fully intelligible.

For many prospective *olim*, the upshot of attempted assessment and decision may be ambivalence, frustration, embattlement, or, simply, dilemma. I am inclined to believe that, at some level, the factors we have noted as militating for *aliyah* are familiar to most religious Zionists. They sense that the quality of their *avodat Hashem* can be enhanced by the move, and they perceive that their relation to the pulse of Jewish history can be likewise deepened. They may refrain from making the leap, but not without anguish — some possibly troubled by the thought that they may be rationalizing, while others may be content that they have sound reason for staying put but are nettled by the need to justify themselves at all.

Perhaps the most ambivalent about *aliyah*, however, are spiritual protagonists who, externally and adversarially, are not embattled at all but are, rather, torn, and possibly tormented; in no way impelled to choose between conscience and convenience, only between contrasting and, at the practical plane, often conflicting, claims of conscience proper. On the one hand, they are truly desirous and even anxious to live and work in Eretz Yisrael — and for all the right reasons. On the other hand, they are concerned by a sense of responsibility to their native community and to the need to minister to its spiritual and educational concerns. Upon completion of his book on Hegel, Franz Rozenzweig is reputed to have said that he had now paid his debt to the German landlord, and could move on to more critical matters. In the cases under consideration, however, at issue is often not so much a specific remission as the determination of lifelong venue and often of career as well. With how many young men have I discussed the alternatives of programming computers in Israel as opposed to *hinnukh* (education) or *rabbanut* (rabbinate) in the Diaspora?

And with how many the respective merit of *hinnukh* at different locales? Many of course seek ways to have their cake and eat it, and these have, collectively, contributed much to the Torah milieu in Israel — particularly, via institutions which cater to foreign constituencies. But there is only so much confection available.

The issues are, in part, general and theoretical: public vs. personal priorities, the value of *yishuvo shel olam* as opposed to *talmud Torah*, etc.; and, in part, obviously entail many private variables. In some instances, spiritual counselors take very sharp positions. I heard of a case in which a Sephardi educator who had done valuable work in France and, contemplating *aliyah*, came to Israel in mid-summer to examine opportunities. Whereupon, despite the fact that he was planning to continue teaching here, Rav Ovadia Yosef sent him a message informing him that wherever he would apply for a position, Rav Ovadia would personally see to it that he should be turned down. Most mentors are, however, far more reserved, and their followers far less obeisant. With an eye to Yeats' comment that one writes rhetoric about his battles with others but poetry about his battles with himself, it may be suggested that this group's collected writings could constitute an impressive volume of verse.

Factually, in any event, the history of *aliyah* since *shivat Zion* bears out the wisdom of Hazal's remark concerning earlier epochs. With reference to the events related to the danger posed by Haman's ascendancy and the process of *teshuvah* engendered by it, the gemara notes that the threat of extinction, symbolized by the transfer of the royal signet from Ahashverosh to Haman, was a more effective purgative agent than much hortatory prophecy and reproach. Moreover, the gemara extrapolates and generalizes:

אמר רב אבא בר כהנא גדולה הסרת טבעת יותר מארבעים ושמנה נביאים ושבע נביאות שנתנבאו להן לישראל שכולן לא החזירום למוטב ואילו הסרת טבעת החזירתן למוטב

Rav Abba bar Kahana said: removing a ring is greater than the forty-eight prophets plus the seven prophetesses who prophesied for [the nation of] Israel, since all of them failed to return them [their audience] to (spiritual) wellbeing, and removing a ring returned them to wellbeing. (Megillah 14a)

That, in a nutshell, is the summary of twentieth-century *aliyah*.

Significant and central as *aliyah* is to religious Zionism, what are the implications of its track record in this critical area? To some, they are, and should be, far-reaching indeed. From their perspective, the phrase, "Diaspora religious Zionism," borders on the oxymoron. On this view, the *raison d'être* of a Zionist movement being conceived as geared, primarily, to the encouragement and implementation of *aliyah*, once that goal is palpably beyond reach, it is time to fold the tent. Its proponents might acknowledge that in earlier days, before the floodgates had been opened, this was too rigorous a standard, but contend that in the era of *hok ha-shevut* it is by no means too exacting. And, as to the waiver postulated by Rabbenu Haym, it might be asserted that it is no longer meaningful, inasmuch as the alleged obstacles upon which it had been grounded had long since been neutralized by the growth of the yishuv and the rise in its level of organization and sophistication. Worse still, these critics contend that the profession of Zionist ideology in the context of continued residence in Hendon or in Woodmere is not only innocuous but hypocritical.

I confess that, in making judgments or drawing conclusions, I myself adhere to a less rigorous standard. For one thing, surprising as it may sound to some, I do not reject all strains of hypocrisy categorically, as I recall an adage Douglas Bush used to cite: "Hypocrisy is the tribute which vice pays to virtue." In a more conventional vein, however, there is much to commend the contribution of Diaspora religious Zionism to varied sectors and different levels — national, communal, and personal — of Jewish life. Even if we focus narrowly on the parameters of *aliyah*, it is self-evident that the many who are bent on remaining abroad assist, in many diverse and meaningful ways, those who elect to emigrate. But why should we feel bound to such a narrow standard? Is the contribution to the spiritual and educational realm of any less moment? There are, to be sure, many communities, flushed with manpower, resources, and commitment drawn from diverse sources, that feel self-sufficient, spiritually, even in the absence of input from religious Zionism; still others, who feel, rightly or wrongly, that, by acknowledging the spiritual worth of competing national and historical values, the Zionist component dilutes Torah education rather than enriching it. In a great many, however, the positive thrust is palpable, and in some, religious Zionism is its very lifeblood. This situation is particularly in evidence in an area which straddles the social and intellectual, that of the youth movements. Relatively speaking, the impact of Bnei Akiva is less powerful in North America than elsewhere. But even in the States, it has gained momentum in recent years, and on other continents, it has long been a lighthouse.

Probably the most meaningful contribution of religious Zionism, at the sociopolitical plane as well as at the level of personal commitment, relates to maintaining and stimulating bonds to Eretz Yisrael — and that, in religious categories, and from a Torah perspective. This may entail no more than an emotional link. Yet, that, too, is not to be dismissed lightly. I believe it was from the Rav zt"l that I heard the story of a couple from Minsk who were sharply divided over the issue of *aliyah*. Unable to arrive at an understanding, they agreed to turn to the Minsker Gadol for guidance and resolution. To the surprise and dismay of Zionist circles, he ruled against the proposed initiative. When asked how this counsel could be reconciled with his consistent advocacy of the Zionist cause, he responded that "it is better to dwell in Minsk and yearn for Jerusalem than to dwell in Jerusalem and yearn for Minsk." This may raise certain questions regarding the balance of practice and aspiration as well as halakhic issues concerning the prerogative of determining where a couple should live. For our purposes, however, it serves to exemplify the significance of pure attitude.

Or, to cite a more contemporary voice, a similar message underlies Rav Yaakov Kaminetzky's reported admonition to some *talmidim* (students). He is said to have urged them that, upon walking down Saddle River Road in Monsey, when returning from shul on Shabbat morning, they should not wear their *tallitot* over their coats, in full sight of local residents, lest they forget the nature of *galut* life as opposed to indigenous residence in Eretz Ha-Kodesh. To the best of my knowledge — based, in part, upon direct personal observation — Monsey *bnei Torah* heed the counsel more in its breach than in its observance; but its substantive thrust is amply clear.

Broadly speaking, one may note three distinct components. The first is the concern that excessive acculturation may impair the religious Jew's ability to serve in the capacity of the outsider, so cherished by Colin Wilson, and designated by Leslie Fiedler as the destiny of *Reb Yisrael* and *Klal Yisrael* — to serve, that is, as the voice of conscience, harnessed to social criticism. It is a role for which an identity of *ger ve'toshav* — the dual status suggested in Avraham's proposal to the Hittites, "I am a stranger and a sojourner among you"²³ — may be requisite, and it is incommensurate with the domestication reflected in wearing one's *tallit* on a main street of a non-Jewish town.

I am not certain of the validity of this point, but I am reasonably certain that this was not Reb Yaakov's intent. Of greater relevance is the concern, here previously noted, of the jading of existential bonds to our own land, should we nestle too comfortably and too profoundly in a country which, to a committed Jew must, at some level, be perceived and experienced as foreign soil; at ease, not, as in Carlyle's celebrated phrase, "in Zion," but beyond its pale. Some may dismiss such discourse as romantic rumination, bereft of practical impact. I am inclined to assume that, in time, pragmatic ramifications may indeed issue. Even, however, if they don't, to a spiritual sensibility, attitude itself is crucial.

This point has been effectively expounded by a comment regarding Hazal's inference, most familiar to us from the Haggadah, from the term ויגר שם, "and he dwelled there," denoting temporary sojourn, rather than permanent residence, in the recitation of *mikra bikkurim*: מלמד שלא ירד יעקב אבינו להשתקע במצרים אלא לגור בה, "This teaches that Yaakov Avinu did not descend to Egypt permanently but only to dwell there [temporarily]." It has been suggested²⁴ that the text should not be read as description of Yaakov Avinu's conscious intent at the time. It seems hardly conceivable that a sickly old man, half-blind, almost totally dependent upon familial support, and saturated with a self-image of impending death, should fantasize that he is only going into temporary exile, in quest of immediate respite, and that he would return presently to set up house once more. Hazal's view of the descent and its presumed aim, rather refer to the quality of the sojourn. Yaakov knew full well that Egypt would be his final destination but wished to emphasize that he was going in the capacity of an outsider, precluded from meshing into an alien culture by an existential and axiological chasm rather than by force of circumstances alone.

A third facet, linked to the foregoing and yet distinct, concerns appreciation of the uniqueness of Eretz Yisrael more than relations to ambient Gentile culture. This, too, may be elucidated anecdotally — only this time by means of an incident drawn from my own experience.

In the course of my initial visit to Israel, during the summer of 1962, I went to visit *mori ve-rabbi*, Rav Y. Hutner zt"l, who, prior to his *aliyah*, often spent the summer at Pension Reich in Jerusalem. After reproaching me gently for having left my wife in the United States (אזא כתובה האסטו געשריבען), he began to question me regarding my impressions — particularly, about what had struck my notice especially. As, at that stage, I had focused upon the Torah world in Israel, I noted a number of phenomena which had struck me favorably, as compared to the American scene: widespread popular talmud Torah, the interaction of the Torah and general communities in the implementation of *Hoshen Mishpat*, etc. Every reply was rebutted with the comment that its subject could have been found in Eastern Europe as well, and so was neither endemic nor unique to Eretz Yisrael. When he sensed that I had exhausted my material, he pressed on, inquiring as to what indeed was special about my visit, and, when it became clear that I could, at best, only respond feebly, the Rosh Yeshivah opened with a volley of sources and dicta — the description of Eretz Yisrael as ארץ אשר ה' א-להיך דרש אתה, "a land that Hashem your God cares for," or as that to which Mosheh and Aharon had been barred access, which was now open to us — דוכתא דמשה ואהרן לא זכו לה (Ketubbot 112a) — all trumpeting forth the sacral, metaphysical, and historical uniqueness of the land and all causing me to realize, in a flash, that I had missed the boat entirely. As he railed on, as perhaps only he could, against tourists he had met on the plane, acting and talking as if they were en route to vacation in

California, the sense of failure cut deeper and deeper. I walked out into the Bet Hakerem evening air like a beaten dog. But I knew I had been beaten justly; and today, almost forty-five years later, I remain deeply grateful to the Rosh Yeshivah for opening my eyes and for opening my heart.

In truth, the subject of bonding with Eretz Yisrael is not merely anecdotal at all. It is rooted in Hazal, in a context which is, at once, both halakhic and hashkafic — namely, the concept of creating and sustaining *zekher le'mikdash*, "a memento of the Temple." The memorialization of mikdash bears a dual aspect. It may refer to its destruction, as, for instance, according to the *Ba'al Ha-Maor*, with respect to *sefirat ha-omer* after the *hurban* (destruction).[25] More commonly, however, it relates to remembering *mikdash* in all its majesty and glory, and entails replicating its practice and aura. Thus, the mishnah states that Rav Yohanan ben Zakkai instituted an innovation with respect to the *mizvah* of *lulav*, and that its rationale was the quest for *zekher le'mikdash*:

בראשונה היה הלולב ניטל במקדש שבעה ובמדינה יום אחד משחרב בית המקדש
התקין רבן יוחנן בן זכאי שיהא לולב ניטל במדינה שבעה זכר למקדש

> At first, the *lulav* was taken in the Temple for seven [days] and in the rest of the country, for one day. Since the Temple was destroyed, Rabban Yohanan ben Zakkai decreed that the *lulav* should be taken in the rest of the country for seven days as a memorialization of the Temple.

The gemara goes on to query whence do we derive the principle of creating such memorials, and it cites a *pasuk* in Yirmiyahu:

ומנלן דעבדינן זכר למקדש דאמר קרא כי אעלה ארוכה לך וממכותיך ארפאך נאם ה'
כי נדחה קראו לך ציון היא דורש אין לה מכלל דבעיא דרישה.

> From where do we know that we should memorialize the Temple? From the verse (Yirmiyahu 30:17) "'I will bring you healing and cure your wounds,' says the Lord, 'since they called you dejected, [and said] Zion has no seeker." ["Has no seeker'"] indicates that it must be sought out.[26]

The source is cited here with respect to a very specific halakhic ordinance, and it presumably serves as the *raison d'être* for similar ordinances. Unquestionably, however, it serves equally to enunciate a principle whose scope extends beyond the explicitly normative to embrace the realm of consciousness and sensibility. To sustain the memory of *mikdash*, that whose locus is in Jerusalem and that which coincides with the boundaries of the concentric country, is to vivify it, to rejuvenate it via mental image and soul's yearning.

Derishat Zion (seeking out Zion), *zekher le'mikdash* — this has, traditionally and historically, been the central charge of Diaspora religious Zionism. Of course, it was not denominated as such; but sans nomenclature, with nary a notion about political structure and activity, with no meaningful prospect of implementing its agenda, for millennia, dispersed Jewry persisted in keeping the dream and its underlying and overarching faith alive. Those abiding elements remain a vital aspect of our collective and personal spiritual existence. We have neither the right nor the inclination to waver in our commitment to them, and this sustenance and transmission continue to constitute a sacred charge. Beyond politics and internecine rivalry, its beck and call challenges us continually; and even were there no other, *derishat Zion* is sufficient cause for the perpetuation of Diaspora religious Zionism. To those who dismiss it as anachronistic, to those who denigrate it as anomalous, we can simply respond that, while they are not wholly wrong, they surely are not wholly right. So long as *derishat Zion* is not comprehensively realized, and quite apart from any political activity, religious Zionists, wherever located, and within the context of their broader identity as members of *Knesset Yisrael*, are charged and challenged.

Response to the challenge is complicated by its character and context. In effect, my perception has focused upon the spiritual aspect of religious Zionism, as opposed to the pragmatic implementation of its vision. I have no doubt that this emphasis is warranted, in light of both fundamental and permanent priority, and with an eye to current need. By dint of its very nature, however, this factor potentially pits religious Zionism against competing distinctive Torah values. Such internecine confrontation tends to be perturbing in any event, but in our case perhaps doubly so. For, in certain respects, depth and scope of palpably and narrowly religious commitment is the Achilles' heel of religious Zionism — particularly, in the Diaspora. To be sure, the portrait, often delineated by detractors, and bordering frequently on caricature, of the average *mizrahnik* as ever cutting halakhic corners in the quest for facile compromise and accommodation, is grossly unjust. There is much genuine and profound Torah, *avodah*, and *gemilut hasadim* in the current *dati-le'umi* community, and in many respects, the situation has improved measurably during the past generation. And yet, as with Tennyson's Ulysses, "Tho' much is taken, much abides." There is no gainsaying that the level of engagement in these critical areas, "by which the world is sustained," needs to be broadened and deepened in much of the religious Zionist community. Hence the pressure to intensify *derishat Zion*, at the possible expense of other essential values, may be fraught with axiological difficulty.

Nevertheless, while priority and balance cannot be ignored, our commitment to *derishat Zion* should be neither abandoned nor diminished. And this, for two reasons. First, it should be obvious that apart from attending to dividing the existing cake, the prospect for enlarging it ought to be very real. We are far from exhausting reservoirs of time, energy, and passion to be harnessed in the pursuit of spiritual goals. Much can be garnered from *hefker*, in Melville's terms, "loose fish;" from resources wasted upon the spectrum ranging from frivolity through pettiness to ennui; and, in this respect, we have a great deal to learn from the haredi world and its standards. The second factor relates to the character and substance of *derishat Zion*. Beyond flag-waving and beyond merely exuding emotion, it is all about search and relation; about bonding and linkage; about developing a thirst for Zion and all that it represents and about seeking avenues to quench that thirst — by remembrance and reenactment of things past in conjunction with anticipation of things future.

Consequently, properly understood and experienced, *derishat Zion* does not compete with other Torah values, but rather reciprocally reinforces and is reinforced by them. To seek Zion is to engage in the ultimate quest described and prescribed by Yeshayahu:

ואותי יום יום ידרשון ודעת דרכי יחפצון כגוי אשר צדקה עשה ומשפט א-לקיו לא עזב ישאלוני משפטי צדק קרבת א-לקים יחפצון.

And day by day they will seek Me out and want to know My ways, like a nation which has carried out justice and has not abandoned the law of its Lord, they will ask me for just laws and pine for proximity to God (Yeshayahu 58:2).

Or, in a normative vein: דרשו ה' בהמצאו קראהו בהיותו קרוב. Seek out God wherever He is found, call out to him when He is near (Yeshayahu 55:6).

Coda

Whilst in no way privy to the process, I presume this year's Forum organizers deliberated more than usual before deciding on the assignation of this topic. The argument for giving the nod to a current *ben huz la'aretz* (Diaspora Jew), appears, in certain respects, compelling. The choice of a person in whose mind the issues are fresh and vibrant, in whom the admixture of resolve and resignation — at times, even of pride and guilt — mesh, intersect, and interact within the matrix of a charged emotional present, would have infused the discussion with a vividness not readily attained in a partially retrospective, albeit empathetic, piece.

If I was nonetheless selected, I would like to think the decision was not grounded upon possibly questionable personal qualities, but rather — even if, perhaps unwittingly — as a vehicle for establishing a point. The choice of a person who, while residing in the United States grappled, together with his wife, with the option of *aliyah*, who went on, subsequently, to carve a niche in Israel, while retaining ties with his former bailiwick, but who never looked back in regret or reconsideration, possibly signifies the bonding power of derishat Zion. Bonding Jew and land, bonding Jew and Jew, it is the charge and prerogative of neither the Diaspora religious community, nor of the indigenous Israeli community. It is part of what links us, vertically and horizontally, with *Knesset Yisrael*.

And, I ask myself, in conclusion: Is it too presumptuous to suppose and suggest that an appreciation of the value of varied perception and perspective, is, in part, the import of a relevant gemara in Ketubbot (75a):

אמר אביי וחד מינייהו עדיף מינן כתרי מינן אמר רבא וחד מינן כי סליק להתם עדיף כתרי
מינייהו

Abbaye [among the preeminent Babylonian *amoraim*] stated: "One of them [i.e., from Eretz Yisrael] is superior to two of us." Rava stated: "And if one of us goes there, he is then superior to two of them."

I hope and trust that I am neither so vain nor so foolish as to fantasize, personally, presumed superiority to peers who have chosen to serve the *Ribbono shel Olam* and to service *Knesset Yisrael* within the context of continued residence in the Diaspora. And yet, without harboring illusions, I also trust that I am fully appreciative of the spiritual benefits harvested by my family and myself due to pitching our own tent on the soil of *eretz ha-kodesh*.

Notes

1. In *The Portable Matthew Arnold*, ed. Lionel Trilling (New York, 1949), 331; widely reprinted.
2. This is, in part, an obvious clash of pragmatic priorities. However, among the priorities concerning the recipient of *zedakah*, the Halakhah has assigned weight to both 1) affinity to the donor, including a common local base, and 2) inherent significance and worth, including residence in Eretz Yisrael. See Devarim 15:7 and the Sifre thereon:

   באחד שעריך. יושבי עירך קודמים ליושבי עיר אחרת: בארצך. יושבי הארץ קודמין ליושבי
   חוץ לארץ.

   "In one of your gates." The residents of your town come before residents of another town. "In your land." The residents of Israel come before residents of the Diaspora.

   This invites the obvious question of which, if any, has the upper hand in the event of a clash. To the best of my knowledge, the point is not raised in primary sources, but was discussed by later *poskim*. The *Bah*, in his comment on *Tur Yoreh Deah*, 251, held that *aniyyei irkha* should clearly be preferred, and this view was accepted by the *Shakh, Yoreh Deah*, 251:6, and by the Netziv in his commentary on the Sifre, *ad locum*. However, the *Pe'at Ha-Shulhan* argues vigorously that *anniyei Eretz Yisrael* should be prioritized as שבנתינתו ליושבי ארץ ישראל מקיים שתי מצוות, להחיות עניים ולקיים

ישיבת ארץ ישראל, "In giving it to residents of Eretz Yisrael he fulfills two *mizvot*, sustaining the destitute and maintaining the settlement of Eretz Yisrael" (Hilkhot Eretz Yisrael 2:29). This position was also adopted by many nineteenth-century European poskim. See M.M. Rothschild, *Ha-Halukkah*, 2nd ed. (Jerusalem, 1986), 66–85. It should be noted, however, first, that, in such a case, possibly no normative position exists and the donor may do as he wishes, as in the clash of *tadir* and *mekuddash* (see Zevahim 91a and Menahot 49a and Rambam, Temidin U'Musafim, 8:20 and 9:2). Secondly, these relatively extraneous factors obviously do not exist in a vacuum and other elements — particularly, the nature, character, and level of the need — must be considered as well; see *Hatam Sofer, Yoreh Deah,* 233. Cf. also my remarks in בעניניני צדקה בארץ ישראל ובחוץ לארץ", שערי שמואל (תל אביב, תש"ס), 22-29.

3. In this connection, it is worth noting David Shatz's observation regarding the paucity of interest in the area of *mahshavah*, within the Torah world, in America, as compared to Israel. See his perceptive analysis in "Remembering Marvin Fox: One Man's Legacy to Jewish Thought," *Tradition,* 36 (2002): 59–88.

4. מצוה ד', ברשימת מצות העשה ששכח הרמב״ם לדעת הרמב״ן, בשולי חלק מצות העשה שבספר המצות להרמב״ם.

5. The Ramban's position is most familiarly associated with his discussion in this locus classicus of the *Sefer Ha-Mizvot,* in which it is fully elaborated, and with reference to many *pesukim*. However, the gist of his view is also expounded in his commentary on the most central text,

> והורשתם את הארץ וישבתם בה כי לכם נתתי את הארץ לרשת אתה: על דעתי זו מצות עשה היא יצוה אותם שישבו בארץ וירשו אותה כי הוא נתנה להם ולא ימאסו בנחלת ה' ואלו יעלה על דעתם ללכת ולכבוש את ארץ שנער או ארץ אשור וזולתן ולהתישב שם יעברו על מצות ה'.

> 'And you shall inherit the land and settle in it, since I have given you the land to inherit': In my opinion, this is a positive commandment that God commanded them to settle in the Land and inherit it since He gave it to them and they should not renounce the inheritance of God. And if they consider going and conquering the Land of Shinar or the Land of Ashur or another land and to settle there, they violate a commandment of God (Bamidbar 33:53).

In the course of this comment, the Ramban later evidently acknowledges that Rashi interpreted the *pasuk* differently. However, inasmuch as he goes on to state that his own view is buttressed by many parallel *pesukim*, he may have intended that Rashi only disagreed with his interpretation of this particular text, but not that he rejected the Ramban's halakhic position.

6. See Melakhim 5:9–12.

7. This distinction is clear in the *Sefer Ha-Mizvot.* However, in the passage in Bamidbar, only one goal is defined: residence, collective and/or personal, in Eretz Yisrael.

8. See, e.g., *Tosafot Rosh,* Niddah 61b.

9. See Kiddushin 36b ff., with respect to the criteria for defining which *mizvot* are confined to Eretz Yisrael.
10. Ramban, Devarim 11:18.
11. See Kelim 1:6. The sacral character of Eretz Yisrael bears a dual aspect. 1) Its soil and the produce thereof is subject to certain halakhot which do not apply elsewhere. 2) It is regarded as the locus of *Shekhinah* — in a sense, as an extension of *mikdash* — beyond the level of presence which obtains universally. This mishnah only relates to the second element.
12. Shemot 25:8. The concept of geographic significance with respect to divine presence raises obvious questions. Just as obviously, however, it is rooted in the mainstream of Jewish tradition. Proper analysis of this problem lies, however, beyond the scope of this paper.
13. Tosefta, Avodah Zarah 5:2. The qualifying term, *ke'vayakhol*, is included in some texts but not in all. The implications are self-evident, but, even if it is included, the formulation is far-reaching. Evaluation of this point would require extensive analysis of the substantive weight of this slippery term in various texts and contexts.
14. Ibid. The qualification, *bi-sh'at shalom*, clearly implies that the pressure of circumstance can legitimize emigration. Elsewhere, this principle is explicitly stated, with respect to dire economic straits; see Bava Batra 90a. However, the Rambam, Melakhim 5:9, held that *middat hasidut* required that this dispensation not be invoked. In a similar vein, the Ramban, Bereshit 12:10, states that Avraham Avinu was judged by a higher standard and punished for moving to Egypt in time of famine. See, however, Nedarim 32a, where, by implication, this assertion appears to be rejected.
15. Rashi, Devarim 4:28.
16. Ketubbot 110b, s.v. *hu*.
17. The salient issues and many of the most relevant sources are discussed in a brief, clearly biased, and nevertheless highly useful, monograph, Zvi Glatt's posthumously published (מעפר קומי: ברור חובת העליה לארץ ישראל בזמן הזה (ירושלים, ללא תאריך).
18. עיין האלף לך שלמה: שו"ת על אהע"ז, סי' קיח.
19. עיין שו"ת אגרות משה, חלק אבן העזר, סי' קב.
20. *Megillat Esther*, in the response to the Ramban's animadversion, cited above, *ad locum*. As noted by Glatt, pp. 57–8, there is some ambiguity and, possibly, some internal contradiction regarding the precise historical situation upon which the *mizvah* of *aliyah* is contingent.
21. See e.g., *Avnei Ezer, Yoreh Deah*, 554:56. It might be noted that the attempt to neutralize Rabbenu Haym's position was taken to an extreme by the sixteenth-century *posek*, Rav Yosef Trani (although, obviously, for reasons very different from *Avnei Nezer's*). Evidently, in part, because he was scandalized by the position, and in part, on the basis of comparison with texts of other Rishonim, he contended that the text of the *Tosafot* was not genuinely Rabbenu Haym's but, rather, a later interpolation.

See *She'elot U'Teshuvot Maharit, Yoreh Deah*, 2:28. It has, however, been noted that his father, Rav Mosheh Trani, in his *She'elot U'Teshuvot Mabit*, 1:245, had clearly assumed the text was genuine.

22. *Pesakim*, 88.
23. Bereshit 23:4. For an exposition of this phrase, see the Rav's *Hamesh Derashot* (Jerusalem, 1974), pp. 48–52.
24. I have a clear recollection of the content of this comment, but, regrettably, am presently unable to recall or trace its source.
25. See his comment at the end of Pesahim, in the Rif, to explain why the *berakhah* of she-he'heyanu is not recited in conjunction with *sefirat ha'omer*.
26. Rosh Hashanah 30a. The mishnah's assertion is predicated on the assumption that, *mi-de'oraita*, the *mizvah* of *lulav* obtains for all seven days of Sukkot in mikdash, as it is to this that the "rejoicing before Hashem," cited in Vayikra 23:20, refers, and not, as interpreted by a contrary view in the Yerushalmi, Sukkah 3:11, to additional *korbanot shelamim*.

Acknowledgements and Sources of Essays

All the essays except for chapters 2, 9 and 10 originally appeared in the Orthodox Forum series of Yeshiva University. Chapter 8 was originally published by Rowman & Littlefield. Our thanks to them for permission to reprint the articles.

We likewise extend gratitude to Dov Karoll, who proofread the current volume, and to Alex Israel, who prepared the indices.

Chapter 1, "Of Marriage: Relationship and Relations," appeared in *Tradition* 39:2 (Summer, 2005), pp. 7–35; and in *Gender Relationships In Marriage and Out*, ed. Rivkah Blau (Yeshiva University Press, 2007), pp. 1–34.

Chapter 2, "Talmud and Ma'aseh in Pirkei Avot," appeared in *Rav Chesed: Essays in Honor of Rabbi Dr. Haskel Lookstein, Volume 2*, ed. Rafael Medoff (Ktav, 2009), pp. 1–25.

Chapter 3, "Communal Governance, Lay and Rabbinic: An Overview," appeared in *Rabbinic and Lay Communal Authority*, ed. Suzanne Last Stone (Yeshiva University Press, 2006), pp. 19–52.

Chapter 4, "Jewish Philanthropy — Whither?" appeared in *Tradition* 42:4 (Winter 2009), pp. 7–32, and in *Toward a Renewed Ethic of Jewish Philanthropy*, ed. Yossi Prager (Ktav, 2010), pp. 193–220.

Chapter 5, "Beyond the Pale? Reflections Regarding Contemporary Relations with Non-Orthodox Jews," appeared in *The Relationship of Orthodox Jews with Believing Jews of Other Religious Ideologies and Non-Believing Jews*, ed. Adam Mintz (Yeshiva University Press, 2010), 187–224.

Chapter 6, "Law and Spirituality: Defining the Terms," appeared in *Jewish*

Spirituality and Divine Law, eds. Adam Mintz and Lawrence Schiffman, (Yeshiva University Press, 2005), pp. 3–33.

Chapter 7, "Contemporary Impediments to *Yirat Shamayim*," appeared in *Yirat Shamayim: The Awe, Reverence, and Fear of God*, ed. Marc D. Stern (Ktav, 2008), pp. 231–264.

Chapter 8, "Formulating Responses in an Egalitarian Age: An Overview," appeared in *Formulating Responses in an Egalitarian Age*, ed. Marc D. Stern (Rowman and Littlefield, 2005), pp. 33–51.

Chapter 9, "Reflections upon *Birkot Ha-Torah*," appeared in *Alei Etzion* 10 (2000), pp. 19–29.

Chapter 10, "To Double Business Bound: Reflections on the Divided Life of *Ovdei Hashem*," appeared in the Yeshivat Har Etzion jubilee volume, *Ha-Har ha-Tov ha-Zeh*, eds. Shaul Barth, Yitzchak Recanati and Reuven Ziegler (Yeshivat Har Etzion, 2011), pp. 9–19 (English section).

Chapter 11, "Diaspora Religious Zionism: Some Current Reflections," appeared in *Religious Zionism Post Disengagement*, ed. Chaim Waxman (Ktav, 2008), pp. 3–30.

Source Index

II. Rabbinic Sources

Talmud Yerushalmi / Jerusalem Talmud

Subject and Name Index